Open Sesame

Goodyear Education Series
Theodore W. Hipple, Editor
University of Florida

Change for Children
Sandra Nina Kaplan, Jo Ann Butom Kaplan, Sheila Kunishima Madsen, and Bette K. Taylor

Crucial Issues In Contemporary Education
Theodore W. Hipple

Elementary School Teaching: Problems and Methods
Margaret Kelly Giblin

Facilitative Teaching: Theory and Practice
Robert Myrick and Joe Wittmer

The Future of Education
Theodore W. Hipple

Popular Media and the Teaching of English
Thomas R. Giblin

Race and Politics in School/Community Organizations
Allan C. Ornstein

School Counseling: Problems and Methods
Robert Myrick and Joe Wittmer

Secondary School Teaching: Problems and Methods
Theodore W. Hipple

Solving Teaching Problems
Mildred Bluming and Myron Dembo

Teaching, Loving, and Self-Directed Learning
David Thatcher

Will the Real Teacher Please Stand Up? A Primer in Humanistic Education
Mary Greer and Bonnie Rubinstein

Social Studies As Controversy
R. Jerrald Shive

Evelyn M. Carswell and Darrell L. Roubinek

Open Sesame

A PRIMER IN OPEN EDUCATION

Goodyear Publishing Company, Inc., Pacific Palisades, California

Library of Congress Catalog Card Number: 73-86434

ISBN: 0-87620-646-1 (paper)
      0-87620-647-X (case)

Y-6461-1 (paper)
Y-647X-7 (case)

Current Printing (last number):

10 9 8 7 6 5 4 3 2 1

Printed in the United States of America
Book design by John Isely
Dolls by Nancy Lawton

Acknowledgments of copyrighted and/or reprinted material
are listed on pages 280-89.

v i   **A Few Words of Appreciation**

vii   **Foreword**

i x   **Preface**

xiv   **To the Reader**

1   **Chapter One: Trust**
Little ideas, big ideas to encourage greater trust in yourself,
in children, and in open education.

27   **Chapter Two: Understanding**
Pertinent extracts of a child's point of view, coupled with examples
of exhibiting understanding in classrooms.

63   **Chapter Three: Children**
The many faces of children are included through poetry and prose.

85   **Chapter Four: Openness**
Wherever you are, you can find ways to open up more—open yourself,
your children, your environment.

125   **Chapter Five: Love**
An open struggle with ourselves to get love legitimately inserted
as an underlying curriculum tenet.

141   **Chapter Six: Living**
Today, and all we do with it, is the theme of the dialogs and readings
in this chapter.

175   **Chapter Seven: Expanding**
Space-time-awareness-perceptions-environments—an expanding
perspective of children and their learning environments.

227   **Chapter Eight: Humanizing**
Soul searching on the part of the teacher must be done for a humanizing
model in the institution faced with pressures to dehumanize the pupils.

255   **Chapter Nine: Open Sesame**
ideas, ideaS, ideAS, IdEAS, IDEAS—for open education!

280   **Acknowledgments**

A Few Words of Appreciation—

To the many people who have assisted in the production of this book, the authors would like to express their sincere appreciation:

To Evelyn's husband, David, and to Darrell's wife, Jerrianne, who fully supported and encouraged our efforts;

To Susan Steiner, of Goodyear Publishing Company, whose faith, encouragement and assistance made this book become a reality;

To the authors and publishers who have so generously permitted quotation from their publications;

To Sally, Dave, Ted, Nancy, John and other good people who trusted us;

To the four special boys in our families and the thousands of elementary school children and teachers we have been so fortunate to know over the years, and from whom we have learned so very much.

emc and dlr

Foreword

I first opened up the manuscript of **Open Sesame** while on a flight over the Rocky Mountains. At 35,000 feet altitude, and with an unbroken view of the snow-peaked mountain range, I was struck suddenly by the fact that what I was reading and what I was observing had much in common.

The statements about the fact that **Open Sesame** had no real beginning and no real end had raised my curiosity. Contemplating that notion as one that might be useful for a professional book, my gaze shifted to the panoramic view all around.

There was design!

There was harmony!

There was majesty!

There was beauty!

BUT there was no real beginning and no real ending within my observation. The peaks were integrated with the valleys; the large was a contrast to the small; the powerful seemed to support the weak; the shadows were a perfect contrast for the brilliant sunshine on the snow.

I thought of each topic as one of the snow-covered peaks down below. Each had a place. Each could be viewed from afar, but seldom conquered through study. Each has a contribution to make to the whole process of opening up a rich and rewarding life for individuals. Like the trickles of water that flow from each snow field, each topic contributes something that may appear to be insignificant, but when joined by other influences becomes a mainstream of life and love.

Few people are concerned with the beginnings and the endings. Most are concerned with the point of personal contact that is theirs.

Time seemed short for me as I turned my view from the mountain peaks to the manuscript. I tried reading "Understanding" and then skipped to "Humanizing" and then back to "Love." Each chapter was self-contained for me and I was glad to have had a chance to read in one place many of the fine jewels of professional literature that focused on my deepest concerns for my relations with students. I found that I was no longer concerned with whether I liked **Open Sesame** as a book, but with the thoughts of Who am I? What can I do? How can I integrate into relationships with students that are meaningful and influential?

Open Sesame had suddenly begun to open up secret doors of my own mind. I was brought to threshold after threshold of wisdom from others, but each one bid me enter for only a fleeting moment to be refreshed and strengthened for my educational journey. **I had to travel alone!** I had to realize anew that teaching is "living at the edge of mystery"—not being able to step across with students, but bidding one after another to trust in great ideas and great people. Students, too, must travel alone on their educational journey.

Open Sesame was no longer a college textbook that I would decide to **like** or **not like** for my classes in teacher education. It had become a unique experience for me as a teacher.

Roach Van Allen
Professor of Elementary Education
University of Arizona

As we begin
this book on open education
we are well aware that each of us has
some open and some closed
feelings, behavior,
and dreams!

Each of us works in a different environment, with different children, with different adults, and with differing degrees of openness. Because we treasure this uniqueness we are committed to a humanistic philosophy; thus this book is our attempt to put into an open-ended framework some ideas that we hope

    will help **you** identify your thresholds of acceptance or rejection in a wide variety of experiences;

    will provide some sources of information and inspiration to foster openness in you;

    will help you test your skills through exercises and activities;

    will encourage you to think and act as an open educator.

Such a purpose makes it impossible to write the usual kind of book that must be read from the first page to the last page. Instead, we would like for you, the reader, to start with whatever topic is most appealing to you. Becoming open and growing in openness depends on the reader's desire to modify his or her behavior, the support one receives when attempts are made to become more open, and on many small, but important items of one's everyday experiences.

We believe teachers MUST become more open in their relationships with the children they teach. All children are required to attend our schools and we are expected to prepare all of them to function in a democracy, a form of government that functions best when its citizens are divergent thinkers, able to converge on issues important for the common good. To ask this same openness of college professors who teach those who elect to come to college is equally essential, since the way we teach prospective teachers often provides the model used by these new professionals. We think of open education as a way for teachers to see more, know more, care more! If this book encourages or helps the reader to see more, know more, and care more, we will have succeeded!

—Evelyn Carswell and Darrell L. Roubinek

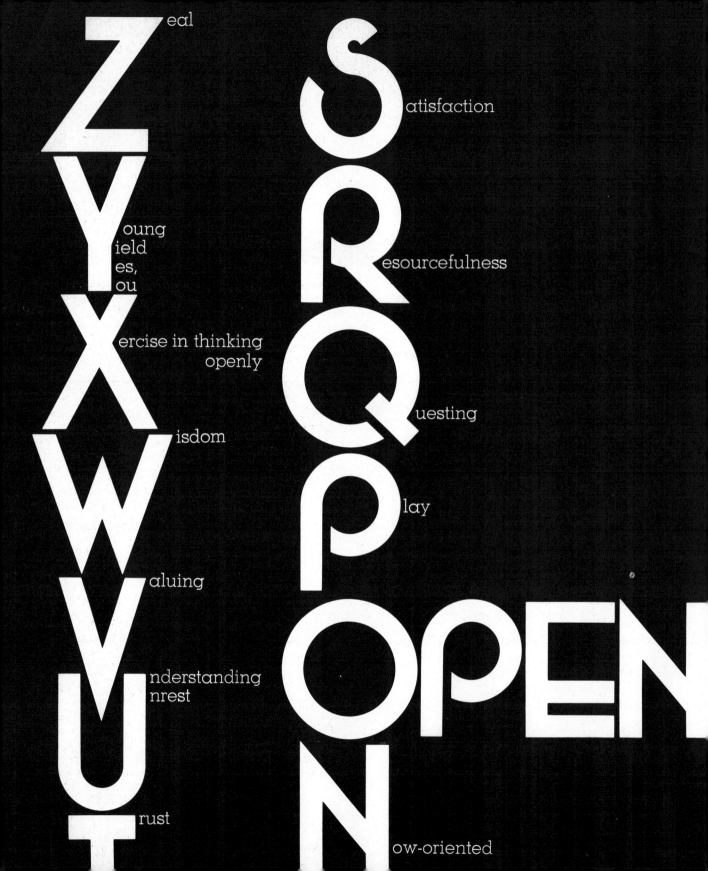

Z eal

Y oung

X ield

W es,

V ou

U ercise in thinking openly

T isdom

S atisfaction

R esourcefulness

Q uesting

P lay

O aluing

N nderstanding
nrest

rust

OPEN

ow-oriented

Movement

Love
Learning
Living

Knowing

Joy
Jumping

Inquiry
Individuality

Humanizing

Growing

Feeling
Freedom

Exploring

Expanding
Exploding

Developing

Children

Change

Creativity

Being
Behaving
Becoming

Accepting

Long before we began working together as professors at the University of Arizona, we had individually explored alternatives to traditional schooling. In our classrooms in Maryland, Kansas, and Arizona we were known as teachers who did not follow the book. As elementary school principals in Kansas, Oklahoma, and Arizona we continually sought to provide more open environments for our schools. We each visited schools attempting to change tradition and discussed philosophy and organization with hundreds of visitors who came to see what we were doing. We found children, parents, teachers, college students, and other educators with whom we could share ideas, programs, materials, and values. Many of these people are characterized in Herb, Suzanna, and others of the Sesame Seven whose dialog is included throughout *Open Sesame,* questioning, finding support, and discussing ideas. While their questions and problems are typical, all characters are fictitious, except the two professors—Evelyn Carswell and Darrell L. Roubinek.

JANICE represents the middle of the road. Sometimes, depending upon what she reads, or with whom she chats, or how she feels, she moves a bit one way or the other from the middle, but never very far. She represents an awful lot of people—educators and laymen—not really against open education but not really for it, either.

CELLA, on the other hand, is a creative rebel. She, being a black woman, is a member of two minority groups, and she is determined to bring about change in schools as quickly as possible.

HERB is the doubter of the group. At times he wants very much to get involved, but he finds it hard to break habits of closure.

TONY, a newcomer, is a long-haired, sandaled, student teacher who is specializing in early childhood education. From his apparent feelings and behavior one wonders why he chose the public school system over private schools.

JOSÉ, the quiet thinker, is somewhere between Tony and Herb in his quest, and, like MORNING STAR, a brand new Indian teacher, wants open education for the Spanish-speaking and the Indian children without their losing their newly acquired chances to be seen and heard as children with unique cultures.

We complete our cast of characterizations with an experienced, very open elementary school principal, SUZANNA. Many teachers tell us they would like to do more toward open education if their principal would so allow, but here we shall express a bias. We find many principals offering all kinds of support that isn't always accepted or utilized by teachers. So, perhaps you'll accept our bias and help us give support to principals such as Suzanna as she and they become even more open.

NOW— TO BEGIN! We have sections called:

TRUST (Morning Star, Herb, and Janice started here, for different reasons)

UNDERSTANDING

CHILDREN (Suzanna starts here)

OPENNESS (José chooses this to read first)

LOVE (You might have guessed that this is where Tony begins)

LIVING (Cella reads this section first)

EXPANDING

HUMANIZING

OPEN SESAME

WHERE DO YOU CHOOSE TO BEGIN?

How about taking your pen and marking the preferred order for **your** exploration? Would you want to jot down some thoughts about you and your ordering?

(Your name)_____

_____

(How would you describe yourself for this, your book?)

My choice for exploring open education with Carswell and Roubinek are:

Trust
   Understanding
      Children
         Openness
            Love
               Living
                  Expanding
                     Humanizing
                       and
                          Open Sesame

Happy Exploring!

CHAPTER ONE
Trust

HERB: Ever since we decided to put our youngest son into the new open school, my wife has been after me to read about open education. She doesn't trust some of the new ideas we've been hearing about. Our boy is very independent for his age—he'll get along all right, I'm sure. He won't have the sort of experience I had when I first started school—I was terrified. And the austere, old school building and the stern-looking teachers didn't help a bit.

MORNING STAR: I well remember the fear I had when the school bus took me from my reservation to the boarding school far away. I didn't trust the strange white people, and my faith in my parents was shaken because they let me be taken away. I hated sleeping in that funny bed under cold, thin things they called sheets. I missed my hogan and sheep and the warm, evening fire. On that first day, as young as I was, I knew I did not trust the people at the school. It was on the second day that I began to learn the most bitter lesson—they did not trust me.

Identify several incidents of childhood when you were trusted.

Are there many or few?

Were they important to you or did you take them for granted?

Think of childhood instances when you were not trusted.

Do you remember more times when you were trusted than when you were not?

Identify those moments of adulthood pertaining to trust and mistrust.

How have all these experiences caused you to feel about trusting children? young persons? other adults?

TRUST ACTIVITIES

Identify your CREDENCE THRESHOLDS—
flying
driving
water
gossip
mistakes,
etc.

for faculties—
List those things your school requires of children and parents that might be considered a lack of faith on your part.

for college classes—
List those things expected of you by professors and/or the university that might indicate a lack of belief in you.

YOU and TRUST

How far do you trust yourself?
with unneeded foods?
with fashion fads?
with gadgetry?
with people's feelings?
with your own children?
with your school children?
with your principal?
with your college students?
with your friends?
with those you dislike?
Do you have confidence only in those who believe in you?
Do you tend to initiate trust? Or do you tend to wait and react?
Why do you have your trust patterns?
Why do you keep these kinds of patterns?
Do you rely on television?
newspapers?
popular magazines?
Do you trust church leaders?
government leaders?
world leaders?
Do you trust all of your children?
most of your children?
all of your faculty?
most of your faculty?
few of your faculty?
your principal?
your department head?
your superintendent?
your Dean?
your Board of Trustees?

"Play was important to headmistresses. They often talked of curiosity. They seemed to trust curiosity as a motive force. They seemed to trust that the forces of a child's development had a forward propulsion..."

From **The English Infant School and Informal Education** by Lillian Weber

"We feel that teachers have to trust their students deeply if alternatives and freedom are to help make school rich, worthwhile places for young people to spend twelve or more years of their lives."

From "The Curriculum-Proof Teacher," by William D. Romey

DOSE OF TRUST

From *Teacher and Child* by Dr. Haim Ginott

Scene: Breakfast.

BETH (age ten): I don't want to go to school. I hate it.

MOTHER (with sympathy): I know. It's not easy for you this year. You have a stricter teacher. I even know that he yells a lot and you don't like it at all.

BETH: You can say that again. He is the roughest teacher I ever had.

MOTHER: I know.

BETH: You can't make me go to school. When you drop me off, I could play hooky.

MOTHER: You could, but I believe you wouldn't.

BETH: How do you know?

MOTHER: I trust you. (Beth relaxes. No amount of logic could have accomplished what a dose of trust did.)

Do children often threaten to do similar things at your school?

How would a trusting teacher respond to—

"I'm going home—I'm not going to stay in this old school!"

WOULD YOU—
   COULD YOU—
   share a moment of your time to find what he is really saying to you?

lead him to some important task and let him know how badly he is needed?

hand him a love-turtle pillow to care for for a few moments?

hug him and share a favorite poem?

find a buddy for him to lean upon?

change his program so he doesn't want to leave?

invite his mother to be a helper for one project or a week?

THROUGH TRUST WE ARE MORE ABLE TO LET GO OF MANY THINGS —SOME OF WHICH MUST BE LET GO!

GIVING UP YOUR CHILD

From *The Prophet* by Kahlil Gibran

And a woman who held a babe against her
      bosom said,
   Speak to us of children.
And he said:
   Your children are not your children.
   They are the sons and daughters of Life's
      longing for itself.
      They come through you but not from you,
      And though they are with you yet they
         belong not to you.
   You may give them your love but not your
      thoughts,
      For they have their own thoughts.
   You may house their bodies but not their souls,
      For their souls dwell in the house of
         tomorrow, which you cannot visit, not
         even in your dreams.
   You may strive to be like them, but seek not to
      make them like you.
   For life goes not backward nor tarries
      with yesterday.

If life goes not backward, why does school deal so much with yesterday's ways?

Have you known teachers who resented sharing "their" students with other adults?

Close your eyes and remember those teachers whose memory makes you feel good. What were they like? How do you want to be remembered?

TRY TO REMEMBER...
Can you recall teachers who tried to force their thoughts on you? How did you react?

Have you recently experienced an encounter with a salesman with an unwanted product? a principal with an unwanted philosophy? a professor with unwanted thoughts?

Will a safe, secure child tend to say to himself, therefore "I am trusted, therefore I trust."?

Are there students in your room whom you do not trust? Are there those who do not have faith in you?

Do you treat your dependable children as you treat those you mistrust?

The Magic Wand

Teacher-fairy godmother
wand of magic
        presto learning
zap!
with many magic
        wands to choose
        any math,
            English, history?
zap!
pinnochio—come to
        learning life
If you weren't
        born with a
        magic wand
        maybe you shouldn't
teach kids who protest for
the magic zap
learning from
their slouch/back
chairs.
        —Janet Bauer

Think of the students in your classroom. Which ones do you trust? Which ones seem secure with you?

Will a student who feels uncertain in your relationship say, "I am not worthy, therefore I place no credence in others."?

MORNING STAR: My head spins as I think of how little trust there was when I went to elementary school. Even though my older sisters and brothers had gone away on the bus to boarding schools, I had always dreaded the day when I would have to say goodby to my pony, my wooly sheep, and my mother. Who would watch over my little brother while my mother was weaving her beautiful rugs? How could I hear the winter stories told by the wise men of our tribe? My fears were great, but I had not imagined the worst.

How could I trust a white teacher who told me to forget that I was an Indian while I was at school? How could I trust a person who took my clothes and washed them, who inspected my hair with an expression of distaste on her face, and who acted as if I were the dirtiest person she had ever seen?

How could I respond to someone who told me that my parents had sent me to this school to learn the white man's ways because they were better ways? How could I feel confidence in a teacher who wouldn't go get my friend's father or the medicine man when my friend was sick?

How much was I trusted when I couldn't go home on weekends because they were afraid I would not come back to school? And when I tried to tell the teacher about the Long Walk of my people, she told the class that my people were bad and were being punished? Trust her after that? I hated her!

It was out of mixed feelings of hate, resentment, hurt pride, and rebellion that I first thought of becoming a teacher. And, later, when I was able to accept the school conditions with less bitterness I decided to prepare for teaching so I could help other Indian children enjoy school—and love learning as I had come to love learning. College, too, was somewhat disappointing. Many of the science and social studies methods courses and materials dealt with so few of the knowledges and ideals of our tribe. And instead of folk tales of native Americans, we studied those of Europe!

Things have improved—my children can go home each evening, and many Indian parents come to help in the school, but I wonder how many of them really trust me? Do I look like a white teacher to them? I wonder!

From Robert J. Fisher in *Learning How To Learn*

RELATIONSHIPS WITH CHILDREN

There is certainly a different quality of interaction in many English classrooms as compared with American ones. There seems to be less fearfulness. The children are not afraid of the teacher, and the teacher is not afraid that the children will take advantage of him. There seems to be greater mutual respect. The teacher is less hesitant about turning responsibility over to the children. Unlike so many American teachers, he does not feel that turning children loose will cause chaos. The teacher works by the side of the children—with them, not above them. He relates to them without placing undue emphasis on his adult status.

The teacher spends a lot of time talking informally with children, and he often goes over their work with them. He seldom talks **at** children; he talks things over **with** them. A nonimposing, accepting quality of spoken and unspoken communication is a distinguishing mark of the ability to relate comfortably to children. The teacher encourages the children to carry out their own tentative plans. Children check with the teacher from time to time, but he will seldom deter them, except to point out where they may be taking on too large a commitment. Respect for a child's ideas implies a basic respect for his integrity as a person.

Too often we let the opportunity slip by, because the prevailing views about good breeding, politeness, and tact have robbed us of our power of independent action. Then we fail to give to others what we should like to give them, and what they long to have. Our human atmosphere is much colder than it need be, because we do not venture to give ourselves to others as heartily as our feelings bid us.

From **Memoirs of Childhood and Youth**
by Albert Schweitzer

Go Ahead! Splurge! Spend yourself! Give!

"These children have no experience," teachers often say, with disdain, despair, compassion or charity. But how can anyone "have no experience"? Why is their own experience treated with such indifference, such contempt? Isnt' it valid? So clearly what the teachers really mean is not that "they have no experience," but that they have no "approved" experience, no cozy well-bred tasteful experience that, talked about openly, would not disturb them, the teachers.

From **Look At Kids** by Leila Berg

Which of your life experiences would be treated with disdain?
Do you have experiences that, if related, might embarrass or annoy other educators?
Are there teachers whose experiences cause you to regard them with charity?

Children with spotless clothes,
Backgrounds similar to ours,
Speech patterns acceptable,
Eager to do well,
These children are The Approved.

—emc

Check Off Your Experiences

People Experiences—
Whom Do You Know By Name?

- ☐ policeman
- ☐ fireman
- ☐ mailman
- ☐ milkman
- ☐ grocery store clerk
- ☐ department store clerk
- ☐ landlord
- ☐ bank teller
- ☐ bus driver
- ☐ gas station attendant
- ☐ (fill in your own)

More People Experiences—
Whom Do You Trust Enough to Call "Friend"?

- ☐ members of the opposite sex
- ☐ young children
- ☐ old people
- ☐ persons of a different race
- ☐ wealthy persons
- ☐ welfare persons
- ☐ foreigners
- ☐ a politician
- ☐ one who has been in jail
- ☐ (fill in your own)

Things Experiences—
What Have you Experienced?

- ☐ ride in an ambulance
- ☐ ride in a patrol car
- ☐ a robbery
- ☐ a murder
- ☐ an unusual wedding
- ☐ a raid
- ☐ a court trial
- ☐ a funeral
- ☐ (fill in your own)

How and Where Experiences—
Which Have You Experienced?

- ☐ flying
- ☐ a train ride
- ☐ being in any kind of boat
- ☐ camping or living in a trailer
- ☐ camping in tent
- ☐ traveling to other parts of this country
- ☐ to Mexico
- ☐ to Canada
- ☐ (fill in your own)

Do you get many experiences vicariously? by reading murder mysteries, the gossip columns, love stories? by attending sports events, concerts, plays? Do you think all of your experiences would be approved by your professor? your principal? your colleagues?

Now Do the Same for Your Children—
But Start Gently
—provide secure environment
—support if experience was fearful or harmful
—respect privacy
—show you care

People Experiences—
Whom Do You Know By Name?
(can be the same as yours)

☐ _____
☐ _____
☐ _____
☐ _____
☐ _____
☐ _____
☐ _____
☐ _____
☐ _____
☐ _____
☐ _____

People Experiences—
Whom Do You Trust Enough to Call "Friend"?
(could be similar)

☐ _____
☐ _____
☐ _____
☐ _____
☐ _____
☐ _____
☐ _____
☐ _____

Things Experiences—
What Have You Experienced?
(could be similar)

☐ ride in an ambulance
☐ ride on a carnival ride
☐ play in a park
☐ ride on a Greyhound or Trailways bus
☐ on an elevator
☐ on an escalator
☐ (fill in your own)

How and Where Experiences—
Which Have You Experienced?
(could be similar)

☐ other sections of our city
☐ camped in a tent or a trailer
☐ to a farm or ranch
☐ into the suburbs
☐ or
☐ into the city
☐ other states in our country
☐ other parts of the world
☐ (fill in your own)

Don't just collect them! Use them creatively!
—through experience charts
—as base for science/social studies explorations
—to develop make-believe experience for others

That age and wisdom are somehow related is not a concept that has been validated, scientifically or otherwise.

And if "experience" is the criterion, then this "child" has probably accumulated more experience from the mass-media electronic society in his 18 years than his parents have in their lifetimes.

From **The Children of Change** by Don Fabun

B.T.V.
   (Before television)
	But D.T.V.
	   (During television)

the style was—	the style is—
group learning	group learning
graded	graded
teacher directed	etc.
regurgitation	
competitive	so, what's new?

Discipline Is Caring by Alvin W. Howard

Ask any teacher, beginning or experienced, what his biggest difficulty with children is and he will almost certainly answer, "Discipline and classroom control." As the second major difficulty, he will probably cite student achievement or lack of it in school, a problem closely related to discipline.

Good discipline is important because no group of people can work together successfully without establishing standards of behavior, mutual respect, and a desirable system of values that leads each person in the group to develop self-control and self-direction.

Good discipline does **not** result if a teacher adopts an inflexible punitive approach or if he is too permissive, pretending that annoying behavior does not exist. In **Schools Without Failure,** William Glasser points out that those who would completely eliminate or substantially relax rules in their eagerness to please children don't realize that firm and fair policies of discipline indicate that adults care about young people and that chil-

dren may interpret the reverse as a symptom of lack of interest in them.

In their relations with pupils, teachers should be firm, fair, and friendly. A teacher needs to take firm positions on many things, but before he does he must determine what he is standing for or against and what his stand implies. Firmness does not imply rigid domination of children nor does it require snarling and growling at them to cow them into submission. Authoritarianism breeds resentment; taking a "Do this or else" position can be exactly the wrong thing for · teacher to do. (For example, a beginning teacher told Dick, a large eighth grader, to take his seat or go to the office. He did neither, and she could not physically compel him to obey her. So, she sent for the principal who, after a quick appraisal of the situation, said, "Come, Dick, you and I need to talk about this someplace else.")

Most children have a keen sense of fair play. If a pupil does something wrong, he expects to bear the consequences, but he also expects anyone else who commits the same offense to receive the same treatment. A teacher should not play favorites or punish the entire class for the sins of a few (e.g. mass detention). A better method is to have a private conference with the erring child as soon as possible about the problem. At best, detention, whether for one student or for many, is of dubious value.

A teacher should be scrupulously fair and courteous—especially if he expects similar treatment. The teacher who makes wisecracks or is flip or arrogant can expect the same from his students and is not justified in resenting their attitude. (Each day, Mr. Johnson, a first year teacher, sent a large number of students to the office for "smarting off." Yet, when the couselor pointed out to him that virtually every youngster complained that Mr. Johnson talked that way to them, the teacher was indignant.)

A teacher should demonstrate friendliness by being understanding, tolerant, and sincere with students. Efforts by a teacher to be one of the gang are seldom, if ever, successful and often prevent development of an atmosphere of mutual respect that is conducive to learning. The teacher who adopts the slang, customs, and behavior of his students will discover that they may be amused or offended by his actions or contemptuous of them. (A group of girls in one home economics class requested a different teacher because theirs was so "cutesy" that they couldn't stand her.)

Some discipline problems, hopefully minor ones, come up in every classroom. But minor problems aren't likely to become major ones if a teacher remembers the following guidelines:

1. Work at being the kind of person children like and trust, and remember that everyone needs success—particularly those with a record of failure. Maintain the respect of the class without being condescending. (Gary, a large sixth grader who had been sent to the office for his "noncooperative" attitude, told the principal he wouldn't respond to his teacher's questions as long as he had to tell his answers to her clown hand puppet.)

2. Maintain a cheerful and attractive classroom rather than a disorderly one which might encourage unruly behavior. Also, remember that a pleasant voice, a neat appearance, and a positive attitude are contagious.

3. Get to know the students. The teacher who knows his students soon develops almost a sixth sense for anticipating trouble before it begins. Virtually every good teacher reports that some of his students say he seems to have eyes in the back of his head.

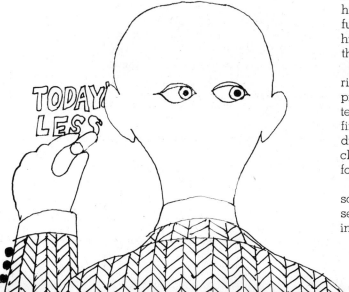

4. Be enthusiastic and courteous and keep your sense of humor. The teacher who really believes that children and learning are important tends to be enthusiastic, and that enthusiasm is contagious. Be as courteous to your class as you wish them to be with you. Also, don't "see" everything that happens; learn to ignore some things and laugh at others.

5. Make education interesting and relevant to children's lives. The teacher who believes he can get by without planning may get away with it temporarily, but before long his lack of organization and imagination will produce dreary lessons, student restiveness, increasing discontent, and ultimate chaos. My guess is that the largest number of classroom offenses occur because the curriculum is dull and the teacher has planned poorly.

6. Don't use schoolwork as punishment. (Linda told her mother that she hated both school and her fifth grade teacher. "Every time we forget to act like prisoners in a reform school," she said, "we have more written work.") Give reasonable assignments, and don't be vague and ambiguous when giving directions.

7. Never use threats in an effort to enforce discipline. What will you do if a child takes up the challenge—as someone ultimately will? A threat that is not carried out only makes the teacher look foolish. (For example, if the teacher threatens to read aloud any notes he confiscates, he may find himself in a confrontation with a militant who refuses to part with a note or the teacher may find himself looking silly after reading aloud a note that proves to be a deliberate plant.)

8. Never humiliate a child. Publicly scolding or ridiculing a student will make him bitter and will probably turn the rest of the class against the teacher. (A ninth grade teacher sharpened the fine-honed edge of his tongue against a borderline dropout. When the boy did drop out of school, the class was extremely antagonistic to the teacher for the remainder of the year.)

9. Don't forget strong-arm students. (A high school physical education instructor abruptly seized a tenth grade boy by the left arm, demanding, "Where do you think you're going?" The boy

COACH

spun with the pull and landed a looping right hook between the teacher's eyes, breaking his nose and knocking him out.)

10. Avoid arguing with your pupils. Discussions about classwork are invaluable, but arguments that become emotional encounters with pupil freedom fighters create ill will on both sides, sometimes with rather surprising side effects. (The group of seventh graders who requested that they be transferred to another class because all they ever did was argue with their teacher knew the difference between discussion and argument.)

11. Don't act as though you expect trouble or you will almost certainly encounter some. (Mr. Potter consistently reported Bennie as a trouble-maker, although no other teacher did. Bennie reported, "No matter what I do for Mr. Potter, it's wrong." Mr. Potter explained, "I had Bennie's brother two years ago, and he was a trouble-maker. I told Bennie the first day of school that I wouldn't put up with any nonsense from him.")

12. Let students know you care. Caring means determining, preferably jointly with the class, what is acceptable and what is not, both in terms of behavior and achievement, continually keeping in mind that all children differ and that what is reasonable and acceptable with one group may not be with another.

Caring means that you are interested in what your students have to say even though it may not pertain directly to the lesson and that you must forego doing all the talking.

13. Establish as few rules as possible and keep them as simple as possible. Examine them carefully from time to time and eliminate those that are unnecessary. (For years, one school enforced a rule that no club could meet on Thursday afternoons. When a new teacher asked why this was so, no one could give a reason. Eventually someone remembered that a long-extinct service organization had conducted activities for children in a nearby building on Thursday afternoons.)

14. Expect to handle the normal kinds of misbehavior yourself, but seek assistance for those problems that need the skills of a specialist.

"What then are **we** to do?"

. . . might we not at least let go of our pretensions . . . and then simply let go of the students?

Let them go. Help them to escape, those that need to escape. Find them cracks in the system's great walls and guide them through, cover their tracks, provide the alibis, mislead the posse . . . the anxious parents, the truant officers, the supervisors and superintendents and officious superegos of the social order.

At least between ourselves and the young, we might begin talking up the natural rights of truancy and the educative possibilities of hooky—which is after all only matriculating into the school without walls that the world itself has always normally been for the inquisitive young.

And who knows? Once we stop forcing **our** education on the children, perhaps they will invite a lucky few of us to participate in **theirs.**

From "Educating Contra Naturam," in **A Man For Tomorrow's World** by Theodore Roszak

---

'Tis with our judgments as our watches; none
Go just alike, yet each believes his own.

—Alexander Pope

AS A CLASSROOM TEACHER YOU HAVE A CHOICE

You can demonstrate your trust of children
or
You can demonstrate your mistrust of children

WHAT KIND OF TEACHER DO YOU WANT TO BE?

1. One who insists that parents sign and return all completed school work

   or

1. One who trusts children to take home all school work

2. One who allows children to leave their assigned desks only with your permission

   or

2. One who demonstrates trust in children by letting them move about without teacher permission

3. One who assigns one student to spy on the class when the teacher is out of the room

   or

3. One who lets the children know that they can be trusted to control themselves when they are alone

4. One who marches all children to and from the classroom

   or

4. One who trusts children enough to allow them to demonstrate their ability to move through the school building on their own

5. One who never allows children to evaluate themselves because they might cheat

   or

5. One who encourages children to become involved in self-evaluation

6. One who manipulates children so that their decisions are your decisions

   or

6. One who trusts children to make decisions about their learning environment

7. One who doesn't share personal feelings with children

   or

7. One who trusts children with personal feelings

Continue this list if this is the kind of teacher you want to be.

Continue this list if this is the kind of teacher you want to be.

—dlr

From *Perceiving, Behaving, Becoming* by Carl R. Rogers

Trustworthiness of Human Nature Is Implied

It will have been evident that one implication of the view presented here is that the basic nature of the human being, when functioning freely, is constructive and trustworthy. For me this is an inescapable conclusion from a quarter century of experience in psychotherapy. When we are able to free the individual from defensiveness, so that he is open to the wide range of his own needs, as well as to the wide range of environmental and social demands, his reactions may be trusted to be positive, forward-moving, constructive. We do not need to ask who will socialize him, for one of his own deepest needs is for affiliation and communication with others. When he is fully himself, he cannot help but be realistically socialized. We do not need to ask who will control his aggressive impulses, for when he is open to all of his impulses, his need to be liked by others and his tendency to give affection are as strong as his impulses to strike out or to seize for himself. He will be aggressive in situations in which aggression is realistically appropriate, but there will be no runaway need for aggression. His total behavior, in these and other areas, when he is open to all his experience, is balanced and realistic—behavior which is appropriate to the survival and enhancement of a highly social animal.

I have little sympathy with the rather prevalent concept that man is basically irrational, and that his impulses, if not controlled, would lead to destruction of others and self. Man's behavior is exquisitely rational, moving with subtle and ordered complexity toward the goals his organism is endeavoring to achieve. The tragedy for most of us is that our defenses keep us from being aware of this rationality, so that consciously we are moving in one direction, while organismically we are moving in another. But in our hypothetical person there would be no such barriers, and he would be a participant in the rationality of his organism. The only control of impulses which would exist or which would prove necessary is the natural and internal balancing of one need against another and the discovery of behaviors which follow the vector most closely approximating the satisfaction of all needs. The experience of extreme satisfaction of one need (for aggression, sex, etc.) in such a way as to do violence to the satisfaction of other needs (for companionship, tender relationship, etc.)—an experience very common in the defensively organized person—would simply be unknown in our hypothetical individual. He would participate in the vastly complex self-regulatory activities of his organism—the psychological as well as physiological thermostatic controls—in such a fashion as to live harmoniously, with himself and with others.

There are two ways of coming at any sort of learning and a moral conduct of life; the one is by instruction in words, the other by practical exercises.

—Josephus 37-96

Even in the kindest and gentlest of schools, children are afraid, many of them a great deal of the time, some of them almost all of the time. This is a hard fact to deal with. What can we do about it?

From **Why Children Fail** by John Holt

How do you react to those who inflict such feelings on you? WHAT ARE CHILDREN AFRAID OF AT OUR SCHOOL?

Close your eyes—picture a young child at school (that child who most closely resembles yourself). What were you afraid of at school? Were your fears justified?

PHYSICALLY ASSUME THE STATURE OF A YOUNG CHILD IN A CLASSROOM. WHAT DOES THE ROOM LOOK LIKE FROM YOUR POSITION? DOES THE PHYSICAL APPEARANCE OF ADULTS ASSUME DIFFERENT PROPORTIONS IN YOUR CHILDLIKE POSITION?

How do you react to these words?
HUMILIATION, PHYSICAL PAIN, FAILURE, LONELINESS, RIDICULE, SUSPICION

From *In Defense of Youth* by Earl Kelley

Many Hold False Ideas About Youth

I have wanted to say that the general public does not understand youth, but this is too mild. Not only do we not understand them, we hold false notions about them. These ideas do not result merely in our being puzzled about young people; they cause us to take action in the wrong direction. These ideas and their results have not only been disproved by research but have failed us again and again through the ages. To cling to them is to fall back far beyond the age of science and reason to the pre-scientific days of witchcraft and even back to voodooism. Some of these false ideas are listed below.

1. Many believe that children are born bad and have to be coerced into being good. This accounts for many acts of aggression committed by adults on babies even in the cradle. These acts are sometimes perpetrated on infants so young that they have not yet even gained their eyesight or their sense of hearing. What such an infant can feel about this is that he has been born into a hostile world. The idea that children are born bad accounts for the "training" concept which rightly belongs to the rearing of animals, such as horses and dogs, but is never successful with humans. This is the opposite of the concept of growth and education. While training seeks to close the mind so that only one response will be available, education in its true sense is designed to open the mind, to reveal the wide world, and to make an infinite number of responses possible. Modern science has shown that children are born neither good nor bad. "Goodness" and "badness" are adult concepts, and they are learned. They are products of the lives people lead from birth on. They depend upon the quality of living available to the young over which the young have no control.

2. Many believe that youth has gone to the dogs. This is an idea which seems to be firmly implanted in the minds of most adults. One is tempted to attribute it to the changed conditions under which we live. But when we realize that this complaint is in the literature almost as far back as

written language goes, we see that we would still have this complaint even if we had not changed the conditions under which we live. The citation of these complaints could fill a large book and would become extremely tiresome. Perhaps it will suffice to quote Socrates, who lived four hundred years before Christ, and to add that this sentiment has been repeated **ad nauseam** ever since, reaching new depths in the last year or two. Twenty five hundred years ago Socrates is quoted as having said:

> Children now love luxury. They have bad manners, contempt for authority. They show disrespect for elders, and love chatter in place of exercise. Children are now tyrants, not the servants of their households.

It seems odd, but the very people who complain about modern youth often like to tell in glowing terms of their own depredations when they were boys. Of course, a story is always improved in the telling, but even after discounting for this, some of the reminiscent confessions are amply horrifying. It is true that more of the shortcomings of youth come to our attention because we live closer together than we did formerly, because we have invented probation officers and juvenile courts, and because people dearly love to read about delinquency. Since we live closer together and there are more of us, there is doubtless more anti-social behavior among some young people.

The over-all evidence, however, is that youth as a whole behave better than they ever did. Careful research has shown that they read better, spell better, and cipher better than they ever did. Not only that, but school discipline and behavior are better than ever before. It is now unheard of for a school to be closed because the students are out of control. But in 1837, one hundred and fifty schools in Massachusetts alone were closed for this reason. In Boston in 1850, it took sixty-five beatings a day to keep a school of four hundred going. About 1875, an uncle of mine decided on teaching as a career and started with a country one-room school. His professional career ended when the pupils tipped the outhouse over, door down, with him in it. I never heard how he got out, but by the time I knew him he was an aging farmer.

Indeed, in my time, the idea that the function of the pupils was to throw out the teacher was not yet dead. The first teaching I did was in a one-room, eight-grade country school where my predecessor had been vanquished. It was a peculiar school in that, though public, it had only boys in it. I learned that nobody would send a girl to the school because it was considered too tough. I have always wondered about it because, although I was only eighteen years old and weighed less than 130 pounds dripping wet (I went into teaching instead of farming because I wasn't very good at farm work) nobody bothered me at all. No pupil ever laid a hand on me, or I on him. The only brush with destiny I had was when one of the fathers came in after school when I was alone and told me that he was going to "thrash me within an inch of my life." This seemed odd, because I thought I was getting along fine with his boy. Since he had stated his errand, however, I picked up the stove poker and said that then was the best time to try. He retreated through the open door, and I never saw him again.

I tell this to make the point that the only trouble I had was with an adult and that I cannot conceive how the former teacher got himself ejected unless he subjected these pupils to extreme aggravation. My success must have come from what I did not do rather than what I did. I did not know any child psychology and my confidence was only exceeded by my ignorance.

Youth, it seems to me, have been getting better instead of worse in spite of living under more difficult circumstances than was formerly the case.

3. It is often said that parents do not love their young these days. Many people believe that parents have become irresponsible and that they no longer care what happens to their young. If parents really cared about their young, they would see to it that their youth did not bother you and me as they now do.

It is true, of course, that some parents care more than others. This has, however, probably always been the case, since people are unique in every way. In the farm community where I grew up, before the automobile had become a factor in our lives, there were parents who seemed to take less care of their young than others. I expect this will always be true.

But in all studies of the nature of the human organism, or of the animals less than human, there is nothing to indicate that parental love has lessened. Parental love for the young is deep-seated and persistent. It can be observed in many of the lower animals. It has had survival value throughout the long history of mankind. How this powerful force, working through the ages, could lessen or disappear in one generation is impossible to explain.

Parents do have to rear their young under more difficult circumstances than they did before America became so heavily industrialized. I shall have more to say about this shortly. There is no reason to believe that they care less; on the contrary, because it is more difficult, they probably are more concerned than ever before. On account of these difficulties they are entitled to our sympathy and understanding, rather than our blame and scorn.

4. Many believe that violence will cure any youth of anything. The same people who believe that parents no longer care about their young accuse them of being over-indulgent. This must mean that parents love their children too much. These people often aver that there is nothing the matter with our youth that a good licking wouldn't cure. They want parents to substitute the knout for love. This belief in the value of violence is so common in our culture that it is frightening. It would seem that the evils of violence would be so apparent, after millenniums of its use, that we would at last be ready to at least try something else. These words may never be finished because we, through our age-long pursuit of violence as a cure for everything, may render this beautiful earth a dead planet, not only devoid of human life but also of blameless, peace-loving animals and the plants on which they depend. Yet many still cry "Hit him!" "Beat him!" "Jail him!"

These people get their impulses from far in the

past, in the pre-scientific days when man was far more naïve than he is now supposed to be. These impulses or beliefs come from the days of the iron maiden and the whipping post. Those were the days when elderly helpless women were thrown into a river. If they floated, they were witches and were taken out, dried off, and burned. If they sank, they were not witches and died an honorable, though watery, death. In those days, the mentally ill were often beaten to drive out the evil spirits.

Although the return of the whipping post is often advocated in the public press (not editorially, so far as I know), the laws of our nation have gradually become more enlightened. Our jails are often degrading and our chain gangs are utterly inhuman, but we no longer beat people in public, and many states in the Union have accepted the futility of capital punishment as a control over behavior.

It seems to me that the biggest lesson the human race could learn, while it can still learn, is that violence never gained anything in the long history of man. "A good beating" never made youth better, even though it might appear to have done so. It never served any purpose except to make youth more fearful, more hostile, more secretive, and more aggressive. It never drew parent and child closer together, but always pushed them farther apart. I would go so far as to say that, unless the youth has been too badly damaged, there is nothing a good loving will not cure. This, of course, applies to our relationships with each other as well as with youth, and if it could spread all over the world, it would be the way to peace. We cannot be at war with our youth and at peace with those more remote from us.

From *Teacher and Child* by Dr. Haim Ginott

Trust

"One teacher I'll never forget. He helped me to change my view of myself and the world. Until I met him, I had a gruesome picture of grownups. I had no father and my mother was working. My grandpa was grumpy and my grandma angry. She argued and accused, and he bullied and blamed. My first teacher was a mean woman, a copy of my grandma. She, too, provoked and punished. My other teachers were indifferent. As long as I was silent, they were satisfied. If I dropped dead quietly, they wouldn't have minded. I was none of their business.

"Then I met Mr. Benjamin, my sixth-grade teacher. He was different. He delighted in our company. In his presence, we felt important; what we thought made a difference. He believed in us and guided us, appealing to our pride and imagination. 'The world needs your talents,' he would assure us. 'There is suffering and sickness and slums. You can be your brother's keeper or his killer. You can bring hell or help. You are each other's agents of agony or of comfort. In every situation, you can become part of the solution, or part of the problem.' His words still ring true in my heart and affect my life for the better."

The Children of Summer

They do not know chromatics,
chlorophyl, nor DNA, but some
spontaneous urge teaches them
the inherent message of flowers.
They do not know the geometric
angle of a lunge into cool water
(nor its molecular structure)
but their souls are happily
submerged in watery being.
They are ignorant of the
thermonuclear power of the sun,
but they know the sun as their
teacher: he shows in their tanned
faces. When shorter days bring
the end of summer, they come
fresh, energetic, and unbridled,
and hushed—They
give themselves in trust to
waves of print and pedant suns.
Summer gave them strength and
natural wisdom—May we do likewise,
their unnatural teachers.

—Jack E. Smith, Jr.

Where are you now?

Trust all children to:
1. sharpen pencils without permission
2. run errands
3. take work home
4. share
5. correct their own papers
6. help each other
7. move around the room with freedom
8. move in a group without marching
9. make choices from a limited number of alternatives
10. share true feelings
11. move throughout the building without a hall pass
12. make personal choices of things to learn
13. choose how to learn
14. choose when to learn
15. choose to learn with others or by self
16. accept your marking or evaluation as fair
17. self-test
18. self-check
19. set up workjobs for and with others
20. discuss with you and give self-evaluation
21. evidence application of learning
22. explore in various degrees and in varied directions

If a man does not keep pace with his companions, perhaps it is because he hears a different drummer. Let him step to the music which he hears, however measured or far away.

—Thoreau

Herb, Janice and Morning Star all began with the chapter on Trust. Herb and Janice both began here because it was the beginning. Morning Star read this chapter first because the concept of trust has a great deal of personal significance to her.

When Herb finished reading "Trust" he called Dr. Roubinek's office and left the following cryptic message:

WHILE YOU WERE OUT

MR. _Herb_

OF _____

PHONE _____

TELEPHONED (✓)   CALLED TO SEE YOU ◯   RETURNED YOUR CALL ◯

PLEASE CALL ◯   WILL CALL AGAIN ◯   WANTS TO SEE YOU ◯

MESSAGE _He said he read the whole first chapter and couldn't find one definition of open education._

For Principals—

What is your "Do Unto Others" policy?
Do you

trust teachers to be as dedicated as you are?
trust teachers to keep growing professionally?
trust teachers to care about all the children?
trust teachers to be honest, sensitive, and kind?
trust teachers to know as much or more than you?

Do you show that you

trust parents to care about their children?
trust parents to know their children?
trust parents to trust you with their children?
attempt to include parents as integral members of the team
    working for your school?
try to help parents and others in the community to understand
    your dreams, your goals, and even your fears?
believe in these people as unique individuals who want and
    expect educators to be successful with children?

From "The Elementary Principal Feature" by Evelyn Carswell
in **Instructor**

How trusting are supervisors?

Supervisors might also try assuming that the teacher, particularly if
he is experienced, is relatively as perceptive as is the supervisor;
they might, in the process, be surprised! Given a colleague
relationship — a relationship of professional respect —
and this is a large "given," the teacher is likely
to bring up most or all of the matters the supervisor considers important. They know when
they have been effective and when ineffectual! But it is very hard to
convince supervisors to trust
the intelligence and percep-
tiveness of teachers.

From **Supervision: The Reluctant Profession**

by Ralph L. Mosher and David E. Purpel

SUZANNA: When Jonathan Kozol wrote about the racism of the Boston public schools, and described so vividly the lack of trust and caring he saw and felt, you would think his book, *Death At An Early Age* would not only have won a national award, but would have led to a radical change in those schools. Yet that book came out six years ago . . .

CELLA (who is a Board Member of the YWCA): In a recent issue of our national magazine I read of a concerned educator pleading with community organizations to help the public school teachers whom she felt "needed help in recognizing the subtle racist traps which they face daily" in the two schools handling children bused largely from the innercity, the Roxbury area of Boston. She found "not an active prejudice, but a subtle, quiet feeling, a different attitude toward these 'different' children—different rules for different people."

SUZANNA: I understand, from what you've told me, that one of the YWCA's prime imperatives is to eliminate racism whenever and wherever it is found.

CELLA: True. On both the local and national levels we are attempting to eliminate racism. I only wish I could get all educators to take a positive stand, and then really commit themselves to that goal!

SUZANNA: I hope you will keep on helping me see the subtle ways I tend to perpetuate racism, Cella.

CELLA: Then you must work at it— but you do work at it, Suzanna.

Cella knows there are many Suzannas who do, indeed, care! But her thoughts run something like this: The Civil War to free the black man ended over a century ago, but the prime facility for reeducating the nation's people—the public schools—still shows consistent evidence of racism. Trust? This sensitive, dedicated young woman knows it is a key need, a key beginning for openness. Many unanswered questions run through her head:

What do you do with those mothers who want their children to succeed in a racist world—will they accept open-education ideas? Or would they think that was another way to continue discrimination?

What do you do with those youngsters already battered by indifference, by subtle neglect?

What do you do with those youngsters whose outlook is shaped by militant, underground groups?

What do you do with fellow educators who really care? With those who pretend to care? and those who don't want to care?

Will more books, more articles help?

What legislation is needed?

Should militancy be encouraged?

How susceptible are you to racism? Is it important to you to eliminate it in yourself? In America? In the world?

Thoughts from You and Creativity

Why is he (the creative person) so different? Or is he really so different after all?

Is he not perhaps like ourselves, except that he has kept something we have lost along the way?

Can you find that "something" in children?
Can you help them to utilize their creativity?

—speculate·on the characteristics of a creative society (among other things) an educational system that rewards and encourages free inquiry, rather than acting solely as a means for transmitting the already discovered and the already "known."

—emc and dlr

Testing Your Certitude with Other College Students

1. Put your name on a strip of paper.

2. List five personal characteristics that you believe will help you be a good teacher; write them on strips of paper of varying sizes, according to their importance to you—most important on widest strip, less important on narrower strip, and so on.

3. Pin them on your clothing in locations that give indication of how you feel about them. (Elbow, back, over the heart, on shoe, etc.)

4. In small groups, be verbally aggressive. Attack each other's characteristics, challenge them, question them. Each characteristic that is attacked must be removed and placed on table or floor.

5. If you would rather give up teaching than give up a condemned characteristic, place the strip containing this characteristic face up. If you are willing to compromise, place it face down.

6. Now examine your certitude.

Can You Trust Yourself To Believe in Your Own Creativity and To Recognize and Nurture the Creativity of Others?

Mirror, mirror, on the wall . . .

What unique characteristics do I have? When I think of myself, do I see only superficial details?

Do I have some traits that I prefer not thinking about? Not discussing?

Do I really know myself?

Do I give my fellow teachers credit for believing in me and wanting to help me?

How am I helping myself?

Am I authentic after all . . .

Assume that you're being interviewed for an elementary teaching position and the superintendent asks only that you describe yourself. List your characteristics. Now, make a check mark by each descriptive term that you think would be significant to children. (Think about the significant teachers in your life—perhaps this will help you select descriptive terms.)

When did I last feel creative?
Why does it happen "sometimes"?
Why to me?

If I want to be a receptive teacher, I must place trust in my fellow teachers, my principal, the children, and—most of all—ME!

Here comes me?

ME? ME. ME!

Student teachers often charge ahead with interesting activities where more experienced teachers hesitate to tread. They play the guitar, teach yoga, take children to controversial public hearings, help them construct geodesic domes, encourage their students to invite VIPs, tie-dye, macrame, cook all kinds of natural-food dishes, and they even play with their children.

One young man, whose native language is Spanish, tackled the language-barrier problem by using a topic common to all his children—food. Here's his summary of problem and project:

A Peso for Their Thoughts ...   by Jim Gibbons

What can you do with a classroom of so-called deprived bilinguals, few of whom read well in English, much less enjoy reading? What can you do to get their attention besides demanding that glazed eyes be focused on your person?

There are a lot of Mexican-American citizens in the Southwest who speak Spanish in a variety of dialects and to be taught solely in English is to be like a long, wadded string with a whole bunch of knots in it.

Mexican-American children speak a language when they come to school. You might say the problem is that the teachers don't speak the children's language. The majority of the schools have tried to solve this problem by teaching the children to speak English. I'm not suggesting that these children shouldn't learn English, but we have no right to reject their native tongue.

If the kids half understand English, they are to be commended. But we, as educators, must do more than scratch our heads. You can't string half beads together to make a necklace. They fall off the string. Neither can you use half-understood words to form ideas.

So I too, scratch my head and wonder what I can do during one semester of student teaching. I am bilingual, speaking Spanish and English. So I think, "Well, these kids know how to speak Spanish already. There is a very systematic relationship between sounds and symbols in the Spanish language. Maybe it won't be such an ordeal to read in their native language."

I have a fondness for Mexican food and I thought it would be a good idea to use a menu so they could read in Spanish. I went to several restaurants in town, but to my amazement, the menus were anglicized. For instance, you order "meat tacos" not "tacos de carne." So I went down to a border town and got a menu with both English and Spanish. It had prices listed in Mexican and American currency. I got another idea. The kids were having trouble in math, so maybe I could get them to convert one currency to the other.

This is what we did in class:

First, I asked the kids to choose the food they wanted. In order to do this they had to read. They wanted to read because they wanted to write on the order forms they had seen in restaurants. (I got this idea from my teacher and purchased the forms at the dime store, for fifteen cents.)

Words that the children had problems with, we tackled by initial letter and then by syllables. Often by tackling the first couple of syllables of a long word, the child could anticipate and predict the whole word. I was delighted that they had enough confidence in themselves and enough oral language background to do this with such conviction as they read. In order to reinforce the sound-symbol relationship, I had them write on the order form.

The next day I brought some papers to hand out. One contained a simplified menu and another contained the description of contents in each type of food. For instance, a cheese enchilada contains cheese (queso), tortilla, and tomato sauce (salsa de tomate).

I asked them to write another order, which they did readily. I then asked them to look at the second sheet and write down the contents of each item of food that they ordered. They did this on a separate piece of paper. On the handout I had a large square subdivided into four smaller rectangles with the headings: carne (meat), verduras or legumbres (vegetables), mois or cereal (cereal) and productos de leche (milk products). In Central America, I had grown up using the words "verduras' and "cereal." But by listening to the children speak, I noticed that they used "legumbres" and "mois." So I used both words for headings

MENU

TACOS DE:	Moneda Mexicana	Moneda Americana
Carne	15.00	1.20
pollo	17.00	1.25
guacamole	22.50	1.80
birria	17.00	1.35

ENCHILADAS DE:		
Queso	15.00	1.20
pollo	17.00	1.35
birria	18.50	1.50

TOSTADAS DE:		
frijol (1)	5.00	.40
pollo (2)	12.50	1.00
Chile con Carne (2)	13.50	1.10
guacamole (2)	20.00	1.60

TAMALES DE:		
Carne	5.00	.40
elote	7.50	.60

CHIMICHANGAS DE:		
pollo	18.50	1.50
Frijol	12.50	1.00
Carne seca	21.50	1.75

ENSALADAS		
de guacamole	12.50	1.00
de pollo	25.00	2.00
revuelta con tomates	6.00	.50

REFRESCOS DE FRUTA		
Piña	5.00	.40
presa	5.00	.40
Coco piña	5.00	.40
mango	6.00	.60

BEBIDAS		
Cola	3.00	.25
naranja	3.00	.25
Fresca ®	3.00	.25
Té helado	2.50	.25
limonada	3.00	.25
café o Té	2.00	.15

POSTRES		
pudín de fruta	6.00	.50
pastel	5.00	.40
(con nieve)	7.00	.55
nieve	3.00	.25
sopapía con miel	6.00	.50

un peso vale ocho (8) centavos en Moneda Americana. Hay veces que los precios salen mas baratos en una moneda que en la otra. Busca los precios de las bebidas a ver cuáles son más baratos.

TACOS TIENEN:
Tortilla
lechuga o repollo
tomate
queso
y _____

TU ORDEN:
_____
_____
_____
_____
_____
_____
_____

ENCHILADAS TIENEN:
Tortilla
queso
salsa
y _____

TOSTADOS TIENEN
tortilla
lechuga o repollo
tomate
y _____

CHIMICHANGAS TIENEN:
tortilla de harina
y _____

TAMALES TIENEN:
masa de maiz
y _____

ENSALADAS TIENEN:
lechuga
y _____

CARNE	MOIS O CEREAL

LEGUMBRES O VERDURAS	PRODUCTOS DE LECHE

with the idea that someday they might be able to use the other synonyms.

After they had written down the ingredients I asked them to write down the contents according to their food group. This proved to be no problem for some, but quite a few needed help. So I took the ones that I thought had the most problems and started with Juanito. I asked him what group he thought **tomato** fit in. He put it with the vegetables and fruits. I made a big chart on the board and they filled it in. I asked if they all agreed when we were finished. If there was a question we discussed it. Then I asked them to take their own order and subdivide it into the four groupings.

The interesting thing about Mexican food is that most dishes are balanced in themselves. The taco, for instance, has meat or beans, lettuce or cabbage for a vegetable, cheese for a milk product, and tortilla for a cereal product. So it was difficult for the children to pick an unbalanced meal. At the same time, I felt that I was teaching the basic concept of a balanced meal. It was a good review in their native language of a concept they had not fully understood in English.

The next step was to figure out the prices. Above each list was the heading "Moneda Americana" or "Moneda Mexicana." I didn't expect their vocabulary to include the word "moneda." So I took a peso out of my pocket and told them "Esta es una moneda mexicana." I passed the coin around and asked them to read the inscription, "un peso." I then said, "Un peso vale ocho centavos americanos. Si un peso vale ocho centavos, cuanto valen tres pesos?" I wrote 3 x 8 on the board. Some answered "veinticuatro"; others said "twenty-four." I accepted both answers and said, "Veinticuatro quiere decir 24 en Ingles." I then brought out some paper currency and asked how much five pesos was worth. Many answered 40¢ right away, but some had problems so I took out some more peso coins. They knew that each coin was worth 8¢ so we took five coins and added them one by one. They agreed that five coins were worth 40¢ and that was the same as the five-peso bill.

We worked up to eleven pesos. This was worth 88¢. I asked if the eight on the left was the same as the one on the right. My question was somewhat ambiguous. We agreed that the numerals were the same. But then with discussion we brought out the idea that the eight on the left, because of its place value, was worth eighty cents. The eight on the right was worth only eight cents. The uncertainties were cleared up when we converted to Mexican currency. The ten-peso bill was definitely not the same as the one-peso coin.

My cooperating teacher had tried much the same procedure with a Sears catalog and accompanying English order forms. During that 45-minute activity one little girl, Lupita, ordered a "Wedding Bells Doll" for $1.98 and filled out her name, address and with some instruction managed to copy the catalog number. During the 15-minute Spanish project, she ordered food for a total of $13.85 in American currency (this is slightly over 172 pesos). Her spelling was perfect except for "Guacamole" which she wrote as "Guamoleo." When it was time to go to lunch, she said her stomach had been rumbling for a long while. She had reacted to what she was reading!

A true alternative to traditional schools might also attempt to find out what the youngsters are really interested in; what they spend their time at when options are open.

—James Cass

Chaos often breeds life, when order breeds habit.
—Henry Adams

For many years, Dr. Carswell has been a strong advocate for outdoor education. At one school where she was principal, she formed a nature club for children of all ages.

1. Two lunch periods weekly, all nature club members met at a school gate to explore a fifteen-acre desert plot adjacent to the school.
2. Each student had a membership card showing what interest group he had joined. Areas of interest were: rocks, lizards and snakes, insects, small mammals, birds, cacti, wildflowers, trees and shrubs.
3. During these exploration periods, children would roam throughout the desert to seek signs of their interest groups. For instance, the bird group found all the birds' nests in the plot, and gathered many loose feathers. They saw tracks in the washes and made sand casts of the tracks. They observed birds flying as the children approached, and they learned to identify the male and female of many species. Occasionally they found a dead bird and this would bring a lesson in anatomy and the principles of flying.

   The other interest groups made similar kinds of explorations, with experiences unique to each kind of interest group.
4. Observation paths were planned and marked with guideposts. A campfire circle was built and this became the discussion center. Certain finds were taken back to school to be compared with pictures in books, or examined under a microscope. Others were returned so other children could see their natural locations.

TRY IT—YOU'LL LOVE IT!

. . . BUT IF YOU AND YOUR CHILDREN ARE INNERCITY PEOPLE . . .

you will have to devise outdoor education activities such as these:

1. Cut a portion from a plastic milk carton, hang it from the ceiling on a pulley that can be raised or lowered by your children; fill it with soil or vermiculite and put plants or seeds in it. This isn't the natural growth, but it may be good enough to help children see the unfolding of new, young leaves, and the turning from shadow to sunlight, etc.
2. Study pigeons — their wing feathers, tail movements, eating habits, droppings, eggs, and what problems they cause.
3. Examine source materials to find what once did grow on the land where your school is built — and make, from paper maché a simulation environment.
4. Most of you city people have zoos — instead of going to stare at animals, why not go to identify those animals the children would like to enjoy in their classrooms, make representative coverings from old scraps and let the children be the personalities of those animals — i.e. the horse in the circus made up of two clowns.

From *How Children Learn* by John Holt

Call It A Faith

In my mind's ear I can hear the anxious voices of a hundred teachers asking me, "How can you tell, how can you be sure what the children are learning, or even that they are learning anything?" The answer is simple. We can't tell. We can't be sure. What I am trying to say about education rests on a belief that, though there is much evidence to support it, I cannot prove, and that may never be proved. Call it a faith.

This faith is that man is by nature a learning animal. Birds fly, fish swim; man thinks and learns. Therefore, we do not need to "motivate" children into learning, by wheedling, bribing, or bullying. We do not need to keep pecking away at their minds to make sure they are learning. What we need to do, and all we need to do, is bring as much of the world as we can into the school and the classroom; give children as much help and guidance as they need and ask for; listen, respect fully when they feel like talking; and then get out of the way. We can trust them to do the rest.

EVERY CHILD IN EVERY CLASSROOM CAN BE TRUSTED!

CHAPTER TWO

Understanding

SUZANNA: The more I read the more I realize how very fortunate I was when I became a principal. My first school was a brand new building and although we found that it was not a perfect structure for teaching, at least we didn't have to struggle with individual, closed classrooms.

CELLA: Remember the slides Dr. Carswell presented at the in-service course you and your faculty organized? Those slides contain innovative ideas for use of buildings all over this country. It seems to me that where teachers and administrators trust themselves to move on to open education, buildings are only a small problem. Any change agent, whether Superintendent, principal or teacher, must build trust in the people with whom he wants to work—but first of all, that person must trust that these same people want to do good things for all children. Included in this trust is the recognition that all teachers want to be better teachers.

SUZANNA: Well, I certainly found this to be true. Trust, like love, seems to be "caught" rather than taught, but either way, it's an essential base for open education!

Don't walk in front of me—
I may not follow.
Don't walk behind me—
I may not lead.
Walk beside me—and just
Be my friend.
                    —Camus

A swift walker, if he happens to be walking with a child, gives him his hand and shortens his stride and does not go too fast for his small companion.

                    —Quintilian

For a great majority of mankind are satisfied with appearances as though they were realities and are often more influenced by things that seem than by those that are.

                    —Machiavelli

TONY: Suzanna, this Machiavelli quote seems to apply to schooling. I have been told by some teachers that children should be made to do things they don't like because this prepares them for the real world outside of school. They give the appearance of educating children, but I think this is appearance, not reality.

SUZANNA: What kinds of practices in your school seem to be appearances of reality rather than real to you, Tony?

TONY: I want you to know that I think my school is more aware of reality than most others—otherwise I would not be doing my student teaching here, Suzanna. Yet, even here, we still try to teach all children how to read by the first year after kindergarten even though we know many children do not have eye muscles developed to read from left to right from a book with small print. We still teach children to add and subtract even though we know they are not ready for the conservation principle. We still act as if art, music, drama and body movement are curriculum frills to be added only after the basic skills are mastered.

What procedures at your school are based on invalid assumptions?
What rules have no real basis?

—Order one set of Understanders; bend gently for proper size. (Understanders: To be worn when working with Children.)

A true story, unfortunately
THE AWFUL BEGINNING by James A. Smith

I looked across the desk at my big girl. She'd come for help in planning her semester schedule.

"Look," I said, "you have some electives. Why don't you take a course or two for fun? You've worked hard and really should take something outside your major that will be pleasurable."

"Like what?" she asked.

My eyes scanned the college schedule of courses. "Like Dr. Mann's Creative Writing or Dr. Camp's Painting for Beginners or something like that."

She threw back her head and laughed. "Who, me? Paint or write? Good grief, Dad, you ought to know better than that!"

"And this," I thought, "is the awful ending."

It was not always like this. I remembered an early golden September day when I went to my garage studio and gathered together my easel, paintbrushes, and watercolors. I sensed someone was watching me and looked up from my activity to see her framed in silhouette in the doorway. The breeze and the sun tiptoed in the gold of her curls. Her wide blue eyes asked the question, "Whatcha doin'?"

"I'm going to the meadow to paint," I said. "Want to come along?"

"Oh, yes." She bounced on her toes in anticipation.

"Well, go tell Mummy and get your paints."

She was off but returned in no time carrying the caddy I had made to hold her jars of paint and her assortment of brushes.

"Paper?" she asked.

"Yes, I have plenty of paper. Let's go."

She ran down the hill before me, pushing aside the long, soft grasses of the meadow. I watched closely for fear of losing her golden top in the tops of the goldenrod. She found a deserted meadowlark's nest and we stopped to wonder at it. A rabbit scurried from under our feet. Around us yellow daisies and goldenrod nodded in friendly greeting. Above, the sky was an infinite blue. Beyond the meadow, the lake slapped itself to match the blue of the sky.

On the lake, a single white sailboat tipped joyously in the breeze. My daughter looked up and saw it. "Here!" she said.

Trusting her wisdom as I always did, I set up our easels. While I deliberated over choice of subject and color, she had no such problem. She painted with abandonment and concentration and I left her alone, asking no questions, making no suggestions, simply recognizing uncontaminated creative drive at work.

Before I had really begun, she pulled a painting off her easel.

"There!" she said. "Want to see?" I nodded.

I cannot describe the sense of wonder that flooded over me as I viewed her work. It was all there—that golden September day. She had captured the sunlight in her spilled yellows, the lake in her choppy, uneven strokes of blue, the trees in her long, fresh strokes of green. And through it all, there was a sense of scudding ships and the joyousness of wind that I experience when I sail, the tilting and swaying of the deck, the pitching of the mast. It was a beautiful and wondrous thing and I envied her ability to interpret so honestly, so uninhibitedly, so freshly.

"Are you going to give it a name?" I suggested.

"Yep! Sailboats!" she responded, as she taped another sheet of paper to the easel.

There wasn't a single sailboat in the picture.

She began school the following week. One dreary November day she came into my study with a sheet of paper in her hand.

"Daddy," she asked," will you help me draw a sailboat?"

"Me? Help **you** draw a sailboat?"

My eyes turned to the wall where her golden September painting hung in a frame I had made for it.

"Me? Help you draw a picture of a sailboat? Why, sweetheart, I could never paint a picture like the one over there. Why don't you paint one of your own?"

Her blue eyes looked troubled.

"But, Daddy, Miss Ellis doesn't like **my** kind of painting."

She held up her sheet of paper in the middle of which was a dittoed triangle.

"Miss Ellis wants us to make a sailboat out of this."

And that was the awful beginning!

CELLA: (having entered the Resource Center with a toadstool, some pine cones and needles, and some rocks) José, are you having fun in your exploration of open education? I noticed at an earlier meeting that your eyes sparkled when Professor Carswell suggested we try creating open education in our group. I thought you'd speak up, but you didn't.

JOSÉ: Cella, I never have found it easy to speak up with adults. I don't even speak up often with children. Guess that's why this open education idea appeals to me. I teach children by having the children do most of the talking.

CELLA: That sounds good to me, José. If you already have children involved, why are you still exploring the open education concept?

JOSÉ: Obviously I haven't been doing it well enough, Cella. My very reticence has prohibited my understanding of those shy youngsters in my classes.

CELLA: (as a few pine cones slipped off her armful of treasures) Oh, dear!

JOSÉ: (replacing the pine cones cautiously) And just what do you intend to do with all those things you are carrying? Have you been up on the mountains?

CELLA: Not today, these things are from a ranch near here. Wherever I go, I gather up some of the things I see, knowing that some children will be able to make exciting learning experiences from anything I collect. Then, too, I hope to encourage the children to share things that seem important to them.

JOSÉ: I'd like to work with you, Cella!

CELLA: (laughing) I'd like that, too!

Teachers, as people, exert an enormous influence on children's attitudes, self-concepts and sense of personal worth.

Any educator knows this.

It is harder for the profession to admit that teachers, as people, can blight as well as foster the personal growth of children.

From **Supervision: The Reluctant Profession**
by Ralph L. Mosher and David Purpel

FAILURE IN FIRST-GRADE by Mary M. Harris

All of us have seen failure and have commiserated with those who failed. Yet how many of us have actually felt the frightening despair of failure? I have.

A veteran teacher with 15 years' experience in several excellent schools, I've been called a born teacher. However, when I recently faced a class of first graders, I was a failure day after day.

My room was set up as a modified open classroom with various activity centers. Theoretically, the group should have been busy and happy. It wasn't. It was a disaster. Noise reached a frenzied pitch. The children didn't listen to me. Once I banged a book against the desk, making a terrific noise. Silence enveloped the room for a moment—perhaps long enough for them to hear my next five words.

My hopes for some small success with an individual or two came to nothing. Amantha wouldn't work unless she received help from me ahead of her classmates. Arlene was sure Elizabeth was getting more of my time than she was. Arnold perched on the edge of his seat as if ready to fly away.

I spent long hours trying to set up interesting lessons, made complete daily plans with several alternatives by way of backup so I could make a quick switch, and tried various methods of control, including formal seating. None of these worked.

My colleagues were sympathetic; the principal assured me things would be better another year.

But nothing helped—I was failing as a teacher.

Beginning to think about former students who had a failure image, I understood, for the first time, their deep fears and realized why verbal encouragement didn't help them.

Praise is only a surface comfort. No one needs to tell a person whether he's a success or a failure. He knows the answer in his own heart, and until a change is made, nothing counts.

It seemed that the only answer to my problem was to try to get through the year somehow. Maybe then I could reach an exit, get straightened out, and start off in the right direction with a new class. But in the middle of the night, a nagging sense of failure still woke me up.

Walking home after one horrible day, I was so immersed in misery that I didn't see Mrs. Walker until her cheery voice called out, "Hello, Mrs. Harris. Let me tell you what Ernie said today. He rushed in from school shouting that this was the most important day of his life."

"Really?"

"Yes! He learned to use the zipper on his pants."

"That's wonderful—wonderful!"

As I left her, she called after me, "He doesn't have to pull them down anymore."

I had never placed much importance on a boy's ability to use a zipper. Suddenly, these questions hit me: Do the children and I have the same interests and ambitions? Do I understand **their** concerns? That night I began the difficult and painful task of figuring out what goals each child was really striving for and whether or not he was aware of them.

Opal didn't care about learning phonics; she just wanted to be as secure as Vicky. That was why she loved to copy things; her papers were beautiful.

Joe wanted to be boss. To hold his position of power, he divided the boys into factions that fought each other in an effort to win his favor. He had little time left for schoolwork.

Patrick was afraid to walk home alone because a gang of older boys tormented him. He spent his day trying to keep on good terms with Tom, his neighbor, so they could walk home together.

Isabel? Now it was clear why she always chose books and projects which were too hard for her. If she chose something sufficiently beyond her ability, success and failure were irrelevant.

Randolph chose the same easy books over and over so he could appear to his parents to be reading well.

While going down through the list, I became more and more aware that the children in my class were not interested in what **I** considered significant. Why was their attitude different from that of young children in my previous classes?

Could it be because of the open classroom, with its freer expression? The longer I puzzled over the problem, however, the more I became aware of factors outside the classroom. Convinced that parents, relatives, and even society in general were involved, I began to conclude that the generation gap has reached the first grade.

Today's six-year-old has grown up in troubled times. He listens to his relatives, his parents, the teen-ager in the park, the boy next door, his teacher, the TV. Who is right? Whom should he follow? No wonder he's confused. He resorts to seeking his own immediate goals. These are important to him, and whether we like it or not, they must be important to us.

With this in mind, I asked myself some searching questions. What about **my** goals? Should I forget my contract to teach boys and girls to read, write, and do arithmetic? Should each child be permitted to work toward his own goals, ignoring those of other people? If Randolph's only goal is to please his parents, should I permit him to keep on choosing the same books over and over? How can I help these children understand what they are seeking and, through their understanding, help them grow emotionally and intellectually? If they can't face their problems in the early school years, how can they face problems which will surely become more disquieting for them and more disrupting for society?

Having thought this through, I began to unfold a plan for my class. Working with me individually, each child developed a list of goals which we both agreed were important for him. These goals were concrete and positive. For example, one of Joe's goals was to help organize games which included **all** the boys. In doing this, he was leading without breaking the group into factions.

Vicky seemed secure, but actually she was shy. One of her aims was to help Opal learn to read. Her efforts served three purposes: Vicky was overcoming her shyness, and Opal was not only learning to read but was getting satisfying attention from her idol.

Patrick set himself the goal of playing with a different person each day. This separated him from Tom and helped him make friends with others. (He found he could still walk home after school with Tom.)

Each child had a written list of his goals. Parent conferences revealed that many boys and girls took the lists home and discussed them with their families.

The children came to realize that all their goals fell under two general headings:

• Try to think of others.   • Try to do your best.

Soon my class began to take on some semblance of order. It was still noisy; there were fights and sometimes emotional outbursts. But now we could discuss these individually, in small groups, or as a class. We became aware of each other. The students didn't always follow my directions, but they tried. (I stopped taking tranquilizers.)

There were many red-letter days, such as the one when the Japanese boy who had entered the class speaking only his native language first answered in English loud enough to be heard. (The class spontaneously clapped.) And there was the day Joe left a game to ask David, a loner, to join up.

My original goals were also being realized. Isabel no longer chose materials that were beyond her. Slowly but surely she was working on her own level of competence and enjoying her success.

Randolph chose a new library book each day and read it well because he wanted to. (His parents were impressed.) Opal and Vicky created a play, and Opal wrote a beautiful note requesting to stage it.

Surveying the situation, I felt warmly satisfied. The children were facing their problems. We didn't have complete solutions, but we were getting someplace.

To Julie

I love you, Julie
I love your little face
And your wrinkled brow.
Pain.
All hidden behind such
Young blue eyes.
I love the shy,
Do-I-dare-take-the-risk smile
That sometimes creeps up on
Your baby old lady face.

I love the tired voice coming
From the depths
Of someplace I cannot go
But even if you took me
I would not
Recognize it.

I love the frightened joy that
Blossoms on your
Face when your answer
Is right. When I reach down
Into that tired mind and let
A shaft of sunlight
Fall on the dead roses in your head.

We must clear them away, Julie,
You and I,
And we must let the smothered
Seeds of morning glory come
Bursting through.

—Kathleen Mulholland

Each person's learning pattern is somewhat like the garden spider's intricate, delicate and beautiful web. While certain similar strands seem identifiable, seldom does the web appear to be the same from day to day.

So it is with each individual's learning. Today it appears orderly, flexible, larger. In tomorrow's environment it may appear battered, shortened—or extended and secure.

The spider adjusts the web each moment. So, too, the learner adjusts his strands of knowledge as the moment dictates. When we, as teachers, want it enlarged, sometimes the learner shortens it, or it appears battered. Sometimes when we aren't expecting enough, the learner suddenly spins a widely expanded, beautifully intricate web.

—emc

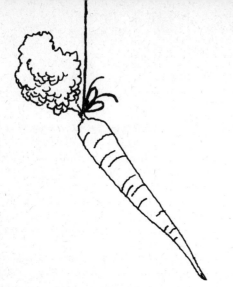

Heavy emphasis on marks, grades, and rank in class results in competition for grades as ends in themselves, prostituting learning and discovery, and generating anxiety.

—Frederick M. Raubinger

The Grading Game
by Brian Patrick McGuire

Last spring I graduated from the University of California, Berkeley, with the highest grade-point average in the College of Letters and Science. In preparing a speech I had been asked to deliver at the annual Phi Beta Kappa dinner, I did some hard thinking that quickly made me realize that my single-minded pursuit of high grades in college had not been worth it. The grade-point game had distracted me from the real goal of education—the development of myself as a person.

My speech at the Phi Beta Kappa dinner advocated the elimination of the letter-grading system and the placing of all courses outside the major field on a pass-fail basis. I recommended that in major areas, each student would be evaluated by means of written appraisals after the completion of each course.

Although my proposals (based on the problems I had experienced in my own university education) were directed to institutions of higher education, I found that high school teachers and students were interested in my suggestions. The very first letter I received after my speech came from a high school teacher in Merced, California, who congratulated me for saying what she had

believed all her teaching life: that grades provide a major obstacle to anyone concerned with teaching or learning.

Since last spring, I have heard from a number of other secondary school teachers and have discussed the matter with many high school students. On the basis of this I have become convinced that the traditional letter-grading system should also be eliminated in precollege education, for it discourages learning more than it encourages it.

Actually, my own experience in secondary school should have been enough to lead me to this conclusion. At the high school I attended in Berkeley, California, my friends and I learned to play the grade-point game with consummate skill. We were preparing for the game of college, and we were told time and again that we had to follow the rules in high school so we would be admitted to the major leagues.

Most of us never questioned the rules. But now that I can look back upon both high school and college, I view the whole system as unfortunate. My major objection to grading as I experienced it is that grades instead of merely symbolizing what had been learned usually became the sought-after goal. In almost all of my courses, my classmates and I were concerned not with how much we were going to learn, but with how much knowledge we had to acquire in order to get a high grade.

Whenever a major examination was imminent, we began to compute exactly how much we had to know in order to get the grade we wanted or needed. As one of my friends summarized his philosophy, we wanted "the best possible grade for the least possible amount of work."

More outwardly idealistic than my friend, I pretended to be shocked by such an outlook. But now, in retrospect, I can see that I was working within the same framework. Like the others, I gauged my efforts on the requirements each teacher set up for the magical "A." Each teacher posed a separate challenge. We would observe his tastes and preferences and then cater to them. Before the first grading period was over, the teachers had revealed their personalities and expectations sufficiently for all of us to know how much preparation was necessary for the first examination.

In high school most of us were too young to be consciously cynical about what we were doing. The problem was more one of adjusting to the system as we found it than of asking ourselves why we were behaving as we were. The classroom was only an extension of the playing field. Good grades were like games won, and points in American history were almost the same as points in a basketball game. The idea of competition was exalted as a good thing in studies as well as in sports.

Knowledge became a matter of discrete packets of information greedily acquired and then unwrapped and displayed on examination papers. Despite occasional orations on the real aims of education and the fulfillment of learning, the difference between what was preached to us and the way we learned did not bother us.

Self-awareness would have been a dubious quality in those days, for so many of our assumptions had in them the makings of disillusionment. As a freshman, I gravitated to a social group that contained the students who accepted the same values I did. We stood on the same spot in the yard at lunchtime for four years and usually spent our time discussing the next examination. Unknowingly we segregated ourselves from the rest of our class. We were the "A" honor-roll group, and somehow students who were not on the honor roll did not get into our group. We never thought of ourselves as being proud or aloof, but of course we never bothered to listen to what those outside our group had to say about us.

It wasn't until my senior year that I realized the resentment felt by others toward the class pecking order. In the spring, the whole class went on a religious retreat. During our discussions, we began to comment on our relations with each other. At one point while I was speaking, another student, Steve, interrupted me: "McGuire, you and all the others like you think you're so good and so much above the rest of us. You get your grades and count your honors and won't have anything to do with anyone else." Before that moment I had hardly been aware of Steve's existence. Now I was stunned to see how disgusted he was by the way of life I represented to him. The very values I had accepted without question had helped make me blind to him and to others like him in the class. I was tempted to dismiss the attack as pure jealousy, but I knew there was much more than jealousy in his words.

For a few days I was bothered by the realization that my unconscious acceptance of the grading system as my criterion for learning and even for friendships had cut me off from many of the people in my class. Then I rationalized that a division between me and "the others" was almost necessary for the continuation of my academic success. I remembered how a friend of mine had summarized the situation by a principle from physics: "A body is buoyed up in a fluid by a force equal to the weight of that fluid which it displaces." In other words, a good student looks good because he is being supported by comparison with the mediocrity of poorer students.

This principle was a ready cure for pre-examination anxiety. I only had to remember that everyone else would score much lower than I, and so my grade would inevitably be an "A" even if I had a limited understanding of the material. Consequently, I would gauge myself and my success not on what I had learned, but on what everyone else had **not** learned. Now that I look back upon this inverse system of learning, I wonder how I could have accepted such a cynical outlook. But I was so caught up in competition for grades that I could be oblivious to my own methods.

Some of my teachers tried to avoid the pitfalls of inverse learning by carefully setting up rigid standards independent of class averages. They would compute everything in points. If someone did not acquire a certain number of points, then he could not get an "A," no matter how poorly the rest of the class did. But such a system made students think of knowledge in terms of individual quanta, each worth a certain number of points. All knowledge-quanta without point value immediately became irrelevant. The demands of academic efficiency deadened intellectual curiosity. If a certain chapter was not required for an examination, we would ignore it. With the guidelines of the point system, we did the minimum work for the maximum grade. With the point system the advantage was that the minimum was more exactly defined.

To those who object to grades, the pat answer is that the grading system is indeed a game, but life is made up of such games, and the sooner one learns how to play with skill, the better. Everyone is aware of the game's inequities, such as varying standards from teacher to teacher, but one finds inequities of this sort on every hand. The point is to learn to cope with situations like this in school so that one will know how to act later on. And sometimes it can even be fun to bluff your way through by pretending to know something.

The fallacy of this argument is obvious: It assumes that the grading system is sound because it follows the patterns of other life systems. The argument tries to excuse the injustice of grades on the basis of the injustice one finds in life in general. But no matter how faithfully the grading system corresponds to life, its basic flaw remains. It forces students to concentrate on marks instead of learning.

Many people would probably agree with some of the preceding observations but claim that if grades were removed, then there would be no motivation for students to learn. Such a fear ignores the real motivation behind the learning process. What I did learn in high school, I learned because I found joy in discovering what I had not previously known about myself, other people, and the world. The moment of recognition gave a reward that no grade could replace. Without such moments the whole structure of grades and preparation for college would never have been able to convince me to study.

Always grades were only the threat, the cattle prod. The real motivation was the satisfaction I acquired from the process of discovery. With some teachers I could almost forget about the grade and simply enjoy the interaction among the teacher, the subject, and myself. Those were the classes where I learned the most, for I was concentrating on the joy inherent in personal discoveries rather than on the punishment of a bad grade or the satisfaction of a good one.

One alternative to the letter-grading system is the pass-fail standard. Pass-fail sets a certain minimum requirement for all students but makes no attempt to classify their achievements beyond that standard. It would be up to the teacher to write an analysis of each student's work at the end of the semester. Such an evaluation would avoid the traditional slots of "A," "B," "C," "D" or word equivalents like "Excellent," or "Good." Instead the teacher would be called upon to outline the exact areas of the subject in which the student had made progress and the areas in which he showed weakness. Also the student himself would be asked to evaluate his own work and to point out the ways he could have done better.

At the beginning, middle, and end of each year, students would take standardized national examinations. Such examinations would compare a student's performance in a subject-matter area over the year. The standard of the class as a whole in relation to other classes could also be noted. Results on such examinations would by no means replace grades. They would be looked upon only as indications of progress, while the main critique would still come from the teacher himself. This individual evaluation would encourage the teacher to think of the student in terms of what he has learned instead of in terms of the student's response to an arbitrary standard of learning.

These proposals are by no means original. Some of them are already in effect in some high schools. The main objection to individual evaluations is that they would take up too much time. But such appraisals would not require significantly more time than is needed by a teacher to compute averages and record grades. If teachers could be less concerned with manipulating point and percentage systems, they would have more time for evaluating each student individually.

Pass-fail and individual evaluation are only suggestions. The main point is that the present A-F, letter-grade system detracts from the quality of learning more than it contributes. In high school I came into contact with many good teachers, but they as well as their students were constantly handicapped by having the system of grades superimposed on the education we were seeking.

Grades do bring a kind of orderliness, but they also put up artificial barriers between people and learning and between people and people. The narrow pursuit of grades becomes a poor substitute for discoveries of the world. The grading system provides a breeding ground for mediocrity and cynicism. Learning gets lost in a maze of points, minuses, and pluses.

We must abolish the grading system and replace it by another means of evaluation that has less tendency to dominate the educational process.

As the grade system has traditionally been used in the past, each student is pitted against the other. Yet in the "real" world in which he will live as an adult, his most important ability will be his willingness and skill in working cooperatively with others. This is particularly true in the business world, which is predominantly a cooperative enterprise and not a competitive one.

No automobile ever got designed, engineered, produced and distributed without the cooperation of literally thousands of people. Competition occurs only in the ultimate market place.

From **On Education** by Don Fabun

Alfred North Whitehead noted accurately that children need a rhythm of learning. People have periods of latency and activity in their learning that must be considered. But in this area of education we have been strangely inconsistent. We are careful to plan our day for children in the elementary school so that they have active and quiet periods following one another, but we have not provided active and passive times during the school year when students can assimilate information that has been given to them over a period of several weeks. We are tied to a "horse and buggy" schedule of September through June school attendance and vacations occur, not for carefully conceived educational reasons but because of historical accidents and tradition. A more logical approach to educating children would be to have specific periods of attendance followed by a specific period of relaxation and recreation.

From "Flexible Scheduling: An Elementary School Need," by R. Dean Gaudette

"carefully conceived educational reasons"—
    for the school calendar?
    for the hours each day?
    for the placement of children?
    for how many things in your school?

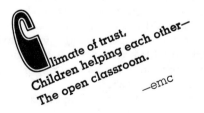

Climate of trust, Children helping each other— The open classroom.

—emc

Thought is deeper than all speech;
    Feeling deeper than all thought;
Souls to souls can never teach
    What unto themselves was taught.

From "Stanza" by Christopher P. Cranch

Suzanna was finding that she was pausing much more often in this chapter than she had done with "Children." She was aware of her personal characteristics of trusting children and teachers, and her ability to expand open environments for both, but she was beginning to realize that she had never really taken the time to undergird her actions with a sound rationale. This chapter on "Understanding" was causing much introspection for Suzanna.

Do I allow time for introspection?
Will knowing myself provide the key to understanding others?
Does understanding others help in understanding myself?
Is it possible—or desirable—to understand people I don't like?

When Gerry Listened—

During a language arts experience in my sixth grade class, one of my students, as he threw his pen across the room blurted, "My writing is lousy!". The lesson, **per se**, stopped abruptly, and an invaluable discussion began that led to one of the most rewarding and satisfying learning experiences for the children and myself.

The discussion began something like this: "What makes you say that?" "Just look at it! I hate it. It looks terrible." "Do you mean you hate to write?" "Yes." "Why do you suppose you hate to write?" "Because I can't do it well." "When did you first realize that you didn't write well and hated to write?" "I guess from the very beginning when I was first learning. I remember my teacher telling me I'd have to try harder if I wanted to write better, and I can remember how my fingers ached, and I guess I just began to hate writing."

From this point on several students freely expressed their feelings toward various school activities they didn't do well in and came to the realization that generally they did not care for these activities. They also went on to expound on those school activities in which they excelled and became aware, that nearly without exception, all students had a good feeling for that in which they excelled. They attributed the fact that they did certain things well to natural ability, encouragement from parents, teachers, and peers, or to some special recognition given them at some time.

During the discussion the thought occurred to me that perhaps the students in our class could perform some valuable services for each other. According to Dreikurs, children in today's society have too few opportunities to be of service to others. It dawned upon me that perhaps here was a golden opportunity to put this bit of theory into practice.

The children were asked if they would consider helping each other become more proficient in areas in which they excelled, and if they would be willing to be taught by those class members whom we agreed were proficient in such areas. The answer was in the affirmative. Each child then made a list of the areas in which he could use some help, and a list of the students in the class whom he thought were capable of instructing in the various areas. The lists were consolidated by subject matter areas. A master list was made up of students who desired help and of students who could give help in the various areas. It was decided that an hour of class time each week would be devoted to helping each other do that which each did well. The class selected a committee of three who scheduled and assigned teachers and students each week. During the rest of the school year, all students had opportunities to be teachers as well as students.

The benefits were enormous. The class came to the realization that everyone in the class excelled in something. They became more tolerant of the strengths and weaknesses of the members of the class. They became more tolerant of me since they had an opportunity to have some first-hand experience in my role. Our classroom was a more congenial place.

As Bernard has said, "To live happily with other people one should only ask of them what they can give." Best of all the students felt good about doing and being of service to others. They seemed to thrive on the idea that someone cared enough to help.

Fringe benefits? Yes. The quality of student work improved immensely!

—Dr. Girolama Garner

Tristan Bernard, "L'Enfant prodigue du Vesinet"
Dreikurs, Rudolf: **Children, The Challenge**

Some people, while conceding that children are happier under the modern regime and perhaps more versatile, question whether they are being fitted to grapple with the world which they will enter when they leave school. This view is worth examining because it is quite widely held, but we think it rests on a misconception. It isolates the long term objective, that of living in and serving society, and regards education as being at all stages recognizably and specifically a preparation for this. It fails to understand that THE BEST PREPARATION FOR BEING A HAPPY AND USEFUL MAN OR WOMAN IS TO LIVE FULLY AS A CHILD.

—The Plowden Report

CELLA: Do you know the main difference between the "haves" and the "have-nots?" The "haves" are able to help their children have a happy and useful childhood.

HERB: I wish my teachers had shared your view.

TONY: Amen!

Me

As long as I live
I shall always be
My Self — and no other,
Just me.

Like a tree.

Like a willow or elder,
An aspen, a thorn,
Or a cypress forlorn.

Like a flower,
For its hour
A primrose, a pink,
Or a violet —
Sunned by the sun,
And with dewdrop wet.
Always just me.

—Walter de la Mare

And, at one lovely school learning is based on the following assumptions:

1. A child is curious, fascinated with the world, eager to try things out, and in need of making sense out of his life experiences.
2. A child is a thinking individual, able to understand and discern; capable of accepting responsibility; eager to make choices and decisions for himself.
3. A child is a unique individual and can best learn at his own rate while following his own ·curiosity and desire to learn.
4. The child is the principal agent of his own education and mental development. Learning is something the child makes happen to and for himself.
5. Given freedom, a child will choose to learn a great deal for and by himself and through his interaction with others.
6. A school based on trust is better than one based on control; one based on questions is better than one based on answers.

From Sacred Heart School, Tucson, Arizona

Can you identify the assumptions on which your school functions? Would you change any of these assumptions?

Statement of School Philosophy

An Action Model

At _____ School, the faculty, students and their parents form a living, Christian community in which people are bound together in mutual aid, responsibility, and cooperation. Freedom exists within this interaction as the liberty persons grant to each other out of their faith in and concern for one another. Such freedom nourished by mutual respect and appreciation; from it, trust grows and individuality flourishes.

Within the prepared learning environment, each child is free to choose from worthwhile options, a sequence of activities unique to his needs and experiences and in which he finds success, interest, and pleasure.

At _____ School, adults and children mutually engaged in the learning process are continually in the process of changing and growing, for to learn is to change. And to experience joy in learning is to delight in life itself, for learning and life are one.

From Sacred Heart School, Tucson, Arizona

From *Freedom and Beyond* by John Holt

Most of the quarrels between adults and children that I see are needlessly provoked by the adults for no other reason than to prove what the child never for a minute doubts, that they are Boss.

This is why, when people say that the teacher must not abdicate his authority, they must be clearer about what kind of authority they mean. They may mean that the teacher should not try to pretend that he does not have more experience than his students, or that his experience does not count, or that there are not things that he is interested in and thinks are important. If so, no argument. But if by the authority of the teacher they mean something else, his power to bribe, to coerce, to threaten, to punish, to hurt, then they ignore a serious difficulty. Teachers with that power cannot get any feedback.

How do you —
  bribe?
  coerce?
  threaten?
  punish?
  hurt?

How can you grow in understanding?

Scapegoating by Beryce W. MacLennan

In ancient times, tribal people would take a goat and with great ceremony heap all their sins on its head and then drive it out into the wilderness. Thus, the scapegoat relieved a tribe of its guilt and freed it from dissension and punishment. In modern times, a scapegoat is essentially a person or thing who bears the blame for others.

Scapegoating is common—particularly in times of fear, frustration, or insecurity, when people are angry and tensions are high. It occurs in situations where the group climate is authoritarian, where the group leaders do not feel secure, where the group is composed of people of different status, and where communication is restricted.

The scapegoat is likely to be the one who is most different from the others in the group. Thus, a member of a minority group, an intellectual in an average group, an unaggressive person in a tough group, or a good child in a delinquent or rebellious group is a likely target.

The scapegoat is often, but by no means always, the weakest or the sickest in the group and vulnerable to attack. He may often provoke the anger and aggression of the group by his self-pity, his irritability, his sense of superiority, or his need for special attention. Anyone may be the scapegoat, however, and anyone may be the one who leads the scapegoating.

Scapegoating occurs frequently in the school and the classroom, with teacher, administrator, or student serving as scapegoat or acting as scapegoater, and teachers need to be able to recognize it for what it is.

Consultants from the Mental Health Study Center and members of the Prince George's County (Maryland) school staff have often found scapegoating to be at the heart of many of the conflicts between members of a school community. In their discussions of various problems, they have encountered some interesting examples of scapegoating in the school.

In one such discussion, Miss Merrihew, a fifth grade teacher, said she was particularly worried about Billy, who, although a conscientious, bright pupil, seemed very unpopular with his classmates. Whenever he started to answer questions, the other boys and girls snickered and made derogatory remarks about what he had to say. When the class was assigned group projects, no one wanted to work with him. There seemed no special reason for the class's attitude except, perhaps, that Billy was new to the group and extremely conscientious.

Billy didn't make any fuss in the class, but in the halls, cafeteria, and playground he was continually getting into arguments with teachers or fights with younger children. These disagreements seemed to be related to the anger he felt toward classmates.

The consultant suggested that the group take a look at what was going on with the class as a whole.

"Who, for instance, is doing most of the cutting down?" she asked.

"Two of the boys seem to be the ringleaders," said Miss Merrihew. "Jim and John are the strongest and largest boys in the class and they really bully all the children. Both do poorly in their schoolwork and have strict fathers who beat them if they bring home poor report cards.

"Jim isn't very smart; and John is defiant, has difficulty concentrating, and is a poor reader. It seems as if both boys are taking their anger out on Billy, who, as a newcomer, has no friends or allies in the group. The other children are afraid to stand up to Jim and John and they join in the attack on Billy. Each one would rather see Billy be the scapegoat than himself."

The teachers suggested that if Jim's work were geared to his level of ability, he might be able to earn better grades and, consequently, be in less trouble with his father. John, on the other hand, clearly needed remedial help and possibly some counseling to discover what was really the cause of his difficulty in concentrating. Both boys might benefit from the teacher's showing more friendly interest and encouraging them to employ their leadership qualities in a more positive way.

The teachers then discussed how they would attempt to effect changes in the class as a whole. Someone suggested taping a series of incidents demonstrating how the children had been unkind not only to Billy but to each other. The class could listen to the tapes and discuss the importance of encouraging and helping one another.

Another teacher suggested that the class might divide into regular subgroups for projects in which leadership would rotate but everyone was expected to work together. If Billy, Jim, and John were separated, the rest of the children might learn to stand up better to Jim and John, and Billy might even make some friends in his subgroup.

Then the discussion returned to Billy again. He, too, was displacing his anger. Angry at his class-mates for bullying him and at his teacher for letting them, yet too weak in the face of group pressure to deal with his problems in the classroom, he expressed his anger by annoying others who were less able to fight back or who had less influence over his life. The teachers decided to wait and see whether reduction in group pressure and a general discussion of human relations in the room would be sufficient to help Billy before recommending counseling for him.

Sometimes a youngster gets the reputation for being a troublemaker and is picked as the problem child in all situations. To understand why he is the one, it is necessary not only to consider him and his problems, but to analyze the total situation.

Betty was regarded by the staff of one junior high school as a troublemaker. When her case was presented to the Mental Health Study Center, she had just been suspended for fighting a white girl who had called a black student a "dirty nigger." When asked how she felt about her situation, Betty said, "The black kids are always the ones blamed. No one cares about us."

In the group discussion of Betty's case, many of the teachers admitted that they felt that the Negroes were more unruly than the white children. Also, they said there was a good deal of friction between blacks and whites in the school.

As the consultant drew these feelings out into the open, the staff began to realize that perhaps Betty thought of herself as a champion of her race at the school. They also saw that they had been denying the larger problem—the animosity between blacks and whites at the school—because they were unsure of how to deal with it.

Face-to-face with this broader issue, the staff decided to form a task force of teachers and students to try to improve feelings between the races. Betty was chosen as one of the Negro representatives. As a result of this recognition and the opportunity for more constructive communication and action, Betty's relationships with the staff and the students improved.

In another class Miss Jones, who was very much loved by the children, was about to leave to get married. The children were happy for her but also upset and rather jealous that she had chosen a mere man over them. Furthermore, they were anxious about having a change of teachers, but they had not talked about any of this.

When Miss Jones was absent one day, the children gave the substitute a terrible time, clearly making her a scapegoat to relieve their upset feelings. Fortunately, the next day Miss Jones said, "I hear you gave the substitute a hard time yesterday. What's the trouble?" The children said nothing, so she continued, "Maybe you're really angry with me because I'm going away and leaving you after all the good times we've had together."

Mary Jane answered, "We don't want you to leave."

"We're not angry; we're sad," added Tom.

"Well, we're all sad at parting and sometimes we're angry that the good times can't continue and that we have to make an effort to get used to a new person," Miss Jones explained. "I'd like to stay with you, too, because I've enjoyed being with you."

Then Miss Jones asked them about how they thought the new teacher would feel coming into the class, knowing that they would be missing Miss Jones. The children thought about this and concluded that she would be anxious. What could they do? Well, at least they would give her a chance. "But, oh, Miss Jones, it won't be the same."

"No, it won't," Miss Jones agreed. "But it can be good in a different way. We never lose the experiences we have lived through and we can go on to gain from new friendships."

The children were still not happy about the change, but they were now able to talk about it and were ready to plan their reception for the new teacher.

Sometimes a child will have special meaning for a teacher and his behavior will stir up an old conflict. The following is such a case.

Jim went to his counselor. "I want a transfer to another science teacher. Nothing I can do will please Mr. Novoric. I really try, but he just shuts me up if I ask any questions. Whenever anyone is talking he always blames me."

The counselor brought this problem up at the weekly meeting with the teachers and the consultant. Mr. Novoric said that Jim was always trying to get attention by asking stupid questions and egging on the other boys to talk and that he was the laziest, untidiest, most irritating boy in his class.

But Mr. Freeman, Jim's English teacher, said he found Jim eager to please. While the boy sometimes did seem slow in understanding and asked some pretty obvious questions, Mr. Freeman thought he sincerely wanted an answer.

Mr. Novoric replied, "Well, I don't know about you, but he bugs me. Why don't we transfer him?"

The consultant had several choices: to agree that a transfer might be best, to suggest that Mr.

Novoric assume that Jim was sincere and answer his questions, or to help Mr. Novoric understand what was especially annoying to him about Jim. She chose the last, because she knew Mr. Novoric was an honest person who could stand looking at himself.

She raised these questions: Why did Mr. Freeman and Mr. Novoric feel so different about Jim's questions? How did **they** feel about asking questions?

Mr. Freeman said that he had always been encouraged at home to ask questions about anything he didn't understand, but Mr. Novoric replied that his father had always insisted that his children think things out for themselves and would punish them if they asked questions which seemed irrelevant or unnecessary. At least, this had been true with all the children except his youngest brother, Henry, who seemed able to get away with murder. He paused a moment and then said in surprise, "I guess Jim reminds me of Henry."

"And how did you feel about Henry?"

"He used to make me furious."

"You would have liked your father to answer your questions, too?"

"Yes, I guess I would." A pause, then, "Maybe I should try that with Jim. Might be a good idea."

Mr. Novoric went back to his class feeling much more sympathetic and interested in Jim. He took the boy aside and suggested they try once more together. Jim was suspicious at first, but when he found Mr. Novoric meant what he said, they were able to develop a good working relationship.

In attempting to understand a problem in which scapegoating occurs, the total situation and everyone involved must be taken into consideration. Often the scapegoater must change his feelings and actions in order for the situation to change. Scapegoating can largely be avoided if feelings can be expressed where they belong and problems dealt with as they arise in their proper context. Free discussion and responsible participation in decision making are prerequisites of a healthy environment.

Teacher, Teacher

Teacher, teacher, tell me why
    You can't be rated for what you do
    But I can be marked and graded by you.
Teacher, teacher, tell me why?

    Teacher, teacher, tell me why
        An A from one teacher is not the same
        As an A from a teacher by some other name.
    Teacher, teacher, tell me why?

Teacher, teacher, tell me why
    Words I use are to you are a "no-no."
    Then why does the dictionary continue to grow?
Teacher, teacher, tell me why?

    Teacher, teacher, tell me why
        You tell us to like differences in our fellow man,
        Yet you treat us alike in all ways that you can.
    Teacher, teacher, tell me why?

Principal, principal, tell me why
    When I dig Mr. Zee do I have Mr. Budd,
    When Mr. Zee likes me, but to Budd I'm a dud?
Principal, principal, tell me why?

Principal, principal, tell me why
    When I learn science fast, but in math I'm so slow,
    Yet the same time for each on my schedule does show.
Principal, principal, tell me why?

—emc

'Tis education forms the common mind:
Just as the twig is bent, the tree's inclined.

—Alexander Pope

Take a poke at your neighbor, and you get sued for damages. Kick a dog, and the SPCA will blacklist you. Beat your wife, and you're a cad. Assault a cop and go to jail. But strike a student, and you're simply a teacher who maintains good discipline.

From "Corporal Punishment in U.S. Schools"
by Diane Divoky

After reviewing a broad spectrum of practices and materials, Miriam Goldberg has stated a number of propositions which characterize approaches considered relatively successful with disadvantaged children:

1. Each pupil's status in each learning area has to be ascertained. Teaching must begin where the pupil is, regardless of grade level, age differential, and materials must be appropriate to his present level. No assumptions can be made about the child's prior knowledge derived from home or neighborhood experiences.
2. Each pupil merits respect as a person, appreciation of his efforts, and understanding of his problems. The teacher must not show by word, look, or gesture that the child's inability to perform adequately or his lack of comprehension of even the most rudimentary concepts is shocking or disturbing.
3. All procedures need to be paced in accordance with the pupil's speed of learning. No assumptions should be made that the child has grasped what has been taught until he is able to demonstrate his grasp over and over again in a variety of contexts.
4. The learning situation needs to have a high degree of structure and consistency so that the child knows what is expected of him at all times and is neither confused nor tempted to test the limits through inappropriate behavior.
5. The learning situation should provide a maximum of positive reinforcement and a minimum of negative reinforcement. Self-teaching materials as well as the teacher should confront the learner

with as few tests as possible in which there is a high probability of error.
6. The classroom as well as the after-school learning activities should provide as much one-to-one, teacher-pupil learning contact as possible.
7. Materials should be related to the world of the learner but not limited to his immediate environment. Stories about cowboys and rockets may prove more exciting and thus a better learning medium than those about the local firehouse and the sanitation truck.
8. One additional proposition needs to be stated, derived not from evidence but from the basic values underlying education in a democracy; although the school should start where the learner is, its responsibility is to enable him to move as far as he can go which is often much further than he himself regards as his limit.

Content, methods, and materials must be integrated in a design which focuses sharply on the role and function of the school in an urbanized and technological society.

Beyond this, however, there is an intangible content which cannot be ignored, because it is significant in ego-development, in motivation, in self-image. This is what is learned from the classroom climate and the teacher as an individual. How to develop a climate in which teachers genuinely believe in the potential ability of disadvantaged children, are committed to its nurture, and convey this respect through their relationships with pupils and parents is part and parcel of the curriculum problem. Those writers who observed that the child "learns what he lives" were not off-target. What the teacher expects or does not expect and how the disadvantaged student perceives these expectations can influence significantly the child's aspiration level and involvement in the educational process.

It is therefore appropriate, and probably necessary, that the goals at any one time may be, not academic achievement as such, but a whole series of underlying competencies which may eventually contribute to the ability to succeed in school.

From **Educating the Children of the Poor**
by Miriam Goldberg

Cella and José were discussing the ambivalent feelings they sometimes faced as they explored open education ideas. If the traditional school programs had helped the great white middle class of Americans to be so affluent, why were these same kinds of people now trying to change schools just when the "children of the poor" were beginning to be included in this educational system.

CELLA: José, I've also wondered how you get along with the parents of your children. Are they hesitant to have you try newer directions?

JOSÉ: Yes, unfortunately they are. They think they understand the 3 R's—and they tend to believe that if we keep pushing these and applying our hands to some pants seats we'll be able to improve our status. I know there are many Anglo parents who feel the same way, but that doesn't help solve my problems.

CELLA: I know what you mean! I wouldn't want my own children to miss the chances they are having in their open school. I see them learning to make decisions, accepting more self-responsibility—and still getting better in the basic skills.

JOSÉ: If it's so clear to us, why can't others see it?

CELLA: I've tried to put down on paper all the really good things I've seen done in a traditional school with self-contained classrooms. Then I've put down on that same paper all the really good things I've seen in more open schools, and I'm convinced that three good teachers caring for a child is better than one good teacher—three styles of relating and seeing different parts of a child are bound to be an advantage for him.

JOSÉ: But don't critics tend to compare the superior traditional teacher with a poor team of teachers in an open school.

CELLA: Often they do because they are reluctant to consider changing their behavior. But that doesn't make open education less valid or less important, José.

And, as Cella and José rose to go, José wondered how he could help more people, both teachers and parents—*understand* the open concepts as he understood them.

Are you sure you're an open teacher?

A Shattered Dream by Mona Mouton

"Everybody wants to know
 Why I sing the blues.
 My kid's gonna grow up
 Gonna grow up to be a fool
 'Cuz they ain't got no more room
 No more room for him in school."

When B. B. King sings this blues, he is singing about the shattered dream of many black, imprisoned ghetto dwellers. That four-hundred-year-old recurring dream of having your children experience less of the hard knocks and more of the good things than you knew. Black people; poor people have always thought of education as the factor that would make the dream come true.

"You better go to school and be somebody!" Not one Black American who has attained any kind of schooling has not heard or been motivated by those very words.

Going to school was the tool with which one was to shatter all of the walls that existed between ignorance and knowledge; black and white; have and have-nots. It was the key to overcoming all of the miseries suffered by a debased, dehumanized society.

Today, in the inner-city school, at an age where technology has landed a man on the moon, no amount of research has enabled educators to eliminate those barriers that impede a cultural group from learning to read and to write. The curriculum, the inner-city school system, and our capitalistic society do not enhance learning. Reading and writing are a secondary issue when you are struggling to survive. Food, shelter, and clothing become primary. Your dignity and privacy are easily bartered for some shallow handouts from the welfare agencies because your hard-earned wages never bought you meat or never enabled you to buy even the necessities.

At a time when much is being said about conservation and pollution of the environment, it is ironic that America has failed to tap her greatest natural resources—the resources lying dormant within poor, unchallenged, unlearned people.

These people are being cheated because they are not being allowed to develop and contribute their individuality and purpose of life.

One popular song today states that it is a "hell-of-a-touchdown just to cross 110th Street." When you see the lives of millions of ghetto dwellers polluted by drugs, hunger, inadequate housing, and despair and realize that all of this indirectly relates to the persons' inability to read and write, then the school, whose job it is to teach, should be held accountable for the fact that many minority children are grossly inadequate in their academic skills. Schools blame the homes and the home blames the school. The home and the school working together is the ideal, and one does not know which contributes what to promote learning. In homes where survival is the pressing issue, schools should revamp to provide those activities found necessary to learning that normally a home might provide.

Parents have not been trained to teach children academic skills even though the parent was his child's first and best teacher.

The children in the inner-city school have the potential for learning, but very little has been done to introduce any material that is relevant to their walks of life or that is even at their interest level.

Sesame Street has been the only agency to have dealt with the culturally-different child's learning in a way that is both relevant and interesting.

One class of youngsters who had been questionably labeled EMR's, could barely recall the alphabet but they were able to recall verbatim all of the current hits played on KGFJ in Los Angeles.

Learning deals with working from the known to unknown, but nowhere is this premise evident in the curriculum in the inner-city school.

More parents are becoming aware of the inadequacy of the inner-city school.

Lou Rawls, in the song, "Tobacco Road," talks about a ghetto, saying, "I hate you because you're filthy, but I love you because you're home." Most families would tolerate the adverse conditions to be near friends and in familiar surroundings but the plight of the schools is causing every able ghetto dweller to flee to the suburbs.

The ghetto schools which generally are about as aesthetic as Folsom Prison are dirty, inadequate, surrounded by high chained fences and masses of asphalt. The school has a lack of everything good and too much of everything bad. The inner-city school is synonymous with the words "tension," "confusion," and "frustration." Much has been said about the over-crowding of slum dwellings and about the oppressive landlord. The same things hold true for the slum schools and their landlords. It is not unusual to receive janitorial services once weekly. The bathrooms are often so deplorable that one would become ill had one to work nearby.

It is not enough that the schools are overcrowded, dirty, ugly, and lack supplies and books but even more appalling is the fact that the inner-city is **racist.**

It is alarming that a growing number of teachers feel that it is not by chance that ghetto schools are inferior. The feeling is that purposely the inner-city children are treated as they are in order to keep them from learning, or, as one person said, "The inner-city school is purposely made inferior so that the end product is manual labor for the ghetto."

Why are school boards not doing anything to make schools equal? Why are principals going along with the trend? Why are teachers not talking to the communities?

Concern is mounting about policies which continue to place untrained and often insensitive non-minorities in the ghetto schools when there are many qualified minority teachers who are told that jobs do not exist. Equally as annoying is the type of teacher often sent to a ghetto school.

The non-minority teacher is not only less qualified but, in most cases, this person physically appears to be different and, in many cases, this person behaves abnormally. It is a rarity to see anyone of striking physical appearance or of a very keen intellect. It seems as though teacher placement of non-minorities in a ghetto school is assigned to those teachers who would be rejected by exclusive or suburban area schools.

On the other hand, the very best minority teach-

ers, because of their expertise, do one of two things. Either a promotion to principal is made or the system considers them too proficient to teach minorities and transfers are made to the suburban school. Both tactics besides being racist are not realistic or humanistic. Being a good teacher has no positive correlation with being a good principal, and transferring of the teacher from the ghetto to the suburbs because of excellence continues to jeopardize the children in the inner-city.

Teaching in an inner-city school is the most difficult teaching there is. Often teachers feel very isolated, morale is rock-bottom low and nowhere can one feel any togetherness. Most times, teachers feel caught in the middle of a hostile community who holds the teacher personally responsible for the lack of academic learning which takes place. On the other hand, the teacher is constantly being reminded by the administration that the teacher is responsible for the gross deficit.

At the same time, when children are not academically performing in accordance with the norms and standards that schools have set, the blame is shifted to the parents by the school—to the fact that the parents have not provided the proper environment conducive to learning.

Parents who are struggling for survival have neither the time, energy, nor the resources for the frills of life.

When you're struggling for survival, chicken and hamburgers become delicacies . . . you can't take your children for a ride when you need that last gallon of gas to go to the unemployment office.

One cannot assume that because of poverty parents are ignorant or uncaring.

It is not the purpose here to mislead anyone and to say that there are not some parents who are just too lazy or too negligent, that their main concerns do not deal with the education of their children. In general, it is found that most parents are less active in school activities and less responsive to any kind of communication because they are tired. Most people who work in the ghetto do hard physical labor, subservient, menial labor; and, after eight to ten hours of hard physical labor no kind of P.T.A. meeting sounds

that inviting! Besides the physical tiredness is the mental tiredness that comes from knowing that the P.T.A. is concerned only with your presence. It seldom deals with or has the power to deal with the real issues in ghetto education.

One parent said, "When I come home tired, I don't want to go. They have the favorite people talk, show 'dumb film' that don't have any relevance. They asked questions and pick their 'favorites' to answer them. It just seems as though they planned it all. Then they bring out the coffee and donuts and gossip."

Most things to be said about the inner-city school are negative and grossly so, but the paradox of it all is that as grossly negative as is the overall situation, there is a factor which is equally as positive—the children.

This is not to mislead or overrule that a certain percentage of every classroom has some children with such serious behavior problems, or bizarre behavior, that the learning of all the other children is so jeopardized and on some days the learning of any academic consequence is negligible.

And, on some days, these children come to school acting so belligerently that their behavior somehow triggers off the behavior of others. On days such as these, and there were many, it was in vain to try to teach.

Teachers complain of their hatred for the inner-city school system and feel little more for their co-workers but over and over again they state that if they could work with just the children, they would find the teaching experience gratifying.

The children in a ghetto school are basically just like the children in any area, in any school; only the problems that inner-city school children face are due to and generated by low income. One cannot assume because the children are poor that they are not loved. One wants to reason why and label what forces are in effect but no one can be sure what psychological, sociological, or ethnic factors are responsible for the fact that in general the children are the loudest, most argumentive, the most garrulous, the most humorous, the most free and the least inhibited of any other school grouping of children.

One would wonder if the school itself does not

produce or preserve such behavior because I do know that when children from inner-city schools attend suburban schools and are in a classroom with children (while constituting a minority) their behavior cannot be isolated from that of all other children.

It is difficult to explain how one feels about being a part of an inner-city but after once being involved in such a school, any other involvement would seem bland.

There is as much difference in teaching in an inner-city school and teaching in a suburban school as there is in drinking Kool-aid and drinking champagne—or listening to Pat Boone and James Brown—or in eating chitterlings and cottage cheese!

From **Live and Learn** by Charles M. Schulz

I know perfectly well that they can read with great understanding without knowing what all the words mean. Semi-literate readers do not need semi-literate books. Bright, average, dull—whatever the classification of the child's intellect, he is immeasurably better off with books that are too difficult for him than books that are too easy.

From **Hooked On Books** by Daniel N. Fader and Morton H. Shaevitz

If we look at children from the height of the little hill we have captured, they are bound to seem unsuccessful adults. Unfortunately we have the power to act on our arrogant and mistaken assessment of the situation, and generally do so.

So we hurry on, desperately trying to organize the chaos that is building up in our own untranquil mind, listening only to what the child would mean if he were adult and not to what the child is saying.

From **Look At Kids** by Leila Berg

understanding can I be?

How friendly

    with each child?
    with all the children?

      with which faculty members?
      with which administrators?

        with which parents?
        with **all** parents?

          How much?
            How often?
              Where is my threshold of acceptance or rejection?
                When I seem to understand, how do I handle conflicts?
                Just how understanding can I be? And still stand
                    where I believe I must stand? What commitments
                are caused by my understanding?

TEACHERS

List your children by name. Next to each name write what you think you are to each child. OR—next to each name write what you think each child is to you.

TEACHERS OF TEACHERS

List your present students. Next to each, list what each means to you and what you think you might mean to each of them. Do the same with members of your department. Are such relationships more distant than your relationships with children?

TEACHERS AND PRINCIPALS

Think of your relationship with each member of the faculty. What are you to each of them. What does each one mean to you?

From an *Anne Arundel Times* supplement featuring the Anne Arundel County Schools, by Larry Nash and Lyn Simmons

Jerome S. Bruner, a leading educator resolves a quandry well. ". . . the very relationship that we have with our pupils is a privileged relationship involving authority and direction; that is, to say, the exchange is uneven. We know; they do not. Since that is the case, it becomes very necessary for us not to use this simplistic authoritative relationship as a means of using our office as a way of establishing truth and falsity."

The teacher must earn respect. It cannot be legislated. He earns it in classroom situations, working with the student, challenging him, encouraging him, leading toward his own solution, respecting him.

By individualizing instruction we begin to put truth into the old educational saw: "We must meet the needs of each child."

The relationship of mutual trust and respect between student and teacher plays an integral part in meeting this goal. If teachers accept their responsibility to encourage successful learning, the child will benefit. Independent and confident learners should be the rewards of an individualized program.

A teacher is a person who can give an understanding to a principle and not just a method to an answer.
—Ruth Manuel, Glen Burnie High School Student

HEY, TEACHERS OF TEACHERS!
HAVE YOU THOUGHT ABOUT—
MODELING AND IDENTIFICATION FOR
TEACHERS OF TEACHERS?

How often have you heard this from college students — especially graduate students — "College professors do not practice what they preach!"

1) They preach individual differences but treat us all alike, as if we come to class with the same experiences, same knowledges, same interests and same rates of learning.
2) They preach about the necessity for higher cognitive level learning yet they test us with lower level test questions, largely recall and regurgitation.
3) They preach about the necessity for learning in the affective domain but deal exclusively with the cognitive.
4) They preach to us about the value of choice in the learning environment but they give us very little.
5) They preach the value of self-evaluation but they never provide us with the opportunity to practice it for ourselves with their programs.

—dlr

This list could go on, and on, and on—Are you a different kind of professor?

The Poor Scholar's Soliloquy
by Stephen M. Corey

I'm not very good in school. This is my second year in the seventh grade, and I'm bigger and taller than the other kids. They like me all right, though, even if I don't say much in the schoolroom, because outside I can tell them how to do a lot of things. They tag me around and that sort of makes up for what goes on in school.

I don't know why the teachers don't like me. They never have very much. Seems like they don't think you know anything unless they can name the book it comes out of. I've got a lot of books in my room at home—books like Popular Science, Mechanical Encyclopedia, and the Sears' and Ward's catalogues—but I don't very often just sit down and read them through when I want to find something out, like whenever Mom buys anything secondhand I look it up in Sears' or Ward's first and tell her if she's getting stung or not. I can use the index in a hurry—to find the things I want.

In school, though, we've got to learn whatever is in the book and I just can't memorize the stuff. Last year I stayed after school every night for two weeks trying to learn the names of the Presidents. Of course I knew some of them like Washington and Jefferson and Lincoln, and I never did get them straight.

I'm not too sorry, though, because the kids who learned the Presidents had to turn right around and learn all the Vice-Presidents. I am taking the seventh grade over, but our teacher this year isn't so interested in the names of the Presidents. She has us trying to learn the names of all the great American inventors.

I guess I just can't remember names in history. Anyway, this year I've been trying to learn about trucks because my uncle owns three and he says I can drive one when I'm sixteen. I already know the horsepower, and number of forward and back-ward speeds of twenty-six American trucks, some of them Diesels, and I can spot each make a long way off. It's funny how that Diesel works. I started to tell my teacher about it last Wednesday in science class when the pump we were using to make a vacuum in a bell jar get hot, but she said she didn't see what a Diesel engine had to do with our experiment of air pressure so I just kept still. The kids seemed interested though. I took four of them around to my uncle's garage after school and we saw the mechanic, Gus, tearing a big truck Diesel down. Boy, does he know his stuff!

I'm not very good in geography either. They call it economic geography this year. We've been studying the imports and exports of Chile all week, but I couldn't tell you what they are. Maybe the reason is I had to miss school yesterday because my uncle took me and his big trailer truck down state about 200 miles, and we brought almost 10 tons of stock to the Chicago market.

He had told me where we were going and I had to figure out the highways to take and also the mileage. He didn't do anything but drive and turn where I told him to. Was that fun! I sat with a map in my lap and told him to turn south, or southeast, or some other direction. We made seven stops, and drove over 500 miles round trip. I'm figuring now what his oil cost, and also the wear and tear on the truck—he calls it depreciation—so we'll know how much we made.

I even write out all the bills and send letters to the farmers about what their pigs and beef cattle brought at the stockyards. I only made three mistakes in 17 letters last time, my aunt said—all commas. She's been through high school and reads them over. I wish I could write school themes that way. The last one I had to write was on, "What a Daffodil Thinks of Spring," and I just couldn't get going.

I don't do very well in school arithmetic, either. Seems I just can't keep my mind on the problems. We had one the other day like this: "If a 57 foot telephone pole falls across a cement highway so that 17⅗ feet extend from one side and 14%7 feet from the other, how wide is the highway?"

That seemed to me like an awfully silly way to get the width of a highway. I didn't even try to answer it because it didn't say whether the pole had fallen straight across or not.

Even in shop I don't get very good grades. All of us kids made a broom holder and a bookend this term and mine were sloppy. I just couldn't get interested. Mom doesn't use a broom anymore with her new vacuum cleaner, and all our books are in a bookcase with glass doors in the parlor. Anyway, I wanted to make an end gate for my uncle's trailer, but the shop teacher said that meant using metal and wood both, and I'd have to learn how to work with wood first. I don't see why, but I kept still and made a tie rack at the school and the tail gate after school at my uncle's garage. He said I saved him ten dollars.

Civics is hard for me, too. I've been staying after school trying to learn the "Articles of Confederation" for almost a week, because the teacher said we could not be good citizens unless we did. I really tried, because I want to be a good citizen. I did hate to stay after school, though, because a bunch of us boys from the south end of town have been cleaning up the old lot across from Taylor's Machine Shop to make a playground out of it for the little kids from the Methodist Home. I made the jungle gym from old pipe, and the guys made me Grand Mogul to keep the playground going. We raised enough money collecting scrap this month to build a wire fence clear around the lot.

Dad says I can quit school when I am fifteen and I am sort of anxious to because there are a lot of things I want to learn how to do and as my uncle says, I'm not getting any younger.

From **Understanding Media: The Extensions of Man** by Marshall McLuhan

In education the conventional division of the curriculum into subjects is already as outdated as the medieval trivium and quadrivium after the Renaissance. Any subject taken in depth at once relates to other subjects. Arithmetic in grade three or nine, when taught in terms of number theory, symbolic logic, and cultural history, ceases to be mere practice in problems. Continued in their present patterns of fragmented unrelation, our school curricula will insure a citizenry unable to understand the cybernated world in which we live.

In an article, "How Fred Andrew Tills The Soil With A Computer," (Saturday Review of the Society, **March, 1973) Dick Hubert and Peter Hauck describe an agricultural enterprise that uses a console for irrigation, computerized analysis and planning for twenty-six different crops over seven hundred miles and two states. The article closes with:** Later, at his neat teakwood desk with his two telephones, radio and intercom, the president of the Superior Farming Company was asked whether he would still like to be running his own farm if it was economically feasible. Sure, he said. "Most of the fun in farming is doing it all by yourself." But it is a way of the past, he said. And for better or worse he is most likely right.

MORNING STAR: I wasn't considered a *poor* scholar, but I do remember feeling frustrated with my teachers' closed minds. I remember many summers when my grandfather would tell tales of our tribe before the white men came in great numbers. He would tell of things his grandfather told him and of things he remembered as a little boy. Then when I saw what the social studies and history books said about our tribe, I tried to tell the teachers the truth. Do you think they would listen? I had to write those things the book said or I would fail my tests. Maybe that's one reason it seemed so important for me to become a teacher. . . . Then she recalled a couplet she had memorized:

'Books cannot always please, however good; Minds are not ever craving for their food.'

(From "The Borough Schools" by George Crabbe)

Do many teachers still cling to tradition because they want the fun of teaching
more than they want children to have the fun of learning?

THE CHILDREN I SEEM
TO SEE MOST...

- THOSE WHO WOULD LIKE TO CHANGE THINGS AT HOME...
- THOSE WHO KNOW THERE IS MUCH EXCITING LEARNING OUTSIDE THESE WALLS...
- THOSE WHO LOVE SCHOOL AND WANT ME TO KNOW IT...
- LOST ONES...
- UNHAPPY ONES...
- CHATTY ONES ...

PRINCIPAL
WALK IN!

THE CHILDREN I SEEM
TO KNOW BEST...

- THOSE WHO CAN'T "COOPERATE"...
- THOSE WHO DAYDREAM...
- THOSE WHO FORGET TO FOLLOW DIRECTIONS...
- THOSE WHO CAN DO BETTER (WHATEVER THAT MEANS) BUT WON'T...
- THOSE WHO HEAR A DIFFERENT DRUMBEAT...
- THOSE WHOSE LEARNING STYLES DIFFER FROM THE TEACHER'S PREFERRED TEACHING STYLE...

THEY ALL COME, HOPING I WILL UNDERSTAND!

Muriel's School

She was one of the smartest girls in her high school class and maybe that's why, after her own children were grown, she decided to go to college to become a teacher. She grew up right across the street from the school and the neighborhood police station and maybe that's why she knew school had to make a difference for some families.

She got to know her children's problems very quickly, and maybe that's why her school looked different from others in the same system.

Children helped keep the school clean so the two maintenance men could teach shop to the elementary school children, many of whom also needed a male relationship;

Children helped with office chores so the principal and her assistant could help with sewing and typing;

Children helped tutor each other, so teachers could offer more alternatives. She was one of the smartest principals I've ever known—long before it became popular to be different.

—emc

A large group of children of a wide range of ages is easier to manage for individual learning than a much smaller group of children of the same age.

From "The Grade School Came From Prussia," by John Henry Martin

Do you believe this? Have you tested its truth?

A classroom, any classroom, is an awesome place of shadows and shifting colors, a place of unacknowledged desires and unnamed powers, a magic place. Its inhabitants are tamed. After years of unnecessary repetition, they will be able to perform their tricks—reading, writing, arithmetic and their more complex derivatives. But they are tamed only in the manner of a cage full of jungle cats. Let the right set of circumstances arise, the classroom will explode.

From **Education and Ecstasy**
by George B. Leonard

Do you believe this?
Have you ever experienced such an explosion?

We sometimes forget that formal education is not a natural institution like the family or the tribe," begins Frank G. Jennings in an article called **"Tomorrow's Curriculum: Future Imperfect,"** (Educational Horizons, **fall 1972). He historically traces some pertinent myths and forms of schooling and concludes with:**
So, let us talk of first things:

The single, most telling indictment of "mass education" is that educators allowed it to remain mass education long after its smothering wastefulness had been discovered for what it was. Its inertia is enormous. How can the mass be deflected and in what direction? How can mass education be converted to or replaced by universal education? And what should this universal education be?

We are talking about system changing and system building. We are concerned to find ways, means, time, energy, patience, and courage to recreate a new educational order out of what we possess. We must have inventories of our physical and human resources. We must build, in large part, with the materials and the manpower of the system we seek to replace, and maintain parts of the old system as we change it. We must assume the dangerously romantic obligation to change people even as we change structures, methods, and goals. We must begin by changing ourselves.

Herewith are some old provocative assertions:

1. The primary mission of education is to make sound citizens.

2. Such citizens are self-validated by the quality of the state they show themselves capable of creating. They must give evidence to each other that they are engaged in that enterprise.

3. The quality of that state is best displayed by the condition of life of the least fortunate, least endowed individual.

4. The quality of that state is enhanced to the degree that each citizen is free to follow a life-style peculiar to himself, limited, sometimes severely, where it impinges upon or limits the life-styles of his fellow citizens.

5. Every citizen, except the severely brain-damaged, must possess a high minimum level of literacy, broadly defined as the ability to get, hold, record, transform, analyze, and transmit subjective and objective information. He should be able to deal with facts and values, know the differences and the relations between them.

6. Every citizen, through his formal education, must have learned how to learn. This is essential if he is to choose and pursue an initial career, be able to decide when to change it, and know how to go about doing so.

7. Every citizen must learn how to identify and tolerate ambiguity; he must have some ability to withstand and to learn from failure.

8. Every citizen must have the ability to understand and assume several social roles beyond that of his suffrage: son, father, follower, leader, worker, user, and critic.

9. All citizens must be capable of performing and possess the will to perform various kinds of community and national service defined and assigned in terms of ability and competing responsibilities.

The preceding assertions are not an exhaustive list. The acquisition of amenities is assumed. So are the roles and peculiar rights of artists. The acceptance of the verities is implicit.

None of this is new. What is new is our conviction that all of this can be accepted as a collective goal for all children and youth. What is new is an awareness that mere talk about goals and priorities never leads to programs. What is new is the realization that beginnings have been made, some of them very long ago, and that we do have the resources and some considerable skill in their employment to realize increasing portions of that goal. What is required is a willingness to settle for small victories, to tolerate provisional defeats, for better roads from childhood to maturity.

TOMORROW'S CURRICULUM:

personal hoppy-copters to move from environment to environment

sensory sentors: sights, sounds, and smells in four or five dimensions

skills in practical application sectors with no great differentiation between child and adult

planet-wide programs

TONY: Janice, do you think educators talk a far better game than they play?

JANICE: I guess so—at least most of the time. What do you think, Tony?

TONY: Looking at myself and my student teaching, I am growing more and more aware that I can talk faster and easier about open education than I can apply it. For instance, I verbalize the idea of every child's desire to succeed in school. Then I find a child whose mother is so eager for him to read that she haunts him and me. She says that if only we would exert more effort, or if only I would demand that he attend to lessons (and she means formal lessons) then he would read and she would be happy. I've talked with him and he feels that success in reading will only bring on another barrage of demands from his mother. So his desire to succeed in school is quite different from the game of success I talk about. But you should see his success in building models—he's a whiz!

JANICE: Can you get him started on reading directions for the models?

TONY: I've tried that—without succeeding. He can read the charts and see the picture on the box cover so he really doesn't need to read the directions. I wonder why I feel uncomfortable with his curriculum instead of mine! Maybe he is more in tune with tomorrow's curriculum than I am.

They that have power to hurt and will do none,
That do not do the thing they must do show,
Who, moving others, are themselves as stone,
Unmoved, cold, and to temptation slow;
They rightly do inherit Heaven's graces,
And husband nature's riches from expense;
They are the lords and owners of their faces,
Others but stewards of their excellence.
The summer's flower is to the summer sweet
Though to itself it only live and die;
But if that flower with base infection meet,
The basest weed outbraves his dignity:

    For sweetest things turn sourest by their deeds:
    Lilies that fester smell far worse than weeds.

—William Shakespeare, Sonnet XCIV

Steve, Go Wash Your Hands!
by Jeanne H. Ward

My silent prayers in school increased in frequency and intensity when Steve entered my third grade class.

Steve had the roundest eyes, dirtiest hands, and wildest imagination I've ever known. These three characteristics worked together toward the disruption of my class's decorum and severely tried my professional patience.

Why couldn't he be quiet and clean some mornings? Why couldn't he at least have clean hands? Why must so many mornings have messy beginnings? End-of-the-day filth was bad enough but more easily forgiven. Trouble every morning? That was just too much. Indoor dirt, mud and snow in season, food, ink from a detonated ballpoint pen, nail polish, glue, malodorous traces of this and that from barn or field—these and more made Steve a frequent visitor to the washbowls in the boys' lavatory. The fact that his goings and comings to the washroom cut into his class and study time considerably gave him not an instant of regret.

Spring was Steve's best season. The reawakening of the earth was an inspiration to him.

One spring morning Steve's always loud voice started the school day with:

"This is a real tick with blood in him. He told me his name is Harold. Watch while I squash Harold!"

(Be patient. Maybe this boy has problems you know nothing of.)

"Steve, throw Harold away and go wash your hands!" Then a little later:

"This bird flew down and asked me to hold it for a while, but it left some little white bugs."

(He must have no one to show things to at home. Act interested!)

"Steve, get rid of all the white bugs. Go wash your hands!"

And again:

"Mr. Craig's dog asked me to help him get a gopher. I did. The gopher cried."

(Why don't his parents discuss the gopher, clean Steve up, and then send him to school?)

"Steve, go wash your hands."

Frustrated and annoyed, I put Steve's name on the list of the school's home visitor. She reported back that there was trouble between the parents but that the home had acceptable standards and there didn't seem to be an obvious reason why Steve shouldn't come to school clean. Steve's mother (who looked chronically worried, the visitor said) insisted that Steve's hands were clean when he left the house but that he had always been inquisitive about animals and things and couldn't resist handling whatever aroused his curiosity.

Soon again at the beginning of the school day:

"This fish in the crick came up three times. The first time he said, 'Steve, make a wish...' "

(Can't you listen and see how the story comes out? Try!)

"Steve, go wash your hands."

Later:

"Look, those smooth rocks are magic. If you rub them and say, 'Rocka-wocka-rock-wocka,' they will make something nice happen."

(Why don't you listen? Why don't **you** make something nice happen?)

"Steve, go wash your hands."

Sometimes it wasn't nature, just the cafeteria that caused a problem:

"Peanut butter is really glue. I made this myself from my own peanuts. Look at these papers stick together."

(It **is** remarkably adhesive, you know.)

"Steve, go wash your hands!"

Days later, I asked for a second home visit. The visitor reported that there was real strife between the parents, but Steve's mother promised that his hands would be cleaner when he came to school.

The next morning:

"A robin gave me one of her eggs, but it's smashed. There was a baby bird in it. I'm sorry."

(When you were young, didn't you ever touch a robin's egg?)

"Steve, go wash your hands!"

And the next morning:

"This caterpillar really had tobacco juice in it, but an elf turned it green."

(Maybe he needs professional help.)

"Steve, go wash your hands!"

The next day:

"Our cat had seven kittens last night. I watched and helped, but she screamed anyway."

(Oh, no!)

"Steve, go wash your hands!"

Desperate, I decided to make a visit to Steve's home myself. As I stepped onto the small porch, I heard a woman's terrified voice saying, "No, you can't. Put it down! At least think of Steve."

"OK, but just once more and you get it!"

I ran away quietly, but my heart pounded for an hour afterward.

The next morning Steve was not in an announcing mood. He said not a word for almost an hour. Then he crept up to my desk and whispered, "My daddy shot my mother in the chest last night and then he shot himself. I touched my mother."

I looked at Steve's hands.

"Oh, Steve! Oh, Stevie! Oh, Stevie, come here."

OPENERS
FOR TEACHERS

Try to understand

that all children do not value knowledge equally

that all children do not enjoy learning all day, every day

that all children do not like the same subjects equally well

that all teachers do not value knowledge equally

that all teachers do not enjoy teaching all day, five days weekly and nine-plus months yearly

that all teachers are not equally comfortable working with all disciplines.

Try to show understanding by

1. Seeing that each child you teach enjoys at least **one thing** each day of each week—and show that you enjoy his enjoying it!
2. Providing a new style of learning in one subject this next week; another the following week, etc.
3. Tackling something new and difficult for yourself so you can feel some of the pain and humiliation of not being immediately successful.
4. Accepting some child behavior that usually repels you.
5. Testing the limits of children's expectations of your behaviors.

Crazy Things

I knew it when I saw you,
that I'd ask you crazy things, like do you
like this or that and hope you'd say
you like me and not care about anything or anyone else and that tomorrow we should get up early in
the morning and begin the
same thing.

—Sam Hamod

Children

CHAPTER THREE

Morning Star had quickly chosen "Children" as her second choice because she considered them to be the very basis for educational thought. "How could any school provide one closed curriculum for the different kinds of children I've seen?"

"Ah," thought Suzanna, "this is going to be a good chapter to explore—children! They're why I wanted to teach, why I want to be a good principal!"

"I hope this isn't full of sickening sentimentality" thought Herb, glancing with haste through these pages. "They are indeed unique, but isn't the purpose of education to force them into some semblance of order?"

**CURRICULUM
From The Children!**

WHICH CHILDREN?

WHOSE LEARNING STYLES?

YOU GOTTA BE KIDDING!

WHAT EXPERIENCES?   WHEN?

WHAT APPROACHES?

Speak to us of Children.

And he said:

You may give them your love but
not your thoughts,
For they have their own thoughts.

You may house their bodies but
not their souls,
For their souls dwell in the house
of tomorrow, which you cannot
visit, not even in your dreams.

You may strive to be like them, but
seek not to make them like you.

For life goes not backward nor
tarries with yesterday.

From **The Prophet** by Kahlil Gibran

On School by Charles M. Schulz

CHILDREN
... **moving, doing, growing**
... **playing, resting, growing**
... **feeling, loving, growing**
... **thinking, reflecting, growing**
... **being, being, being—**
            CHILDREN

From WHAT IS A CHILD? by Ashley Montagu

It is with these **capacities** (the ability to love, to cooperate, the development of educability and intelligence) that the human infant is born, capacities that await the training he will receive from others so that they may become **abilities.** Obviously, none of the behavioral needs is quite as imperative as the need, say, for oxygen. Nevertheless, the behavioral needs are basic to the survival of human beings as human beings.

Human beings incapable of learning are incapable of survival in a human environment without the support of others. Obviously, it is important for a human being to learn to speak; it is even more important for him to learn to think; and most important of all for him to learn to love—to love, because relatedness and involvement are of the essence of the human condition, of mental health; to love, because as the principal factor that has been operative in bringing man safely through the vicissitudes and perils of a long and strenuous evolutionary history, love is the principal behavioral need and capacity of the newborn and of the human being all the days of his life.

My own studies as an anthropologist were not at all concerned with the investigation of love and its significance for human development. However, the mounting evidence of the studies of others and of my own on the nature of the human nature cumulatively and most consistently points to the most neglected form of behavior as having been a most important factor: 1) in the evolution of man, and 2) in the growth and development of the person, not only socially, but also physically.

The notion that man is born with innate aggressive drives is the very opposite of the truth, for man has evolved as a highly cooperative creature, among whose basic needs is the avoidance of painful and harmful situations. . . . Aggressive behavior is learned, just as love is learned. But while the capacity to love constitutes an innate need, aggressive behavior does not. Aggressive behavior constitutes a pathological response arising from the thwarting of the need for love.

A child is a promise seeking fulfillment in performance. His basic needs and his need for love constitutes his inbuilt value system. What he desires is to have his needs satisfied in the manner conditioned by that value system. In brief, just as the child is physically the product of evolutionary adaptation to millions of years of environmental pressures, so his behavioral potentialities are the product of several million years of similar evolutionary adaptations. And just as the child is born with potentialities for physical growth and development within the pattern of those physical potentialities, so he is born with behavioral potentialities for growth and development that, like the physical potentialities, require the appropriate environmental stimulations if that growth and development are to be realized.

We must study **human beings**, not individuals. An individual is a unit; a human being is a constellation of human interrelationships.

One Child

Lying in the bow of the boat
the child feels pressures.
As the oars dip thin cedar
trembles against the weight of water.
Fear tingles, half-delicious, half-painful.
At night darkness presses
held at bay by the night-light.
No pleasure here, only terror.
In winter teachers loom heavy with learning,
and the words in books overflowing thin covers.
No time to toss a word lightly,
to turn and test it for meaning,
only to cut through quickly
like a boat through water.

—Candace T. Stevenson

**3 ships from UNICEF
     (for Bruno Bath, age 8, in Brazil)**

they are afloat on three boats
Bruno Bath comes out
Bru No Bath which is
great for three boys out
boating on the sea of purple
blue and white
black boats white squiggle
waves, I'd like to join them
but it's all on paper.

—Sam Hamod

(Bruno Bath's painting appears in the third week
of March, 1971 UNICEF Calendar Book.)

From *Freedom and Beyond* by John Holt

Thoughts on Children and Freedom

"If we give children freedom how will they ever
learn discipline?"
This is a common question—really a statement.
When people talk about their children "learning
discipline," what is it that they really want him
to learn? Probably, most or all of the following:

1. Do what you're told without questioning or
   resisting, whenever I or any other authority
   tell you to do something.
2. Go on doing what you're told for as long as
   you're told. Never mind how dull, disagreeable, or pointless the task may seem. It's not
   for you to decide.
3. Do whatever we want you to do, willingly. Do
   it without even having to be told. Do what
   you're expected to do.
4. If you don't do these things you will be punished and you will deserve to be.
5. Accept your life without complaining even if
   you get very little if any of what you think you
   want, even if your life has not much joy, meaning, or satisfaction. That's what life is.

6. Take your medicine, your punishment, whatever the people above you do to you, without
   complaining or resisting.
7. Living this way is good for your soul and
   character.

Rather like the sermon the rich used to preach to
the poor in the early days of the Industrial Revolution: accept the station in life, however humble,
to which God has called you, and there meekly
and gratefully do your duty. This preaching still
goes on —.

Children, because they are small and weak,
     because they have had little experience, and
          because it suits us to condition them quickly
               before they have more experience,
     become secretly convinced we are omnipotent,
          and that any catastrophe is the result of our wrath,
               our wrath with them.

From **Look At Kids** by Leila Berg

The greatest joy in life, I believe, is to have the
pleasure of a child's company; and one of the
greatest tragedies is to be denied this pleasure.
This we do, I think, by being too insistent on
inflicting adult purposes and goals on our young.
We need not pretend to be children ourselves
and indulge in such nonsense as baby talk, but
we do need to be genuinely interested in the
thoughts and interests of those with whom we
would communicate.

From **Humanizing The Education of Children**
by Earl C. Kelley

Trick or Treat*

Zack and Sally and Susie and Chris
Lurch by doorways in dextrosal bliss
Mumbling their thanks and screeching their glee
Claiming their homage, demanding their fee
Reminding their fathers, who sit by the fire,
Of the fog-thin film of manners, the liar.

The slick pink flesh, the shiny hair,
The nails that are cut till hardly there,
The toes that are shod in a dead cow's skin,
Disguise so well the primal sin.

Hardly ever is sloughed the refractive sheen
That never mirrors what the race has been.
Hardly ever is punctured the membrane of charm
That keeps the goblins so quietly warm.

It takes October, and leaf-stripping gusts
and hysteria of dark, for unmasking lusts,
for showing the barbs that thorn the hooks
that stretch the smiles and disguise the looks.
It takes the mask and it needs the coal
to bare, for once, the twitching soul
that was birthed in the dusty, whirling black
cycles, aeons, and ages back,
when Zack and all his little friends
were thoughts of germs in swamp-side sands,
when manchild could've gone in either way,
to sweet repose, or to midnight play;
but as it happened, the new germ fell
heir to the trick that gave him hell,
the wild delight of wanting mad,
and the iron code that made him sad.

For all days, then, the law is firm;
parental brow, though kind, is stern;
we count on order—think we know
the child's heart feels what the face will show,
until we chill by the fire's gleam
at the fleeting grimace, scarcely seen—
and sense the stifled, primal scream—
of our little children, on Halloween.

—Peter F. Neumeyer

*For Zack and Chris—and Danny, who is too young.

TREASURES

I lay my treasures in a row
To let my Mother see.
But she thinks things are only trash
That mean the most to me.

I do not see how she can fail
To love that tiny little snail.

—Anna Bird Stewart

Navajo Girl

My spot is here
at this desk
open book piled
upon open book.
Behind me the fire
mumbles its elf-song
making company
warmth,
nearly human.
She
would like it here
to read, to study.
The door opens east;
the walls, the rugs,
the books, the spirit,
all are hers.
(Curious that I should know her spirit
before I know her.)
I would put her in my place,
small shoulder blades
to feel the fire's warmth.
I would put her in my place, and
sitting at the other desk
would talk to her
without words.

—Christopher Nye

This Is A Child

A child is innocence meeting the world
With a trusting, outstretched hand,
Curiosity discovering the world
Unhurriedly, unplanned,
Honesty laying bare the world's
True joys and hidden flaws,
Excitement never allowing the world
To stop, but briefly pause.
A child is Laughter conquering the world
With an open, smiling face.
A child is Love uplifting the world
To a happier, higher place.

—Kay Andrew

Children are a bridge to heaven.—Persian Proverb

A child goes to school to wonder. The school is where he enters the Anglo world with shy curiosity; it is a magical microcosm of society to him. The teacher is his sorcerer, a mother who is worldwise, knowing all sorts of facts and magic, powerful as the policeman, but human as an aunt or uncle. In the beginning that is how school seems to the child.

He is lost at the thought that he cannot enter that wonderful world because he speaks the wrong language or is the wrong color. The child is proud of his father; he boasts of his barrio heritage. He doesn't know that he is supposed to be "culturally deprived."

If the teacher ridicules the language of his father, his way of thinking, the beliefs and behavior his mother taught him, the child is bewildered. He is told he must choose between being "American" or "Mexican." It is no choice for him, for he is neither but is both. He will argue, or grow silent. Either way the child will be in conflict with the teacher. And his idyll of education is ended.

From **La Raza: The Mexican Americans**
by Stan Steiner

Children and Movement

Children.
They move. Sometimes slowly; sometimes quickly.
They breathe. Sometimes they pant. Sometimes they seem to be holding their breath.
They're alive. Sometimes they're warm and cuddly.
Sometimes they seem to be all elbows and knees sticking out every which way.
Sometimes they're frigid and rigid.
They're always growing!

—emc

Children in Open Education—

They are much more free to move. They can often choose to move slowly. They can choose to move quickly. They tend to be accepted when they are dynamic and alive. They tend to be accepted when they seem pensive, almost apathetic. They can be warm and cuddly, and warm and cuddly behavior in the open education environment is clearly visible. Sometimes they seem to be all elbows and knees sticking out every which way. Open education provides open spaces, variety of furnishings, options in time, space and activity so that elbows and knees can be acceptable. Sometimes they're frigid and rigid, but not for long in an open climate. There's a place for rigidity if the learner so chooses, but with viable alternatives, frigidity and rigidity tend to be absorbed and flexibility and warmth are the replacements. They're always growing, but the wide differences and the lesser similarities accentuate the philosophy of the open education environments that each child is unique, and it is "meet, right and salutary" that his uniqueness be respected!

—emc

Think of the most active
child you know. How long can you be
comfortable with him? How do you reject
his activeness? What kinds of things do you
do to and with him to restrict his activity?
At what point does your acceptance
threshold change to rejection?

Do
children
look at you as
an active person?
What kinds of physical
activity do you share with
them? What new physical activity
are you doing this year? Are you on the
growing or declining edge of your physical
activity? Is that
good for you?

What is your favorite physical activity. Take
enough time to recall the sensory details.
Now think! Have you given each child
some opportunity to have an
exciting physical activity?

What kind of child do
you favor—the warm, cuddly,
inactive child, or the aloof, independent child?

HUG-O-GRAM

Make your own Hug-O-Gram!
Mentally, or in writing, move from
the children you'd most like to hug to
those you probably never would hug.
(This is not exclusively a
primary age activity!) Can you
identify why you feel as you do?

Children and Movement—

See how small each child can get.
How wide can each one become?
How tall can each one stretch?
Move back to the most comfortable size.

See how quickly all the children in any one learning center can line up from shortest to tallest.

Then have the two ends stand together to show
that children are not all the same size.
Do this several times a year to see what changes
occur during the school year.

Trace one of each child's feet and one of
each adult's feet. Arrange them by
size from BIG to little
or from wide to narrow.
Check them out to see if they
match height or weight of
owners. Why not?

Make a bar graph
showing how far each
person can jump from a
standing position. What
other kinds of movements can
you graph?

Think of a very slow-moving child. How comfortable are you with this child? When
are you supportive? When do you become irritated? How do you try to help this child?

Make a collection of thumb prints.
Study each with a magnifying glass.
How are they similar? How do they
differ? Compare thumbs with bird
claws and animal paws. Focus
on movement!

How big a circle can your group make
when your arms are flat against your
sides? When your arms are spread-eagled?
Measure the radius, the diameter, the
circumference of each circle.

Each day play a recording or
tape (preferably children's choice)
and with eyes closed, have
children move to the music.

Find photos of
children from other
countries. Bring a large
mirror. Compare children's
facial characteristics
with those in photos.

TO DANCE IS TO FEEL

(For Ellen, from the wounded, the stuck, and the dying . . .)

In the Dance of Life, some people choose to seek
A Master Choreographer; some persons dance out their own lives.
But all men, in the face of the music of the universe
Shall open their pores and loose the sweat of existence
Becoming one with the surrounding air,
From the moment of birth, dancing the life-death struggle
Rhythmically enlarging the collective mind-body experience.

Dance, like touching, comes from within.
Reflecting from without, the body firms and relaxes
To realign with gravity, fulfilled with gentle control
Muscles and shadows deepened with devotion,
Some through quiet introspection, some howling in the night.

Two people, three, more, moving through each other's space
But never in time, try though we may to share spontaneity,
Flowing together in harmonic creation.
Having shared, we sometimes part
Choosing to dance with another.
Sometimes we leave the mainstream
Moving inward, to be by ourselves.

So, like consciousness, spacial awareness a part of being
We move, time and space relative.
The whole person inherent in confluent environmental participation
In one's own life.

To dance is to feel.
To feel is the essence of being.
Oneness evolves from the frenzied motion of all the parts.
So let us put on the costumes
And move together, freely.

—Wron Carswell

Children are sensory creatures, but they sometimes need help in the development of their sensory perceptions.

1. Take a group of 8 to 10 children on a sensory walk outdoors.
2. Let the children choose which way they want the group to face.
3. Facing one direction, have them stand side by side at arm's length.
4. Have them take ten giant-steps forward, looking and listening as they step.
5. Have them identify what they saw or heard. Let other children see (i.e., an ant hill, an insect gall, or a small trail in the weeds).
6. Have them reverse positions and see if they missed anything on the way.
7. Expand in different directions, or compass points, or number of steps, or a particular number of minutes to watch and listen, etc.

Try this each month. What positive things come from such experiences?

The Eyes of a Child

A child's eyes, those clear wells of undefiled thought—what on earth can be more beautiful? Full of hope, love and curiosity, they meet your own. In prayer, how earnest; in joy, how sparkling; in sympathy, how tender! The man who never tried the companionship of a little child has carelessly passed by one of the great pleasures of life, as one passes a rare flower without plucking it or knowing its value.

—Caroline Norton

To Be a Child

Doomed as absurd adults, we can forget
That stories run through children's heads, the way
Young children run all through a summer day.
Hot in the blazing of the alphabet.
We watch her reading there, wearing her wild,
Utterly-given-up, ravenous look.
But see! It is as if a breathing book
Has picked her up and reads the living child.

This is to be a child: To heighten
Each thing you handle, to be shyer
Than rabbit in wide field, to frighten
Deep dark that scared you, to fly higher
Than kite or hunting hawk, to brighten
Daylight, because you are a fire.

—Paul Engle

A Sense of Wonder

A child's world is fresh and new and beautiful, full of wonder and excitement. It is our misfortune that for most of us that clear-eyed vision, that true instinct for what is beautiful and awe-inspiring, is dimmed and even lost before we reach adulthood.

If I had influence with the good fairy who is supposed to preside over the christening of all children, I should ask that her gift to each child in the world be a sense of wonder so indestructible that it would last throughout life, as an unfailing antidote against the boredom and disenchantment of later years, the sterile preoccupation with things that are artificial, the alienation from the sources of our strength.

If a child is to keep alive his inborn sense of wonder without any such gift from the fairies, he needs the companionship of at least one adult who can share it, rediscovering with him the joy, excitement and mystery of the world we live in.

—Rachel Carson

Yes, child of suffering, thou mayest well be sure,
He who ordained the Sabbath loves the poor!
And, when you stick on conversation's burrs,
Don't strew your pathway with those dreadful **urs.**

From "Urania" by Oliver Wendell Holmes

What do you want for children?

Janice sat thinking about "A Sense of Wonder" and the statement about children needing at least one adult to share and keep alive their inborn sense of wonder. "What a neat way to approach our principal about increasing the number of adults in our classrooms for next year. All this time I've been planning to talk about our need to have more human resources to plan and prepare more things for children, and yet, perhaps our most pressing need is to have more teachers who have the time to be with children who want to share."

Some Things to Ponder

Why do we want more adults in the learning environment?

Is it because we desire to create an environment that contains a multitude of activities and choices for children—so that children will always have something to do—always be kept busy?

How do you feel about children who choose to do nothing?

Is it a requirement in your classroom that everyone must be busy. Even though you may allow children to talk while engaged in an activity—how do you react when they talk without being engaged in an activity?

Somewhere the Child ✓

Among the thousands of tiny things growing up all over the land, some of them under my very wing—watched and tended, unwatched and untended, loved, unloved, protected from danger, thrust into temptation—among them somewhere is the child who will write the novel that will stir men's hearts to nobler issues and incite them to better deeds.

There is the child who will paint the greatest picture or carve the greatest statue of the age; another who will deliver his country in an hour of peril; another who will give his life for a great principle; and another, born more of the spirit than of the flesh, who will live continually on the heights of moral being, and dying, draw men after him.

It may be that I shall preserve one of these children to the race. It is a peg big enough on which to hang a hope, for every child born into the world is a new incarnate thought of God, an ever fresh and radiant possibility.

—Kate Douglas Wiggin

Know You What It Is To Be a Child?

Know you what it is to be a child? It is to be something very different from the man of today. It is
to have a spirit yet streaming from the waters of
baptism, it is to believe in love, to believe in love-
liness, to believe in belief. It is to be so little that
the elves can reach to whisper in your ear. It is
to turn pumpkins into coaches, and mice into
horses, lowness into loftiness and nothing into
everything—for each child has his fairy godmother in his own soul. It is to live in a nutshell
and count yourself king of the infinite space; it is

To see the world in a grain of sand,
  Heaven in a wild flower,
To hold infinity in the palm of your hand,
  And Eternity in an hour.

—Francis Thompson

**To each educator:—You once knew what it was
to be a child. Do you remember? Do you remain
childlike? Or have you forgotten?**

A Little Child

A little child, a limber elf,
Singing, dancing to itself,
A fairy thing with red round cheeks
That always finds, and never seeks . . . .

—Samuel Taylor Coleridge

Half-past Three

My friend has a yacht, a house by the sea,
But I have a boy who is half-past three.

I have no jewels, no satin gown,
But I have a boy who is butter-nut brown.

My friend has an orchid, my friend has a rose,
But I have a boy with a freckled nose.

O gull, tell the waves that I have no yacht.
Wind, tell the wild forget-me-not

That I have no jewels, no shimmering gown,
No satin slippers, no pillows of down,

But I have a robin, a wind-swept hill,
A pocket of dreams, a heart to fill,

And I have a boy who is half-past three—
A little lad who looks like me.

—Emily Carey Alleman

The Excursion

                    I have seen
A curious child, who dwelt upon a tract
Of inland ground, applying to his ear
The convolutions of a smooth-lipped shell.
To which, in silence hushed, his very soul
Listened intensely; and his countenance soon
Brightened with joy; for from within were heard
Murmurings, whereby the monitor expressed
Mysterious union with its native sea.

—William Wordsworth

Water finds its level,
    the swallows fly south in winter,
        children learn.

—Tolstoy

from *Leaves of Grass* by Walt Whitman

THERE WAS A CHILD WENT FORTH

There was a child went forth every day,
And the first object he look'd upon, that object he became,
And that object became part of him for the day or a certain part of the day,
Or for many years or stretching cycles of years.

The early lilacs became part of this child,
And grass and white and red morning-glories, and white and red clover, and the
    song of the phoebe-bird,
And the Third-month lambs and the sow's pink-faint litter, and the mare's
    foal and the cow's calf,
And the noisy brood of the barnyard or by the mire of the pond-side,
And the fish suspending themselves so curiously below there, and the beautiful
    curious liquid,
And the water-plants with their graceful flat heads, all became part of him.

The field-sprouts of Fourth-month and Fifth-month became part of him,
Winter-grain sprouts and those of the light-yellow corn, and the esculent
    roots of the garden,
And the apple-trees cover'd with blossoms and the fruit afterward, and wood-
    berries, and the commonest weeds by the road,
And the old drunkard staggering home from the outhouse of the tavern whence
    he had lately risen,
And the schoolmistress that pass'd on her way to the school,
And the friendly boys that pass'd and the quarrelsome boys,
And the tidy and fresh-cheek'd girls, and the barefoot negro boy and girl,
And all the changes of city and country wherever he went.

His own parents, he that had father'd him and she that had conceiv'd him in
    her womb and birth'd him,
They gave this child more of themselves than that,
They gave him afterward every day, they became part of him.

The mother at home quietly placing the dishes on the supper-table,
The mother with mild words, clean her cap and gown, a wholesome odor falling
    off her person and clothes as she walks by,
The father, strong- self-sufficient, manly, mean, anger'd, unjust,
The blow, the quick loud word, the tight bargain, the crafty lure,
The family usages, the language, the company, the furniture, the yearning and
    swelling heart,
Affection that will not be gainsay'd, the sense of what is real, the thought
    if after all it should prove unreal,
The doubts of day-time and the doubts of night-time, the curious whether and how,
Whether that which appears to is so or is it all flashes and specks?
Men and women crowding fast in the streets, if they are not flashes and specks
    what are they?
The streets themselves and the facades of houses, and goods in the windows,
Vehicles, teams, the heavy-plank'd wharves, the huge crossing at the ferries,
The village on the highland seen from afar at sunset, the river between,
Shadows, aureola and mist, the light falling on roofs and gables of white
    or brown two miles off,
The schooner near by sleepily dropping down the tide, the little boat slack-
    tow'd astern,
The hurrying tumbling waves, quick-broken crests, slapping
The strata of color'd clouds, the long bar of maroon-tint away solitary by
    itself, the spread of purity it lies motionless in,
The horizon's edge, the flying sea-crow, the fragrance of salt marsh and
    shore mud,
These became part of that child who went forth every day, and who now goes,
    and will always go forth every day.

HERB (to himself): Why, when I'm struggling with some school modification, do I always try the old academic route first—define my terms, list my objectives, identify my processes, and set up my standardized measurement tools? I know I need some new models. All I have to do is remind myself of my attempts to be a good father to our three children.

First, Joel—
    we wanted to do everything right with Joel, and of our three he's the most orderly, the most upset when things don't go right—as he thinks right should be.

Next, Michelle—
    we relaxed a bit more with her. We had learned that children were indeed flexible. And Michelle's whole being was so different from Joel's. He ran on a tight schedule, and Michelle never seemed to settle into any schedule—she never seemed to need one.

Then, Jonathan—
    guess we were a little too relaxed with this one. He's really flexible and unpredictable. Course he's as independent as they come.

All three of them are good kids, and each talented in his own way. I guess if one just looks at children, their need for open education is obvious, and if that's what they need, that's what they'll get from old Herby, here!

Children and Feelings

Children.
They feel. Sometimes happy, sometimes sad.
They laugh at funny little things. They laugh at surprises. They often giggle.
Sometimes they cry. They hurt.
Sometimes they hurt themselves; sometimes they hurt others.
    They are frequently very sensitive and kind.
Sometimes they are cruel.
Whether they hurt or help is often dependent on what happens in school.
Sometimes we cause children to hurt!

Children in Open Education—

Children can feel more freely. They can express a wider release of feelings because exposure is encouraged. In open environments children are frequently happy. There is a buzz and movement that indicates the satisfaction of involvement. Sometimes they are sad. But they seldom stay sad for long—there are too many adults with whom to share one's sadness and too many alternatives to entice the child. They laugh at funny little things and at themselves, because the open environment allows them to look at themselves with security. They often giggle, and there is much more time and opportunity for giggling in the open classrooms. Sometimes they cry and sometimes they hurt. Sometimes they may hurt themselves and occasionally they may even hurt others. But more frequently, hurts are diminished in environments of openness since there is not the basic need to compete against each other— cooperation is far more prevalent! They are frequently very sensitive and kind and because they make so many decisions about their activities, they are commonly involved in doing things for their school, for their friends, for their families. With an accepting climate, their needs to be cruel are greatly diminished, as are their own chances of being hurt by unfair competition, by impossible task requirements, by treating children as "products" of the school. The open education environments are designed to help children feel good about themselves!

—emc

Are there a good number of "belly-laughs" in your class each day?

Do you believe some children are "too sensitive"? How do you handle such children? Do you try to reduce their sensitivity? Why?

Do you laugh readily? Or occasionally? At people? Or with people? Do you ever laugh at yourself?

How do you respond when children cry? Do you respond differently to girls' crying than to boys' crying? Have you ever cried in front of children?

How do you respond to an angry child? How do you respond to a child's anger toward another child? Toward you, his teacher?

Do you cry easily? Or seldom? Or never?

How do you help bring out the anger hidden in children?

How sensitive are you? Does your sensitivity vary with specific children?

Children and Feelings—

ACTIVITIES FOR CHILDREN

Have
you
thought
of
having
children
DANCE
their
feelings?

BRING
ONE
OF
YOUR
CUDDLY
TOYS
TO
SCHOOL
TO
BE
HUGGED
BY
ANYONE
WHO
FEELS
THE
NEED
TO
HUG!

Giggle together. Laugh together. Hug yourself. Hug two friends. Give your teachers a big bear hug. Hug your knees. Sit on the floor in one big circle and hug the persons on either side of you.

Prepare an attractive desk arrangement with two boxes. In one box put a form, if needed, or some pretty writing paper to encourage children to write about nice things they see happen in school, on the bus, on the playground, etc.
I liked_____

_____

Put the finished paper in the second box and have a friendly postman deliver all papers just before school ends each day.

Collect small animals and insects. Make appropriate carrying cages for them with food and water dispensers. Enable them to be loved, and checked out (like library books) to be taken home and shared.

Make a BIG punch pillow out of materials stuffed with old plastic cleaning bags. Make your stitches strong. Throw the punch pillow all around your big circle so everyone can get the "mads" out. Now, everyone give the BIG punch pillow a big hug before you put it away!

Before feelings build to an explosive pitch, it is wise to sit in a big circle and talk everything over eyeball-to-eyeball.

He who knows nothing, loves nothing.
He who can do nothing understands nothing.
He who understands nothing is worthless.
But he who understands also loves, notices,
    sees, . . .
The more knowledge is inherent in a thing,
    the greater the love.
Anyone who imagines that all fruite ripen
    at the same time as the strawberries
    knows nothing about grapes.

                —Paracelus

More Thoughts on Children
From *Freedom and Beyond* by John Holt

Deny children—or anyone else—the chance to do 'nothing,' and we may be denying them the chance to do 'something'—to find and do any work that is truly important, to themselves or to someone else. There is tension here. A child who appears to be doing nothing is not necessarily doing something more important. Perhaps much of the time he is not doing anything important. Perhaps any one of a number of things that we might suggest to him might be better, even in his terms, than what he is doing. But when we act as if this were always so, the child never finds his true work, and worst of all, never thinks of himself as capable of finding it.

Child's Country

Nothing is strange to the child for whom everything is new.
Where all things are new nothing is novel.
The child does not yet know what belongs and what does not;
therefore for him all things belong.
The ear of the child is open to all music.
His eyes are open to all arts.
His mind is open to all tongues.
His being is open to all manners.
In the child's country there are no foreigners.

              —Kenneth L. Patton

> My Thought for Today Is . . .
>
> Being Alone!

My thought for today is—

SUZANNA: How many children in our school would prefer being alone today?

CELLA: As long as I've been studying about children I'm amazed at how much more there is to know.

HERB: Sometimes I think if it weren't for children, teaching school would be EASY!

DR. ROUBINEK: Funny how some college kids seem more immature than some of the children with whom they work!

JOSÉ: Children! What a drab world this would be without them.

DR. CARSWELL:
  A child's face today
  Chases my doubts away—
  Open education must come to our schools!

What is your thought for today?

The Dump

The Dump is full of the loveliest prizes,
Boxes, and bottles, and bright tin cans.
The billy-goats find the best surprises
And drink rain water from kettles and pans.

I took my mother a beautiful pot
With just one hole—it was almost new.
I thought she really would like it a lot,
But she threw it away, and she scrubbed me,
    too.

The Dump is a place where treasures are found,
But if we give them we get no thanking.
We might carry home all that's on the ground,
And we might carry home a spanking.

—Anna Bird Stewart

Thus a Child Learns

Day by day the child comes to know a little bit of
what you know; to think a little bit of what you
think; to understand your understanding. That which
you dream and believe and are, in truth,
becomes the child.

As you perceive dully or clearly; as you think
fuzzily or sharply; as you believe foolishly or
wisely; as you dream drably or goldenly, as you bear
false witness or tell the truth—thus a child learns.

Thus a child learns; by wiggling skills through his
fingers and toes into himself; by soaking up habits
and attitudes of those around him; by pushing and
pulling his own world.

Thus a child learns; more through trial than error,
more through pleasure than pain, more through
experience than suggestion, more through suggestion
than direction.

Thus a child learns, through affection, through
love, through patience, through understanding,
through belonging, through doing, through being.

—Frederick J. Moffitt

Childhood shows the man as morning does the
day.

—John Milton

The dreams of childhood—its airy fables, its
graceful, beautiful, humane, impossible adorn-
ments of the world beyond: so good to be believed in once, so good to be remembered when
outgrown.

—Charles Dickens

Children and Knowing

Children.
They seek. They quest. They test. They teach.
Sometimes they listen. Sometimes they tune us out.
Sometimes they trust us; sometimes they doubt us!
They know so much,
but sometimes they don't show us what we want to see.
They think. They plan. They scheme. They organize.
Sometimes they think about world affairs.
Sometimes they think about home and Mother and about Dad's job.
Sometimes they wonder about butterfly wings.
Sometimes they daydream.
Their patterns of thinking differ—from day to day,
from activity to activity, from one another.

Children in Open Education—

In open schooling each child sees many models of height, of posture, of joy, of thinking, of listening, of playing, of becoming, of being—and from them he can pick and choose those most appropriate for him at any given moment. He is not limited to an adult's preconceived idea of growth for him. Because he is free to explore many possibilities, he develops perceptions of his potential, his being, his becoming. He does not have to measure up to some imagined "third grade boy" or to a "1" as an evaluation of his skill or knowledge or collection of attitudes. The climate in which he is learning shows that his growth over his own prior accomplishments is what enables him to live comfortably with himself. He knows that responsibility accompanies each free choice he makes because he lives this way in the open learning environment. He goes home with a sense of personal worth because he is aware of his achievement and he returns to school on the morrow with joy and excitement because he knows he will be able to continue to quest!

—emc

What about the child who knows little? How do you truly feel about him? Why?

How many times must a child show you he knows something? Once? Ten times? Every day? Once a year? How do you make this kind of decision?

What about the child who knows "everything"? How do you truly feel about him? Why?

What can you do for the child who knows a little about many things but doesn't seem to want to know much more?

What about the child who knows quite a bit about many things but has a few "Do Not Disturb" areas?

Children and Knowing—

ACTIVITIES FOR CHILDREN

Play "I'm thinking of . . .". After each incorrect guess another clue
must be given by the thinker until the correct guess is made.

Put a photo of "The Thinker" on a bulletin board.
Have children put what they think about in envelopes marked "Thoughts."

Piaget emphasizes two requirements for learning.
First, a child must be allowed
to do things over and over again
and thus reassure himself
that what he has learned is true.
Second, this practice should be enjoyable.

Take a few minutes
every day
to name some topic,
process or concept.
See what children
know about it.
Try it!

Take time one day
to write on the boards
all the words any one
group can say. Surprise
everyone with the sheer
number—as well as the
difficulty.

Have each child identify
one thing he thinks he can teach
to another child—or to an adult.
Put each name and topic on an "I
can help . . ." bulletin board.

Play—

Sounds like this make me think of . . . .
Smells like this make me think of . . . .
Touching this makes me think of . . . .
Tasting this makes me think of . . . .
Seeing this makes me think of . . . .
Doing this makes me think of . . . .

Would we ever say that a ten-year-old who can't
play hockey is retarded? Well, when it comes to
intellectual skills, that's what we do. We say if
this child can't multiply, he's retarded.

From "Do The First Two Years Matter?"
by Jerome Kagan

We need say only one thing to young children:
COME AS YOU ARE!

From **Teaching the Child Under Six**
by James L. Hymes, Jr.

The institutions continue to be run by a generation that finds it increasingly difficult to be in tune
with the technological environment in which it
finds itself. The Children of Change, on the other
hand, have never experienced any other world
but the technological one in which they are living.

For them two highly significant things happened:
time collapsed and the horizon disappeared.

From **The Children of Change** by Don Fabun

CHAPTER FOUR

Openness

From *Live and Learn* by Charles M. Schulz

© 1963 United Feature Syndicate, Inc.

Peace on Earth

I shall pass through
this world but once.
If therefore,
there be any kindness
I can show,
or any good thing
I can do,
let me do it now;
let me not defer it
or neglect it,
for I shall not pass
this way again.

—Hallmark Cards, Inc.

From *Radical Ideas and the Schools* edited by Jack L. Nelson, Kenneth Carlson and Thomas S. Linton

The reflective, protective, status quo education system is consistent with aspects of socialization that call for noncritical assimilation of the traditions and mores of a society but is inconsistent with the dynamics of an open society based on enlightened citizens and persistent change.

Schools exist not only to pass on the historic wisdom and folly of the society but to provide the means for new directions, different mistakes, and alternative truths.

Why is it so hard for schools to move forward, and so easy to slip back?

From Freedom and Beyond
by John Holt

Key
to
Change

---

teacher change—

No teacher is going to teach differently until he believes differently, and can see himself in a new role. Any change which he may contemplate must seem reasonable to him.

From **Education and the Nature of Man**
by Earl C. Kelley and Marie I. Rasey

---

teaching—

The greatest thing about teaching, in my opinion, is that it brings the mature, educated, love-giving teacher in direct contact with the immature, uneducated, love-seeking child. If we lose this human relationship, our young will become automatons; and the light will have gone out.

From **Humanizing the Education of Children**
by Earl C. Kelley

---

hidden message—

It is, after all, how we treat people, not what we tell them, that most affects what they do. Our acts carry a hidden message much stronger than anything we say.

From **Freedom and Beyond** by John Holt

---

feelings—

Like many children, and many adults, too, Stephen is far more concerned with hiding his abased condition from the view of the world than he is with escaping that condition.

From **Death At An Early Age**
by Jonathan Kozol

From *Illuminating the Lives of Children: More Effective Use of Resources in the Elementary School* by Leland Jacobs

The teacher must attend to the sources before the resources can become meaningful.

But who are the sources? For a real teacher the answer is perfectly clear. The sources are the children. And how do teachers work with the sources that are essential before the resources ever get a chance? Real teachers attend to the sources first by respecting the dignity of being of every child. This is where real teaching starts. There isn't any use of you having all that fancy equipment in your school if you don't start with respect for the dignity of the one who is going to use it.

And this all goes back to the fact that a child comes to school with his life, not his case history, but with a living, dynamic life. Nor should he immediately be labeled with disadvantaged or underprivileged or something of that sort, for from the minute that we as professionals begin to put those words into our vocabulary, we begin to put blinders on and we hunt for the disadvantageness and the underprivilegeness. And I don't see any value in talking about such things. They come with the lives they have got and real teachers start with the dignity of just their being.

The basic right of the individual is to be who he is. There is nothing in our contracts that says that the children should come to school the way we want them. That's not part of the educational enterprise. To get them the way we want them. All clean. All starchy. Or, however we want them.

The contract says that in our great experiment in education that we take all of the children of all of the people the way they are. And a real teacher starts right there. The way they are.

A famous child psychologist, once said: "The child who comes to school not only has the right to be the age he is, he has the right to be the kind of child he is."

The dignity of being grows out of the idea that the child walking into my classroom has the right to be the child he is.

I have seen the most defeated students, the ones most thoroughly oppressed in school, coming back year after year, looking fresh and open on the first day of school, ready to put their failure and despair and cynicism aside and begin again, if only it were made possible for them to do so.

From **The Open Classroom** by Herbert Kohl

The single most significant aspect about the school that works toward developing a more humane experience for children is its quality of openess.

From "To Make a Difference in the Lives of Children," by T. Darrell Drummond

SUZANNA: Listen to this, Herb. "The dignity of being grows out of the idea that the child walking into my classroom has the right to be the child he is." I can't help thinking what a wonderful experience school would be if all teachers carried this thought. This one thought might be a good theme for next fall's in-service education program.

HERB: (With disbelief and amazement): That statement makes me think of the physically aggressive child. These children would ruin a classroom and bloody the noses of half the kids in a week if allowed to be what they are. But when I visited my own child's open classroom, he appeared natural and comfortable in the classroom. I was pleased to see him being himself and enjoying every minute of school. His teacher did not permit harmful, physically aggressive behavior, and often talked to individual children about their behavior toward others. This classroom was not being ruined by children who appeared to be themselves. Perhaps I should spend more time visiting open classrooms and relating what I read to the things I see.

JOSÉ: I am impressed with Jacobs' statement. I can remember being punished for speaking Spanish in the classroom and even on the playground when I was a child. Thank goodness this seldom happens anymore. And yet, I fear that teachers are still discriminating against the Mexican-American child even though they aren't punishing children for speaking Spanish. Because of the experiences of my youth and subsequent experiences as a young adult, I still have doubts and fears. Yet the more I read about open education and open teachers the more convinced I am that open education holds great promise for the Mexican American child and for all children.

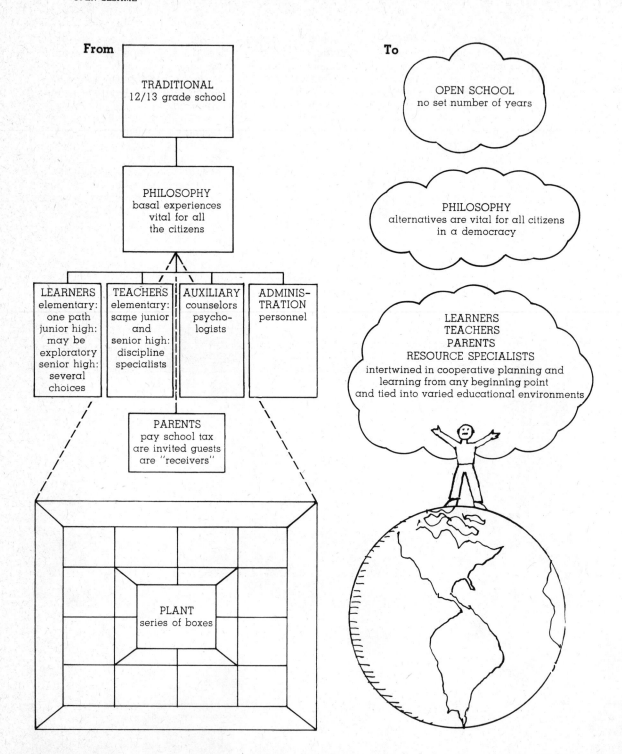

From

TRADITIONAL
12/13 grade school

PHILOSOPHY
basal experiences
vital for all
the citizens

LEARNERS
elementary:
one path
junior high:
may be
exploratory
senior high:
several
choices

TEACHERS
elementary:
same junior
and
senior high:
discipline
specialists

AUXILIARY
counselors
psycho-
logists

ADMINIS-
TRATION
personnel

PARENTS
pay school tax
are invited guests
are "receivers"

PLANT
series of boxes

To

OPEN SCHOOL
no set number of years

PHILOSOPHY
alternatives are vital for all citizens
in a democracy

LEARNERS
TEACHERS
PARENTS
RESOURCE SPECIALISTS
intertwined in cooperative planning and
learning from any beginning point
and tied into varied educational environments

CURRICULUM

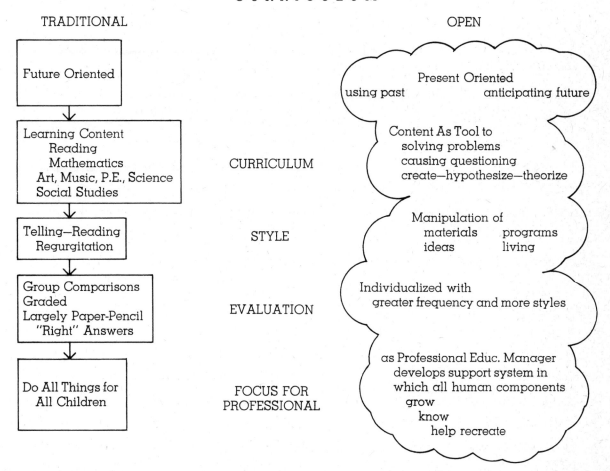

TRADITIONAL

Future Oriented

↓

Learning Content
   Reading
   Mathematics
Art, Music, P.E., Science
Social Studies

↓

Telling—Reading
Regurgitation

↓

Group Comparisons
Graded
Largely Paper-Pencil
  "Right" Answers

↓

Do All Things for
All Children

CURRICULUM

STYLE

EVALUATION

FOCUS FOR
PROFESSIONAL

OPEN

Present Oriented
using past   anticipating future

Content As Tool to
  solving problems
  causing questioning
  create—hypothesize—theorize

Manipulation of
  materials   programs
  ideas   living

Individualized with
  greater frequency and more styles

as Professional Educ. Manager
develops support system in
which all human components
  grow
    know
      help recreate

The curriculum should be like a
fan, opening up to more and more
things, to bigger and bigger
things.

From **What We Owe Children—The
Subordination Of Teaching To Learning**
by Caleb Gattegno

From *Education and the Personal Quest* by Lloyd W. Kline

Quite succinctly, there are at least six different approaches available in designing and implementing various curricula: skill, data, concept, theme, attitude, process.

It would be interesting to be able to determine such secondary and unintentional results of our curriculum and instruction, then to line them up one by one with the "positive" results of our stated primary mission, and to see which outstrips which in magnitude and lasting effect. The timeless stereotypes of "school" and of "teaching"—whether wardens, welts, and work or simps, saps, and silliness—may be the most valid indicators of the pedagogical effectiveness of our schools up to now.

I am ready to act on the belief that an individual can be as pluralistic as a society can be, that he therefore can legitimately seek an assortment of educational experiences that might look like a hodge-podge to someone else, and that he therefore can legitimately want to "change his course of study" far more often than once a year—or than once in four years, or eight, or twelve, as is now the case in many school careers in which eighth or ninth graders are asked to choose, essentially, between "college prep" or "non-college prep." I am certain that he is a unique combination of a far greater diversity of unities and partial unities and processes and faltering processes than even he himself is capable of verbalizing and that every moment finds him to be a different combination than he was the moment before. For all the labor, for all the sustained attention, for the cohesion it requires, a book is no more synonym for its author than a poem is for its poet, or a statement for its speaker, or a birdhouse for its builder.

I will now entertain—indeed, welcome—for its own sake and in its own size and shape, any learning experience, any instructional activity, any notion that comes along for the curriculum. We have lost or debilitated too many valuable moments or exchanges or ideas simply because they have come in packages either too short or too shallow or too simple to turn into one-semester courses. Or else we have stretched them beyond the breaking point to make them fit.

RECALL:
   Peak **learning experiences!**
Aren't they ALWAYS **experiences that broke out of the "expected curricula"? What keeps us from breaking out more often?**

Reform must begin with this fact: Schooling is not all of education, and the other parts of education require just as much explicit planning and organization as does schooling.

From "How Do The Young Become Adults?" by James S. Coleman

Then—
WHY shut?
WHY sealed?
WHY tied?

Open vs. authoritarian

. . . if the school is to be a place for the young to grow physically, psychologically, and emotionally, the authoritarian technique can hardly be called efficient. This method has too many losers.

From **Humanizing the Education of Children** by Earl C. Kelley

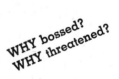

WHY bossed?
WHY threatened?

Open personalities will learn if given something to learn; closed personalities, filled with fear, are not free to learn. But, because the open learner brings unique experience and purpose to the lesson, what he learns will not necessarily coincide with the learnings of the person sitting next to him. It is therefore impossible to guarantee that all members of a class will grasp the same relationships and knowledge. This has been the despair of the authoritarian teacher throughout the ages.

From **Humanizing the Education of Children**
by Earl C. Kelley

These things we have learned—

Simply doing "more of the same but harder" will scarcely dent the problem. New concepts of the total educational program are demanded. Such rethinking may impel us to new policies, different arrangements of time and organization, more effective deployment of professional staff, an extended role for the school in the community, and a reshaped curriculum. It is unrealistic to expect improvement from a moderate amount of tinkering.

From **Educating the Children of the Poor**

But at least educators are becoming aware of the fact that learning is dependent on much more than how hard pupils work, and how zealously teachers teach.

From "How Do We Learn?"
by John I. Goodlad

A TEACHER IS MANY THINGS by Roy Wilson

Looking for a handy definition of a teacher?

Roy Wilson, director of the NEA's division of press and radio relations, passed along several in the course of his speech at the recent AEA Tri-Conference in Phoenix.

An editor, said Wilson, gave this definition: "Teachers are people with brains in their heads, love in their hearts, energy in their bones and chalk on their noses. They come in all sizes and shapes and in both sexes—which makes it nice for other teachers. They work at top speed, arrive early, stay late, have the wisdom of Solomon, the patience of Job, the drive of a jet engine, the calm of a June night and the glamor of Grace Kelly."

An educator said: "A teacher is a person who can enter a room some enchanted September morning with 30 lively American youngsters, stay with them all day and survive."

A TV writer said: "Teachers are the influential Americans."

An education reporter said: "A good teacher is like the smell of hot biscuits . . . nice to have around but very hard to describe."

A major national magazine said: "A teacher is educator, foster mother, psychologist, janitor—and one of the most important people in our national life."

A teacher should be someone willing to give assistance but reluctant to give directions.

—Donna Schueler
Glen Burnie Senior High Student

God guard me from those thoughts men think
In the mind alone;
He that sings a lasting song
Thinks in a marrow-bone.

—Yeats

**What foibles
do we impose
under the
guise of schooling?**

Below are a number of categories, each with a list of words and phrases. Select any one category, read the words aloud. Which ones are pleasing to you? Which are offensive? How do these words relate to the children you teach? Are your expectations based on the pleasing/offensive responses you made for yourself? Try a category or two.

APPEARANCE	LANGUAGE	MUSIC
clean	frequent use of slang	rock
long hair	use of dramatic speech in everyday life	opera
heavy make-up	incorrect grammar	symphonic
no hosiery	use of big words	country
neat	swearing	jazz
cut-off jeans	use of metaphors	singing
no bra	frequent analogies	guitar
messy	Southern drawl	drums
chic	twang	strings
heavily jeweled	nasal tone	organ
dirty	idiosyncrasies	brass
hand-me-downs	excellent English	modern
bare feet	foreign accents	classical
fat	poetry	synthesizer
short	murder mysteries	transistor radio
skinny	history	stereo
freckled	novels	televised
ugly	short stories	marching bands
smelly		recordings
beautiful		folk songs
missing teeth		movie scores
runny nose		composing
coiffured hairdo		performing
matted hair		
strong perfume		

As you've grown older, have you found pleasure in wider variety of the items under any one category, or do you find more and more new or changed things that are more offensive? Again, are your acceptances used as standards for the children you teach?

ARTS AND CRAFTS	SPORTS	FAITH	PEOPLE
paintings	swimming	in yourself	uneducated
sculptures	football	in other people	opposite sex
macrame	basketball	organized religion	different race
pottery	hockey	meditation	transient
photographs	baseball	upward movement of society	highly religious
sewing	gymnastics	in government	creative
cookery	exercises	in school officials	from New England
woodwork	bowling		physically handicapped
metalwork	cycling		revolutionary
knitting	hiking		on welfare
beadwork	fishing		Asiatic
leathercraft	hunting		talkative
jewelry making	sailing		a cowboy
knick knacks	running		politician
collages	walking		very bright
models	competitive		quiet
	amateur		a Texan
			from the South
			highly opinionated
			conservative
			a policeman
			ex-convict
			always right
			famous
			very wealthy
			pusher
			ignorant
			Chicano
			beautiful
			Indian
			do-gooder
			teacher

A teacher is someone that teaches you and help you learn. If you have a problem you can always tell it to your teacher.

—Linda Itter
Ft. Smallwood Elem. School

A teacher is someone that teaches you how to read, write, do math, English, spelling and lots of stuff that kids don't like.

—Missy Selander
Ft. Smallwood Elem. School

Teacher in Individualized Instruction . . . A Relationship of Guidance towards Discovery

One of the most important features of the individualized program is the interaction between the teacher and the student. The teacher is more relaxed and is able to establish greater rapport with the student. The student is not limited to one teacher confined within one room. Teachers have time to know students in the small instruction groups which grow from common needs or interests and through individual teacher-pupil evaluatice conferences.

It is not the student, in all cases, who fears shared confidence with a teacher. Often teachers have misgivings about getting to know students as intimately as individual conferences allow. The teacher asks himself, "If a student gets to know me as a person, will he respect my authority any less?"

Is it always necessary for teachers to hide what they are really like under a pretence or to magnify social distance between teacher and student?

From **Anne Arundel Times**

Gather your own collection of

"A Teacher Is . . ." from your children.

The relationship between environment and learning needs much more study and exploration. Despite a growing consensus among educators that the learning environment can crucially affect the quality of experience a child encounters during a school day, relatively little change has occurred in most classroom design over the years. Today many schools are **containment centers**—designed to hold classes while students memorize the "stuff" necessary for advancement to the next higher instructional level. The typical classroom still serves to satisfy objectives predicated on teacher domination and print-verbal learning resources; it personifies emphasis on keeping group order.

From "Designing Tomorrow's School Today: The Multi-Sensory Experience Center," by Henry W. Ray

Just so. Just so the public school practices alienation on the land, and it is a practice which affects its teachers, its kids and the parents of its kids alike, some obviously more harshly than others. You may be sure you know everything about your kid, or about how you want to teach, or about yourself as a kid, but if the school tells you different you'll find that wedge driven in there between you and your child, between you and your class, between yourself as you know yourself and yourself as the school tells you about yourself.

From **How To Survive In Your Native Land** by James Herndon

Federal Fashions—

Every year brings a new fad in the federal education establishment. Last year's was "accountability." This year, it may be "competency-based education," which is the catch-phrase for a new approach to teacher education. In a CBE program, students work through a series of "instructional modules" at their own pace, using any means of learning that seems best suited to them. They evaluate their own progress but must in the end meet specified behavioral objectives.

—The Education Digest

—timely and richly textured books.

From **Death At An Early Age**
by Jonathan Kozol

For those of us who teach, the return to first principles means a return to Tolstoy's critique of compulsory, public education: an honest admission that what our existing pedagogical machinery is programmed to produce is the man that industrial society in its benightedness thinks it needs; and what industrial society in its behightedness thinks it needs of us is but the shriveled portion of our full humanity—how small a portion one must almost weep to say.

But lest we despair, we must remember that for Tolstoy this bleak fact was only a minor blemish on the face of an abidingly beautiful truth; that the spontaneous splendors of the human personality return to us whole in every child and will struggle fiercely to be educated in accordance with their nature.

From "Educating Contra Naturam,"
by Theodore Roszak

WHAT THEN ARE WE TO DO?

One of the most grim things about teaching in such a school and such a system is that you do not like to be an incessant barb and irritation to everybody else, so you come under a rather strong compusion to be quiet. But after you have been quiet for a while there is an equally strong temptation to begin to accept the conditions of your work or of the children's plight as natural.

From **Death At An Early Age**
by Jonathan Kozol

Another study conducted by the Center reveals that students from an open elementary school face a smoother transition into a traditional junior high school than do students who enter from a traditional elementary school.

From "Research Results For The Classroom,"
by E. Joseph Schneider and Mary Kennedy

From "A Little Bit of Chaos," by Beatrice and Ronald Gross

The theoretical basis of the Open Classroom is found in the work of the Swiss child psychologist Jean Piaget. His work began to influence many other experimental psychologists in the 1950s when his studies were published, but not until recently has his work been interpreted and popularized in the mass media.

Piaget is best known for his finding that intelligence—adaptive thinking and action—develops in sequence and is related to age. However, the ages at which children can understand different concepts vary from child to child, depending on his native endowment and on the quality of the physical and social environments in which he is reared.

But Piaget's books, based on his research on how children learn, also proved that it is a waste of time to tell a child things that the child cannot experience through his senses. The child must be able to try things out to see what happens, manipulate objects and symbols, pose questions and seek their answers, reconcile what he finds at one time with what he finds at another, and test his findings against the perceptions of others his age. Activity essential to intellectual development includes social collaboration, group effort, and communication among children. Only after a good deal of experience is the child ready to move on to abstract conceptualizations. PIAGET IS CRITICAL OF CLASSROOMS WHERE THE TEACHER IS THE DOMINANT FIGURE, WHERE BOOKS AND THE TEACHER'S TALKING ARE BASIC INSTRUCTIONAL MEDIA, AND WHERE LARGE GROUP INSTRUCTION IS THE RULE, AND ORAL OR WRITTEN TESTS ARE USED TO VALIDATE THE WHOLE PROCESS. CLEARLY FROM HIS FINDINGS, TRADITIONAL TEACHING TECHNIQUES ARE INEFFECTUAL. BUT FOR CHILDREN WHO MUST DEPEND ON THE SCHOOL ENVIRONMENT AS THE RICHEST THEY ARE TO ENCOUNTER, IT CAN BE DOWNRIGHT DAMAGING; DENIED A CHANCE TO GROW, THEIR MINDS MAY ACTUALLY ATROPHY.

. . . There are four operating principles of the Open Classroom. First, the room itself is decentralized: an open, flexible space divided into functional areas, rather than one fixed, homogeneous unit. Second, the children are free for much of the time to explore this room, individually or in groups, and to choose their own activities. Third, the environment is rich in learning resources, including plenty of concrete materials, as well as books and other media. Fourth, the teacher and her aides work most of the time with individual children or two or three, hardly ever presenting the same material to the class as a whole.

The teachers begin with the assumption that the children want to learn and will learn in their fashion; learning is rooted in firsthand experience so that teaching becomes the encouragement and enhancement of each child's own thrust toward mastery and understanding. Respect for

and trust in the child are perhaps the most basic principles underlying the Open Classroom.

characteristics of learning:

a general atmosphere of excitement
virtually complete flexibility in the curriculum
interpenetration of the various subjects and skills
emphasis on learning rather than teaching
focus on each child's thinking and problem-solving processes and on his ability to communicate with others freedom and responsibility for the children.

physical layout:

. . . There is no up front, and one doesn't know where to look to find the teacher or her desk. She is usually to be found working intensively with one or two children, or, if things are going as they should, often standing unobtrusively aside but observing each child's activities with great diligence. There are no desks and few chairs—fewer than the number of children. And the children are everywhere: sprawled on the floor, in groups in the corners, alone on chairs or pillows, out in the hall, or outside in the playground if it's good weather. . . . Each child uses the room differently, according to his own interests, concerns, and feelings on a particular day.

The layout of the room supports the program. An aerial view of a typical second-grade class in the middle of a morning would show that the room is divided into six sections, defined by open bookshelves that hold appropriate equipment, all of which is easily accessible to the children.

The child is free to choose, but whatever choice he makes he will be confronted with a wealth of opportunities for exploration and discovery. In the math section is everything he can use to measure and figure, including the Cuisenaire rods, balance scales, rulers and a stop watch, workbooks, and counting games such as Sorry and Pokerino. Similar riches await him in the language arts section, where he can read, make a tape recording or type, write, and play word-games and puzzles; or in the arts area with its paints, clay, dyes, and sand. Other corners are devoted to science, music, and blocks.

In the Open Classroom, each child's day is distinctive and different from every other day. To give him a sense of his progress, each child may keep a diary, which is also used to communicate to the teacher.

The variety of the activities mentioned in the diaries suggests the highlights of each child's day, but many educators and most parents find it difficult to define clearly what is being learned at any one moment and are usually resistant to the idea that a relaxed and unpressured atmosphere can stimulate serious work.

Conventional educators observing an Open Classroom for the first time are often so fixated on the children's informality and spontaneity that they fail to note the diligent planning and individual diagnosis by the teachers and the intellectual and sensuous richness of the prepared environment. These latter qualities, however, are hard-won, and to "open" the classrooms without having developed these strengths is to invite mere mindlessness and frustration.

. . . the Open Classroom seems precariously based on a kind of trust little evident in education today. Teachers must trust children's imagination, feelings, curiosity, and natural desire to explore and understand their world. They also must learn to trust themselves—to be willing to gamble that they can retain the children's interest and respect once they relinquish the external means of control: testing, threats, demerits, petty rules, and rituals. School administrators, in turn, must trust teachers enough to permit them to run a classroom that is not rigidly organized and controlled but, rather, is bustling, messy, flexible, and impulsive. Parents must trust school people to do well by their children, without the assurance provided by a classroom atmosphere recognizable from their own childhoods and validated, however emptily, by standardized tests.

Innovation

When I was young
   down in the grades as they used to say
   I ran home from school one bubbley day
"Dad! Buy me a pen!
I shall write in Ink!
  Tomorrow"
The ancient one smiled with pride
His work huge hand offered
A black hatted orange log.
"Here, my son, is the latest device.
An innovation.
  Its New!
It's called a fountain pen."
My reply stumbled
  for I coveted the marvelous machine.
"No, Dad. My teacher says
A steel quill in a wooden holder
  For we must learn the proper way
And you must scorch the point
When you light your pipe."

Now I am old.
  More bald than gray
My daughter ran home today
     Bubbley and gay.
"Dad! Buy me a pen!
I shall write in Ink!
  Tomorrow"
"Here, darling Kit. Here is the most modern machine."
I offered a ball point pen
  efficient in its slender silver beauty.
Over her covet clogged eyes
  she choked a cruel echo
"No, Dad. My teacher says
A fountain pen.
  For we must learn the proper way.
And you must buy me
     bottled ink."

—Gerald T. Kowitz

From Master of Arts thesis
by Kathleen Gee Haight

Open Education

Open education expresses a new point of view about children, learning, and knowledge which results in a changed classroom organization and atmosphere. This author contends that this changed classroom might possibly affect both anxiety and creativity in children. The principles and characteristics of open education then become relevant here.

Open education resists specific definition. No one definition exists because there is no one specific model. It is best understood in terms of certain underlying assumptions. Many of these assumptions are attributable to the work of Swiss genetic espitemologist Jean Piaget. Others involve points of view about children and about the nature of knowledge.

Assumptions about children, underlying open education, include:

1. Children are competent, desirous of learning, and trustworthy.
2. They can take responsibility for their own learning.
3. They are innately curious, and can initiate their own learning.
4. Children develop physically and intellectually at their own rate.
5. They learn at their own speed, in their own way.

Assumptions about learning include:

1. Learning proceeds from the concrete to the abstract through active exploration of and interaction with a rich learning environment.
2. Play is the principle mode of learning in childhood, and as such is not distinguished from work.
3. Self-motivated learning is self-perpetuating and more lasting.
4. Expression is an important source of learning, and feelings have their place in the classroom.

5. Learning which is most important is not necessarily that which can be measured.

Assumptions about knowledge include:

1. Little or no knowledge exists which it is essential for everyone to acquire.
2. It is important to help children learn how to acquire knowledge, what is worth knowing.
3. The thinking process is more important than the product.
4. In our increasingly complex world, a problem-solving approach is more appropriate than rote memory of facts.
5. The emphasis should be on learning instead of teaching, should be person-oriented instead of subject-oriented.
6. "Being" is more important than knowing. The final test of an education is not what a man knows, but what he is.

Open education has certain characteristics implicit in the underlying assumptions. First, teachers and children share in the decision-making processes. The teacher does not automatically decide what, how, and when specific learning will take place. However, the amount of freedom of choice involving learning varies greatly from classroom to classroom. But children have some freedom to move about and choose their own activities. The classroom is characterized by a rich learning environment. Usually, an open classroom includes many learning centers, or interest areas. They are also characterized by small group or individual activities. There are few large group activities. The role of the teacher is also changed. He becomes a manager, observer, director, facilitator of learning. He is usually supportive, non-authoritarian.

From *Freedom and Beyond* by John Holt

There are certainly great differences between the traditional classroom and the open or free classroom that I and many others are urging. But this difference is not made clear at all by calling these classes "structured" or "unstructured." Or even by pointing out that the open class has if anything **more** structure than the traditional, not less. Let us instead speak of two different kinds of structure, and to see how they differ. We might say that the structure of the traditional classroom is very simple. There are only two elements in it, only two moving parts, so to speak. One is the teacher and the other is the students. The children may be all different but in such a class their differences do not make any difference. They all have the same things to do, and they are all expected to do them in the same way. Like factory workers on the assembly line, or soldiers in the army, they are interchangeable—and quite often expendable. The second thing we can say of this structure is that it is inflexible, rigid, and static. It does not change from the first day of school to the last. On the last day as on the first, the teacher is giving out information and orders, and the children are passively receiving and obeying or refusing to obey. The third thing we can say of this structure is that it is arbitrary and external. It does not grow out of and has nothing to do with the life and needs of the class, what the children want, what the teacher has to give. It is dropped on them from above like a great glass box. The teacher is as much a prisoner and victim of this structure as the children. He has little more to say than they about what it should be, and can do little more than they to change it.

By contrast, the structure of the open class is complicated. It has as many elements as there are teachers **and** children in the classroom. No two of these elements are alike, and their differences make all the difference, since no two children will relate to the class and teacher, or make use of them, in quite the same way. Secondly, the structure is flexible and dynamic. The relationship of each child to the teacher and to the class changes from day to day, and may change enor-

mously in the course of a year. Indeed the nature of the whole class may change. Finally the structure is organic, internal. It grows out of the needs and abilities of the children and teachers themselves. They create this order, in ways vividly described by James Herndon in **The Way It Spozed to Be,** or George Dennison in **The Lives of Children**—or like the children in my opening story. When and because they create it, the order works. By that I don't mean that it looks neat and pretty; it often does not. I mean that it helps people to get things done, helps them to live, work, and grow. It does not squelch life. It enhances it.

The structure of a class can also be clear or unclear, straightforward or contradictory. This has not much to do with its being open or not, except that a very strict and traditional classroom is often both clear and straightforward—**anything** you do in there can get you into trouble. What the child wants to learn about the class is, are the rules easy or hard to find out? Once you have found them out, can you count on them? Some communities say, no problem about rules here, it's all out in the open, all down in black and white. Others say, we have no rules, don't believe in rules. Neither is true or possible. All communities have some rules, and all have more than they could write down. One of the things that makes a community is that it has more rules than it knows. People in the community do a lot of things the same way, and never even think about it—until an outsider comes in and does something completely different. A school I once knew used to boast that its only rule was No Roller Skating In the Halls. Nonsense. As the students well knew, there were plenty of things that you could get in trouble for doing.

In any classroom, traditional or open, rigid or flexible, kids want to know how to get along, how to become an insider instead of an outsider, how to get whatever good things are going. Most of all, to use the phrase everyone loves, they want to know where are the limits. If doing and saying something is going to get them in really bad trouble, they want to know beforehand what it is. Like the Constitution, which forbids it, they don't like **ex post facto** law—having the government

(teachers) say that what you did was a crime, but not saying it until after you did it. Tyrants are on purpose vague about the law. Tearful child: "But what did I do?" Avenging adult: "You know **very** well what you did!"

It is not so important that the structure of the class, its rules and customs, be clear in the sense of explicit. Children are used to figuring out the rules in complicated human situations. What they don't like is a structure that is contradictory. In the early progressive school, and, I suspect, in quite a few alternative schools right now, the adults have strong expectations about the way the children will and should behave. They project onto children their theories about right human behavior in general. They think, if the children are healthy they will behave the way we think everybody should behave. For that matter, this is probably true for all teachers, progressive or not. The difference is that the traditional teacher tells the children how he wants them to behave. The progressive or so-called free teacher says, "Behave any way you like." So the child has to look for clues, which the adults can't help giving, to show whether he is doing the right thing or not. This can be exhausting. Sometimes the kid gets fed up with it, and like the famous (probably made-up) child in the progressive school, says, "Teacher, do we have to do what we want today?", meaning do we have to figure out what you want us to do today? Why don't you just tell us?

When I first started visiting a lot of schools and classes, I saw, by furtive glances darted toward me, by plaintive voices and strained movements, that in some classes the children were very anxious; in others, much less so. This didn't necessarily have anything to do with how strict the class was. From all I heard and saw a notion that I call the Behavior Gap began to form itself in my mind. Imagine a spectrum of behavior from very Good to very Bad. If we start at the Good end of the line and move toward the Bad, for every teacher we come to a point on the line, call it point A, which represents behavior that is bad enough to annoy her and to make her wish that it would stop, but not bad enough so that she thinks she can or needs to or ought to do anything to stop it. If we keep moving toward the Bad end, after a while we get to another point, point B, which represents behavior so bad that she feels she can, must, and will take some kind of action to stop it. The distance between A and B is the Behavior Gap. When it is wide, the class is going to be uneasy; when it is narrow, they are probably going to be more at ease—unless point B is impossibly close to the Good end of the behavior spectrum. For the most part, how wide or narrow the gap is counts much more than where it is on the spectrum. This is another possibly useful meaning for the old saw about children and limits. Children certainly don't like adults who are bugged by everything they do. But they equally dislike being around an adult who lets them bug him. It is too mysterious and threatening. What is he going to do when he does cut loose?

If a kid is doing something that annoys a teacher, better to say, "Hey, cut that out, it's driving me crazy." Or, "Please don't do that, I really don't like it." Then the structure is clear, and the kids get information about the teacher from which they can build up a fairly good picture of him and learn how to live with him.

HERB (to the group): Have any of you read John Holt's *Freedom and Beyond?*
TONY: I've seen several selections from *Freedom and Beyond,* Herb.
HERB: I was thinking of his discussion about the structure of an open classroom and that of a traditional classroom.

Several members indicated that they had read this selection.

HERB (with an air of accomplishment): Holt really gets specific about defining open education. He says that children get fed up with doing their own thing. They (children) want teachers to tell them what to do and how to behave. The really important thing in an open classroom is to make the structure clear to the children.
CELLA (choosing her words carefully): Herb, what did Holt say about structure? The reason I'm asking this question is because to me it is extremely important to understand structures, as Holt defines them, before isolating those two statements.
HERB: Holt says that in a traditional classroom the structure has two main elements—the teacher and the children.
TONY: How does he describe the structure in an open classroom?
HERB: The structure is the same, the teacher and the children, but in an open classroom the children know the limits.
CELLA: Wait a minute, Herb; Holt said more than that! He said that in an open classroom there are as many structures as there are teachers and students and that no two of these elements are alike. Furthermore, in an open classroom

the structure comes from the needs and abilities of the children, not from the desires of only the teacher.
HERB (after glancing at the selection): O.K., you're right. But he did say children should know the limits.
CELLA (smiling): I'm not arguing that point, Herb. I'm simply saying that the real issue is *where does the structure come from.* You see, Herb, if I decide what the limits will be for all my children and make sure they understand these limits, I've really got a closed classroom.
HERB (somewhat angrily): Holt said that if something bothers you, as a teacher, just tell the kids that their behavior is driving you up the wall. Do you disagree with that?
CELLA (thinking it's about time to change the subject): No, Herb, I don't disagree with that at all, so long as your children feel free to say to you or to another child: "Hey, would you please stop that; it's driving me nuts." Talking about nuts, why don't we take a break? Coffee anyone?

During the coffee break, Herb went for a walk. He was disturbed about getting angry, and he wanted to think about his feelings.

At times I fight certain ideas about open education, and at other times I accept it. Why am I this way?

Rather than returning to the discussion group, Herb walked along the road that led to the mountains. He examined the ideas that he found disagreeable and soon realized that these were the practices he felt most unsuccessful with in the classroom. He considered his angry reactions—they were personal and emotional. His problems

were with himself and not with the children.

I disagree with some tenets not because I'm convinced that they're bad for children but because I feel inadequate or fearful of being involved with them.

While dealing with this thought, he remembered reading somewhere that schools are for adults and not children.

This could be true, especially if I continually have to deal with my emotional problems while making classroom decisions. To make that statement false, I will have to put aside my personal problems and consider the welfare of the children in front of me.

Dear Cella:
During the break at our last meeting I went for a walk. I wanted to be alone. After I got home, it occurred to me that you might have felt I was angry with you. I wasn't. In fact, I was angry with myself for getting upset during the session. I came to some interesting conclusions while walking along the old road—will tell you about them sometime soon.

Sincerely,
Herb

"Open Education: Yes!" by Ella Q. Forman

In an article in **Saturday Review,** September 18, 1971, writer Marilyn Hapgood warned that the open school has reached a critical stage in this country. Here is a promising trend that can go the way of "progressive education" and other innovative movements which in the past have been enthusiastically espoused and then discredited by their own proponents.

Charles Slack, in "Three Essays on Our New Movement," in **Educational Technology** (January, 1972), comments on "informal education" and offers the following seriocomic description:

> There is definitely a week-end, summertime holiday, Fourth of July, anything you want, hot dogs and ice cream, comic books and ring-o-leary-o sound to the very word "informal."
>
> It brings to mind kids yelling and running around, kids not knowing where their seats are, . . . kids who forgot their homework (or, God forbid, teachers who forgot to give them any). It makes you think of sincere lib-gal teachers, . . . all pants-suits and owlish horn-rims brimming over with expansive ideas, but not exactly knowing how to, well, how to keep things under **control.** It makes you think of long and dirty hair on male teacher-aides with ratty old sneakers and torn fringe jeans and a look in the eye that says they've done more than just read about drugs. It is positively scary, "informal is." What about setting limits? . . . I mean, a little chaos is all right, but a constant racket **all** the time! Who's in charge here? I can't hear myself think.

On the other hand, a writer named Caleb Gattegno, in his book, **What We Owe Children**, points out that

> Teachers in the traditional schools make the assumption that what they know and have to teach is unknown to learners. They believe that they are making the unknown known by imparting information to the students. All they need to do is teach—the learner is on his own. How many readers, for example remember—let alone understand—everything their teachers taught them? Sixty or forty per cent of what they were taught? And to what extent has that sixty or forty per cent of the subject matter retained enabled them to meet what is new and strange in life? The answers are self-evident.

Indeed they are. Even allowing for large doses of scapegoatism, it has become apparent that the system which has served American society successfully for so many years no longer satisfies its patrons.

The hue and cry from the marketplace merely echoes demands that the profession has placed upon itself—that new and better ways be found to deal with our rapidly changing world.

The reasons leading to these new demands have been well documented. Sputnik, the population explosion, the knowledge explosion, rapid societal change, the traumatic impact of change, and so on. All these have contributed to the growing belief that the focus of education must now be on learning rather than on teaching. A whole series of objectives and procedures must be orchestrated to the key of the individual student and at the same time be manageable in a group situation.

The open school provides an enticing promise to all who will listen. It offers school districts the versatility necessary to effect change at a rational and manageable rate. An open school climate can be initiated by knocking out a wall between two classrooms. Usually housed in facilities constructed to facilitate its objectives, it may even be found in a store front or on an inner city street.

Within its walls (or nonwalls), lies an infinite variety of organizational and curricular possibilities. These can be used by the teaching teams exploiting their special skills in order to do more with and for the students. Higher cognitive skills and the affective domain can be included in the curriculum. The key is providing the student with alternatives in activities which relate to his life experience. Planning and making choices calls for decisionmaking in a controlled environment. The learner experiences the consequences of his decisions. Content is presented in challenging and relevant ways, using technological and human resources. The basic textbook is only one of many tools. All this is possible because of the team approach and the new roles assumed by both the teachers and the learners.

Concerns have been expressed that are not entirely without foundation. An open classroom is much like the little girl with the curl in the middle of her forehead of nursery rhyme fame. When it is good, it is very, very good . . . and when it is bad, it is HORRID! An open classroom can appear at times to be chaotic, and if it is not properly managed, it is! Also, a so-called open classroom with teachers and students functioning in four teacher directed corners scarcely justifies the expense of tearing down walls. Third, some fear that the advent of the programmed materials and performance objectives will lead to a purely mechanistic type of curriculum. And it could. Fourth, others are concerned that the humanistic approach will result in a lack of attention to the basic skills necessary for literacy. This too, is a possibility. Was it not ever thus, whenever incompetent or unprepared or misassigned personnel were in charge? These criticisms cannot be reserved for the open settings alone. Similar ills can exist in any classroom; they are simply more visible where no doors exist behind which to hide.

The characteristic picture of an open classroom has become familiar. Large carpeted areas, the hum of sound, the students participating in a variety of simultaneous activities. They move around the room working at will, individually, in pairs, or in small groups—using many materials and media—under the direction of a team of teachers and para-professionals. To the uninitiated, it indeed appears informal, even suspiciously like Charles Slack's tongue-in-cheek description. But with two very critical differences.

The reality is that the more informal a class appears, the more rigorously and skillfully it is planned and managed. Every movement, every activity has been based on a sound objective. Scarey informality? Not to the students! They know what they're doing and why; they've shared in the planning. Who's in charge? The teachers, but in new roles, using new skills and insights.

The second reality holds the key to the potential inherent in the open school concept. The movement, the color, the innovative hardware and software are merely the tip of the iceberg, hinting dimly at the size and shape of the unseen mass below the waterline.

Rather than a single concept, several strategies form the foundation and shape the program. And, to pursue the iceberg analogy one step further, it is upon those same principles, so necessary to its success, that a learning center program can founder unless they are accepted by the practitioner.

1. **The curriculum provides strategies for developing skills in both the cognitive and affective domain.** In addition to the traditional content the following must be included and planned for: communicating effectively, learning how to think, to accept oneself, and to get along with others. This involves skill building strategies, small group interaction, and one-to-one encounters with peers and teachers.

Four teachers, for example, can divide the responsibility for 120 or 130 children in many ways, numerically. Individualizing to this degree is not difficult; however, providing avenues for students to earn success and/or accept incidents of failure, without failing as human beings, is less simple. Resources for training are available; it is unrealistic to expect teachers to succeed without it.

2. **The learner assumes the responsibility for his own behavior.** Although this statement has assumed almost cliché status, it is widely misunderstood. Apprehensive parents interpret it to mean that children "decide what they want to learn"—so what is the teacher paid for? Misinformed teachers tend to overwhelm children with masses of dittoed booklets or commercial kits in which the child "works on his own."

What it really means is that students are offered

alternative ways of reaching clearly defined objectives: learning how to add fractions, for instance, or discovering what causes rain. The alternatives are limited, possibly to either one set of materials or another. Once he is committed to a choice, the student must have an opportunity to evaluate his progress and set new goals for the next step on the continuum. Without the evaluative process, often accomplished at regularly scheduled pupil-teacher conferences, the concept of self-directed learning can be meaningless.

3. **Continuous Progress Learning becomes a reality rather than an ideological myth.**

This is one where we say we should take the child "where he is" and move him along in a manner consistent with his learning style and rate. CPL is eminently possible in the open school but not without the accountability factor. Management by objectives is plugged in here, beginning with an assessment of needs. Obviously, teachers must first ascertain where the pupil is. Diagnostic —and if need be remedial—procedures can be started. (This can happen when there are others right there to maintain the total group.)

The "copout" comes if the desired behavior is not established, preferably with the commitment of the student and if records are not kept which can be easily and accurately interpreted to the parents. Mother and Dad need to know if Suzy is not yet up to grade level, whatever that means. If they can be shown that she's gained a year and a half in nine months, however, this is acceptable.

For the accelerated student the process is equally valuable. He doesn't need to relearn what he demonstrates he already knows. Both vertical and horizontal experiences commensurate with his ability can be offered. And the child in the middle gets his fair share too.

4. **The combined resources of the team provide expertise and flexibility.** True, so long as total commitment is part of the package. Probably one of the most severe constraints in the open school system is the building and maintenance of the teams.

Teachers must cope with changing roles in terms of interaction with students and the curriculum. They must also relinquish some of their au-

tonomy and much of their ego involvement with "my kids." They must learn to give each other feedback, to encounter and even confront without destroying the team morale.

Some teachers are unwilling or unable to cope with the tremendous effort and trauma involved in becoming a team teacher/facilitator of learning. While there should be no stigma attached to such teachers, it is fatal to include them in open school teams.

To teachers who accept the assumptions, however, the rewards are a more than adequate trade off for the constraints. Working with students for whom the joy of learning provides the only discipline necessary is still the greatest reward that teachers can enjoy. The challenge of developing a truly humanistic curriculum which includes solid academic progress as a key goal, but only one of the goals, can be irresistible to the highly intelligent, "tuned in, turned on" teacher of this decade.

5. **The principal wears a new hat.** It is an open secret that principals have found their traditional roles eroded, with frustration the inevitable result. Nevertheless, the building principal is still the key person in the implementation of change and innovation.

The autocratic or **laissez-faire** leader will not see exemplary programs developed in his building.

But a "new breed" of principal has internalized the role of instructional leader. This principal and his staff are mutually united in the development and pursuit of objectives. He trains himself in new techniques of team building and problem solving. He or she involves staff decision-making. He models attitudes and behavior patterns of trust and valuing humans of all ages and pigmentation. His creation of a support system is essential, absorbing, and mutually appreciated by staff, students, and the community.

6. **Accountability can be established from several informal sources.** Rather than rating students subjectively or on the basis of standardized tests, the focus is on reporting progress. The establishment of shared objectives serves to delineate what schools can accomplish and what they cannot.

We can no longer assume implicit responsibility for social, physical, and spiritual needs of children. We should, however, learn how to report to parents how a child functions alone and with others. Observation, performance criteria, taped interviews, and anecdotal records are merely a few of the ways in which information can be gathered.

Objective measurement techniques of critical thinking and the affective processes have not been widely developed. It is, however, possible to describe desired behavior and to indicate "yes" or "no."

The crucial responsibility lies with the team informational retrieval system. It need not be complicated; it **must** be easily accessible. Every member of the team must have both input and access. A teacher who responds, "I don't know what Jimmie is doing in reading, I see him only for spelling," instantly annihilates his credibility with that parent.

7. **Learning to feel is feeling to learn.** Learning is enhanced or constrained by the attitude and/or valuing reaction of the learner. Awareness of this becomes a powerful tool in the open school. When students are involved in planning and setting objectives, a natural concomitant becomes commitment to responsibility.

Children are instinctively aware of the interaction of the cognitive and affective, and their response supports independent behavior with responsibility. Students are busy, involved, happy, and **learning**.

The skill of teachers makes this happen. The teaching of responsibility and decisionmaking skills are contingent upon learner readiness, in the same way as readiness is involved in the reading process. Thus, the elusive, but quite tangible condition known as "climate" is established.

8. **It's all based on research**. The literature abounds with thoroughly researched models and strategies for every aspect of open education, many more than can possibly be used. From these come the support and the rationale for putting innovation into practice. Sophisticated, systematic procedures are mandatory. The particulars of the program start with needs assessment and evolve from the allocation of resources made available by the district. Resources are: personnel, facilities, materials, and time.

9. **It is an evolving process.** The open school is not a panacea nor, as some seem to think, a goal in itself. It is a collection of procedures with the specific goal of meeting the needs of modern youth and providing them with life skills in their world of future shock. It can begin when two teachers plan for one segment of thirty minutes a day. It can grow to be a highly complex, totally absorbing way of life for students, educators and the community. As one problem is solved, others emerge, at successively profound levels. Teaching in open education can become a highly complex, sophisticated occupation, simultaneously frustrating and utterly satisfying.

In my view, the fact that change is difficult and threatening does not obviate the necessity for it nor dim the challenge. It is also a fact that the information giving function formerly monopolized by schools has been weakened by early childhood experiences in an information rich, technological society. Traditional methods cannot compete with real world experiences, whether they be vicarious, such as landing on the moon with the astronauts or as actual as a ratbite. The eclectic, evolving nature of open education contains both its weakness and its strength.

Its weaknesses dictate support of administration, teacher competency, and training in innovative strategies. Viewed from that angle, perhaps constraints become strength. It requires talent and devotion; isn't that what teaching is all about?

On the positive side, open education offers a viable set of principles which, through time, can help public education to achieve a renewed and valued position as a fundamental institution in American society.

JANICE: (having read "Open Education: Yes"!): *Surely there must be more to open education than the mere removal of a wall.*

(to Dr. Roubinek): I've just finished reading "Open Education: Yes"! and came across a sentence that indicated that an open school climate can be initiated by knocking out a wall between two classrooms. Do you agree with this?

DR. ROUBINEK: That would depend upon the definition of an open school. If we are talking about open space, I agree. However, if we mean openness in respect to the instructional program, I'd say, not necessarily so. Open space does not guarantee an open school.
(pointing to sign) This sign should be hung over the door of every open classroom, every open school!

JOSÉ: Dr. Roubinek, what do you mean, "an open classroom is open to parents?"
DR. ROUBINEK: In open classrooms parents *are* encouraged to participate in the learning environment. Many open teachers use parents as helpers and resource people, and without exception, open teachers actively seek out parents to discuss children and learning. How else do you get input about the child's attitude towards school as he expresses it at home? How else do you find out the parents' attitudes toward school?
JOSÉ: Does this mean that parents have more of a voice in their child's education in an open classroom?
DR. ROUBINEK: Yes. Especially in an out-in-the-open manner. Certainly the parent's attitudes greatly influence children in any school environment. If the parents, for instance, hated school—don't you think the child is going to pick up some of this and start school with a few misgivings? Open education brings the parents to the fore—opens their minds about school. It could make all the difference in the world to their children's chances of deriving the benefits schools have to offer.
JOSÉ: Do you think parents understand open education?
DR. ROUBINEK: Parents who have experienced an open teacher probably do, but so few parents have had this experience that I'm sure we'd have to say that as a group, parents do not understand. And you see, José, if parents could understand it, then they wouldn't be so fearful of open education. *This is something that teachers and principals must not forget to deal with when discussing open education with parents.*
DR. CARSWELL: It's really unfortunate that you were unable to visit the St. Paul Open School in Minneapolis. You really would have enjoyed seeing all the wonderful learning activities for children.
DR. ROUBINEK: That's what many people have told me. Did I hear correctly that the St. Paul Open School has children from kindergarten through high school?
DR. CARSWELL: Yes, they do, and you should see how well children of different ages work together.
DR. ROUBINEK: Why don't we plan to spend some time during our next discussion session talking about this school? Were you able to bring back any handouts?
DR. CARSWELL: I brought back quite a lot of printed material—such as their goals, their reasons, their design and implementation, and a brief description of their program. On every one of the four floors of that big old building I saw a number of exciting ideas. I have slides of some of these activities to show you.

NOTICE TO PARENTS
An Open Classroom Is Open To Parents As Well As To Their Children

St. Paul Open School Goals

WE SEEK TO ESTABLISH A PROGRAM IN WHICH PEOPLE:

1. Approach learning with confidence and joy.
2. See themselves as worthwhile persons and have an active positive regard for every person as an individual.
3. Develop an understanding of human social systems and physical environments.
4. Develop and reassess personal values.
5. Develop social skills including conciliation, persuasion, honest communication and group decision-making.
6. Develop the skills of reading, writing, speaking, listening, computation, learning and critical thinking.
7. Develop and maintain good health habits, physical fitness, recreational skills and positive body awareness.
8. Are willing to take risks, make commitments, become involved and be accountable for their actions.
9. Have a sense of awe and wonder, a capacity for esthetic appreciation and enjoyment.
10. Are creative, curious, self-directed and open to new experiences.
11. Recognize that individual actions can influence the course of events.
12. Recognize the humor and incongruity that is a part of the human experience.

From "St. Paul Open School: Design, Rationale, and Implementation" by Wayne Jennings, Ph.D., Director

The Design of the St. Paul Open School

Any project begins with certain assumptions of what is to be included—in short, a design which guides development of the project. Often in the beginning stages of a project, there is a gap between actuality and design. It is important, however, to understand the design, the key elements, of which include:

1. Advisor-Advisee Roles. Each student selects an advisor from the staff. The advisor meets with each student **weekly** to help the student write goals and devise a program. The advisor meets periodically with both the parents and the student to discuss expectations and the student's education. The advisor is the student's advocate, champion, expeditor and facilitator. The advisor acts as an "educational broker" by helping arrange learning experiences in and out of the school that achieve the student's goals. The advisor's responsibilities are crucial to the school's functioning. The advisor helps students approve their strengths and weaknesses to the end of becoming lifelong designers of their own education.

2. Major resource areas. Each of the resource areas or "theaters of learning" provides a **kaleidoscopic variety of learning experiences.** The shop area, for example, has students at work on projects of their choosing in wood, metal, plastics, electronics, printing, duplicating, motors, welding, crafts, etc. Students may be building bookcases, polishing stones, fiberglassing a canoe, or designing a school intercom. Each of the resource areas contains sub-activity areas and the possibility of thousands of projects to be pursued independently or with others.

The music/drama/dance areas provide oral and instrumental music for individuals, ensembles, large groups in such areas as opera, symphony, popular, jazz, etc. Listening areas for music and dramatic readings are available. Tape recorders, video tape recorders, stereo, Moog synthesizers, and musical instruments are essential. Classic, modern and folk dance, free or creative movement helps students gain coordination, grace, beauty, posture and rhythm—not to mention vocabulary, expressiveness and artistic appreciation. Drama, formal or extemporaneous, enhances self-discipline, creativity and understanding of self and others.

Each resource area contains a small library of books, magazines, films, etc. The student is encouraged to look things up, explore, delve into a topic, follow how-to-do-it materials and conduct research.

The major resource areas in total provide an incredible array of learning activities: repairing a clock, upholstering silk screening, mastering trigonometry, organizing a political party, interning on a job or in a community agency, planning and preparing a television script, electronic cooking, writing school publications, researching the development of air transportation, conducting traffic surveys, experimenting with the effects of light on plants, discussing Shakespeare—in short, the kind of activities most schools want but somehow aren't sufficiently geared for as a regular diet.

3. Integrated learning. The student building a chug in the shop reads directions, plans, designs, orders materials, measures and calculates, engineers and researches for reduced friction and wind resistance, decorates the body, writes for race entry blanks and evaluates the project. Building a chug involves math, reading, physics, art and working with others.

Teachers seek to integrate learnings from many areas into projects and activities. Such efforts build vocabulary and aid concept development so that the student continually expands learning and relates material in other areas. Learning fractions is not an isolated math activity into which the math teacher tries to breathe life, but rather is useful knowledge in such areas as shop, home economics and photography. Accelerated learning in many areas related to building a chug is the result of integrated learning practices.

4. Curriculum Choice. Students select courses and activities, then devise their own schedule. Their program is constructed from the array of activities and courses available in the resource areas. The student becomes an active agent in designing an education. The school's design exploits the child's tendency to concentrate on tasks of interest, tasks he assigns himself. There are no required courses. Instead, the child's natural curiosity and drive for mastery lead to a considerable range of exploratory activities and self-initiated learning pursuits. Compared to the usual school where young students are walked in lines, seated within the grasp of the teacher and controlled in all dimensions, **even very young students in the Open School rapidly learn to find their way about a complex building, go to lunch, devise and follow a schedule independently.** This is surprising to visitors accustomed to more structured school procedures.

5. Teacher as facilitator. The teacher's role changes from information giver and prodder to that of a facilitator arranging exciting learning experiences, clearing obstacles and barriers to learning, suggesting possibilities, helping students with personal goals and purposes, and being a friendly guide. **Each teacher in a sense becomes a director and planner of a learning empire in which the child's interests are stimulated and catered for.**

6. Resource people. Many kinds of people in the Open School enterprise teach and help young people grow and develop. Parents assist as volunteers. **People with expertise** teach or prepare materials under the direction of certified personnel. **Paid aides** provide a variety of services from clerical to teaching. The teacher's specific knowledge and skill with students becomes extended manyfold through the use of resource people. One of the best categories of resource people are the **students themselves.** One teaches leatherwork, another has an extensive stamp collection, another is skilled and patient at helping young children read, another organizes a paper airplane club (along the lines of the **Scientific American** contest), another knows German, and so forth. **When students teach, they not only learn their subject more thoroughly, but also learn presentation, how to organize information, some psychology of learning, personal effectiveness, and how to be more articulate.** They learn these things in one of the most efficient ways—**by doing, by experience.**

7. The community as classroom. Learning occurs in many places and trips are planned to take advantage of courses, activities, people, and events in the community. **Students work as interns, volunteers and employees. Field trips** make the community a part of a larger classroom. Some schools operate entirely in the community without a school building and have found the students more resourceful and knowledgeable about the world. For too long schools have built high walls and have turned inward, away from life. The Open School is involved in the world and all of life. Open School students have been **all over America** and **on other continents.**

8. Affective emphasis. How one feels is frequently more important in personal action than what one knows. The self-concept, values, attitudes, a can-do spirit, acceptance of others, enthusiasm, responsibility and initiative are areas of emphasis in the learning activities of the Open School. The results are an increased appetite and interest in school and lifelong learning. **The goals and methods of the Open School which place a special priority on affective dimensions create cumulative learnings.**

9. Life skills. The actual skills and competencies needed to be a successful person are valid and important goals of education. Being articulate, knowing how to find information, how to solve problems, critical thinking, reading skills, computation skills, conciliation skills, physical fitness and good health habits are among the important life skills taught at the Open School. They are not only the goals listed in a curriculum guide but are essential to function well in the school since the school is patterned like life. One of the most important drives in life is being able to cope with daily tasks. The school that is like life encourages —actually makes necessary—learning to be an effective person in life.

10. Cross age grouping. Students do not develop skills or interests at the same age and rate. Organizing students into single age groups or fixed groupings decreases opportunities for satisfying the various personal growth patterns. Many schools are moving toward non-graded approaches. Activities in the Open School are based on interest and what the student can actually do rather than on age restrictions. Students learn much from one another and are in many instances natural teachers. The immediate presence of older students provides leadership models for younger students to study. For the older child, responsibility and leadership opportunities enhance feelings of importance and reduce the teenage anti-establishment subculture.

11. Heterogeneous student body. Life in a pluralistic world requires exposure and contact with people of many backgrounds. Diversity provides richness, stimulation and opportunities to examine one's values. The student population at the Open School has been structured to reflect the diversity of the city.

12. Shared decision making. The school should resemble a miniature democratic society. The Open School's problems are examined by all affected and decisions reached through careful study, discussion and negotiation. The likelihood of acceptance and commitment to decisions is enhanced when one has helped shape their outcome. Staff meetings are open to participation by students and parents. An Advisory Council of staff, parents, students and citizens-at-large study problem areas and suggest policy.

Rationale for the Open School

Somewhat different theories of learning support the rationale of the Open School's design. **Learning is considered to have occurred when there is actual change in the person.** Learning does not automatically result from schooling; nor does success at rote memory; nor does the usual routine of assign, study, recite, and test. These activities often do not change the person in positive directions.

Learning occurs most naturally during periods of intense involvement, during active doing, and as part of living. Learning results **from experiencing:** reading an appreciated poem, attempting to explain feelings in speech or writing, playing an instrument, drawing, acting, planning, etc. Learning occurs easiest and most thoroughly when interest and personal motivation are high. Educators talk of individualized and personalized instruction because they know its powerful effect on learning. This is precisely why each child's program in the Open School is based on interest.

Much experience and research suggests that children learn in different ways, at different times, from things around them that interest them, and from each other. And that children learn fastest when pursuing their own interests.

The innate urge to explore so evident in an infant is self-perpetuating if the child receives pleasure and satisfaction from such activities. In ordinary schools exploratory activity is restricted to certain times and places, and is to be done only in limited ways for all children at a specified pace. When this happens, curiosity is reduced; creativity and spontaneity are not fostered and natural drives to learn in school are reduced.

An example of the natural drive to learn occurs with one of the most difficult areas—learning to talk. The infant recognizes the power of speech. Without lessons, textbooks or tests (except performance in life) the child masters the entire grammar and structure of the language (or two languages in a bi-lingual home) intuitively by age five. This whole process occurs even though the brain is not highly developed. In addition, the child incorporates incredible inflection and subtle nuances of tone into his repertoire, as all parents know.

If an infant were constantly criticized, graded and prodded in learning to speak, it is likely the same blockages would occur as too often occur in reading. Rather parents are patient with mistakes, the seeming nonsense talk and the word play of infants. In good time, nearly every child masters the language.

The same drive for mastery of something personally important, for gaining the mental tools of those around him, is a part of the delightful curiosity and energy of the child. The desire to read is a powerful drive of young children, for reading unlocks many treasures and secrets of how to do things and how things are. The same is true with other life skills; they are obviously important to the needs for mastery and well-being.

The Open School attempts to harness such drives for learning. However, even more fundamental drives cause blockages for some children: does the child feel good about himself; does the child feel protected and safe from harm; and, does the child have enough nourishment? Each of these primary drives must be reasonably satisfied from the child's view before more complex learning and risk-taking activities can take place.

In the Open School the timetable for learning is within, rather than artificially established by age. The school's task is to provide an environment in which the skills for effective living are important and needed, a personally supportive, nurturing and safe climate, and exciting, stimulating activities for the mind to explore and speculate about.

Such a setting encourages a child to learn in many directions, to develop talents and interests, to continue learning, to be excited about new things, to be in awe and wonder of the unknown —in short, to be an enthusiastic lifelong learner. Such a person is not bored easily, does not flit or dabble from one thing to the next. Such an adult is sought after as a worker, as a friend, and as a mate. Such a person possesses a solid sense of self-worth and does not require egotistic antics. Such a person is self-disciplined and understands the need for an orderly society.

Implementation of the Open School

The implementation of the Open School design is a challenging task. The decision to begin the school in September, 1971 came too late to permit planning, adequate budget allotments and preparation of the building. The staff, none of whom have worked in such a program before, met for the first time just two weeks before the students arrived. One week before the students came, a rough office building was acquired and had to be converted. The hard surfaces and high ceilings echoed every sound and made ordinary conversation difficult. School began without a typewriter in the building, no Ditto machine, no mimeograph machine, and literally no equipment. Material was begged and accumulated from any source.

Teachers suddenly had to cope with the tough problems of student accountability, scheduling, responsible freedom, control and direction, how to intervene, providing stimulating choices, and messiness. Their thinking was yanked to and fro on concerns such as order and structure vs. disorder, the value of play, and how to develop self-discipline. Far from the appearance of being permissive and endorsing lack of structure, teachers needed to learn great organizational and planning skills to reduce chaos and random wandering by children. They needed to learn to keep records of a child's progress in dozens of areas, to maintain an exciting environment by changing it often, to explain to children the **why** of reasonable behavior, to be in charge because they were needed rather than by arbitrary authority, to organize students for cleaning up and putting things away. The subtle differences in guiding rather than directing needed to be understood. The personal involvement with children by the teacher and the small band of helpers, aides, volunteers, older students and college youth had to be organized and trained. There was no abdication of authority but arbitrary authority had to be replaced with earned respect, cooperation and responsibility. The teachers shaped elements of the program toward these ends. Teachers didn't lecture about cooperation but had to arrange for it to happen—a highly challenging, creative task.

The program improves as perplexing problems are mastered. Progress is rapid but several years will be required to accomplish most elements of the design. Students and parents join with staff to seek solutions and to establish new norms of expectations and humanistic procedures. A common task builds strong bonds that sustain the school through its design shortcomings. In a sense, the building itself, the curriculum, the need for materials, becomes everyone's responsibility, everyone's problem, and everyone's pride as progress is achieved.

The St. Paul Open School by Wayne Jennings, Director

What makes school exciting?

At first, maybe it's fat orange pillars, and purple, yellow, white, blue or green walls and doors stretching down the corridors.

Maybe it's knowing that students and parents and teachers painted most of them, working together—changing an old four-floor building from factory-drab to bright colors in a few weeks' time.

Maybe it's the exciting exploration you witness in the art area, where learners from 4 to 40 are at work on such projects as ceramics, silk screening, painting, carving, jewelry-making, leather-work, photography, and more.

Or maybe it's the quiet, intense comradeship in a 10-year-old helping a 6-year-old learn to read; a tall redhead showing a small blond tyke how to use a camera; a 12-year-old black girl helping a small boy take his first panful of cookies from the oven.

Whatever turns you on—the St. Paul Open School has got it. A research and demonstration unit of the St. Paul public education system, the school (which opened in September, 1971) has 500 students, **age 5 through 18, representative** of the city's geographic areas and its citizens' socio-economic and ethnic backgrounds.

It manages to turn the students on, too—so much, that they showed up in droves a week before opening day when the newly rented building was opened for renovation. On opening day they cheered for minutes at a time when the principal spelled out some features of the school: no report cards; no grades; no required classes; no lecture-memorize-test routine from teachers.

HOW DOES IT WORK?

Without those familiar ingredients, what does go on in the school?

Many things are happening simultaneously. Students are working alone, in groups, teaching one another, making discoveries together, discussing, exploring, watching demonstrations, taking short courses, going on field trips.

The school is organized into major learning areas, or **"theaters of learning":** art; music-drama; humanities; math-science; industrial arts; home economics; and physical education. Each area has a library-resource center and a "smorgasbord" of activities to choose from—some of which are conducted by volunteers or are out in the community. There is also a central library-resource center. Many areas have rooms for quiet study, short courses, and group or individual projects in addition to large open spaces.

When a student is not actively involved in one of the multitude of activities going on at all times, he may be meeting with his advisor. The two of them together are continually charting his goals and means of achieving them, and evaluating progress. When a given project or course of action doesn't work out, there is no stigma of failure. Instead, either the goals are changed or different ways of working toward them are found. The student learns to know his own strengths and weaknesses, what he needs to work on and what comes easily, what areas he avoids, and how he reacts

to different people. Eventually, he comes to know himself well. Students determine their schedules, learn to design their own education on the way to becoming self-initiating learners. Such students will be lifelong consumers of learning.

DO THEY REALLY LEARN?

This approach integrates learning of many kinds. Basic skills like reading and writing are part of many learning situations, and teachers seek ways to weave them in. In the case of a film project, for example, students read manuals, photo magazines, and books on the subject, keep logs or records, write letters, design instructions for others, calculate distances, arrange demonstrations, purchase materials, determine proportions and ratios for enlargements; and thus constantly use and become familiar with reading, writing and math, at whatever level they're operating at. Every plunge is an opportunity for making mistakes, learning from them, and growing in skills and confidence.

Years of research into educational practices suggest that in a setting of intrinsically interesting and extensively equipped "theaters of learning" young people are stimulated and learning occurs more easily, more naturally and more thoroughly than in conventional schools. Psychological research indicates that more learning takes place when an individual is predisposed to want to learn—when his emotional state is ready to grasp new knowledge.

Learning, at the Open School, is conceived in terms not only of the 3 R's and other basic "subject matter" of so many curriculum manuals, but also of the other important qualities needed for living in a rapidly changing society: flexibility, openness, initiative, an appetite for lifelong learning, enthusiasm, constructive human relationships, responsibility, continually broadening perspectives and deepening self-discoveries.

DO TEACHERS TEACH?

Teachers—or **learning facilitators** as they prefer to call themselves—spend their energy and thought on maximizing learning for students.

They are assisted by **aides, volunteers, student**

teachers and various **resource people** on call. But more than any others, they are assisted by the students themselves—who, by the very nature of the entire enterprise, are in natural roles of teachers-and-learners. **The student deeply involved in an interest area attracts others following an old dictum, one doesn't truly understand an area until one teaches it to another.**

Older students serve as a model to younger students by providing **leadership** and **teaching**. This responsibility role effectively combats the useless feeling of many teenagers and enables them to spend more of their great energy in creative directions and less in resentful, anti-adult, anti-establishment teen sub-culture so common today in a world with little use for teenagers. Younger children benefit by more individual attention and personal help **from others not so distant from their problems as are adults.** In turn, young children help even younger children.

Teachers were selected for the Open School on the basis of **interest, competence** and **educational philosophy**—a distinct advantage over reassigning or retraining a traditional staff. Democratically organized, **the teachers themselves make decisions on additional personnel, training, budget—** thus increasing their understanding of these decisions and their feeling of responsibility toward making them work. They agreed with gusto to level with one another, to be open and honest, to welcome suggestions from anyone, of whatever age or expertise. Students and parents are welcome and participate in the frequent faculty meetings. Where staff lack the skill to handle a situation or a task, they help each other—through training sessions or more informal means. They work closely with parents and interested citizens, as well as students, on an elected Advisory Council.

DOES EDUCATION COST MORE THIS WAY?

Seldom have so many exciting features and concepts been put together in a single project. In addition, the economic ramifications are exciting to speculate on.

The staff consists of just seventeen professional teachers for five hundred students. **A principal** directs the school, assisted by a **program coordina-**

tor (teacher on special assignment) and **two community resource specialists** (ordinary citizens) who coordinate volunteers, resources, information dissemination and visitors.

If quality education is the result, as desired, the Open School will demonstrate that the usual attempted solution to individualizing and improving education—the reduction of class size—is not necessarily valid. In the city of St. Paul, with 50,000 public school students, a reduction of just one pupil per classroom for all classrooms in the system would cost over $1-million. A significant reduction of, say, 5 or 10 pupils would cost between $5- and $10-million. It can be seen that, conversely, if class size is increased, then savings of a similar magnitude are realized.

One of the goals of this project is to demonstrate that, with sufficient equipment and materials, as much learning can take place with fewer professional teachers. Initially, the money saved on teaching staff will be put into the "stuff" of learning. Eventually, it is hoped, real financial savings will result. If, in addition, learning is improved, then a real breakthrough in education will have occurred.

At this point in the St. Paul Open School anything seems possible.

Is Open Education For All Children?
by Darrell L. Roubinek

This question always stimulates a lively discussion in the open education seminars at the University of Arizona. As one might suspect, graduate students hold varying points of view concerning this question.

Those students who do not believe that open education is for all children can sight countless incidences where children have created all sorts of problems in an open classroom. Their solution is usually to reassign these children to self-contained classrooms. The rationale for this position goes something like this:

1. Some children prefer to be told what to do, how to do it, and when to do it.

2. Some children are "aimless wanderers" and "non-choosers."

3. Some children cannot maintain self-control in an informal learning environment.

4. Some children never seem able to create a balanced program for themselves.

Those students who support open education for all counter this rationale with statements such as:

1. We agree that some children do not make choices in the learning environment, but they never can change this behavior in a closed environment where choices are not available.

2. We do not believe that children are non-choosers. Children make many choices before and after school. Children who do not choose any activity in a classroom probably do not care for any of the options.

3. We agree that children are at varying stages of self-control, but again, we assert that children cannot develop self-control if they are not permitted opportunities to control themselves.

The purpose of the seminar is to provide students with the opportunity to explore their feelings and attitudes toward open education; therefore, no attempt is made to make all agree that open education is for all children. However, after the following activity, some students tend to modify their positions. In general this activity seems to help students become more committed to their position on the question.

First, some of the generally accepted goals for open education are identified:

1. Self-reliant learners
2. Positive attitude towards learning
3. Problem solvers
4. Creative learners
5. Appropriate choice making
6. Responsible learners and citizens
7. Etc.

The question, **"Are the identified goals of open education appropriate goals for all children in our society"?**, is then considered. As one might guess, we find considerable agreement about the appropriateness of these goals.

Secondly, the manner in which open education

attempts to reach these goals is briefly described. Some of the most common descriptions are:

1. Choices of learning activities
2. Children help create the learning environment
3. Curriculum is based on the needs, interests, and concerns of children, and thus is more individualized
4. Children have free access to a wide variety of materials
5. More free movement of children within the classroom
6. Etc.

Thirdly, this question is considered: **"Are the identified approaches to learning and living in an open classroom necessary in order to reach the goals we have agreed upon?"** This question usually generates considerably more discussion and disagreement than does the first question. This situation reinforces something we've known in education for a long time—educators are in closer agreement on the broad goals of education than they are on how to reach these goals.

Is open education for all children? How would you answer this question?

Perhaps the most important prerequisite for your success in running an open classroom is a careful and honest examination of your attitudes and values.

From **The Open Classroom: Making it Work**
by Barbara Blitz

So You Want To Change To an Open Classroom by Roland S. Barth

Another educational wave is breaking on American shores. Whether termed "integrated day," "Leicestershire Plan," "informal classroom," or "open education," it promises new and radical methods of teaching, learning, and organizing the schools.[1] Many American educators who do not shy from promises of new solutions to old problems are preparing to ride the crest of the wave. In New York State, for instance, the commissioner of education, the chancellor of New York City schools, and the president of the state branch of the American Federation of Teachers have all expressed their intent to make the state's classrooms open classrooms. Schools of education in such varied places as North Dakota, Connecticut, Massachusetts, New York, and Ohio are tooling up to prepare the masses of teachers for these masses of anticipated open classrooms.

Some educators are disposed to search for the new, the different, the flashy, the radical, or the revolutionary. Once an idea or a practice, such as "team teaching," "nongrading," and (more recently) "differentiated staffing" and "performance contracting," has been so labeled by the Establishment, many teachers and administrators are quick to adopt it. More precisely, these educators are quick to assimilate new ideas into their cognitive and operational framework. But in so doing they often distort the original conception without recognizing either the distortion or the assumptions violated by the distortion. This seems to happen partly because the educator has taken on the

---

1. For a fuller description of this movement, see Roland S. Barth and Charles H. Rathbone, annotated bibliographies: "The Open School: A Way of Thinking About Children, Learning and Knowledge," **The Center Forum,** Vol. 3, No. 7, July, 1969, a publication of the Center for Urban Education, New York City; and "A Bibliography of Open Education, Early Childhood Education Study," jointly published by the Advisory for Open Education and the Education Development Center, Newton, Mass., 1971.

verbal, superficial abstraction of a new idea without going through a concomitant personal reorientation of attitude and behavior. Vocabulary and rhetoric are easily changed; basic beliefs and institutions all too often remain little affected. If open education is to have a fundamental and positive effect on American education, and if changes are to be consciously made, rhetoric and good intentions will not suffice.

There is no doubt that a climate potentially hospitable to fresh alternatives to our floundering educational system exists in this country. It is even possible that, in this brief moment in time, open education may have the opportunity to prove itself. However, a crash program is dangerous. Implementing foreign ideas and practices is a precarious business, and I fear the present opportunity will be abused or misused. Indeed, many attempts to implement open classrooms in America have already been buried with the epitaphs "sloppy permissivism," "neo-progressive," "Communist," "anarchical," or "laissez-faire." An even more discouraging although not surprising consequence has been to push educational practice further away from open education than was the case prior to the attempt at implementation.

Most educators who say they want open education are ready to change **appearances.** They install printing presses, tables in place of desks, classes in corridors, nature study. They adopt the **vocabulary:** "integrated day," "interest areas," "free choice," and "student initiated learning." However, few have understanding of, let alone commitment to, the philosophical, personal, and professional roots from which these practices and phrases have sprung, and upon which they depend so completely for their success. It is my belief that changing appearances to more closely resemble some British classrooms without understanding and accepting the rationale underlying these changes will lead inevitably to failure and conflict among children, teachers, administrators, and parents. American education can withstand no more failure, even in the name of reform or revolution.

I would like to suggest that before you jump on the open classroom surfboard, a precarious ve-

hicle appropriate neither for all people nor for all situations, you pause long enough to consider the following statements and to examine your own reactions to them. Your reactions may reveal salient attitudes about children, learning, and knowledge. I have found that successful open educators in both England and America tend to take similar positions on these statements. Where do you stand?

Assumptions about Learning and Knowledge[2]

INSTRUCTIONS: Make a mark somewhere along each line which best represents your own feelings about each statement.

Example: School serves the wishes and needs of adults better than it does the wishes and needs of children.

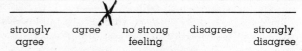

| strongly agree | agree | no strong feeling | disagree | strongly disagree |

I. ASSUMPTIONS ABOUT CHILDREN'S LEARNING

Motivation

Assumption 1: Children are innately curious and will explore their environment without adult intervention.

| strongly agree | agree | no strong feeling | disagree | strongly disagree |

Assumption 2: Exploratory behavior is self-perpetuating.

| strongly agree | agree | no strong feeling | disagree | strongly disagree |

---

2. From Roland S. Barth, **"Open Education,"** unpublished doctoral dissertation, Harvard Graduate School of Education, 1970.

Conditions for Learning

Assumption 3: The child will display natural exploratory behavior if he is not threatened.

strongly agree	agree	no strong feeling	disagree	strongly disagree

Assumption 4: Confidence in self is highly related to capacity for learning and for making important choices affecting one's learning.

strongly agree	agree	no strong feeling	disagree	strongly disagree

Assumption 5: Active exploration in a rich environment, offering a wide array of manipulative materials, will facilitate children's learning.

strongly agree	agree	no strong feeling	disagree	strongly disagree

Assumption 6: Play is not distinguished from work as the predominant mode of learning in early childhood.

strongly agree	agree	no strong feeling	disagree	strongly disagree

Assumption 7: Children have both the competence and the right to make significant decisions concerning their own learning.

strongly agree	agree	no strong feeling	disagree	strongly disagree

Assumption 8: Children will be likely to learn if they are given considerable choice in the selection of the materials they wish to work with and in the choice of questions they wish to pursue with respect to those materials.

strongly agree	agree	no strong feeling	disagree	strongly disagree

Assumption 9: Given the opportunity, children will choose to engage in activities which will be of high interest to them.

strongly agree	agree	no strong feeling	disagree	strongly disagree

Assumption 10: If a child is fully involved in and is having fun with an activity, learning is taking place.

strongly agree	agree	no strong feeling	disagree	strongly disagree

Social Learning

Assumption 11: When two or more children are interested in exploring the same problem or the same materials, they will often choose to collaborate in some way.

strongly agree	agree	no strong feeling	disagree	strongly disagree

Assumption 12: When a child learns something which is important to him, he will wish to share it with others.

strongly agree	agree	no strong feeling	disagree	strongly disagree

Intellectual Development

Assumption 13: Concept formation proceeds very slowly.

strongly agree	agree	no strong feeling	disagree	strongly disagree

Assumption 14: Children learn and develop intellectually not only at their own rate but in their own style.

strongly agree	agree	no strong feeling	disagree	strongly disagree

Assumption 15: Children pass through similar stages of intellectual development, each in his own way and at his own rate and in his own time.

strongly agree	agree	no strong feeling	disagree	strongly disagree

Assumption 16: Intellectual growth and development take place through a sequence of concrete experiences followed by abstractions.

strongly agree	agree	no strong feeling	disagree	strongly disagree

Assumption 17: Verbal abstractions should follow direct experience with objects and ideas, not precede them or substitute for them.

strongly agree	agree	no strong feeling	disagree	strongly disagree

Evaluation

Assumption 18: The preferred source of verification for a child's solution to a problem comes through the materials he is working with.

strongly agree	agree	no strong feeling	disagree	strongly disagree

Assumption 19: Errors are necessarily a part of the learning process; they are to be expected and even desired, for they contain information essential for further learning.

strongly agree	agree	no strong feeling	disagree	strongly disagree

Assumption 20: Those qualities of a person's learning which can be carefully measured are not necessarily the most important.

strongly agree	agree	no strong feeling	disagree	strongly disagree

Assumption 21: Objective measures of performance may have a negative effect upon learning.

strongly agree	agree	no strong feeling	disagree	strongly disagree

Assumption 22: Learning is best assessed intuitively, by direct observation.

strongly agree	agree	no strong feeling	disagree	strongly disagree

Assumption 23: The best way of evaluating the effect of the school experience on the child is to observe him over a long period of time.

strongly agree	agree	no strong feeling	disagree	strongly disagree

Assumption 24: The best measure of a child's work is his work.

strongly agree	agree	no strong feeling	disagree	strongly disagree

II. ASSUMPTIONS ABOUT KNOWLEDGE

Assumption 25: The quality of being is more important than the quality of knowing; knowledge is a means of education, not its end. The final test of an education is what a man **is**, not what he **knows.**

strongly agree	agree	no strong feeling	disagree	strongly disagree

Assumption 26: Knowledge is a function of one's personal integration of experience and therefore does not fall into neatly separate categories or "disciplines."

strongly agree	agree	no strong feeling	disagree	strongly disagree

Assumption 27: The structure of knowledge is personal and idiosyncratic; it is a function of the synthesis of each individual's experience with the world.

| strongly agree | agree | no strong feeling | disagree | strongly disagree |

Assumption 28: Little or no knowledge exists which it is essential for everyone to acquire.

| strongly agree | agree | no strong feeling | disagree | strongly disagree |

Assumption 29: It is possible, even likely, that an individual may learn and possess knowledge of a phenomenon and yet be unable to display it publicly. Knowledge resides with the knower, not in its public expression.

| strongly agree | agree | no strong feeling | disagree | strongly disagree |

Most open educators, British and American, "strongly agree" with most of these statements.[3] I think it is possible to learn a great deal both about open education and about oneself by taking a position with respect to these different statements. While it would be folly to argue that strong agreement assures success in developing an open classroom, or, on the other hand, that strong disagreement predicts failure, the assumptions are, I believe, closely related to open education practices. Consequently, I feel that for those sympathetic to the assumptions, success at a difficult job will be more likely. For the educator to attempt to adopt practices which depend for their success upon general adherence to these beliefs without actually adhering to them is, at the very least, dangerous.

At the same time, we must be careful not to assume that an "official" British or U.S. government-inspected type of open classroom or set of beliefs exists which is the standard for all others. Indeed, what is exciting about British open class-rooms is the **diversity** in thinking and behavior for children and adults—from person to person, class to class, and school to school. The important point here is that the likelihood of successfully developing an open classroom increases as those concerned agree with the basic assumptions underlying open education practices. It is impossible to "role play" such a fundamentally distinct teaching responsibility.

For some people, then, drawing attention to these assumptions may terminate interest in open education. All to the good; a well-organized, consistent, teacher-directed classroom probably has a far less harmful influence upon children than a well-intentioned but sloppy, permissive, and chaotic attempt at an open classroom in which teacher and child must live with contradiction and conflict. For other people, awareness of these assumptions may stimulate confidence and competence in their attempts to change what happens to children in school.

In the final analysis, the success of a widespread movement toward open education in this country rests not upon agreement with any philosophical position but with satisfactory answers to several important questions: For what kinds of people—teachers, administrators, parents, children—is the open classroom appropriate and valuable? What happens to children in open classrooms? Can teachers be **trained** for open classrooms? How can the resistance from children, teachers, administrators, and parents—inevitable among those not committed to open education's assumptions and practices—be surmounted? And finally, should participation in an open classroom be **required** of teachers, children, parents, and administrators?

---

3. Since these assumptions were assembled, I have "tested" them with several British primary teachers, headmasters, and inspectors and with an equal number of American proponents of open education. To date, although many qualifications in language have been suggested, there has not been a case where an individual has said of one of the assumptions, "No, that is contrary to what I believe about children, learning, or knowledge."

FOR TEACHERS

From	To	To	To	From	To	To	To
Activity	Activities	Ideas w/or w/out activities	?	Texts	Many Sources	Original Sources	?
Curriculum Guide	Curriculum Explorations	Explorations	?	1 room	Suites, Entire School	Community	?

...a child comes to school with his life, not his case history, but with a living, dynamic life.

Welfare family   WHAT IS UNIQUE, DYNAMIC, FASCINATING ABOUT THESE CHILDREN?

Child #1_____

Child #2_____

Child #3_____

Cuban refugee_____

Mexican child_____

Migrant child_____

Indian child_____

Black child_____

City child_____

Rural child_____

List the new ideas or things YOU have tried to use or learn in this present calendar year. Are there few or many? Do your expectations for children differ in this respect from your expectations for yourself? WHY????

And from here, as you might guess—Herb went on to chapter five; Janice went on to chapter five; Cella went on to chapter five. And you, reader, where do you go from here? And why?

CHAPTER FIVE

Love

Have the big,
soft, love-bugs we've
placed around the school
provided a temporary
refuge for loving?

♥

By letting children choose
their favorite teachers to
work with once a week, have
we provided a little extra
loving?

♥

When I put that red velvet heart
in a colleague's mailbox for some loving act
she performed, am I helping the loving cause?

Any theory of love must begin with a theory of man, of human existence.

—Erich Fromm

What about man? Who is he? What is his basic nature? Are the answers to these questions important?

CONSIDER
1) Can you trust man (children)
if you believe man to be basically
a. good
b. evil
c. neutral
2) Can you exhibit faith in man (children)
if you believe man to be basically
a. good
b. evil
c. neutral

—dlr

Many believe that children are born bad and have to be coerced into being good. This accounts for many acts of aggression committed by adults on babies even in the cradle. These acts are sometimes perpetrated on infants so young that they have not yet even gained their eyesight or their sense of hearing. What such an infant can feel about this is that he has been born into a hostile world. The idea that children are born bad accounts for the "training" concept which rightly belongs to the rearing of animals, such as horses and dogs, but is never successful with humans. This is the opposite of the concept of growth and education. While training seeks to close the mind so that only one response will be available, education in its true sense is designed to open the mind, to reveal the wide world, and to make an infinite number of responses possible. Modern science has shown that children are born neither good nor bad. "Goodness" and "badness" are adult concepts, and they are learned. They are products of the lives people lead from birth on. They depend upon the quality of living available to the young over which the young have no control.

From **In Defense of Youth** by Earl C. Kelley

But, for today's child, it is a far cry from the world in which seven-year-old Alice walked with Lewis Carroll in a mood of trust and love that led to his present of a fantasy world for her pleasure.

From **The Learning Child** by Dorothy H. Cohen

Tony had a beard and wore sandals. He was of the generation that valued the peace symbol. Some of his friends were interested in Zen. Some became followers of new religious groups. Tony had friends in Canada, hoping for amnesty. He helped build a geodesic dome in a commune. His companions talked openly about love of one's fellowmen.

TONY: Dorothy Cohen makes sense. And it isn't only children who need trust and love.
CELLA: Do you feel your friends are providing this kind of environment for their children, Tony?
TONY: To a much larger degree than was provided for me and my brothers, Cella, but when the children go to school, this isn't so. At least not in many schools that I've visited or heard about.
CELLA: Is that why you chose to do your student teaching in an open education school?

TONY: You bet! Even there it's hard enough to show the love kids need—at least I'm in a situation where the children and their parents believe love is an essential part of school life. This is important to me—and I hope to find even more ways of supporting this trend. I agree with Oscar Wilde:
   "To love is the rarest thing in the world.
   Most people exist, that is all."
CELLA: And Shakespeare: "Then Happy I, that love and am belov'd."

IS THERE PLENTY OF LOVE AT YOUR SCHOOL?
...AT YOUR COLLEGE?
HOW HAPPY ARE YOU AT SCHOOL?
ARE YOUR STUDENTS HAPPY?

. . . love is, without any question, the most important experience in the life of a human being.

—Ashley Montagu

If it is true, as I have tried to show, that love is the only sane and satisfactory answer to the problem of human existence, then any society which excludes, relatively, the development of love, must in the long run perish of its own contradiction with the basic necessities of human nature. Indeed, to speak of love is not "preaching" for the simple reason that it means to speak of the ultimate and real need in every human being.

From **The Art of Loving** by Erich Fromm

Thoughts of *Open Sesame*'s characters:

HERB: I must admit I feel inhibited talking about love. I wonder why I'm this way?

CELLA: Expressing love, acknowledging the need to openly express it, and developing and encouraging love in schools is essential. I see many teachers intellectualizing the idea that children of the poor, and children of minority groups can succeed, but because it may be hard to really love these children, much of the humanistic movement is still in the token stage.

SUZANNA: The children I see with big problems are the children who are crying inside for love.

TONY: This is where it's at!

DR. ROUBINEK: I see too many teachers who don't love themselves. How can they love others?

MORNING STAR: Love and beauty are a deep source of strength for our Indians as they leave the reservation—and it's a good thing these are so strong—the outside world is often so hostile to us!

JANICE: I think love is most important. I love all my children!

DR. CARSWELL: If I truly love a person, shouldn't I support and free that person rather than attempt to possess him?

JOSÉ: To really love someone is to be interested in everything about them.

**What kind of atmosphere
exists in your teachers' lounge?
Do teachers speak for or against
individuals? What type of behavior
do you exhibit in the lounge—rejective
or accepting?**

♥

**Do you feel you are a loving
person? How do you
demonstrate your love
to others?**

Have you thought about the atmosphere that exists in your room? What kinds of signals are sent to a visitor? Positive? Negative? Do you think a visitor to your room might say, "This is a good place to be. I sense warmth, love, understanding and trust." Have you received signals as you first entered another classroom? If adults can receive these signals, can children receive them as well?

WE THINK SO!—emc and dlr

Thoughts on love from William Shakespeare

For shame! deny that thou bear'st love to any,
Who for thyself art so unprovident.
Grant if thou wilt thou are belov'd of many,
But that thou non lov'st is most evident;
For thou art so possess'd with murderous hate,
That 'gainst thyself thou stick'st not to conspire,
Seeking that beauteous roof to ruinate,
Which to repair should be thy chief desire.
O change thy thought, that I may change my mind!
Shall hate be fairer lodg'd than gentle love?
Be, as thy presence is, gracious and kind,
Or, to thyself, at least, kind-hearted prove;
Make thee another self, for love of me,
That beauty still may live in thine or thee.

—Sonnet X

Love looks not with the eyes, but with the mind.

—Midsummer Night's Dream

And then, the whining school-boy, with his satchel,
And shining morning face, creeping like snail
Unwilling to school.

—As You Like It

We live in deeds, not years; in thoughts, not breaths;
In feelings, not in figures on a dial.
We should count time by heart-throbs. He most lives
who thinks most, feels the noblest, acts the best.

From "Festus," by Philip James Bailey

Game Theory
Sum-Zero

COMPETITION

If I have a coin
And you have none
If I give you my coin
then you have one
and I have none.
Non Sum-Zero.

EDUCATION

If I have a thought
And you have none
If I give you my thought
then you have one
and I have one.
Non Sum-zero.

REALIZATION

If I have love
And you have none
If I give you my love
then you have my store
but I gained more.

—Gerald T. Kowitz

Parent's Creed

If a child lives with criticism,
    He learns to condemn.
If a child lives with hostility,
    He learns to fight.
If a child lives with ridicule,
    He learns to be shy.
If a child lives with shame,
    He learns to feel guilty.
If a child lives with tolerance,
    He learns to be patient.
If a child lives with encouragement,
    He learns confidence.
If a child lives with praise,
    He learns to appreciate.
If a child lives with fairness,
    He learns justice.
If a child lives with security,
    He learns to have faith.
If a child lives with approval,
    He learns to like himself.
If a child lives with acceptance and friendship,
    He learns to find love in the world.

—Dorothy Law Nolte

Aren't teachers "parents in absentia"?
How do you apply this creed?

He prayeth well, who loveth well
Both man and bird and beast.

He prayeth best, who loveth best
All things, both great and small.

From "The Rime of the Ancient Mariner"
by Samuel Taylor Coleridge

Like as the waves make towards the pebbled shore,
So do our minutes hasten to their end;
Each changing place with that which goes before,
In sequent toil all forwards do contend.
Nativity, once in the main of light,
Crawls to maturity, wherewith being crown'd,
Crooked eclipses 'gainst his glory fight,
And Time, that gave, doth now his gift confound.
Time doth transfix the flourish set on youth,
And delves the parallels in beauty's brow;
Feeds on the rarities of nature's truth,
And nothing stand but for his scythe to mow.
And yet, to times in hope, my verse shall stand,
Praising they worth, despite his cruel hand.

—William Shakespeare

Discuss a love assignment and encourage each child to participate in a love project after school. The following day, discuss in class any love projects the children want to share with class.

RECIPIENT	ACTIVITIES			
Animals	Feed birds	Carefully give a horse a handful of green grass	Scratch a cat's neck	_____
Your town or city	Pick up broken glass or trash on or beside sidewalk	Write a complimentary note to your mayor	Do some small chore to improve the appearance of your house or yard	_____
Nature	Plant a flower	Water a wilting plant	Clear away weeds that are choking a plant	_____
People you don't know	On a hot day, offer a drink of water to mailman	Pay attention to someone, ask a question about their job	Say good morning or good afternoon to a passerby	_____
People you know	Make an "I love you" card for a friend	Give a flower to someone	Compliment someone, praise someone	_____
Your family	Offer to do the dusting for your mother	Carefully polish a pair of your father's shoes	Tell your sister or brother that you love them	_____
Yourself	List all the good or special qualities that you have—your assets.	Wash your hair with special care, so that it really shines	Put some flowers or some pretty leaves or branches in a glass or vase in your room or in any room in your home	_____

From *The Art of Loving* by Erich Fromm

The Art of Loving

For most children before the age from eight and a half to ten,* the problem is almost exclusively that of **being loved**—of being loved for what one is. The child up to this age does not yet love; he responds gratefully, joyfully to being loved. At this point of the child's development a new factor enters into the picture: that of a new feeling of producing love by one's own activity. For the first time, the child thinks of **giving** something to mother (or to father), of producing something—a poem, a drawing, or whatever it may be. For the first time in the child's life the idea of love **is** transformed from being loved into loving; into creating love. It takes many years from this first beginning to the maturing of love. Eventually the child, who may now be an adolescent, has overcome his egocentricity; the other person is not any more primarily a means to the satisfaction of his own needs. The needs of the other person are as important as his own—in fact, they have become more important. To give has become more satisfactory, more joyous, than to receive; to love, more important even than **being loved**. By loving, he has left the prison cell of aloneness and isolation which was constituted by the state of narcissim and self-centeredness. He feels a sense of new union, of sharing, of oneness. More than that, he feels the potency of producing love by loving—rather than the dependence of receiving by being loved—and for that reason having to be small, helpless, sick—or "good." Infantile love follows the principle: **"I love because I am loved."** Mature love follows the principle: **"I am loved because I love."** Immature love says: **"I love you because I need you."** Mature love says: **"I need you because I love you."**

To respect a person is not possible without **knowing** him; care and responsibility would be blind if they were not guided by knowledge. Knowledge would be empty if it were not motivated by concern. There are many layers of knowledge; the knowledge which is an aspect of love is one which does not stay at the periphery, but penetrates to the core. It is possible only when I can transcend the concern for myself and see the other person in his own terms. I may know, for instance, that a person is angry, even if he does not show it overtly; but I may know him more deeply than that; then I know that he is anxious, and worried; that he feels lonely, that he feels guilty. Then I know that his anger is only the manifestation of something deeper, and I see him as anxious and embarrassed, that is, as the suffering person, rather than as the angry one.

Knowledge has one more, and a more fundamental relation to the problem of love. The basic need to fuse with another person so as to transcend the prison of one's separateness is closely related to another specifically human desire, that to know the "secret of man." While life in its merely biological aspects is a miracle and a secret, man in his human aspects is an unfathomable secret to himself—and to his fellow man. We know ourselves, and yet even with all the efforts we may make, we do not know ourselves. We know our fellow man, and yet we do not know him, because we are not a thing, and our fellow man is not a thing. The further we reach into the depth of our being, or someone else's being, the more the goal of knowledge eludes us. Yet we cannot help desiring to penetrate into the secret of man's soul, into the innermost nucleus which is "he."

*Cf. Sullivan's description of this development in **The Interpersonal Theory of Psychiatry**, W. W. Norton & Co., New York, 1953.

Can you trust children if you have no faith in children?
Can you love without faith and trust?
Can you trust, love and have faith in children without knowing man?

Who is it that says most? which can say more
Than this rich praise,—that you alone are you?

—William Shakespeare

Many kinds of people look at love—

A SCIENTIST LOOKS AT LOVE
by Ashley Montagu

From the evidence which is thus far available, it seems clear that love is indispensably necessary for the healthy development of the individual. Love is the principal developer of one's capacity for being human, the chief stimulus for the development of social competence, and the only thing on earth that can produce that sense of belongingness and relatedness to the world of humanity which is the best achievement of the healthy human being. And what is health? Health is the ability to love and the ability to work.

Love is creative—creative both for the receiver and the giver, greatly enriching the lives of both. It confers survival benefits upon others and upon oneself in a creatively enlarging manner. When we understand the meaning of love we understand that it is the only thing in the world of which one can never give too much. The counterfeit of love—overprotectiveness and "smothering"—is really a disguised hostility. Genuine love can never harm or inhibit; it can only benefit and create freedom and order. Love has a firmness and discipline of its own for which there can be no substitute. No child can ever be spoiled by love, and there are few if any human problems which cannot be best solved by its application.

Scientists are discovering at this very moment that to live as if to live and love were one is the only way of life for human beings, because, indeed, this is the way of life which the innate nature of man demands. We are discovering that the highest ideals of man spring from man's own nature, that what is right for man is what is right for his nature, and that the highest of these innately based ideals is the one that must enliven and inform all his other ideals, namely, **love.** This is not a new discovery in the world, of course; what is new is that scientists have rediscovered these truths by scientific means. Contemporary scientists working in this field are giving a scientific foundation or validation to the Sermon on the Mount and to the Golden Rule: to do unto others as you would have them do unto you, to love your neighbor as yourself.

In an age in which a great deal of unloving love masquerades as the genuine article, in which there is a massive lack of love behind the show of love, in which millions have literally been unloved to death, it is very necessary to understand what love really means.

We have left the study of love to the last, but now that we can begin to understand its importance for humanity, we can see that this is the area in which the men of religion, the educators, the physicians, and the scientists can join hands in the common endeavor of putting man back upon the road of his evolutionary destiny from which he has gone so far astray—the road which leads to health and happiness for all humanity, peace and goodwill unto all the earth.

In our inner cities, where children are at the bottom of the totem pole in people value, where playgrounds are concrete, and the few trees in the park are NOT TO BE CLIMBED, can it be then that there, any evidence of love might be as disturbing as violence?

Do teachers, and social workers, and other authorities cause children to feel that love, kindness, and tenderness are threatening feelings? Does the hurry and flurry of big-city living inhibit the feelings of trust, love, understanding?

Do city schools, then, open up alternatives in programs so children can feel real feelings, can express those real feelings, can know the teacher loves and cares?

—emc and dlr

I think all over London, maybe all over England, there are babies growing up in their deprivation into children who think they are not loved unless they are shouted at and beaten, and adults who think they are not cherished unless they are betrayed.

From *Look At Kids* by Leila Berg

———————————

The love needs involve both giving and receiving ... We must understand love; we must be able to teach it, to create it, to predict it, or else the world is lost to hostility and suspicion.

From **Motivation and Personality**
by Abraham Maslow

———————————

I tell thee, Love is Nature's second sun,
Causing a spring of virtues where he shines;
And as without the sun, the world's great eye,
All colours, beauties, both of Art and Nature,
Are given in vain to men; so without love
All beauties bred in women are in vain,
All virtues born in men lie buried;
For love informs them as the sun doth colours;
And as the sun, reflecting his warm beams
Against the earth, begets all fruits and flowers;
So Love, fair shining in the inward man,
Brings forth in him the honourable fruits
Of valour ,wit, virtue, and haughty thoughts,
Brave resolution, and divine discourse.

From the play "All Fools" (1605)
by George Chapman (1559-1634)

**Could it be that some
  teachers do not
    show love to
      their students
because they, themselves,
  do not have enough
    love to "go around"?**

TEACHING THE YOUNG TO LOVE
by Jack Frymier

In such a world as this, the need for teaching young people to love transcends anything else. It goes far, far beyond teaching young people to add and subtract and to read and write. It goes far, far beyond most of the substantive things we teach in school today. It should not be necessary to substantiate that argument, but as educators we do not seem to talk in those kinds of terms. We seem willing to deal at tremendous length with the cognitive aspects of education. However, when we talk about feelings, attitudes, values, or relationships, we are uncomfortable. We don't deal directly with them. We don't organize the educational effort necessary to achieve goals in the affective domain. And yet we must. We must teach young people to behave in positive, loving ways. There was a time, perhaps, when it didn't make too much difference, a time when only a few people might be hurt or killed. That time is now gone and we all know it. The young people in this world today seem to know it and feel it more than the older generation does. They represent the only generation that has grown up completely within the parameter of awesome destruction and thermo-nuclear holocaust as a possibility. Right now, they are protesting the teaching of killing, and I refer to ROTC. ROTC is organized instruction in teaching man to kill. Many of us have been a part of ROTC and a part of war and killing. But the time has come for us to move in a different direction.

How can education teach young people to love? Let me cite a few things that I think are pertinent. Young people on college campuses these days are striking out, striking back, striking down. At root is their concern for our negative attitude. Whether they see this negative attitude represented in the form of a contract to build death-dealing devices or in the form of a university's arrangement with the government to teach ROTC or in the form of the rigid, insensitive, and inhumane institutions they feel exist in this country, they protest such negativism. Moreover, they are protesting it in drastic ways—ways that upset, discourage, and even frighten us. But whatever the form of the message, they are trying to say to us, "Can't you provide an education that does not teach us to have negative feelings toward our fellowmen, an education that does not teach us to be proficient in destroying life?" What they are demanding is an education that teaches them to be humane, to engage in those things that are life supporting and life creating. Education can teach them such positive ways of living, and I think there are some concepts in particular that can help us accomplish the task.

I am intrigued, for example, by some major developments in the field of social psychology. In the past 30 or 40 years, we have seen a tremendous amount of research in the field of human relationships, prejudice, social interaction, and so forth. One such study is Gordon W. Allport's **The Nature of Prejudice.** The book is a classic study of the idea that prejudice is the opposite of love. Prejudice means relating to people in negative ways rather than positive ways. In his book, Allport points out that there are five levels of rejective behavior, five degrees of prejudice, if you please. He goes on to say that these levels of rejective behavior are interrelated: that they are sequentially organized in such a way that one has to precede the other. In other words, number five, which is the most serious, cannot manifest itself until the first four have occurred, and number four cannot appear until the first three have, and so forth. According to Allport, these five levels of rejective behavior are as follows:

1. **Anti-location behavior.** The mildest form of rejection is speaking out against other people, saying things about them which are harmful or degrading. It is, however, the preliminary step in what may ultimately become much more dangerous behavior.

2. **Avoidance.** The second level of rejective behavior is represented by avoiding people, staying away from them, not having contact with them.

3. **Discrimination.** When a person discriminates, he subjects another person to an unpleasant or undesirable experience that he, himself, would be unwilling to endure.

4. **Physical attack.** When we strike out against another person, physically harm him, we have reached the fourth level of rejective behavior.

5. **Extermination.** The fifth and most serious form of rejective behavior has been reached when one man kills another.

These five levels of rejective behavior constitute a theory of prejudice in Allport's terms. They constitute what I would call one-half of a continuum about the way in which we relate to other people. But there is another half—another five levels—of that continuum which is aimed in a positive direction. To discover what these levels are, we need simply to mirror Allport's five levels of rejective behavior and view the five levels of accepting behavior. Perhaps these other five levels will help us understand what the notion of love is and help us also to teach the young to love.

1. If the first level of rejective behavior is speaking out against another person, then we might view the first level of accepting or loving behavior as speaking out in favor of another person.

2. If the second level of rejective behavior is avoidance, then the second level of accepting behavior is to seek out other people, to approach them, to deliberately have interaction with them in a positive way.

3. Discrimination is the third level of rejective behavior. The third level of loving behavior might then become altruism—doing positive things for other people, giving of yourself.

4. In contrast to the rejective behavior of physical attack, the fourth level of loving behavior might be touching, caressing, hugging, behaving in positive ways in a physical sense toward other persons. We all recognize these physical actions as being indications to other that we feel they are good, worthwhile, important; that they are loved.

5. If the fifth level of rejective behavior is destruction of life, then, at least theoretically, the fifth level of loving behavior would be the creation of life. Obviously, that is what the sexual act is—the ultimate intimate relationship between man and woman. It represents the epitome of loving behavior.

Why can't we use these ten aspects of behavior, ranging as they do from the very negative to the very positive, as a handle that we can take hold of and talk about when we try to teach the young to love? By utilizing such ideas as Allport's, we can teach students cognitively to understand the concept of love.

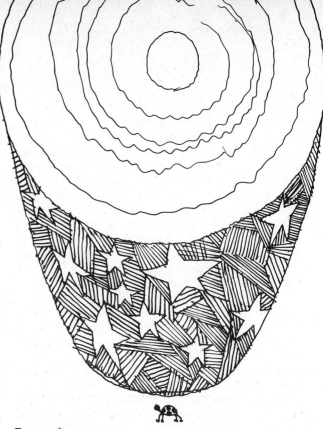

From WHAT IS A CHILD? by Ashley Montagu

Obviously, it is important for a human being to learn to speak; it is even more important for him to learn to think; and most important of all for him to learn to love—
　　to love,
because relatedness and involvement are of the essence of the human condition, of mental health;
　　to love,
because as the principal factor that has been operative in bringing man safely through the vicissitudes and perils of a long and strenuous evolutionary history, love is the principal behavioral need and capacity of the newborn and of the human being all the days of his life.

Remember:
The sky for a bug
may be
the bottom of his log.
What does your sky look like?

Suzanna read the Frymier article and thought about the unloving incidents that had happened to some of her students and about some of their problems. Each child's situation raises another question which Suzanna cannot answer.

There is Cheryl, who feels she will receive her Mommy's love only if Cheryl is the top scholar in the school. How can Cheryl love those who are her intellectual superiors?

Why must schools practice competition? Especially unfair competition?

Suzanna recalled Joey, who bears the burden of being a mulatto in a family of dark blacks who want everyone to "think Black!"

How does school eradicate negative family influences? How does one decide which influences are negative?

Last month, one of Suzanna's students, Maria, experienced a death in her family. Maria's aunt and godmother died. In a family of twelve children, Maria misses the attention she had received from her Tia.

Can schools become involved in patterns of subcultures?

Hermie will not willingly produce —because this is what his father most wants from him. Hermie's father runs the family home like an army camp and believes the school should be run the same way.

Where does love enter this picture?

Little Frankie's alcoholic mother lets him know he is an unwanted burden to her. Frankie loves, with hugs and kisses, each of his teachers—and lots of little girls, as well.

What will happen to Frankie in junior high? Who'll love him then?

CIPHER IN THE SNOW
by Jean E. Mizer

It started with tragedy on a biting cold February morning. I was driving behind the Milford Corners bus as I did most snowy mornings on my way to school. It veered and stopped short at the hotel, which it had no business doing, and I was annoyed as I had to come to an unexpected stop. A boy lurched out of the bus, reeled, stumbled, and collapsed on the snowbank at the curb. The bus driver and I reached him at the same moment. His thin, hollow face was white even against the snow.

"He's dead," the driver whispered.

It didn't register for a minute. I glanced quickly at the scared young faces staring down at us from the school bus. "A doctor! Quick! I'll phone from the hotel...."

"No use. I tell you he's dead." The driver looked down at the boy's still form. "He never even said he felt bad," he muttered, "just tapped me on the shoulder and said, real quiet, 'I'm sorry. I have to get off at the hotel.' That's all. Polite and apologizing like."

At school, the giggling, shuffling morning noise quieted as the news went down the halls. I passed a huddle of girls. "Who was it? Who dropped dead on the way to school?" I heard one of them half-whisper.

"Don't know his name; some kid from Milford Corners," was the reply.

It was like that in the faculty room and the principal's office. "I'd appreciate your going out to tell the parents," the principal told me. "They haven't a phone and, anyway, somebody from school should go there in person. I'll cover your classes."

"Why me?" I asked. "Wouldn't it be better if you did it?"

"I didn't know the boy," the principal admitted levelly. "And in last year's sophomore personalities column I note that you were listed as his favorite teacher."

I drove through the snow and cold down the bad canyon road to the Evans place and thought about the boy, Cliff Evans. His favorite teacher! I thought. He hasn't spoken two words to me in two years! I could see him in my mind's eye all right, sitting back there in the last seat in my afternoon literature class. He came in the room by himself and left by himself. "Cliff Evans," I muttered to myself, "a boy who never talked." I thought a minute. "A boy who never smiled. I never saw him smile once."

The big ranch kitchen was clean and warm. I blurted out my news somehow. Mrs. Evans reached blindly toward a chair. "He never said anything about bein' ailing."

His step-father snorted, "He ain't said nothin' about anything since I moved in here."

Mrs. Evans pushed a pan to the back of the stove and began to untie her apron. "Now hold on," her husband snapped, "I got to have breakfast before I go to town. Nothin' we can do now anyway. If Cliff hadn't been so dumb, he'd have told us he didn't feel good."

After school I sat in the office and stared bleakly at the records spread out before me. I was to close the file and write the obituary for the school paper. The almost bare sheets mocked the effort. Cliff Evans, white, never legally adopted by step-father, five young half-brothers and sisters. These meager strands of information and the list of D grades were all the records had to offer.

Cliff Evans had silently come in the school door in the mornings and gone out the school door in the evenings, and that was all. He had never belonged to a club. He had never played on a team. He had never held an office. As far as I could tell, he had never done one happy, noisy kid thing. He had never been anybody at all.

How do you go about making a boy into a zero. The grade school records showed me. The first and second grade teachers' annotations read "sweet, shy child"; "timid but eager." Then the third grade note had opened the attack. Some teacher had written in a good, firm hand, "Cliff won't talk. Uncooperative. Slow learner." The other academic sheep had followed with "dull"; "slow-witted"; "low I.Q." They became correct. The boy's I.Q. score in the ninth grade was listed as 83. But his I.Q. in the third grade had been 106. The score didn't go under 100 until the seventh grade. Even shy, timid, sweet children have resilience. It takes time to break them.

I stomped to the typewriter and wrote a savage report pointing out what education had done to Cliff Evans. I slapped a copy on the principal's desk and another in the sad, dog-eared file. I banged the typewriter and slammed the file and crashed the door shut, but I didn't feel much better. A little boy kept walking after me, a little boy with a peaked, pale face; a skinny body in faded jeans; and big eyes that had looked and searched for a long time and then had become veiled.

I could guess how many times he'd been chosen last to play sides in a game, how many whispered child conversations had excluded him, how many times he hadn't been asked. I could see and hear the faces and voices that said over and over, "You're dumb. You're dumb. You're a nothing, Cliff Evans."

A child is a believing creature. Cliff undoubtedly believed them. Suddenly it seemed clear to me: when finally there was nothing left at all for Cliff Evans, he collapsed on a snowbank and went away. The doctor might list "heart failure" as the cause of death, but that couldn't change my mind.

We couldn't find ten students in the school who had known Cliff well enough to attend the funeral as his friends. So the student body officers and a committee from the junior class went as a group to the church, being politely sad. I attended the services with them, and sat through it with a lump of cold lead in my chest and a big resolve growing through me.

I've never forgotten Cliff Evans nor that resolve. He has been my challenge year after year, class after class. I look up and down the rows carefully

---

LOVE IN A CLASSROOM IS—

A teacher who cleans
your bloody knee!

Being asked
to
join a group!

A teacher who senses your fear
and understands how it feels!

A teacher who allows the little ones to
crawl into her lap, and sits on love pillows
beside the big ones!

A friend who
helps you clean
up your mess!

A teacher who listens!
(I mean **really** listens!)

When your teacher smiles at you
at some very special moment!

A teacher who asked
YOUR mother to come
to class to help out!

When children are
kind to you!

Caring   **Accepting**

Sharing   **Feeling**

Touching   **Helping**

Understanding

each September at the unfamiliar faces. I look for veiled eyes or bodies scrouged into a seat in an alien world. "Look, kids," I say silently, "I may not do anything else for you this year, but not one of you is going to come out of here a nobody. I'll work or fight to the bitter end doing battle with society and the school board, but I won't have one of you coming out of here thinking himself into a zero."

Most of the time—not always, but most of the time—I've succeeded.

Affective Conditions—

Love and apprehension, joy and discord are endemic to the open classroom; teachers and students have a responsibility, first to acknowledge and then to cope with the release of strong emotions. Teachers especially must be sensitive to the fear and humiliation children may experience while learning; their task is not so much to cushion stress as to help children understand it.

Teachers also have a special obligation, it is held, to know themselves in some depth—since insensitivity to their own needs often permits gross misuse of praise and punishment in classrooms. Finally, proponents of these new alternatives are aware that all groups of thirty-six children are not identical; every social group, if allowed to develop naturally, evokes its own unique life-style, which is to be fostered and respected, not put down or neglected.

From "Assessing the Alternatives,"
by Charles H. Rathbone

AND—IN OPEN EDUCATION CLASSES
—to include all those things on the opposite page, **plus**

An **adjustability** that meets a wide set of circumstances for children.
>   EVERY TIME a group votes on any issue, negative voters know they can have alternatives.

A **responsiveness** to children.
>   A recognition of high and low energy points of children, and an open school schedule responsive to these energy patterns, with teachers readily accessible to all children at all times.

An **enlightenment of learning.**
>   A wide variation in tasks, in styles of goal accomplishment, in environments and in pacing, so teachers can see that children are actually **eager** to learn, to become skillful.

A **freeing of hampering obstructions.**
>   An active operation making school fit for children to travel through; the elimination of serious obstacles to the success of each child.

A **tolerance for internal change.**
>   Once the movement of openness begins, it will not always be contained as teachers might have planned on paper. Children will be candid and sensitive, ingenious and yet unsophisticated, forthright and free.

Teachers and Teachers of Teachers

Have students identify their
feelings of love. Illustrate
or find pictures to
illustrate.

Are you familiar with
Leo Busgalia and
his love-ins at the University
of Southern California?
Would you feel free enough to
lead a love-in with your
students? Your faculty?
Your friends? Your parents?

Can you talk about love?
about how you show love?
about how you feel when
others show they love
you?
about how you feel when
you see others show-
ing love for each
other?
about love as a positive
power?
about possessive love?
about many kinds of love?

"Love sought is good, but given unsought is
better."

From "Twelfth Night" by William Shakespeare

♥

Living

CHAPTER SIX

Toynbee, in describing formal education, said, "In fact, the art of playing with words was substituted for the art of living."

Happy the man, and happy he alone,
He who, can tell today his own:
He who, secure within, can say,
Tomorrow do they worst, for I have lived today.

From **Imitation of the 29th of Horace** by Deyden

From the Preface of *The Aims of Education* by Alfred North Whitehead

One main idea runs through the various chapters, and is illustrated in them from many points of view. It can be stated briefly thus: The students are alive, and the purpose of education is to stimulate and guide their self-development. It follows as a corollary from this premise, that the teachers also should be alive with living thoughts. The whole book is a protest against dead knowledge, that is to say, against inert ideas.

---

a natural high

2 apples on a plate
sun falls through the open window
I am utterly happy.

—Sam Hamod

From "Children of the Apocalypse" by Peter Morin

The paradox, of course, is that the dissolution of culture has set us free to create almost anything—but it also deprived us of the abilities to do it. Strength, wholeness, and sanity seem to be functions of **relation**, and relation, I think, is a function of culture, part of its intricate web of approved connection and experience, a network of persons and moments that simultaneously offer us release and bind us to the lives of others. One "belongs" to and in culture in a way that goes beyond mere politics or participation, for belonging is both simpler and more complex than that: an immersion in the substance of community and tradition, which is itself a net beneath us, a kind of element in which men seem to float, protected.

That is, I suppose, what the young have lost. Every personal truth or experience puts them at odds with the "official" version of things. There is no connection at all between inner truth and what they are expected to be; every gesture demanded and rewarded is a kind of absolute lie, a denial of their confusion, and need. The "drifting free" is the sense of distance; it is distance—not a "generation" gap, but the huge gulf between the truth of one's own pain and possibilities and the world's empty forms. Nothing supports or acknowledges them, and they are trapped in that gulf, making the best of things, making everything up as they go along. But it is the most basic and awful task of all, for it is so lonely, so dangerous, so easily distracted and subverted, so easily swayed. The further along one gets the more alone one is, the more fragile and worried, the deeper into the dark. It is there, of course, that one may need help from adults, but adults have no talent for that at all; we do not admit to being in the dark—how, then, can we be of any use?

If all this is so, what sense can one make of the public schools? They are stiff, unyielding, microcosmic versions of a world that has already disappeared. They are, after all, the state's schools, they do the state's work, and their purpose is the preservation of things as they were. Their means are the isolation of ego and deflection of energy.

Their main structural function is to produce in the young a self-delusive "independence"—a system of false consciousness and need that actually renders them dependent on institutions and the state. Their corrosive role-playing and demand systems are so extensive, so profound, that nothing really human shows through—and when it does, it appears only as frustration, exhaustion, and anger.

That, of course, is the real outrage of the schools: their systematic corruption of the relations among persons. Where they should be comrades, allies, equals, and even lovers, the public schools make them "teacher" and "student"—replaceable units in a mechanical ritual that passes on, in the name of education, an "emotional plague"; a kind of ego and personality that has been so weakened, so often denied the experience of community or solitude, that we no longer understand quite what these things are or how to achieve them.

Whatever ones hopes or loves, each teacher is engaged daily in that same conspiracy to maim the young. But I am talking here about more than the surface stupidities of attendance requirements, grades, or curriculum. Those can be changed and updated. But what seems truly untouchable is what lies behind and beneath them: the basic irredeemable assumptions about what

is necessary, human, or good; the treatment of the person, time, choice, energy, work, community, and pleasure. It is a world-view so monolithic and murderous that it becomes a part of us even while we protest against it.

The authors feel the following statement from The Plowden Report is so important that it bears repeating—and rereading.

Some people, while conceding that children are happier under the modern regime and perhaps more versatile, question whether they are being fitted to grapple with the world which they will enter when they leave school. This view is worth examining because it is quite widely held, but we think it rests on a misconception. It isolates the long-term objective, that of living in and serving society, and regards education as being at all stages recognizably and specifically a preparation for this. It fails to understand that THE BEST PREPARATION FOR BEING A HAPPY AND USEFUL MAN OR WOMAN IS TO LIVE FULLY AS A CHILD.

—The Plowden Report

TODAY IS THE FIRST DAY OF THE REST OF YOUR LIFE EVERYBODY'S

Isn't it better to begin to live fully today than never to have
lived fully at all?
Regardless of their background, can you help
your children live more fully today
than they have ever lived before?
A belly laugh a day might keep
the psychiatrist at bay;
Helping children see the beauty
around them; wherever they find themselves.
Honest contributions by each child towards the creation
of the learning environment, with ensuing successes and failures;
As each child goes home each day,
he carries positive feelings
about himself and the school day.
THIS MEANS: music   laughter   movement   projects   decisions   compromises

problem solving

Of all the skills we teach, problem solving is the one thing that we can be sure the learner will need as he becomes an adult.

———————————

The question is often raised of whether young children can work at problem-solving projects. Children have been doing this up until the time they enter school. To be sure, the young child may not pick the problems we think are important; but although we adults find it difficult, we must encourage him to live in a young child's world.

Problem solving can best be done with others. The individual never comes to know others completely, but he has a better chance of doing so if he works with others toward an agreed-upon, worthwhile goal. This is the way to assuage, to a degree, the loneliness of the human spirit. We all have unique experiences and purposes; and while no one can share them completely, we can know about and have empathy with them. This is an important reason for people of all ages to do things together.

From **Humanizing the Education of Children**
by Earl C. Kelley

———————————

In your school, do your
children help to solve
problems of the school?—
vandalism
orderliness
wanderers
etc.

If not, why?

How about problems of—
advanced curricula
interests groups
futuristic ideas

Lessons From Life

A CHILD that lives with ridicule
　　learns to be timid.
A CHILD that lives with criticism
　　learns to condemn.
A CHILD that lives with distrust
　　learns to be deceitful.
A CHILD that lives with antagonism
　　learns to be hostile.
A CHILD that lives with affection
　　learns to love.
A CHILD that lives with encouragement
　　learns confidence.
A CHILD that lives with truth
　　learns justice.
A CHILD that lives with praise
　　learns to appreciate.
A CHILD that lives with sharing
　　learns to be considerate.
A CHILD that lives with knowledge
　　learns wisdom.
A CHILD that lives with patience
　　learns to be tolerant.
A CHILD that lives with happiness
　　will find love and beauty.

　　　　　　　　—Ronald Russell

———————————

So perhaps it is not a completely vain hope that one day, even in our schools, we will have many persons who are helping to grow persons.

From "Can Schools Grow Persons,"
by Carl R. Rogers

———————————

O suffering, sad humanity!
O ye afflicted ones, who lie
Steeped to the lips in misery,
Longing, and yet afraid to die,
Patient, though sorely tried!

From "The Goblet of Life"
by Henry W. Longfellow

The Right Not To Read—

We ... propose that people who are concerned about the academically underachieving child switch their focus.... In this technological age, it is difficult to understand why literacy has maintained such importance. With education focusing almost solely on a curriculum based on literacy, we are excluding a sizable number of potentially capable citizens from an opportunity to be educated, informed and employed in meaningful jobs.... Can't we teach children about the world around them, their own and other cultures, the similarities and differences of other peoples, the social and ecological needs of people, past, present and future? The child's right to learn these things should outweigh his right to read.

From "Reading Rituals," by Norman E. Silverberg and Margaret C. Silverberg

Suzanna and Janice were walking toward the University where they planned to meet Herb and Cella. They were striding briskly and chatting vivaciously.

JANICE: Did you read Silverberg's "The Right Not To Read"? I guess I'm just an old-fashioned teacher who believes every child MUST learn to read! I guess I believe this is the very most important thing to be done in school.

SUZANNA: Janice, have you ever tried to find out how much your weak readers have learned about your science, or social studies, or math, without reading?

JANICE: What do you mean, Suzanna?

SUZANNA: I often sit in on conferences with children and their parents, so I try to be as positive as I can be with them. So I ask many questions of each child, and I've always been amazed at how much some of them learn even though they can scarcely read. I often wonder why we grade children on a test that requires reading if we want to know how much they know about the science or the social studies unit.

JANICE: But if they could read, wouldn't they be apt to know even more?

SUZANNA: That's quite possible, but I interpret Silverberg in light of what I know about children. I believe it's far more important for children to share what they already know, build on those things, and from there go into reading skills as another avenue to learning.

Status Takes Over the Schoolhouse

Miss Wilson, who distributes chalk,
Clips, ink eradicator,
To fellow teachers, now is called
"Supplies co-ordinator."

Miss Josephs has the job of keeping
Bookroom records straight; her
Official billing's "Books and films
And maps co-ordinator."

Joe Fry, who disciplines unruly
Boys in alma mater,
Subscribes beneath his name the tag
"Morale co-ordinator."

Miss Morse was drafted for the lunchroom
By an unkind fate; her
Reward is that she's known to all
As "Eats co-ordinator."

Our old friend Ed, the man who runs
The teachers' elevator,
Is hoping for the title "Ups
And downs co-ordinator."

—A. S. Flaumenhaft

Comments and Conjectures from "Patriotism and All That Goes with It" by Val D. Rust

9:30 A.M.:

A great buzzing of children's voices as they come in from the playground. These are the oldest group in the nursery school.

Mrs._____ takes the flag from the shelf. From habit they begin to cluster at the edge of the large circular rug which is situated in the middle of the classroom.

"Sit down, everyone," she calls; "don't touch the flag," she cautions a small girl. "Peggy, you must put your bear in the locker."

"I don't care if you sit together, children, but PLEASE DON'T TALK," she calls in a high voice.

"Are we ready, are we ready?"

"Mrs._____, Mrs._____," calls a girl, "Ann pushed me out of the way."

"I heard her say she was sorry, you have to forgive her when she says she is sorry."

"I see someone with a hat on. Would you put it in the locker?"

"Alright, all ready to sing our good morning song?"

"Yes," they chorus and to the tune of **Happy Birthday to You** they sing:

> Good morning to you
> Good morning to you
> Good morning dear children
> Good morning to you
> Good morning Mrs._____
> Good morning Mrs._____
> Good morning Mrs._____
> Good morning to you.

"Now who is going to hold the flag this morning?"

"Now let me see—please don't get up—Let's see who hasn't had a turn in a long long time."

All the children call, "I haven't, I haven't."

"Please Debby, sit down . . . uh . . . I don't think Scott has had a turn in a long long time."

"I didn't, I didn't," calls another little boy.

"But let Scott have it today," she states emphatically.

"Alright, come on Scott," and she pulls him gently to her side handing him the flag.

"Unwind it carefully, carefully," she directs him.

"Everyone is to stand up when they see the flag," she calls to the group.

"Straight and tall, right hand on your left breast."

"She has her left hand," calls a little child pointing to her neighbor.

"Don't let it touch the floor," Mrs._____ cautions Scott.

"May I go to the bathroom, teacher," calls a little girl.

"Alright, we won't start until you get back," assures Mrs._____.

"Alright, don't jiggle around," she calls and begins circling the group making certain they are all in the proper position.

"Right—right—right,—don't put your hands in your pocket,—right,—right,—please leave your beads alone,—shhhh, you're talking,—that's right, Gail . . ."

"OK, let's see a better circle," she calls to all. "It's a little bit sloppy today, just a little bit sloppy."

"Don't move your hand, I put your hand in the right place, don't move it."

"Paul, stand tall, put out your chest, look at the flag."

"Are you proud of the flag of the United States of America?"

"Yes," they all yell as she urges them on.

"Then show it. . . ."

And from out of the silence following the union of all comes a clear small statement, "Some people . . . Some people burn the flag."

"Right, they're not very nice, are they?" she says with a taint of bitterness. "They should live in another country."

And a small child agrees, "No, where they can't come to this country and burn our flag."

"Right, if they don't like us, they should live somewhere else."

"I wish somebody would kill them people," adds another tiny girl.

"Oh, no, we couldn't do that," admonishes Mrs._____, "they're just very disrespectful, and they don't like the flag."

"If some people kill the other people they. . . ."

Mrs._____ cut in, "Then we would have a big war."

"Then the police would come and put them in jail," calls a little girl.

"If they don't love the flag, maybe that's where they belong," Mrs._____ says, "people who don't love the flag, maybe that't where they belong—jail."

"But we MUST respect the flag of the country where we live."

A small child calls out, "Some people are in jail all their life."

"That would be a long time," says Mrs._____.

"Alright, let's start now," she interrupts, "let's start now, 'We love the flag of our country—right hand on left breast, and let's look at the flag . . .'"

I pledge allegiance to the flag,
Of the United States of America,
And to the Republic for which it stands,
One nation,
Under God,
Indivisible,
With liberty and justice for all.

Then they all burst into singing:
My Country tis of thee,
Sweet land of liberty
Of thee I sing.
Long may thy land be bright
With freedom's holy light
Protect us with thy might
Great God, our king.

What Are Your Priorities For Your Children?

_____ to demonstrate empathy for others
_____ to respect the individualities of people
_____ to read
_____ to be an active learner
_____ to enjoy learning
_____ to add, subtract, multiply, and divide
_____ to love
_____ to communicate with others
_____ to be honest
_____ to cherish all living things
_____ to leave a work area clean and ready for another child
_____ to show that I think of other children as well as myself
_____ to listen to other ideas
_____ to enjoy learning about my city, my country
_____ to spell
_____ to conform to rules and regulations
_____ to solve problems
_____ to have a sense of achievement
_____ to have self-confidence
_____

List additional priorities if this list isn't complete enough for you. Rank the priorities (1 for highest, 2 for next, and so on). Circle your top 5 priorities. Think about your classroom. Does your classroom exemplify your identified priorities? Reevaluate your priorities! Are they really important??

Suggest to your principal that your entire staff create a list of priorities and then evaluate how effectively your school deals with each priority. Be open about your priorities! What priorities would the parents of your children select? Why not involve them too? **And,** don't forget your children and their priorities!!

WHERE HAVE WE BEEN AND WHERE ARE WE GOING?

John Jarolimek, in the April 1973 issue of **Educational Leadership,** shared this thought about the curriculum reform movement of the 1950's and 1960's.

"Looking back, even after this short a time, it does seem strange, indeed, that while the reformers were searching for basic concepts from the disciplines, society was desperately searching for its soul."

Do you suppose twenty years hence someone may write: "While the behaviorists were searching for behavioral objectives in the 1970's, society was fighting for its basic survival."

Let's hope not!

___

If you give a child the gift of seeing the intricate patterning of bare trees etched against the monochromatic world of snow and twilight, you have added richness to every winter of his life.

—Mary Harbage

From *Look At Kids* by Leila Berg

Only when they leave school do they begin to learn. (This is true of vast numbers of our children; in fact, it may be still true of most of them.) I sometimes think we are simply taking a chunk out of their lives—ten years when we drive them and beat them and disintegrate them and undermine them, 'till at last they can escape from us; and all they have ever learn't that is going to be any good to them and that will compensate for ten years of legal captivity is the bare technique of reading—not the pleasure in reading nor the companionship of books which luckier children learn before they come to school, but just the bare painful technique, and some children only learn that when they escape into life.

LIVING ACTIVITIES

WITHIN WALLS—

Gather children's words
and children's stories
of their living
outside of school.
Show that you accept the
children as they really are.

Get the children to
share their dreams. Help
them to face themselves.

When dealing with social studies,
make the ideas as REAL as possible—
i.e. studying a farm, line the walls
with rural scenery; make a BIG barn;
steep them in the feeling of living
as a farm child.

WITHOUT WALLS—

Each year, bring a **real** artist,
a **real** poet, a **real** actor,
a **real** businessman, a **real**
elected official, . . . to share
himself with your children.

Do as many things in your curriculum
in the real world as you can
manage: real stories, real
music, real newspapers, etc.
1. List as many occupations as
   you can collectively think about.
2. Show how each and everyone must
   use some math.
3. Identify how many places all of
   us trust someone else or some
   machine to do our math for us.

From "Play, The Essential Ingredient" by Ruth E. Hartley

Many of us, including parents, teachers and psychologists, are still anxious and uncertain about the values of child-oriented, rounded basic early education, of which the child's own eager play is the chief tool.

"Play," said Lawrence Frank, "is the way a child learns what no one can teach him." More than ever before, we need to deepen our understanding of the power of this spontaneous, absorbed activity. We need to see what enormous and necessary contributions play and creative activities can make toward the learning and thinking abilities of children—toward the desired cognitive growth that is currently being emphasized almost to the exclusion of all other facets of development.

COGNITION—PROCESSES AND CONCEPTS

To acquire all these understandings, a child needs, first and most basically, a wide variety of **repeated, concrete** experiences. Both the variety and the chance for repetition are essential. Only in this way can a child master the quality of objects—through his own relationship to them.

By giving the child access to many different kinds of materials and freedom to explore them in his own way, we make possible the first cognitive layer—his ability to recognize objects, and actions, to distinguish them from each other, to become aware of similarities and differences, and finally to abstract, to classify and to symbolize. All this comes naturally and zestfully from a rich, active play life.

SOME PLAY ACTIVITIES

Fingerpainting and Mindbuilding
Playing with Water
Blocks and Spaces
The World's a Stage

VALUES AND PLAY

Research data and models are available for the teacher with courage to pursue a "play-centered" or "child-centered" program for systematic academic learning. Perhaps the most compelling research is that of Dorothy E. M. Gardner, who has received the Order of the British Empire for her contributions to education. She compared children who had spent their school lives in child-centered schools, where **their** interests largely served as drive and directive, with a carefully matched group of others from good traditional schools. She evaluated mathematical skills, language usage, science knowledge and creative abilities. She found that in none of the traditional subject matters were the pupils from the child-centered schools inferior, while they were clearly superior in activities calling for invention and originality. The relevance of this research is undeniable. Few will disagree that, of all things we need now and in the future, original thinkers and problem-solvers head the list.

DO YOU KNOW WHAT, HOW AND WHERE YOUR CHILDREN PLAY? HOW DO YOU USE THIS INFORMATION?

WHAT TELEVISION PROGRAMS DO YOUR CHILDREN WATCH? HOW DO YOU USE THIS INFORMATION?

WHERE HAVE YOUR CHILDREN TRAVELED? NOT FAR AWAY? HOW DO YOU EXPAND THEIR HORIZONS? ...FAR AWAY? HOW DO YOU USE THIS INFORMATION?

Photo by R.A. Gregoire, © 1974 by CRM, a division of Ziff-Davis Publishing Co. Used with permission.

CELLA: I plan to return to an inner-city school after my year of study at the university and I hope to be able to improve that inner-city school. But what a tremendous task! Especially as I think:

- How foreign these schools seem to be from the real lives of the children!
- How difficult it is to interest children in reading when little need for reading is demonstrated at home.
- How difficult to adjust to so much aggressive physical behavior.
- How difficult to adjust to the language of the children!
- How difficult to adjust to standards that are a part of the child's life but so foreign to most teachers!
- How difficult to teach and live in a school that is locked to keep the drug pushers out!
- How difficult to be physically close to children who are not clean!
- How easy it is to give up and just get through the day so I can drive out of the inner city to my home!

JANICE: When you think about these problems, open education seems like the only hope.

CELLA: Why not open education in the inner-city school? Where have traditional educational practices gotten most of the inner-city children? At least with open education, teachers may feel more secure in dealing with children's interests and their world 'as it is.'

JANICE: What makes you think that inner-city teachers will be any more receptive to open education than other teachers? And, how about the inner-city parents, how will they feel about open education?

CELLA: I'm sure that many inner-city parents will be concerned even though they know how ineffective traditional schools have been for so many of their children. And, oh yes, I nearly forgot the inner-city administrator! I wonder how he will react?

JANICE: And what about America? What does America want for the inner-city child? Do you suppose they hope that by just ignoring the situation it will 'go away'?

CELLA: I'm not sure what America wants for the inner city but I know what I want and I feel that open education can provide what's needed, such as:

1. An accepting environment to live in.
2. A success-oriented environment to learn in.
3. More parent involvement.
4. A chance to explore many interests.

JANICE: And how about:

5. A chance to practice self-reliance in the classroom.
6. A chance to see just how responsible I can be with some freedom in the classroom.
7. A chance to move around the classroom.
8. A variety of activities for a variety of learning styles.
9. Several open, trustworthy, loving adults to guide children.

Those of you who are knowledgeable about or interested in the inner-city schools can extend this list:

10. _____
11. _____
12. _____

TOY TALK by Betty Jane Stielau

Toy Talk was initiated in fall, 1970, with fifteen kindergarten children from Phoenix's inner city, their mothers, and an equal number of university students enrolled in a course called "The Acquisition of Language," taught by Dr. Carol Steere, assistant professor of elementary education, Arizona State University, Tempe.

They started with little space, no toys, zero funding, a willingness to work hard, one hundred per cent involvement, and a great deal of interest. Ideas were solicited from faculty members, husbands, neighbors. The specific goal of the project was to sponsor parent-child relationships in such a way that both parties could serve as teachers and share dominance. "Bridging the gap," in the words of the project's founder and director, Robert D. Strom, chairman and professor of elementary education, Arizona State University, Tempe. Because a child's natural ability to fantasize and to create "pretend" situations is equal to, if not superior to, that of adults, toys were selected as a medium for enhancing communications among grownups and children. A child's awe of adult authority, theorized project founders, might diminish if parents allowed a child's natural tendency to imagine to take the lead in a learning situation.

Also, would verbal facility increase if toys served as the basis for adult-child conversations? This is what the initial project was designed to explore. Sorting through a box of nine toys that included soldiers, Indians, an ambulance, and a boat, the volunteer elementary school teachers drew up a group of words relative to these toys and to situations in which they could be used. The only criterion used for selecting words was whether they seemed applicable. Later, each teacher selected 20 of the 120 words which she felt were most appropriate for use in the play situation.

A teacher team consisted of a player partner and an observer. The observer wrote down verbal exchanges among the adult player and each of the three- to six-year-olds in the test group.

Suggested plots state a situation for which the child must find a solution. The plots are simple statements that ask a child to pretend and imagine. A typical situation: "You are a helicopter pilot and I am your co-pilot. A family is trapped by a forest fire in the mountains and they need our help."

The parent is encouraged to ask open-ended questions that require the child to spin a story in response. "How did this happen?" the parent may ask, holding up the helicopter. Or, "What shall we do to help these people?"

This first experiment showed that talking and fantasizing about toys can be a natural way to develop and test vocabulary and concepts. By venturing into an area in which a child excels, by respecting his imagination, and therefore by sharing interpersonal power, a skilled adult can easily introduce new vocabulary, define words by acting, and raise questions to assess the child's comprehension. Toy Talk makes it possible to discover the extent of a child's vocabulary as well as the meanings he attaches to words.

As an instructional method, Toy Talk fosters a respect for a child's creativity, provides immediate feedback, and allows for mistakes to be corrected without embarrassing the child. Because imagination and free expression of feelings are encouraged, most children, especially those from low income families, Strom found, enjoy and benefit from Toy Talk. Disadvantaged children, like those from middle income families, are daily exposed to a wide range of vocabulary on television; they are inundated with words without having the benefit of word definitions. The difference is that poor children rarely can turn to an adult for information that will enable the child to link events and action with verbal symbols.

As adult teams continued Toy Talk teaching, play observation, and curriculum development, group evaluation sessions were held concurrently. The willingness of parents and college students to be self-critical, as well as constructive suggestions offered by children, helped pinpoint obstacles that would have to be overcome or attributes, such as patience and good humor, that needed to be encouraged.

From the adults' viewpoint, Toy Talk represents

a teaching opportunity through play that is without parallel.

There is now a parent-child lab specially constructed for project Toy Talk by Arizona State University architectural students under the direction of Richard Britz. (The lab was developed in cooperation with the Department of Elementary Education.) The students constructed four different rooms, or modules, before the lab was finally completed. Entering the play area is like entering a part of Fantasyland. There are four structures on the floor that convey an impression of moon craters, and similar structures on the ceiling. The material used to construct this area was polyurethane foam, applied with a gun type dispenser, which becomes rigid in less than a minute. Highly insular, the result is long lived, preserves warmth, has high dimensional stability, is non-flammable and nontoxic, is self-adhering, and possesses great structural strength. (The foam is used commercially for insulation, floatation packaging, and sealing.)

Variable color lighting encourages creativity. Most important of all, the polyurethane foam has solidified into an environment that bears no relationship to any cultural or economic level. The child and parent can enter the lab, forget the outside world, and give their imaginations free rein.

Interest in the Toy Talk project has been keen. The Rockefeller Foundation gave a growth grant of $8,000 to help continue the program. Eighty members of the Toy Manufacturers of America have donated toys to the project.

The Arizona State University College of Education, also favorably impressed with the potential of Toy Talk, gave $5,800 to further the program. Interested parents wanted to participate. Educators who read about Toy Talk, or who heard it described at conventions, requested sample curriculum. School superintendents volunteered their districts as sites for field testing.

The faculty team of Toy Talk believes it would be unwise to over-estimate its present readiness for offering any instruction or curriculum at this time. The project is still in the development stage and although it has come a long way since fall, 1970, much remains to be accomplished.

An ASU architecture student, Jim Garrison, works on one of the Toy Talk structures.

ASU architecture graduate Charles Thums of Tempe stands in a futuristic landscape constructed of wire, wood, and polyurethane foam.
Photos courtesy of The Arizona Republic.

Future projects include designing and developing a special workshop and creating multimedia presentations for parent trainers. (The majority of parent trainers will not be certified teachers, and their variety of self-instructional aids is desirable to allow them a more practical than academic influence. Orienting parents calls for visuals, audio tapes, slide narratives, film strips, videotapes, and monograph materials.) Toy Talk supervisors also would like to define and develop further module curriculum units.

But Toy Talk holds real promise for adult-child communications. As Robert Strom has said in an article "Toy Talk" (**Elementary School Journal,** May, 1970):

In my estimate, part of the parental problem of how to win the child's respect and how to share more may be related to the decline of parent-child associations that are rooted in a learning context. In the past parents served as teachers of skills, a task that brought gratitude and respect from the young.

However, many parents today teach less and appear inclined to turn most learning situations over to professional teachers. With this transfer, parents lose the gratification of teaching their young as well as the learner's esteem.

As long as adults refuse to teach with toys, they are telling the young, "I cannot tolerate a curriculum in which imagination has priority because it would demand that I respect you, allow your power to affect our relationship. At the time in life when you are most inclined to learn, I am least disposed to teach you." To retain this position ignores a reasonable medium by communication between the generations. . . . We have already learned that by respecting a child's strength we can better equip him with the several skills required for a successful adult life. At the same time, our grownup play partners are able to win the respect they so urgently need. In Toy Talk, both goals are possible because each is necessary."

AN EXPERIMENT IN COOPERATION by the NTL Institute for Applied Behavioral Science

Team learning is a powerful learning device that is often neglected because many students know cooperation only as cheating. Joint problem solving requires legitimate giving and receiving of help. This month's Brief will have been effective if the members of the class become more sensitive to how their behavior may help or hinder joint problem solving.

The Cooperation Squares game, described below, can be played by students in the upper elementary grades or above. It takes about 45 minutes.

Before class, prepare a set of squares and an instruction sheet for each five students. A set consists of five envelopes containing pieces of stiff paper cut into patterns that will form five 6" x 6" squares, as shown in the diagram. Several individual combinations will be possible but only one total combination. Cut each square into the parts

a through j and lightly pencil in the letters. Then mark the envelopes **A** through **E** and distribute the pieces thus: Envelope **A**, pieces **i**, **h**, **e**; **B**, pieces **a**, **a**, **a**, **c**; **C**, pieces **a**, **j**; **D**, pieces **d**, **f**; and **E**, pieces **g**, **b**, **f**, **c**.

Erase the small letters from the pieces and write instead the envelope letters **A** through **E**, so that the pieces can be easily returned for reuse.

Divide the class into groups of five and seat each group at a table equipped with a set of envelopes and an instruction sheet. Ask that the envelopes be opened only on signal.

Begin the exercise by asking what **cooperation** means. List on the board the behaviors required in cooperation. For example: Everyone has to understand the problem. Everyone needs to believe that he can help. Instructions have to be clear. Everyone needs to think of the other person as well as himself.

Describe the experiment as a puzzle that requires cooperation. Read the instructions aloud, point out that each table has a reference copy of

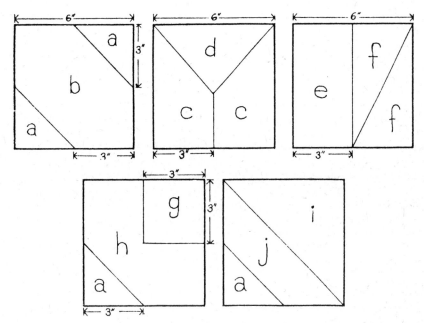

By using multiples of 3 inches, several combinations will form one or two squares. Only one combination will form five 6" x 6" squares.

them, then give the signal to open the envelopes.

The instructions are as follows: Each person should have an envelope containing pieces for forming squares. At the signal, the task of the group is to form five squares of equal size. The task is not completed until everyone has before him a perfect square and all the squares are of the same size.

These are the rules: No member may speak. No member may ask for a card or in any way signal that he wants one. Members may give cards to others.

When all or most of the groups have finished, call time and discuss the experience. Ask such questions as: How did you feel when someone held a piece and did not see the solution? What was your reaction when someone finished his square and then sat back without seeing whether his solution prevented others from solving the problem? What were your feelings if you finished your square and then began to realize that you would have to break it up and give away a piece? How did you feel about the person who was slow at seeing the solution? If you were that person, how did you feel? Was there a climate that helped or hindered?

If students have helped to monitor, they may have observations to share.

In summarizing the discussion, the teacher may wish to review behaviors listed at the beginning. He may also want to ask whether the game relates to the way the class works from day to day.

It is said that our schools are geared to "middle-class values," but this is a false and misleading use of terms. The schools less and less represent any human values, but simply adjustment to a mechanical system.

From **Radical Ideas And The Schools**
by Paul Goodman

When we suggest that schools educate for peace, we do not equate peace with quiet, harmony, order, or perpetuation of the status quo. Instead, educating for peace means preparing students to respond maturely to frustration and conflict.

From "Peace: Today and Tomorrow,"
by George Henderson

The group for which we are educating the child must not ask too much of the individual—if by too much we mean the loss of selfhood—nor the individual too much of the group—if by too much we mean its disintegration as an entity.

From "The Individual In The Group,"
by Elizabeth L. Simpson

But Where's Our Wisdom?

About the time when hay was mown, the heavens
Rained hosts of little legendary frogs,
The whole green world leapt wild with wonderment,
Imps among smaller imps, we laughed and danced
Our echoes and shadows out of breath, and then,
No less impulsive and precipitate, fled
From dragonflies with crocodilian mouths
And bat's-wing vampires down the darkening fields.

In that far country myths were true enough
Though long since proven false to minds grown old
In habits of a scientific time.
But where's our wisdom that we feel no more
The joys of jubilating earth and sky,
The dance of frogs and stars within the blood,
And the wholesome terror too of boundless being
Inside us, and about us, and beyond?

—Geoffrey Johnson

From "Human Beings As Learning Resources" by Alexander Frazier

Now we are learning better how to free up space and time in open-structure classrooms and schools so that children can move ahead at their own pace in pursuit of learnings expected of all and also engage sometimes in the independent investigations or undertakings that enable them to develop understandings and competencies of their very own.

For what kinds of purposes, then, may we need to recall children from individual study to work or learn together?

As we reconstitute learning groups of various sizes, we may find quite a number of "people uses" to hold onto. Here is one quick list to illustrate the range of resources for learning that children themselves represent:

1. A child gains information and ideas from interaction with other children.
2. He also learns how to give information and ideas to others.
3. He profits from the correction and extension of many kinds of partial insights or incomplete perceptions as he tests what he thinks he knows with other children.
4. He learns to understand what feelings have to say, both his own and those of others, as he lives and works with other children.
5. He learns to give and take help in many one-to-one relationships where size, age, level of competency, and the like may make for inequities among partners.
6. He learns to create new ideas from the contributions of himself and others in a group setting.
7. He learns to plan with others to get work done by thinking ahead, defining and assuming responsibilities, keeping target dates in mind and bringing plans to a satisfactory completion.
8. He builds enduring personal relations with a growing number of other children from participating in varied work and play projects.
9. He develops competence as a performer and team member through playing games and engaging in sports with other children.
10. He tests out and strengthens acceptable sex role behavior by interaction with other boys and girls of his own age.

From *Look At Kids* by Leila Berg

At the end of 1966 I wrote six stories about a large family such as might live in the East End of London—stories that in structure would make a six or seven year old's first read-for-yourself book, but with real conversation, real emotions, real people —and I took them to a school in the East End and read them aloud to a class of seven year olds.

The effect was extraordinary. The children began to laugh. They laughed physically, like a very small child laughs—helplessly. They laughed till the tears streamed down their faces. They couldn't sit down. They stood up and jumped up and down, hugging themselves . . . and hugging their neighbours. At first I thought I would wait till the laughter subsided before I read on, but the laughter never subsided. As I finished each one, they demanded the next. I read one after the other, marvelling all the time at the very young looseness and floppiness the children's bodies had taken on, and the quite extraordinary quality of their constant laughter. I have often read stories to children, and they have often laughed, but not like this.

I was still puzzling over it when I got home. . . . it suddenly clicked. The physical laughter of release from tension, the laughter of acceptance, of recognition. For the first time with a shock of joy those children (. . .) had seen themselves portrayed in preserves that hitherto were middle-class and alien. They didn't have to pretend to be someone else any more. They were released.

Heads wrote in about these books, scandalized and vehement, from both middle-class and slum areas. Such subjects, they said, should not be mentioned. Such subjects did not exist. Children do not play on bomb-sites or dumps. There are no bomb-sites or dumps. They have all been built over long ago (this was the beginning of 1967). All children play in parks or pleasant play areas.

All homes have hot and cold water and proper bathrooms, and nobody uses tin baths. Fish and chips must not be mentioned. No children play in old cars. The head of the family must not be held up to criticism.

It was evident that some heads flatly denied their pupils' identity. Also they had no sense of humor.

Statistics save us the bother of facing each moment of life for whatever it brings. Statistics help us to pigeonhole our little bits of existence, to set them all in order, to add and multiply, subtract and divide them until the moment of living has been lost in computations, and "truth" stands absolute and proven, as obvious as 2 plus 2.

Oh, the arrogance involved! The arrogance of teachers who think they "have" a student in the number or letter that they scratch on his report card, who think they can judge him absolutely and capture the immeasurable complexity and grandeur of his essence in a digit or two.

The arrogance of those parents who judge their children to be successes or failures by the numbers that are recorded on impersonal graphs stored in cold rows of steel file cabinets in a school office.

The arrogance of students who willingly default their own humanity, their sense of their own dignity and worth, in their pursuit of such an abstract and arbitrary thing as a numerical grade!

From **Education and the Personal Quest**
by Lloyd W. Kline

We could ask, with Jerome S. Bruner, "How does the culture in which a child lives affect his way of looking at the world?

Studies in Cognitive Growth

Have you ever thought what the world looks like through the eyes of your children? How different is their world from your world?

Music   T.V.   Food   Peace
        Drink   Dance
Art   Drama   Play   Work
        Love   Friends   Money
Adults   Authority   Fun   War

Can you list two songs that are most popular with
    your children?
What does peace mean to your children?
How do they describe love?
What constitutes work for your children?

From "Education for Genuine Community" by Samuel D. Proctor

We have had so much experience, so much rehearsal in exclusion tactics that we would have an awful lot of reeducation to do to start building a strategy for inclusion.

We want education to prepare us to live in a society of variety and make it work, to live among people with widely differing starting points and find joy in seeing them all moving forward at their optimum pace, to find happiness and fulfillment not in power — in domination — in self-destructive greed and materialism — but in helping others to find value in their lives. We want education to define a new goal for us that is more satisfying than affluence, more humane than race and class strife, and more decent than self-indulgence.

COMMON WAYS TO EXCLUDE CHILDREN

1. Fail to recognize certain children when they raise their hands.

2. Purposely exclude a child from those special activities.

3. Limit your positive reactions to his contributions.

4. Make a special effort to give recognition and approval to values not commonly held by the child or his family.

5. Don't touch him but touch others.

6. Don't smile at him but smile at others.

7. Don't listen to him but listen to others.

8. Ignore other children's verbal attack on him.

9. Don't invite his mother to help with special activities but invite the parents of others.

10. Be quick to criticize and slow to forgive.

11. Create classroom standards that are beyond his reach.

12. Be sure he knows that his actions frequently displease and disgust you.

13. Always compare him to others.

14. Say to him such things as: "Good boys don't behave that way." or "People who live like that are disgusting."

How often do you exclude children???

**From *A Man For Tomorrow's World*
by ASCD 1970**

New or Renewed Commitments —

1. The prime mover of man is the quest for meaning in life beyond the satisfaction of material wants.
2. The community to which each of us must hold himself ultimately responsible is the community of world opinion and universal law.
3. An elementary and essential criterion for evaluation of any society is the feeling of being fully alive within it.
4. Individuality in behavior and belief is not only a basic human right but the major resource of any dynamic society.
5. Authenticity in the expression of feelings is essential to both personal well-being and social health.
6. Access to and participation in the arts are an essential human heritage on which the quality of life in any society in large part depends.
7. The processes by which society tends to renew rather than merely maintain itself have to be understood and properly managed if a society is to remain dynamic.
8. The allocation of its resources to meet basic human needs characterizes the good society.
9. Women remain the largest and most neglected resource in our society, both under-educated and under-employed.
10. The communication of reliable information is crucial in a society served by mass media.
11. Peace comes at home and abroad from the constructive management of conflict.

Do you really believe that a most essential criterion for evaluating the classroom is the feeling that the teachers and children are fully alive within it?

Do you apply this same criterion to the college classes you attend?

Shouldn't there be the same kind of vivaciousness present?

Or are you too tired after teaching all day to care?

Or has the system incorporated a path of least resistance?

Do you feel your way is not to question "Why"?

Have you given up hoping for that "fully alive" feeling in the college classroom?

Can or do you revive it for the elementary classroom?

CHILDREN OF TECHNOLOGY: IMAGES OR THE REAL THING by Dorothy H. Cohen

Elementary teachers of long experience who look at children these days often shake heads in bewilderment. "They are different, definitely different, but it's hard to put your finger on just what it is. They seem harder to deal with somehow, but not in the old familiar ways."

As teachers talk to each other, details begin to mount. "They flit," says a teacher of first-graders. "They can't seem to stay with anything for very long. It's as though they have no patience with themselves." "They seem to expect quick results without understanding that some things take time," says a teacher of third-graders. "They don't understand about the effort it takes to go deeply into something. They give up too easily and put up a fight against trying." "But I've noticed," remarks another teacher, "that when they resist it's because they don't know what to do. When I give them the specific skill they need to take them over the next step they're grateful and pleased—until the next hurdle." "That's just it," says a teacher of pre-teens, "they're so rooted in the immediate. They have no tolerance for delay, no sense that tomorrow will come." "Oh, yes, instant gratification," all chorus knowingly. "But what can you do about **that**?"

Teachers of younger children talk of differences too. A veteran kindergarten teacher notes that "my children today prefer the stapler to the paste, which is harder to manage; and they will not stay with a project when several steps are involved that take longer than a few minutes." To this a teacher of four-year-olds adds her concern about the casualness with which the children wander over to the clay table for a few lackadaisical moments and as casually wander away from it. Far from investing themselves in the sensory satisfaction the clay offers and from that going on to creations of some kind, the children jab at the clay, poke it a bit, smooth it, smack it and leave it in a matter of minutes. "Only when I sit at the table and encourage children to stay and do a little more," says the teacher, "do they experience the delight of becoming really involved and even productive." ("At their own level, of course," she hastens to add.) And that comment reminds another kindergarten teacher that her children no longer respond enthusiastically to the suggestion they take broken equipment or toys to the custodian to repair. "Not only is fixing things unglamorous to these five-year-olds, but they act as though the very idea is absurd."

Clues from a First Grade

What does this behavior mean? Evidence of noninvolvement and the disinclination to exert effort are appearing in homes and classrooms where good choices and interesting activities are consistently offered to children. It is not the same as the passive resistance to traditional programs that were dull. Something seems to be happen-

ing that eludes good teachers' efforts. It is possible children are indeed taking on unfamiliar patterns.

Some stories by first-graders about their baby sisters and brothers offer a clue. Most of these stories tell of babies who do things and who stimulate positive and negative feelings in the bosoms of their older siblings or parents.

My Baby Sister
One day my sister was in bed. I heard her crying. I heated her bottle of milk and I gave it to her.

Little Babies
Little babies have diapers. And they crawl on the floor. Their mothers scream because they get all dirty.

Baby Joe
Once upon a time there was a little boy. His name was Baby Joe. He had a snowball. He threw it through a window and his mother had to pay.

But a different perception of babies appears in the next story. It may be the aberration of one peculiar child, but it may also be a straw in the wind.

My Baby Brother
This is my baby brother. He is watching television. Then he went to bed.

Environmental Feedback

Joseph Church (1961) points out:

It is the way the environment feeds back to his actions that forms the baby's schemata: the paper that crackles or tears, the plastic toy that skitters away from his awkward fingers, the chair that refuses to budge, the toy car that rolls backward and forward but not sideways, the food that sticks to hands, the flavors and odors and sounds that come from everywhere, the pliancy and resiliency and intractibility of things.

What is today's environment feeding back to children? All around, children see adults who place greater reliance on mechanical aids than on their own capacities and resources. All around are symbols and symbol systems that do not relate in comprehensible ways to the sensory reality children understand best. Technology mushrooms like a genie to create a magical quality of efficiency without human effort. Man as toolmaker and man as symbolizer have always existed. But tools and symbols were never so cut off from primary experience as they are now. Men and women who use tools to extend the capacities of their hands experience satisfaction and frustration as a realization of the struggle for personal competency. Men and women who operate machines experience a more tenuous, diluted relationship between self-competency and productivity. But as people push buttons to make things happen, productivity becomes more and more disassociated from the direct effort that generates solid feelings of competency in an individual. The loss of involvement creates a subtle devaluation of the person—which probably accounts for some of the feelings of alienation so common in our society. We are the slaves of our technology, not the masters of our environment through technology.

Adults decry this condition, but accept it as the price of comfort. They do not see the dangers to children. Busy with problems of war, pollution and racism, we have not really looked at the impact of technology on children. Yet what is feeding back to children from the environment of the adult world is that the personal effort of any individual makes very little difference. Except within the family itself, where technology has reduced the need for physical effort but not eliminated entirely the personal effort required for the satisfaction of needs, the message rings out that technology makes it easier, so don't bother. The message comes embossed in symbols and symbol systems carried by billboards, magazine advertisements, television loud-speakers and neon lights.

The Price Children Pay

Ought we to be upset when children shrug their shoulders at a task and say, "It's too much trouble."? Yes, we ought. Not because children are lazy or won't learn unless forced, as the traditionalists always said, but because children

are being engulfed by the anomie, the impersonalization and the desensitization that have already harmed so many adults and caused havoc among so many adolescents.

Piaget speaks of sensory-motor learning in children as the underpinning for their understanding of the world. The way of children has been to learn by doing: to try, to test, to experiment, to find out for themselves by using their bodies and their bodily senses. For centuries people have struggled to keep children from being so active and experimental and have forced them to sit, listen and repeat what adults thought they ought to know. What a heartache that at this point in educational history, when the insights of Dewey are supported by the investigations of Piaget and teachers everywhere are ready to concede the nature of childhood that must be accommodated in curriculum, growing numbers of children are not responding with delight to the opportunity to learn in their own, time-honored way! It is almost as if technology's side effects, which are destroying the very quality of life even while material comfort increases, are undermining healthy childhood growth as well. Witness the role of television in exacerbating these effects.

TV as Mediator

The phenomenon of being informed about the world by television imagery is easily enough contrasted with the pre-World War II experience of firsthand learning which prevailed everywhere for children except at school. Pre-World War II children lived in a considerably more bounded child world of their own in which parents were clearly the arbiters of what was good for children. While individual parents may not always have been successful in influencing their children, the yardstick of judgment was acknowledged to be in their hands.

Television has extended the boundaries of the child's world to include heavy doses of adult life. In addition, the men (and more recently women) who write shows and commercials have by the overwhelming magnitude of their operation usurped the parental role of mediator between children and the adult world. But they have not done so with the same sense of responsibility as parents might be expected to have. On the contrary, just as technological development has inevitably been tied to creating weapons of increasing destructiveness even as material conditions were improved, so the expanded world offered by television has been tied to a potential for serious damage to children by being heavily an instrument of salesmanship. In the contemporary child world—where extraordinary pressures exist to achieve within symbol systems, where adult organization and management restrict children's free time for sensory learning, where space to play is curtailed by urbanization—television has set out to turn children into passive, compliant consumers.

This has happened because the period of television's growth coincided with the adoption by the economy of a policy of planned obsolescence. Notions of durability and quality have been drastically altered as technology made it possible to foist upon the nation a pattern of constant and rapid turnover of goods on the basis of replacement of materials that do not last and the development of appetites for the superficial and the meaningless. Almost instantaneously with the availability of tremendous audiences all able to hear and see the same thing at once, television has turned into the greatest huckster of all times. The cynicism of planned obsolescence in a world that has millions of deprived people accounts for the ruthlessness with which first adolescents, and then younger children, came to be perceived as suitable markets. At the cost of staggering sums of money, technology has been used to shape child tastes and interests toward buying.

How Not To Grow Up

Normally children incline toward being active and productive, toward mastering materials and knowledge. Normally their conformity is to each other as their direct and honest responses create a subcultural value system that clarifies their struggle with adult norms. But in the drive to bring them into the fold, the weaknesses of children have been used to trap them into new directions. Their known resistance to giving up the pleasure principle in favor of delaying gratification, their rootedness in the immediacy of present time, their experience in the adult world, their lack of judgment and above all their need to conform to each other have been manipulated in order to entice, beguile and seduce them into wanting what they never dreamt of, what they do not need, and what may even not be good for them. Some parents have fought back. But the children, backed by their seducers, frequently outsmart parents or wear them down by persisting. Sales of toys and tempting foods have gone up. But the price seems to be the infantilization of the children, for whom the message not to grow up is loud and clear:

The most important thing in life is to buy something new.
Feel greed, envy and desire for gratification.
Indulge your appetite for what the sponsor has said you ought to have.
Gratify your desires at once. Rush to the store NOW, before it's too late.
Do not become too attached to a toy or play material; there will be something new tomorrow.
Trust your seller; he is your best friend.
There is a magic ingredient to solve every problem. It can be bought.
Technology accomplishes miracles, like magic.
Only a fool holds onto something simply because it still works.
There are technical (magic) ways out of everything.
It is ridiculous to try to figure things out yourself when others (sellers) or machines will do it for you.

And it begins in babyhood. As the little first-grader said:

This is my baby brother.
He is watching television.

Next Questions

That technology has changed our world for the better in many respects no one can gainsay. We do need technological help to eradicate hunger and destitution. But Norbert Wiener warned long ago that technology would destroy human beings if it was not directed to human ends. Surrounded by the model of adults without stature in the present organization of a highly technical society, children are further reenforced by TV in the denigration of their own effort before they have the chance to become productive through their own bodies and senses. They not only do not see why they should put out effort for a goal that is not immediate, but they fail to learn that they have the necessary competency to try.

As we move at an unprecedented pace toward living with images of the real thing, ought we not worry about whether we are creating children who are losing strength to function in human ways, who will be overdependent on technology, who will not find competency in mastering their environment or feel the surge of joy in being active, feeling doers? Will they be images of the real thing themselves? Is this what teachers are sensing?

Must it be?

Bibliography

Callahan, Raymond E. **Education and the Cult of Efficiency.** Chicago: University of Chicago Press, 1962.

Church, Joseph. **Language and the Discovery of Reality.** New York: Random House, 1961. P. 40. Reprinted with permission of publisher.

Goulart, Ron. **Assault on Childhood.** Los Angeles: Sherbourne Press, 1969.

Rudolf, Marguerita, and Dorothy H. Cohen. **Kindergarten: A Year of Learning.** New York: Appleton Century-Crofts, 1964.

Wiener, Norbert. **The Human Use of Human Beings: Cybernetics and Society.** Garden City, N.Y.: Doubleday, 1954 (also available in paperback from Avon Books, 1969).

From *Reality Therapy—* *A New Approach To Psychiatry* by William Glasser

Using Reality Therapy, there is no essential difference in the treatment of various psychiatric problems. . . . From our standpoint, all that needs to be diagnosed, no matter with what behavior he expresses it, is whether the patient is suffering from irresponsibility or from an organic illness.

Responsibility, a concept basic to Reality Therapy, is defined as the ability to fulfill one's needs, and to do so in a way that does not deprive others of the ability to fulfill their needs. A responsible person also does that which gives him a feeling of self-worth and a feeling that he is worthwhile to others. He is motivated to strive and perhaps endure privation to attain self-worth. When a responsible man says that he will perform a job for us, he will try to accomplish what was asked, both for us and so that he may gain a measure of self-worth for himself. An irresponsible person may or may not do what he says, depending upon how he feels, the effort he has to make, and what is in it for him. He gains neither our respect nor his own, and in time he will suffer or cause others to suffer.

In their unsuccessful effort to fulfill their needs, no matter what behavior they choose, all patients have a common characteristic: **They all deny the reality of the world around them.** Some break the law, denying the rules of society; some claim their neighbors are plotting against them, denying the improbability of such behavior. Some are afraid of crowded places, close quarters, airplanes, or elevators, yet they freely admit the irrationality of their fears. Millions drink to blot out the inadequacy they feel but that need not exist if they could learn to be different; and far too many people choose suicide rather than face the reality that they could solve their problems by more responsible behavior. Whether it is a partial denial or the total blotting out of all reality of the chronic back-ward patient in the state hospital, the denial of some or all of reality is common to all patients.

The therapist who accepts excuses, ignores

reality, or allows the patient to blame his present unhappiness on a parent or on an emotional disturbance can usually make his patient feel good temporarily at the price of evading responsibility. He is only giving the patient "psychiatric kicks," which are no different from the brief kicks he may have obtained from alcohol, pills, or sympathetic friends before consulting the psychiatrist. When they fade, as they soon must, the patient with good reason becomes disillusioned with psychiatry.

Psychiatry must be concerned with two basic psychological needs: the need to love and be loved and the need to feel that we are worthwhile to ourselves and to others. To develop the underlying problem—**we all have the same needs but we vary in our ability to fulfill them.**

But, whether we are loved or not, **to be worthwhile we must maintain a satisfactory standard of behavior.** To do so we must learn to correct ourselves when we do wrong and to credit ourselves when we do right. If we do not evaluate our own behavior, or having evaluated it, we do not act to improve our conduct where it is below our standards, we will not fulfill our need to be worthwhile and we will suffer as acutely as when we fail to love or be loved.

If we do not learn to fulfill our needs, we will suffer all of our lives; the younger and the more thoroughly we learn, the more satisfactory our lives will be. However, even if we learn at a young age to fulfill our needs moderately well, we may not be able to continue to do so all of our lives. From time to time in everyone's life the world and our situation in it changes, requiring us to learn and relearn to fulfill our needs under different conditions and stresses.

As the many instances of abandoned children show, man is not driven by instinct to care for and teach responsibility to his children. In place of instinct, however, man has developed the intellectual capacity to be able to teach responsibility well. Children ordinarily learn by means of a loving relationship with responsible parents, an involvement which implies parental teaching and parental example. In addition, responsibility is taught by responsible relatives, teachers, ministers, and friends with whom they become involved.

Children want to become responsible, but they won't accept discipline and learn better ways unless they feel the parents care enough to show them actively the responsible way to behave.

The parents must not only hold the child to the correct course of action, they must also show by example that they are capable of taking the responsible course. Parents who have no self-discipline cannot successfully discipline a child. A parent who sits watching television, who never reads a book or demonstrates any of the values of using his intellect, will be hard pressed to teach the value of doing well in school through diligent study.

It takes a long time to give up ingrained beliefs about mental illness and to learn instead that the child's behavior is the best way that he has discovered to fulfill his needs.

Grades are not important; learning is measured by the ability not to repeat my words but to put the concepts being taught into action. These abilities are not necessarily related.

We must reject the idea that it is good to be objective with people; objectivity is good only when working with their irresponsible behavior. Treating children as objects rather than as people who desperately need involvement to fulfill their needs only compounds the problem.

From "Curriculum Development From a Psychoanalytic Perspective," by Louise L. Tyler

Atmosphere. There has been much discussion about the kind of atmosphere desirable in a school or in individual classrooms. Terms such as permissive, accepting, open are frequently used to describe the desired atmosphere. These terms are also used to characterize the atmosphere and behavior of the analyst. Analysts are supposed to be accepting, understanding, and permissive with patients. However, there is a general structure which underlies the openness, acceptance, and permissiveness which also sets a tone. This is a structure of regular appointments, certain routines for both analyst and patients, and certain rules to appropriate behavior in the treatment hour.

It would seem that the implications for schools and individual classrooms or teaching situations should be characterized by acceptance, permissiveness, and openness. However, all experienced teachers know that this can be the road to chaos, particularly in some difficult situations and at times in the best of situations. Even if the statement to the group is that you can **say** anything you want and do anything you want, children are not able to cope with what may be directed at them or what they hear directed at the teacher and, incidentally, the teacher may not either.

It is obvious that acceptance, permissiveness, and openness must be set in a general structure of some constraints which are supportive.

HOW TO KILL INDIVIDUALITY: TWO VIEWPOINTS by Margaret Greer, Michael Langenbach, and Thomas W. Wiggins

The classroom is a world in which events occur in rapid succession. As a teacher seeks to cope with the myriad of details involved in a day's teaching, pressures can mount, and he may focus primarily on the tasks, not the children. The teacher may forget that his responses to his pupils strongly influence their feelings and attitudes. The episodes that follow are provided as reminders.

Recognition (Nursery School)

Scotty: (quietly delighting in his reflection in an ornament on the Christmas tree) Hi, Me.

Mrs. Scrooge: Scotty, go on to the office and look for your glove in Lost and Found.

Rabbits (Grade One)

Teacher: (to herself) It's nearly Easter, so that means the rabbit business again. Guess we might as well get it started today.

(Teacher gives usual bunny buildup, and 31 potential bunny makers get busy with their assignment. Teacher visits among the pupils and finally pauses beside the desk of Denny, who has hardly started with his project.)

Here, Denny, let me help you with your bunny. First you draw the head like this. Then you put two big ears on top like this. Now you put some whiskers on the mouth. Now the feet. And then the tail. There. Isn't that a fine bunny?

Now maybe you'd like to cut it out.

Denny: (to himself) No I **wouldn't** like to cut it out. It isn't **my** rabbit.

(Denny cuts out the bunny and presents it to the teacher for judgment.)

Teacher: That looks fine, Denny.

Denny: (to his "production") You're not **my** rabbit!

Sanitation (Grade Three)

Adam: (to teacher with animation upon entering the room at the beginning of the school day) Mrs. Lymm, you'll never guess what happened at our house last night! You know my dog that's got fat? Well, she—

Mrs. Lymm: Adam, blow your nose. It's running all over.

A Hole (Grade Four)

Mrs. Playground Patrol: (to the diggers) Boys, why are you digging that hole? Cover it back up before somebody comes along and falls in and breaks a leg. You'd feel pretty sorry if that happened, wouldn't you?

(Diggers cover up hole.)

A Winner (Grade Five)

Mrs. Analysis: Children, today we will work with just three things—colors, water, and paper. Everyone will create his own design.

Take your paper and sprinkle water on it like this. Then, dip your brush into the paint and let

a drip or two fall on your wet paper. Now, see how the color runs to make an interesting design? That's water magic.

After your painting is dry, see if you can give it a name. Have fun and try not to spill paint all over yourselves or the floor.

(Mrs. Analysis walks about the room, commenting on her pupils' work. Presently she pauses beside John's creation and says to herself) Ye gads, what mad colors! Black, purple, and that one greenish-yellow splotch. I've wondered about you before, John.

(Mrs. Analysis continues on without comment but later returns and says to herself) Well, for-

ever more. Look at that! Pastels this time—pink, blue, orange. Maybe I'd better ask him to explain.

(To John) You used all those dark colors the first time. Now you're using lighter ones. What made you use such different combinations?

John: Oh, well, on the first design I had to use black because Sue spilled some all over my paper. Then, Gail wouldn't let me have yellow so I had to take the purple left over at the sink. The green's mine.

I used pink and blue on the second one because I could reach 'em. Pete had 'em right there. And Nathan had too much orange in the lid, and it was about to spill, so I helped him use it up.

Mrs. Analysis: Oh.

What children say and what they do are important to them. When the teacher responds in such a way that children know their contributions are of value, he is creating an atmosphere in which learners can thrive. Acceptance is a form of reinforcement that says to the child: "What you say and do is important. Therefore, **you** are important."

—**Margaret Greer,** assistant professor, College of Education, University of New Mexico, Albuquerque.

Recently, a first grader asked his teacher why there was a fuss about trying to put Humpty Dumpty together again. The teacher exclaimed, "Well, we can't have poor Humpty on the ground in pieces when he should be on the wall where he belongs." She went on to ask, "And by the way, Billy, where do you belong?"

It appears as though the primary purpose of the elementary school is to mold young children to fit various cultural roles dictated by society. Educators in the elementary schools emphasize conventional, middle-class values and behavior. They "grant" implicit and explicit rewards to children and place constraints on them in order to induce them to trade in their individuality for a socially acceptable role, and, thereby, like Humpty, stay in one predictable piece.

During the course of a one-day visit to a typical elementary school, we heard teachers make many statements that demonstrate how elementary schools can manipulate children and mold their behavior so that it becomes predictable and culturally acceptable. The following are some examples:

"Big boys don't cry."

"I don't want to see anyone sitting idle."

"It's time to go to the lavatory."

"Dolls are for girls."

"John, your hair is too long."

"Good workers always sit tall."

"You should all be finished by the bell."

"Don't touch anyone else."

"Always be nice to David; he's hard of hearing."

"Don't work ahead."

"Don't color outside of the lines."

"Smile and we'll know you're happy."

"If you work slowly, you won't make mistakes."

To induce children to comply with the above, we heard:

"If you're naughty, no one will like you."

"Good students make good leaders."

"Why can't you behave like a good little girl?"

"Your records will go with you to the other school."

"Perhaps you should talk with the principal."

"Do you want your parents to know?"

"Remember, report cards are coming out soon."

Teachers could unquestionably add to this collection. So could administrators, who use an equally convincing collection of statements in their efforts to socialize behavior.

Although teachers and principals frequently talk about programs that foster individuality and promote human development, one is hard-pressed to find the empirical evidence.

—**Michael Langenbach,** assistant professor of education, and **Thomas W. Wiggins,** associate professor of education and human relations, University of Oklahoma, Norman. Dr. Langenbach and Dr. Wiggins have taught in elementary school.

TEAM LEARNING by NTL Institute for Applied Behavioral Science

Why not experiment with making assignments to small groups? And why not allow some children to tutor others? **Team learning** might be even more revolutionizing than team teaching.

Before getting to team-learning assignments, groups have to be built. Members need to get to know one another and to have some experience that shows them the value of working in a group where members help one another.

Some Action Suggestions:

1. Form groups of three to six students, employing one of the following options:

• Use existing groups already formed for some other purpose.

• Decide what achievements and skills a learning group needs and compose groups accordingly. Also take into account personality mixes and compatibility.

• Form random groups by counting off or by some other mechanical means.

• Ask students to move around the room until they find three or four others with whom to form a group—perhaps with students they don't yet know very well. (By moving around himself and allowing for flexibility of group size, the teacher should be able to ease into a group anyone about to feel left out.)

2. Help the group get acquainted.

Use the "egg carton exercise" (about 20 minutes).

Bring an egg carton to class and ask individuals to list as many uses for it as they can in about two minutes. Then give each group about three minutes to develop a group list. Ask whether individuals got new ideas from their group and whether everyone had a chance to get at least one idea into the group list. (If not, allow another minute for adding to the list.)

Have each group see if it can agree on the three to five best uses to be shared with the other groups.

List on the board the "best uses" from each group. Are lists different or similar? Do they suggest differences among the groups? (Is one group practical, one group unusual, one group funny, etc.?)

Did the groups work differently? Did some groups find it easier to build a group list? Did some groups get ideas from all members and some from only one or two?

Another warm-up activity is a story-completion exercise (about 15 minutes). The teacher writes a sentence on the board, for example, "I wondered what the man had in the odd-shaped package."

Each member of the group adds a sentence until the group completes a story. The teacher then asks each group to name a member to report the story to the class and instructs or coaches him so that he will report accurately.

The groups share their stories, and again the teacher leads a quick discussion to bring out differences among the groups and ways in which groups might work better.

Still another activity is the "cooperation squares exercise," described on page 57 of the October 1969 issue of TODAY'S EDUCATION (about 45 minutes).

3. Discuss with the class what they have learned about working in small groups and explain the idea of team learning. Points include: Much learning has to be done alone, but often we can learn better by sharing resources and helping one another. With experience in both methods of learning, we are better able to decide when to work alone and when to work as a team. In team learning, the team succeeds only if each member succeeds. Some of the labor can be divided. More material may be covered if reading assignments can be divided and reported back. Assignments will be to the team. The team will decide who does what. If anyone "goofs off,' this becomes a problem for the team to work on. If anyone has special difficulties, the team will have to help him. If no one in the group can help, then the team can ask the teacher for assistance.

4. Give the first small-group assignment.

This might be: Try to arrive at your team's definition of what responsibility for self and others means and be prepared to share this with the other teams.

You might make an assignment more specifically related to what the class is studying.

Or you might give a current events assignment with each team choosing some news area for reporting to the class.

5. Discuss with the class what kinds of assignments they would like to do as teams.

"In the first place it seems clear that when students perceive that they are free to follow their own goals, most of them invest more of themselves in their effort, work harder, and retain and use more of what they have learned, than in conventional courses."

From **Freedom To Learn** by Carl R. Rogers

"When children are encouraged to have intellectual freedom, they seem spontaneously to exhibit emotional freedom as well."

From **The Open Classroom: Making It Work** by Barbara Blitz

For Helping Kids Live Together—

"Those big kids think they're so smart!"
"Go away you little punk!"
"I'm scared to go to the library where all those big kids are."
"Big kids are always bossing me!"
"Get lost!"
"They won't let me play because I'm littler."
"Those 6th graders took the ball and the baseball diamond away from us!"

Statements like these led us to explore the possibilities of improving relationships among the elementary children in our building which maintains a self-contained classroom type of organization. Two of us embarked upon a year-long project aimed toward improving the human relationships between our classes. The two classes were composed of a combination of third and fourth grade students, and another combination of fifth and sixth grade students.

Various activities that incorporated the concept of cross-age helpers were regularly planned and scheduled each week during the school year. The first semester ten of our fifth and sixth grade children worked on a one-to-one basis with ten of the third and fourth graders. Various reading activities were engaged in depending upon the individual need and interest of the younger students. The second semester the emphasis was on math. Throughout the entire year, there were times of total involvement of both classes. These activities were mainly in the physical education and fine arts areas. With each additional experience both teachers and children became aware of the increasing acceptance and respect exhibited between the younger and older students as well as among the students in each class.

Of the many neat "happenings" that took place during the year, perhaps the most unique of these was an ecology tour of our city late in the spring. By this time of the year, bonds between the younger and older children had become quite firmly established. The fifth and sixth graders planned a bus tour of the city. The purpose of the tour was to look for evidences of growth, pol-lution, and abuse of natural resources. A dittoed sheet was prepared for use in recording what was observed. A camera was taken along, and a team of students organized to take photographs of highlights of the trip.

The fifth and sixth grade class invited the third and fourth graders to accompany them on this field trip. Without hesitation, the younger children selected for their teammate an older child with whom he had worked on several prior occasions. The older children briefed the younger ones on the purpose of the trip and explained the responsibility of each member of each team during the tour. It was decided that the older child would do the written recording; however, both members of the team were responsible for making observations and communicating ideas.

During the two and a half hour trip, conversation between the team members had definite purpose. The children seemed awakened and impressed with what they saw. Upon return to the classroom, teams combined and consolidated their recorded information which was then shared orally with the entire group. A lively, revealing discussion followed. Later, on-going activities were pursued in the individual classrooms in the areas of math, language arts, social studies and art. The classes shared the fruits of these activities with each other.

We felt that our endeavors during the year were most worthwhile, and that through the interaction of the students in the two groups the attitudes and the relationships of the children toward each had improved.

> American the Beautiful
> More beautiful would be
> If Thoughtless Toss—it
> Didn't roam from sea
>   to shining sea.
>
> —Third and Fourth Grade

—Miss Evelyn Badger and Dr. Girolama Garner Teachers, Hudlow Elementary School, Tucson

TEAM TEACHING—A NEW MODE OF LIVING
by Darrell L. Roubinek

Increasing numbers of elementary schools are creating team-teaching learning environments. This trend towards team teaching appears to have been facilitated largely by the creation of open space schools; however, teachers in self-contained classrooms have also demonstrated interest in teaming within the confines of their physical limitations.

Many kinds of team-teaching models have been created. Each model has its own unique characteristics which evolved from the uniqueness of each team and its individual team members. Teams come in varying sizes, ranging usually from two to eight members. Leadership roles vary from team to team as do role assignments for individual members. Some teams group children according to ability or achievement, other teams have rejected this concept, and yet others utilize a wide variety of grouping patterns.

Even though teams vary in respect to their organizational and instructional patterns, they nevertheless share come common elements. First, they all are experiencing, or have experienced, a new mode of living (teacher togetherness). Second, this new mode of living has created some new problems that self-contained teachers have not faced. And, third, children are facing a new mode of living, too (more than one teacher and living with a greater number of children).

Experience has shown that many team teaching situations have failed to live up to expectations. Teams have been dissolved and walls go up, individual teachers leave teams disenchanted and hurt, and some teachers live in misery for most of the school year. Yet, while some teams do encounter serious problems, there are a great number of successful teams whose teachers are firmly committed to teaming.

In my observations of teams, both in preparation and in actual teaching operation, I have observed that teams who effectively prepare themselves for teaming have a much greater chance for success than those teams who fail to consider some crucial aspects of teaming. If this is true, then preparation becomes a crucial issue for teachers who are considering teaming.

The following suggestions may assist you in discovering some of the decisions that must be made prior to and during teaming:

1. A successful teaming situation must have its origin in an atmosphere where teachers have time to explore and are encouraged to innovate. **Teachers who are considering teaming should first determine the administrative attitude toward teaming and innovation.**
   a. May we create learning centers?
   b. May we individualize our instructional program?
   c. May we provide choices for children?
   d. May we work with a multi-aged group of children?

2. Unsuccessful team-teaching situations, almost without exception, fail to establish interpersonal relationships. **Teachers who are considering teaming must give top priority to interpersonal relationships!**
   a. Seek professional assistance from qualified people who can assist your team with interpersonal relationships before school, during the school year, and/or whenever the need arises. **Inservice must be continuous!**
   b. Select team leaders with care. Identify and describe the role of the team leader. What kind of leader do you want?
   c. Spend time discussing individual team members' viewpoints about such things as:
   (1) Student control—how much, who, and when?
   (2) Student behavior—what constitutes misbehavior?
   (3) Discipline—what kind, when, and by whom?
   (4) Movement of children—what kind of restrictions, if any?
   (5) Choices—what kind of choices for children and how many?
   (6) Learning centers—what kind, how many, teacher directed, child directed, process centered, etc.?

(7) Noise—what is the noise tolerance level of team members? How can we deal with our differences?

(8) Teacher comparisons by children—children will compare teachers and discover favorites. Can each team member accept and live with this reality of life in teaming?

(9) The list could go on and on.

3. Organizational tasks are important for a successful teaming venture. These kinds of questions should be considered:

a. How much scheduling will be permitted on our team?
NOTE: Teams which become obsessed with scheduling become less flexible than self-contained classrooms. How important is flexibility for your team?

b. What roles will each team member assume?
NOTE: Some teams become nothing more than a departmentalized team: One teaches math to all, one teaches social studies, etc. What do you consider best for your children? Surely an elementary school can become more than this!

c. What types of grouping patterns are best for children? How do you feel about ability and/or achievement grouping? Why not consider student initiated groupings (let children find someone to share their learnings with).

4. All team-teaching situations, whether considered successful or unsuccessful, have experienced conflict in some form or other. Prepare yourself for dealing with conflict.

a. Plan carefully your approach for receiving a new team member. A well-functioning team—demonstrating poise, experience, confidence, and a high degree of effectiveness—can threaten a newcomer. Make the newcomer feel that she has something to offer and that indeed you need her!

b. Remember that team leadership is seldom vested only in the official leader. Leadership is often shared by several teachers, especially those with seniority. Senior

teachers may form a strong clique which can cause severe conflict.

c. Cliques of teachers within a team are far too common. Teachers often form alliances because of different philosophies about how to deal with individual children, how much choice should be available for children, how much restriction should be placed on the movement of children, etc.

Even though some of the problems of team teaching have been outlined, a negative response by the reader towards teaming was not intended nor desired. Rather, this writer is convinced that children can best be served by teams of open adults who can and do demonstrate their openness towards each other and children in the learning environment.

RECIPES FOR LIVING

DECORATE

1. Locate one old sofa.
2. Open the cushions enough to stuff in surplus foam chips.
3. Restitch with bright yarn.
4. Buy inexpensive throw cloth or bedspread.
5. Cover sofa—enjoy it!

TURNABOUT

1. Take one precious half-hour daily.
2. Use it to let some children teach **you** something.
3. Enjoy learning—showing children that you are learning.

LAUGH

1. Talk, talk, talk with the children about their ideas of "fun" and "funny things."
2. Together write, edit, and bind your own funny stories.

LOVE-RUG

1. Collect carpet samples.
2. Have each child make his favorite geometric design. Cut that design from a square.
3. Bind or sew the pieces together for a love rug or living rug.

MAKE MUSIC

1. Identify some musical instrument your children would like to play.
2. Locate someone who knows that instrument. Ask that person to help you.
3. Make this a music project for you and those who want to learn.

OPENERS
FOR TEACHERS

Begin—
With an almost barren room. Provide as much time as needed the first few days of school to create with the children an inviting learning environment.

Add—
A beauty corner or center. Enable children to bring what they think is beautiful for sharing.

Suggest—
Building upward in your room. Make a rope ladder up to a tree house or a reading nest or an observation porch.

Solicit help from your parents—
To make your room look more like a living room rather than a clean, sterile kitchen.

Move—
To a living environment that brings laughter and joy to each day's living.

Original thinkers in schools?

Remember how many innovative persons we've identified who were either "shifted" or "weeded out" of schools? How many times have **I** been told: "Go easy—just don't go too fast"!

—emc

"Pro" Statistics—

Working in education is not the easiest kind of task. My brother owns a small business and he can tell how things are going by gathering data that gives the end results of a gain or a deficit. He thinks, and I tend to agree with him, that we are careless in education. We gather data—how many kids are absent, how many tardy, and how much it costs per student to educate each child in our district. BUT, gathering data on what children learn is not as easy. We give group tests that enable us to rank them, and we can identify how far from the norm each child deviates, but— is that **real data**? And what of the other things each learns? How do we really know?

"Pro" Unique Cultures—

HOPI CHILD: My Indian home is on a collection of mesas, surrounded by the Navajo Indian tribe. My people are close to the sun and sky. We love our land. In our culture we are taught to help each other—to cooperate. So when I first went to the white man's school, I found that I did not please the teacher. She kept urging me to get my work done fast so I could be "first." Being "first" meant to show my cousin that he wasn't as fast as I was. Maybe he couldn't do his work as fast as I did, but he certainly could find the homes of the rattlesnakes faster than almost any other boy in our village; and those snakes are important for our rain dance.

—emc

CHAPTER SEVEN

Expanding

Secretly, or not so secretly, you always wanted to change education.

Open Education Requires Expansions of Many Kinds

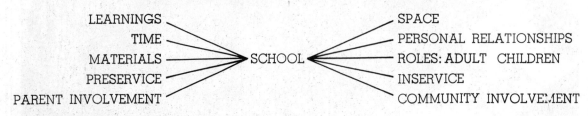

LEARNINGS
TIME
MATERIALS ——→ SCHOOL ←——
PRESERVICE
PARENT INVOLVEMENT

SPACE
PERSONAL RELATIONSHIPS
ROLES: ADULT CHILDREN
INSERVICE
COMMUNITY INVOLVEMENT

From *How To Survive In Your Native Land*
by James Herndon

The first characteristic of any institution is that
no matter what the inevitable purpose for which
it is invented, it must devote all its energy to doing
the exact opposite. . . . The second characteristic
is that an institution must continue to exist. . . . The
school must encourage its students not to learn.
For if the students learned quickly, most of them
could soon leave the school, having Learned. But
if the students left the school it would cease to
exist as an institution and then the students would
have No Place In Which To Learn.

---

celebration

he was high
          "dance" he said to the chipmunk
          chipmunk didn't answer, not believing he was addressing him
          "dance chipmunk" he said, so that the chipmunk knew he was
                              talking to him—because sometimes chipmunks
                              can't be sure that men really want to talk
                              to them
      "fizz" said chipmunk
      "o.k." he said
                    so they fizzed

                                        —Sam Hamod

TUNNELED RESTRICTIVENESS
by Darrell L. Roubinek

The education of America's youth which has been entrusted to the public school institution has traditionally and is currently taking place within the confines of a physical structure. These physical structures were supposedly designed for education, which specifically implies the enhancement of learning. As one observes these structures and what takes place within them, it is quite possible for the astute observer to question whether or not schools were designed for education because what often takes place within them does little to enhance learning.

Educators often feel limited by existing structures, and rightly so, because physical limitations are a reality. However, physical limitations cannot be used as an excuse for a sterile and gloomy learning environment. Modifications and creative minds can always be employed to overcome many of our physical limitations. Even though we can overcome many of our physical limitations, we must also be aware of other limitations that are imposed by the behavior of the teacher and the structure of the instructional program. These nonphysical limitations can be, and many times are, more restrictive on the individual child than are physical limitations.

The functionality of space includes three concepts of life space: **personal life space,** of which the school environment is only a part; **structural life space,** and **functional life space,** both of which the schools control while the child is in school. Even though life space has been described as having three parts, it is not three independent spaces. A child's personal life space determines largely his ability to handle structural and functional space, and, on the other hand, his experiences with varying structural and functional spaces influence his personal life space.

Personal Life Space—The personal life space of an individual consists of the universe. His personal life space therefore contains all potential meaning, purpose, and value for the individual. Assuming that the concept of the total universe

THINK! How often do you use your physical classroom structure as an excuse for the lack of action? Just how limiting is your classroom or school?

Look at your classroom. How do you use the space you have? Could you use the space you have differently?

is limitless, then the personal life space of an individual is limitless as well. However, that part of the total universe which any one individual can experience is limited, and these limitations are both self-imposed and other-imposed.

Based on the definition and description of personal life space presented here, it is assumed that personal life space can become enriched, broadened, and made more meaningful for the individual through his personal involvement with life. It is further assumed that parents, teachers, and other individuals with whom the child interacts can influence and enhance the richness and meaningfulness of a child's personal life space. These assumptions, if valid, indicate that it is indeed possible to assist the child in becoming more aware of the total universe by helping him overcome self-imposed limitations and by eliminating other-imposed limitations.

We know that the individual is not capable of receiving and internalizing all that is offered within the total universe; therefore, the human organism is selective of what it attends to in the universe. In this respect, the individual limits himself. If an individual is to have the opportunity to be a successful selector, he must not only be in tune, but he must be equipped to sense, have the opportunity to select, and, above all, must have the desire to explore his environment.

Functional Life Space—The instructional program of a typical elementary classroom is also restrictive in nature. Many elementary classroom teachers consider silence as next to Godliness, and in order to maintain silence, the movement of children must be restricted. The best way to restrict movement is to keep children at their own desks with activities designed for the desk. When children are physically restricted to a desk, then they must function at the desk. Their functional life space therefore becomes progressively more restrictive in nature as well.

The nature of youth does not appear to be congruent with a tightly restrictive structural and functional life space. To observe children at play (and don't forget that children learn through play), one cannot fail to notice the amount of time de-

What kind of life spaces do your children bring to school? Would you like to know more about them? Try listening more and talking less! Try watching more while "doing" less!

Instead of saying, "I didn't have time to do...," wouldn't we be more honest by saying, "I didn't take time to do..."

time to do
to do...

voted to physical movement, learning through physical contact, and the wide range of interests demonstrated by children during a given interval of time. The human spirit, as demonstrated by the young, is not nurtured by compartmentalization, restrictive space, and restrictive time. This is not to say that space and time are not important; they are extremely important, and this, therefore, is why excessive restrictions on children can become a hindrance to the development of the child.

Self-imposed limitations are not the only limitations that affect the personal life space of children in our schools. The typical elementary school, through its structure and organizational patterns, is a limiting factor for a child's personal life space as well. Rather than enriching and broadening, which should be top priority for education, many aspects of the educational process stifle and delimit life space for children. These are other-imposed type limitations.

Structural Life Space—The school building and the classroom imposes upon the children structural boundary limits. A self-contained classroom can restrict the scope of a child's environment to a space of 750 square feet. The assignment of children to individual desks further imposes a restriction of life space.

In this type of situation, the structure tends to become progressively more restrictive in nature—from home, to the school, to the classroom, and finally to an individual desk. Because of this progressively more restrictive nature of the typical elementary school, educators have suggested for years that elementary education needs to expand and broaden the boundary limits. Many of the early suggestions centered around the concept of taking the children into the community for first-hand experiences. This concept has validity and is practiced in many elementary schools; however, the amount of such experiences is often administratively restricted, and whether or not a significant amount of broadening is allowed to occur at this time is questionable.

The concept of broadening through actual community experiences can in fact decrease the

Consider for a moment just how many time restrictions are forced on you as a classroom teacher. Perhaps there aren't as many as you think!
How many time restrictions do you impose upon your children?
—Time to begin school day
—Time to end school day
—Time to eat
—
—

How about self-imposed limitations of teachers? Do you limit yourself? Why?

amount of structural restrictiveness of the elementary school. At given times the child can, through these experiences, escape imposed structural limits and have a shot at a larger portion of the total universe. The assumption that learning occurs best only within the confines of a physical structure called a school has little validity in light of the evidence we have about learning and the learner.

Begin a list of places near your school where you could take your class for learning experiences.

1. _____
2. _____
3. _____
4. _____

WHY:
- Are children assigned individual desks?
- Are movements of children teacher-controlled?
- Are desks lined up in neat rows?
- Are children not allowed to share and work together?
- Is the teacher and her desk up front?
- Are children marched to various places within the school?
- Are all children working on the same project and on the same task?
- Is it that the room is very quiet?
- Is the school day broken up into small segments of time?
- Is it that children do not explore their community on school time?
- Does the teacher make most, if not all, significant decisions for children?

Do your children sit in rows? After they leave one day, sit in any seat, but the first of any row, and look all around you. Imagine the children who would be in the closest desks. Can you tie the behavior of the child in whose seat you're sitting to his position in your room?

Think about your classroom. What restrictions have you placed on children? Why have you restricted your children?

PERHAPS BECAUSE:
- These practices tend to restrict the physical life space of children, and if a teacher desires control and order then this kind of restriction on space and movement has value. It is common knowledge that control and order is better maintained when the available space for movement is limited.
- Teachers who employ tunneled restrictiveness cannot, at their present stage of development, trust children enough to allow more free movement.
- Teachers are more concerned about and interested in established input systems, such as scope and sequence patterns, standardized norms, etc., than they are about children's needs, interests, questions, and concerns.
- Teachers believe themselves to be the most significant ingredient in the educative process and therefore place themselves up front in command of everything.
- Teachers believe they teach children how to participate in a relatively free and open society by living at school in a relatively closed and restrictive learning environment.
- Teachers believe that children do not have the competence and the right to make significant decisions about their own learning.

WHAT DO EDUCATORS BELIEVE?

As we observe the educative process in many elementary schools, we begin to wonder what it is we really believe about children, learning, knowledge, and school, and just what concepts are guiding our behavior. Would it not be possible for an observer to conclude that the following generalizations are guiding far too many educators in America's elementary schools:

Military Marching .... teaches .... self-disciplined movement
Silence .... denotes .... effective learning
Ridicule .... enhances a .... positive self-image
Children .... are .... miniature adults
Extrinsic motivation .... creates .... self-motivation
Rat psychology .... is .... human psychology
Passivity .... is .... (functional) learning
Schools .... are for .... adults
Children .... cannot be .... trusted
Learning .... takes place only at .... school
Children .... have .... (no) rights
Violence .... teaches .... nonviolence
Humanism .... denotes .... weakness

I sincerely hope that these generalizations are not true, but of this I am convinced: Open teachers who operate open learning environments would not demonstrate these kinds of beliefs about children, learning, knowledge, and school.

What do you believe about children, learning, and knowledge? Is the learning environment in your classroom consistent with your beliefs?

(Suzanna, Janice, and Herb are enjoying a cup of coffee.)

SUZANNA: How do you feel about the suggested reasons why teachers tend to restrict children in the classroom?

JANICE: It's pretty obvious when you think about it. A teacher can have more control over children if she restricts their allotted space and their amount of movement. But what I'm struggling with right now is "beliefs." Do teachers behave according to what they believe about children, learning, and knowledge, or do they just do what comes naturally?

HERB: What do you mean, "do what comes naturally"?

JANICE: I guess I'm talking about behavior patterns which a teacher exhibits without thinking about them. I'm so busy in my room that I don't take time to always think about my beliefs.

SUZANNA: But, Janice, don't you often, at the end of the day, look back over the school day and think about how you treated certain children and how your class was organized that day?

JANICE: Quite often, and many times I can't sleep because of something I've said to a particular child. I feel terrible about my lack of understanding at times.

HERB: Maybe I've got an example of what you're talking about. Last summer during a seminar class we were asked to identify some of our beliefs about children, learning, and knowledge. We all agreed on many things such as "children have different rates of learning" but at the same time some of us admitted that we had all children working in the same math book, on the same page, and moving at the same rate. The professor pointed out that a discrepancy existed between what we professed to believe (Children have different rates of learning) and what we often practiced (Children have the same rates of learning). If you have all children working in the same book, on the same problem, and all trying to go at the same rate, can you, or do you, believe that children have differing rates of learning?

How would you answer this question?

Take a few minutes and list what you believe about children, learning, and knowledge. Take some time after school to evaluate your behavior and the day's activities against your beliefs. Ask another teacher or your principal or a professor to visit your room and to look for consistency between what you profess to believe in and what actually happens in your room. Help that person do the same for her situation.

From "The American Schoolhouse, Historical Perspective" by Charles William Brubaker

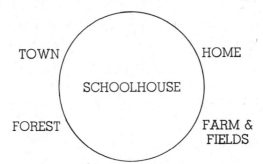

TOWN   HOME

SCHOOLHOUSE

FOREST   FARM &
FIELDS

The One-Room School Was A Home Base For Education With Extensions Out Thru Farm and Town

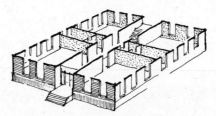

Then . . . a major innovation . . . separation of grades into classrooms

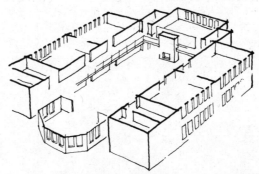

Before World War I special rooms, as a kindergarten and assembly hall, were added

In the 1920s . . . schools were often formal monuments with rows of classrooms along corridors

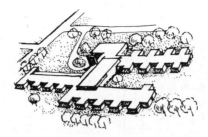

After 1940 Crow Island and other new schools rediscovered humanism

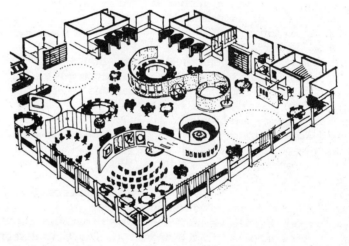

Then—new scheduling and groupings, air conditioning, systems design,
and team teaching generated the open space school

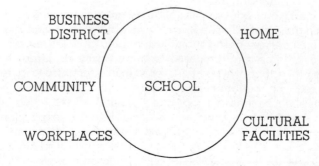

Next—the school may reach out with satellites in the community . . . and we'll have come full circle!

Consider!
**Is there a difference between an open space school and an open school?
Does open space signify openness?**

From "The Vanishing Schoolhouse" by Evans Clinchy

Found Space

"Found" space is space that is in almost every community but is rarely seen because it doesn't look like school space. Such space can be "found" in some very unlikely places:

• An ancient loft-type factory in the Bronx has been converted by one of New York City's community school districts into a superb, open space elementary school. The space was available on a short-term basis for the cost of modernization— about fourteen dollars per square foot.

• This same school district is in the process of converting an abandoned movie house into a learning center and administrative space.

• An underused bathhouse in Boston has been converted into a modern annex for one of the city's older and most overcrowded high schools. Total cost: eleven dollars per square foot.

• Boston has also recently converted a bowling alley into a first-rate, open space elementary school at a total cost of about thirty dollars per square foot.

• A supermarket in Harlem has been converted into Harlem Preparatory School, perhaps the country's leading private school for black and Spanish-speaking students.

• New York City is contemplating converting a large hotel—again in the Bronx—into a high school.

Found space in most cases has not only the virtue of low cost, but also the virtue of speed. It is already there and requires only modernization and conversion to school purposes, a process that usually takes far less time than the complicated procedures required for building new schools. Found space can often be leased space which again is a considerable saving in time and often money.

The St. Paul, Minn. Public Schools has converted a four-story factory into the St. Paul Open School, housing early primary through high school students.

The teachers at Sacred Heart School in Tucson, Arizona, have found some space in their existing classrooms. They are using the ceilings. What uses could you find for your ceiling? Art work, yes; numberlines, certainly; frequently misspelled words—why not!

The British Infant Schools are famous for their found space—the out-of-doors. Surely we could use this found space much more than we presently do!

Where is your found space to be "found"?

From *Teaching In A World of Change* by Robert H. Anderson

Expansibility: Permanent and Temporary.

There are several ways of looking at adaptability or flexibility in school structures. For instance, capability of enlargement by temporary or permanent additions is desirable whenever school enrollments promise to increase or future improvements of the plant itself are contemplated. Architects usually have little difficulty in making provisions for future expansion when doing the original design, but sometimes an exciting building that was not planned for expansion presents a frightful problem when a community wants to enlarge it.

Inventive designs and new approaches to construction and transportation have in recent years boosted the use of temporary, relocatable school buildings in solving the problem of space shortage. . . .

The use of operable walls and acoustical carpeting provides a versatile and comfortable atmosphere. Through arrangements of this sort a school district can achieve an unusual degree of flexibility while maintaining high standards of quality.

OTHER TYPES OF FLEXIBILITY. In addition to expansibility, a modern school building should possess other kinds of flexibility. First, it should be versatile—that is, it should lend itself to a variety of uses, both immediately and over the long run. Second, it should be capable of on-the-spot internal rearrangement (some architects use the metaphor "malleable" to describe this quality) with minimum effort. It might, for example, have folding partitions that permit spaces to be combined or separated. Third, it should be capable of economical modernization when educational requirements change. "Convertibility" is the term generally used for this kind of flexibility.

There are several ways to achieve these kinds of flexibility. One is to build a school with a variety of spaces, each suited to a different function. ... A second way of achieving flexibility is through the use of the so-called loft plan. Here the architects locate roof-supporting and other load-bearing partitions in such a way that the interior space of the building is left relatively free and open. It is then possible to subdivide the interior space by means of operable walls or movable partitions which, when retracted, provide one or more large unrestricted spaces. These spaces can then be used for large, medium-sized, and small groups with relatively little difficulty or loss of time. The great majority of new schools in which provision is being made for flexible grouping have chosen the loft plan.

Yet another way of achieving flexibility is to deny the need for many space partitions either permanent or temporary. Open plans have become increasingly popular in the past few years. ...

SCHOOLS WITHOUT PARTITIONS. Some schools are experimenting with the elimination of partitions altogether. Large open spaces of various geometric shapes (spheres, hexagons, squares, and even a volute), each containing the equivalent of three to five conventional classrooms, are to be found in an increasing number of new schools. The teachers in these spaces usually work as a team, and often the programs are nongraded as well. There is already an impressive literature in support of wall-less classrooms, and the feasibility and desirability of teaching in large open spaces are becoming evident to the profession.

In most of these schools the teachers have unusual opportunities to pool their talents and to work closely together. They can observe and help one another as they teach, and they usually share a team office in which professional planning and conversation are easily carried on. The pupils enjoy a close working association with one another and with their teachers, in an unusually flexible setting.

BUILT-IN FLEXIBILITY

One can discover really neat ideas about built-in flexibility by visiting new buildings. For example, in Casa Grande, Arizona, I visited a school that will have clip-on walls. These walls provide the opportunity to create rooms of all sizes. But what about lighting and ventilation? Both the lights and air vents are movable, which means that lights can be moved to any small room that is created and so can the air ducts.

No more excuses about physical limitations! ! !
OR
At the Matske School at Cypress-Fairbanks, Texas, the school space, except for some private kindergarten space, was entirely visible from corner to corner.

And,
the playground was under and around the open plant.

—emc

**Is There a Difference
Between an Open-Space
School and an Open School?**

TONY: Suzanna, could we talk about the differences between an open-space school and an open school? I've noticed that the terms "open-space school" and "open schools" are often used interchangeably in education literature.

SUZANNA: Have you visited some open-space schools?

TONY: Yes, but while teachers and principals carefully referred to their schools as either "open schools" or "open-space" schools, I found that many of the so-called open schools only had open space—not open education. They were just like traditional schools.

SUZANNA: How would you describe an open-space school?

TONY: An open-space school is a school that has large classrooms with several teachers and many children in each large area.

SUZANNA: Were all of the schools you visited new schools?

TONY: No, one was an old building where some walls had been removed to make large instructional areas.

SUZANNA: Did you consider this old building to be an open space school?

TONY: Yes, I would consider an old building with some interior walls removed to be an open space school. Do you agree with my description?

SUZANNA: Yes, Tony, I do. In fact, the only requirement for the title, open-space school, appears to be that the school have some open space. Of course some schools have more than others, so perhaps some distinction might be made as to the amount of open space. When you visited open-space schools that referred to themselves as open schools did you agree that they were open schools?

TONY: No, but I must admit that all of the schools were involved, in varying degrees, with some of the things we consider characteristics of open education. Some schools, however, were doing so little, as far as I could see, that I could not consider them open schools. In my opinion, they should be called open-space schools.

SUZANNA: Well, Tony, it sounds to me as if you have answered your own question. *Open space does not guarantee an open learning environment.*

TONY: I've noticed that teachers and administrators do not always agree on what an open learning environment is. They seem to agree about the individual characteristics, such as choices, movement, discovery, etc., but they often disagree about how much movement, how many choices, and how many discovery activities constitute an open environment. Why is this so?

SUZANNA: Well, Tony, I guess each of them is putting it together in his own unique way so that it makes sense to each one, just as children do! I sometimes wonder what the children think of this open space vs. open education. I get the feeling most kids I know would think what you and I call open learning environments are only a beginning to really open education.

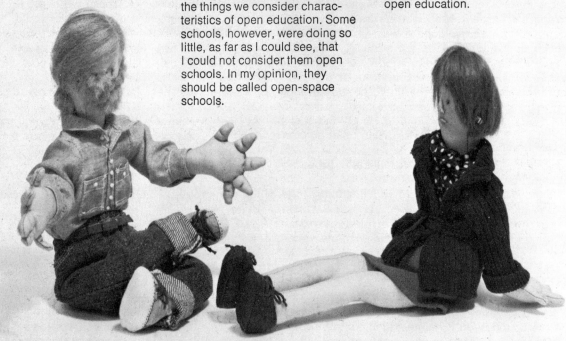

WHAT CAN YOU DO WITH CLASSROOM SPACE?

1. Open closet doors and let this space be available for all.
2. Replace individual desks with a few tables.
3. Have fewer chairs and table work space than you have children. All children do not need to be sitting down and working at table space at the same time.
4. Convert the top of the teacher's desk to a general work bench; add sturdy casters.
5. Stack open ended boxes on top of each other to store things.
6. Painted ice cream cartons provide spaces for storing and are colorful. In addition, they are easily moved.
7. Use the hallways for various kinds of centers. Don't hesitate to try—talk to the fire marshal and try to work out an agreement. Consider table tops on hinges and chains that can be folded against walls when not in use.
8. Use the hall walls for displays of various kinds.
9. Cover walls with paper for writing or for additional art space.
10. Use the ceiling for displays of various kinds.
11. Use the ceiling for pull-up storage.

Take:
A. One pulley
B. Piece of strong cord
C. Col. Sanders Chicken bucket, ice cream cartons, or pickle or mayonnaise buckets from school cafeterias
D. One willing custodian or teacher or parent

Add:
A. Crayons
B. Blocks
C. Brushes
D. Puzzle parts
E. Model parts
F. Chess or checker sets, etc.

From *Schools Are For Children*
by Alvin Hertzberg and Edward F. Stone

The Physical Environment
In order to create the appropriate climate for open education, we have to rethink how we can best use the space in which children are to live. Although there is no "best" way of arranging a learning environment, some general considerations can serve as a guide to reorganizing the classroom.

As a point of departure, let us look at a model of an English primary classroom. What is there about the use of space and the arrangement of furniture in this classroom that is typical of an open environment?

The classroom is divided into various learning centers or bays. Each bay is a mini-classroom, designed to accommodate a particular interest of children. For example, the bay devoted to science contains apparatus, tables, display space, specimens, books, and other materials that will help children investigate by themselves. The reading bay is arranged to help children cultivate a love of reading. It is a pleasant corner of the room with a shaggy rug, a lamp, rockers and soft chairs, and attractive displays of books. It is an inviting place to be, warm and cozy—the best place in the room to curl up and enjoy a good book. The arts bay has a fine display of dried wildflowers and a collection of different shells, as well as materials for mobiles, mosaics, and paintings. It is a busy place, where children can see elements of beauty and find ways to express personal ideas. In another bay, a single child can look at filmstrips, or listen to music or recorded stories. The size of a bay depends primarily on how many children will be accommodated at a time and on the amounts of material to be used and stored while children are working.

Each bay or learning center is set up in such a way that materials are readily available for selection by the children. Small racks or bookshelves are combined with cardboard cartons, shoe boxes, plastic containers, and a variety of other storage devices so that children can have what they need in the very place they are learning. The storage facilities help children to develop a sense of order. Adequate storage also helps them learn to arrange and classify materials, and to care for them so that the next child can also find what he needs.

In the open classroom one notices that there are not as many desks or tables as there are children. Children stand while painting, get down on their knees while measuring, and are not often at a desk for very long. A large number of desks is unnecessary since children are actively at work all over the room. This mobility is characteristic of the entire day.

An important point about reorganizing the physical environment for children is that it is not necessary to buy much new furniture for the room. Most of the furniture in a conventional classroom can be readily adapted to create this more open learning environment. Seating units fixed to the floor, however, are not suitable for creating learning bays; they should be removed and replaced by individual desks or tables. These tables need

not serve as a permanent base for each child; instead, they can be used as the boundaries for specific bays. They can also be used for display space, for storage of materials, and in a variety of other ways depending upon the imagination of the adults and children in the room. Movable bookcases and cardboard cartons can also be used to establish working bays in much the same way. An additional advantage of using bookcases and cartons this way is that the backs can be adapted to create additional display areas. In a sense, they become miniature and portable bulletin boards.

The flexibility and ingenuity with which the teacher arranges the room can also be seen in his use of teaching materials. In this newer physical environment, they are always available for children's use. Paints are not stored away in a cupboard; they are within easy reach in a container near the sink. Books are not put away by the teacher and reserved for use at specific times of the year; all books are always available to children when they need them. Not only are the materials accessible, but the teacher provides a wide variety of them to satisfy the varying abilities and interests of children. This idea of accessibility and variety is at the heart of the open learning environment.

A large number of materials for children are concrete and manipulative. A variety of counting items such as beans, buttons, acorns, washers, dog biscuits, wooden cubes, and coins are stored in the learning bays. A variety of measuring devices such as lengths of string, foot rulers, plastic measuring cups, pill bottles, bottle caps, and pint containers are kept there neatly. The child can also find all sorts of materials for creative writing, such as paper, pencils, pens, leaves, shells, photographs, sculpture, models, and books. The teacher constantly seeks ways of adding richness and meaning to the physical environment. He finds ways of supplementing the existing materials, and he invents and improvises new ones as needed. In addition, he encourages children and parents to bring in and share materials that enhance the environment.

A most important part of the physical environment is its sense of order and beauty. The establishment of bays and the organization of materials help bring about the needed sense of classroom order, but this is enhanced by a conscious effort to make the environment as pleasant and beautiful as possible. Bulletin boards are functional but attractive. Children's work is displayed with dignity and taste, and includes a range of drawings, paintings, etchings, and prints. The room holds displays not only of children's work, but of flowers, hobby work, art books, embroidery, and sculpture. There is often in the center of the room a display of the most ordinary objects arranged in new and attractive ways so that children are helped to see beauty in everyday things. A drab wall is covered with brightly colored paper; a piece of used velvet transforms an empty table top into a lovely exhibition area for dolls; wires are hung between the front and back walls of the classroom so that the children will have a place for their mobiles. In these ways, children learn to make beauty an everyday part of their lives.

The physical environment is not static; it is always changing. It is necessary, therefore, for the teacher to constantly study and evaluate the use of space. For example, he notices that few children are using the music bay. Is it because the bay is too small, so that some children who would like to use it don't have a chance? Are there enough bells or triangles in the bay, so that a small group of children can get together naturally and make music? Do the children working in the center of the room block access to the music area? Does the wood corner in the adjoining bay interfere with the listening pleasure of children who want to hear records or tapes? The key to effective evaluation is careful observation of what the children are doing. If the bay is not being used effectively, the teacher must try to identify the difficulty and work with the children to make that area more functional and satisfying.

Finally, the teacher who attempts to build a good physical environment for children is conscious not only of the arrangement of his own classroom, but of the child's experience in a large context. If the child is to have a greater chance to make intelligent choices and to satisfy a wider range of interests, the learning environment can no longer be confined to his classroom. It must include the classroom next door, the halls, the yards, and the entire school community.

How Many?

. . . ways can you rearrange your room to expand curriculum alternatives?
. . . ways can you use the halls to expand your program?
. . . ways can you use your building to expand curriculum alternatives?
. . . ways can you use your local neighborhood to provide alternatives?
. . . ways can you redeploy personnel to offer a better program?

From *Learning How to Learn*
by Robert J. Fisher

Flexible Work Space

Arrangements for centers of interest can be traced to nursery school practices. The classroom is divided into numerous teaching areas where many small groups can carry on a variety of learning functions simultaneously. Classrooms tend to have so little floor space that teachers often construct temporary dividers to form work bays that separate one activity from another. Many heads have created extra work areas in older buildings by erecting temporary walls or by converting cloakrooms and passageways.

Some of the newer schools have been planned specifically to accommodate more openness. These schools attempt to use almost all covered area as teaching space. Semiprivate bays and working spaces are skillfully arranged so that the teacher can maintain eye contact with various corners of the extended classroom (D.E.S., 1961).

Instead of teaching from the front of the class, the teacher moves about from bay to work area to library corner, stimulating investigation, answering questions, and offering encouragement.

Open- or semi-open-planned schools are designed to promote team teaching with a variety of learning activities planned for purpose-built corners and sections. There are quiet areas for reference work or contemplation, noisy areas for construction and dramatic play, messy areas for pottery-making and painting, well-organized areas for scientific investigations. Children can carry their work outside of the classroom into cupboards, corners, hallways, and outdoors. The library corner is often carpeted, tucked out of the way of traffic, and furnished with comfortable chairs or benches. One village school has been furnished in a manner similar to a home: it has a bedroom, study, kitchen, and sitting room with electric fireplace, which should help to ease the transition from the warmth and familiarity of the family setting (D.E.S., 1961).

Photo by Jane Bown, © 1974 by CRM, a division of Ziff-Davis Publishing Co. Used with permission.

Versatile Furniture

One solution to an overcrowded class with too many desks blocking easy movement is to remove some of the traditional furniture. Some teachers no longer consider it necessary for each child to have his own desk. Children sit at work tables, stand at tabletops or easels, or lean over workbenches. Instead of forty cluttered desk drawers hiding the children's paraphernalia from view, there are trays stacked in accessible storage racks, which save space and allow children to move from one work area to another. Corners, tabletops, booths, countertops, sinks, and shelves are devoted to pottery, scientific collections, libraries, structural apparatus, handicrafts, and props for dramatic play.

Neat rows of desks no longer separate children from one another in order to prevent talking. Children spend as much time on their feet as they do sitting down, and the furniture is arranged to promote conversation rather than restrict it. Children seem to survive well enough without desks of their own; the added space allows for a much wider use of the learning environment. More traditional teachers balk at the thought of not having a desk for every child. They claim that each child wants to possess his own little space. More likely, it is the teacher who wants to restrict the child's movement. Children seem happy with the opportunity to move about, and their sense of private ownership is seldom offended by the request to share furniture.

A GLANCE AT: CREATING AN OPEN CURRICULUM FOR AN OPEN CLASSROOM
by Darrell L. Roubinek

Create activities that demonstrate the interrelatedness of a variety of subjects or disciplines	Search for relationships
Organize activities on a variable time schedule	Individualize time based on the needs and interest of children
Create activities that stress processes	De-emphasize the right answer syndrome
Strive for activities that stretch the imagination of children—illuminate and magnify each child's vision of himself and of his world.	Push beyond the child's present scope of awareness by stimulating each child's natural thirst for new thoughts and new experiences.
Emphasize goals which improve the quality of life for children	Nurture creativity, self-direction, valuing, beauty, intellectuality
Utilize the individual learning styles of your children—	Observe children and discover their uniqueness—nurture the individuality of children
Become a designer of curriculum	Cooperatively design and create, with your students, a learning environment that best meets the needs and interests of the children.

JOSÉ: Dr. Roubinek, I'd like to visit with you about your "A Glance At Creating An Open Curriculum." I think I understand the direction I should take but I'm not sure of the changes involved. Do you understand what I'm trying to say?

DR. ROUBINEK: I think so, but to be sure, let's explore one of the ideas to see if we agree. Where shall we begin?

JOSÉ: Interrelatedness.

DR. ROUBINEK: O.K. What do you think this means?

JOSÉ: Rather than organizing the classroom into short time-blocks for reading, spelling, and math, we should move towards large blocks of time where children could use all of these skills in relation to a topic or theme.

DR. ROUBINEK: That's the main idea. However, I was thinking also of concepts and generalizations. But let's talk about time blocks. Many self-contained classrooms and some open-spaced schools for that matter are really departmentalized environments. And what really is happening to children is that the educative process is, for them, merely taking their world apart and segmenting it into bits and pieces. It seems to me that our main goal is helping children find meaning, and the best way to accomplish this is by assisting children in seeing relationships and making a meaningful whole out of all the things they experience.

JOSÉ: Then, you think that the way to do this is by creating large blocks of time?

DR. ROUBINEK: Well, the creation of larger time blocks will certainly be helpful for the teacher, but the mere creation of larger time blocks will not assure interrelatedness. In the first place, the teacher must recognize the possible relationships that are available, and, in the second place, she must be aware of how children can be guided into activities that demand the identification of relationships.

JOSÉ: For example?

DR. ROUBINEK: Let's assume that a class of children, or even a small group of children, are interested and concerned about automobile pollution, and with the help of the teacher, have set out to learn about the problem and the possible solutions. The central focus of this study might be science in respect to emissions from internal combustion, effects of pollution on life, both plant and animals, and maybe the specific problems faced by Los Angeles and its particular climate and location.

JOSÉ: Location, which would deal with geography. Then, of course, the health problem which could lead to concepts about public health and health services. And, let's see—oh yes, the concern for constructive social action and the many problems that face industry, the politician, and concerned people.

DR. ROUBINEK: The list could go on and on. The possibilities are nearly limitless, but, what about skill development?

JOSÉ: The children would need to read to find out information, and they would need to read a wide variety of materials. They would probably write letters to find out more information, and they might interview some people. And, I can see a need for math, spelling, and note taking.

DR. ROUBINEK: You see, José, this is the kind of involvement that I see as really providing the opportunity to discover relationships.

JOSÉ: We can illustrate this idea like this:

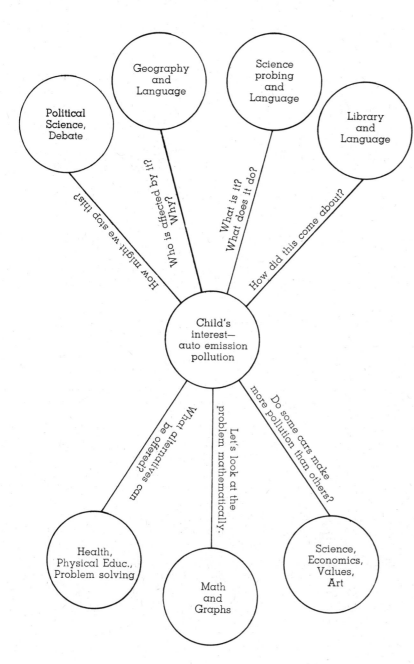

DR. ROUBINEK: I've seen that technique used for other kinds of curricula explorations, José, and I think it's great for helping lots of children see interrelatedness.

JOSÉ: But you know, this kind of interrelatedness is the very thing that the self-contained classroom teachers in my district keep saying they can do even better than teams.

DR. ROUBINEK: Don't let them get away with that limited assessment. Granted, they can do many things in a cross-discipline way, but the very fact that there is only one of them to move from that webbing experience on to other explorations limits them. Think what three adults with three kinds of experiences and three collections of talents could do. For instance, what I see happening in open education environments is that in the auto-emission web, one child might have been involved only in the actual printing of a PR poster, not because he was interested in auto emission, but because he had the talent to design and letter an attractive poster. What he was initially involved in was an entirely different webbing experience dealing with printing a booklet on "No-Heat Recipes" for younger children.

JOSÉ: So you're talking about webs around webs, and webs into and out of webs, and a much more individualized program for children, aren't you?

DR. ROUBINEK: Indeed, José, indeed!

INDIVIDUALIZED IN-SERVICE EDUCATION
by Leonard L. Stillwell

Individualize teachers' in-service education? Why not! Teachers and administrators are constantly trying to find new ways to individualize instruction for children. Why not accord the teacher the same treatment? After all, teachers are individuals too; they differ in intelligence, interests, and needs.

At present, the after-school teachers' meeting, the one- or two-day vacation workshop, or the two-week summer workshop (sometimes for extra pay), complete with resource speakers and a carefully structured activities agenda, are par for teachers' in-service education. But how often do teachers (like some of their students) "tune out" such programs—especially the ones in which they're given little, if any, chance to develop activities that suit their interests and needs?

The Kamehameha schools have been trying to put new life into their in-service education program. Teachers there are required by contract to paritcipate in a two-week summer workshop once every three years. Understandably, not all of them approach the assignment with enthusiasm.

The problems of organizing meaningful productive workshops were apparent; the solution was much simpler than anyone anticipated. The first of a series of consecutive workshops was organized in 1965. Their purpose was to demonstrate the potential of audiovisual media in schools and to help teachers develop some skill in the use of media in their classrooms. Our motto was "Have Fun," and we felt that individualizing each person's program would fulfill that goal.

Having agreed on the need to select a project that would be worthwhile to all participants, we chose the development of graphic instructional materials, with emphasis on overhead transparencies but with provision for some teachers to prepare photographic slides, filmstrips, and tape recordings. Next, we decided to be a working workshop and therefore eliminated all passive activities except such essential ones as lectures, demonstrations, and presentations by outside resource people. Finally, we decided to encourage teachers to create instructional materials particularly suited to the interests and needs of their students.

Recruitment of an expert staff and collection of a wide assortment of materials and equipment were essential if the workshop was to be successful. We were fortunate at Kamehameha to have well-qualified professionals and paraprofessionals who could guide individual teachers in the workshop sessions. The director of instruction; the audiovisual coordinator; and the graphic artist, photographer, technician, and office clerks of the Audiovisual Department assisted participants during the entire workshop. We purchased graphic material for producing overhead transparencies in quantities more than sufficient to meet our needs and supplied each participant with a drawing board and a kit of basic graphic artist's tools. (The cost of the materials was de-emphasized so that participants would use them freely without undue concern about their expense.) The workshop area had the necessary equipment to produce transparencies for overhead projectors and attractive bulletin boards with displays of typical graphic instructional materials and production techniques.

The results more than exceeded our expectations, not only in the quantity and quality of the instructional materials produced, but in the positive attitudes that participants developed toward audiovisual media as teaching tools. Each teacher produced materials that fit the needs of his unique teaching tasks.

The flourishing growth of audiovisual services at Kamehameha can be directly traced to this and subsequent workshops conducted with the individual rather than the group in mind. A similar workshop was carried on the following summer. Then at the request of teachers who had not been scheduled to attend the summer workshop, a week-long, evening one was held in early fall.

Despite their evident success, these in-service education efforts did not completely fulfill the requirements for true individualization. First of all, the workshops were limited in scope, because participants worked with audiovisual media only. Second, the activity was scheduled for a specific time and place. Finally, it was a professional assignment, not necessarily one of personal choice.

What additional steps might be taken to expand the concept of individualizing in-service education? What further application of audiovisual techniques might be used to facilitate individual opportunity for professional improvement? The experiences gained at Kamehameha in individualizing student learning activities provide a partial answer.

Student use of audiovisual materials and equipment in carrels is increasingly becoming an accepted method of instruction at Kamehameha. Why not adopt this approach for teachers?

At present a modest amount of materials and equipment is being assembled for such a program. A variety of educational materials in an audio or visual form and the equipment for individual viewing and listening will be placed in teachers' lounges in much the same manner as they are in student carrels. Then, teachers will have an opportunity for increasing their professional knowledge—by choice.

The advantages of this approach seem limitless.

1. Teachers will be free to choose from available subjects those of interest to them, or they may ignore the materials entirely.

2. They can examine and reexamine materials at their convenience and at their own pace in a comfortable, relaxed atmosphere.

3. In-service education can become a continuous activity as long as there is a constant, changing flow of materials.

4. Information presented in this manner need not be restricted to any specific topic or topics as was the case in the workshops. In fact, the success of the program may well be determined by the number and variety of materials available.

What are some program possibilities for this type of teacher in-service training? A number of tape recordings of presentations at meetings and conventions attended by representatives of the Kamehameha schools that are already available enable fellow teachers to share these events.

Media specialists are preparing a tape/slide program of the behavioral characteristics of Hawaiian and part-Hawaiian children. They are also adapting existing tape/slide programs depicting the historical backgrounds, instructional programs, administrative policies, and procedures in the Kamehameha schools. (These should be particularly helpful to new teachers.)

Audio tapes and 16mm films from colleges and universities, professional educational organizations, and educational foundations are other possibilities for the in-service education program. Additional projects might include preparation of step-by-step training programs to illustrate school management procedures. Teacher-prepared programs describing successful classroom methods and materials are another possibility. Teachers might even preview commercially produced instructional materials for students.

The ultimate success or failure of individualized in-service education may or may not depend upon the application of audiovisual technology. It may finally depend upon the attitudes of teachers and the way the program is organized. Think a bit. Isn't it time for school systems to break out of the traditional patterns and attempt new ways of providing for the educational needs of teachers as well as students?

BRAINSTORMING IN-SERVICE EDUCATION
by Darrell L. Roubinek

In many ways the in-service program being created in the Kamehameha Schools, Honolulu, complements the efforts of teachers who are attempting to create open classrooms. Leonard Stillwell and the Kamehameha administrative staff are attempting to create a more individualized in-service program for teachers, and open teachers are struggling to create more individualized and personalized programs for children. These two endeavors are compatible and mutually beneficial.

It would seem that teachers who are attempting

to create a more individualized and personalized program for children will be highly motivated to continue their efforts if they have an administrative staff that wants to create the same kind of in-service program for the teachers. In such a situation the administrative staff models the type of professional behavior that is required of open teachers. **How beautiful!**

What alternatives might be available for a principal or the central administrative staff should they desire to create a more individualized and personalized in-service program for teachers? Add your ideas to this list and share these ideas with your administrator. Who knows what exciting things might result from a few minutes of your time?

1. Sharing learning center ideas
2. Acquiring manipulative materials
3. Visiting other teachers and schools
4. Sharing creative teaching ideas
5. Spending time with outside resource people
6. Planning field trips for teachers into the community
7. Visiting and discussing current social and educational problems with:
   a. parents
   b. school board members
   c. local city officials
   d. state officials
   e. businessmen
   f. high school students
   g. university students
   h. administrators
   i. university professors
   j. _____
   k. _____
   l. _____
8. Attending university or school district sponsored workshops, classes, or seminars
9. Improving personal skills in art, music, literature, drama, physical education, role playing, etc.
10. Exploring ways of individualizing time for children in the classroom
11. _____
12. _____

Have you ever participated in a teacher in-service program that was designed as if all teachers have the same interests or needs? How do you feel when the selected topics have no value for you?

Do you think children in your classroom might feel the same way if your activities have no apparent value for them?

After attending an in-service meeting that had little value for you, have you often heard yourself say something like this: "Why don't they let us plan our own in-service; after all, who best knows what we are in need of or interested in"?

Again, don't you think that children might say the same things about you?
THINK about this!

One team in one school where Dr. Carswell and Dr. Roubinek work brought all children together for a large group exploration. It went something like this:

Step 1. Children decided what kinds of study trips they would like to take the following month. (There were many!)

Step 2. They also decided what kinds of behaviors were expected while on these trips and how school behaviors might indicate probable study-trip behaviors.

Step 3. They worked out a plan for making two first and two second choices. (NEAT! Most adults would have named them first, second, third, or fourth, while to the children it made much more sense to choose two firsts and two seconds.)

Step 4. They signed up and got both a first and a second choice.

Step 5. Parents were elicited and organized by the aides. They did not necessarily go on the same trips chosen by their children.

Step 6. Because of many small groups going to many different places, and seeing many different things, the preplanning and post-sharing created many individualized and highly motivated learning activities of all kinds of styles and products.

From "Open Schools: Tempering A Fad"
by Joseph Featherstone

As schools move in informal directions, there will be an increasing criticism of our system of training and credentialing teachers and administrators. (Here, with the exception of outstanding institutions like London's Froebel Institute, the English do not have examples to emulate. Their teacher colleges are improving, but they have trailed behind the work of the best schools.) The training of administrators will come under attack, and in some places separate training programs for administrators will be abolished. The inadequacy of teacher training will also become more evident, although it is far from clear how to improve it. What we do know is that theory has to be reunited with practice. Without a solid ground-ing in child development, much of our informal teaching will be gimmickry; and without a sound base in actual practice in classrooms, theory will remain useless.

The enormous variety of the American educational landscape makes it difficult to speak in general terms. In certain areas, education schools willing to restore an emphasis on classroom practice may unite with school systems ready to move in informal directions. In other areas, where the education schools are unable to change their mandarin ways, school systems will have to assume more and more of the responsibility for training and credentialing teachers. Whichever the pattern, a central feature of successful programs will be periods of work in good informal settings. Thus a prerequisite to any scheme of training will be the existence of good schools and classrooms to work in. The single most important task is the reform of schools and classrooms, for good informal classrooms provide the best teacher training sites.

Whether the current interest in informal teaching leads to cumulative change will depend on many things. Two are worth repeating: whether enough people can understand the essentially different outlook on children's intellectual development which good informal work must be based on, and whether our schools can be reorganized to give teachers sustained on-the-job support. I'm somewhat optimistic about the first: the ideas are in the air, and many teachers, on their own, are already questioning the assumptions behind the traditional classroom. The second question will be much harder to answer satisfactorily. In some places, the schools are ripe for change; in others, change will come slowly and painfully, if at all; and in others, the chances for growth are almost zero. Those promoting informal teaching ought to be wary of working in institutional settings where real professional growth is out of the question. In such a setting, all obstacles mesh together to form what people rightly call the System. Right now, it seems unlikely that the System in our worst school systems will ever permit teachers to teach and children to learn. But things may have looked that way to some British educational authorities in the 1930's, too.

A final word on the faddishness of our educational concerns. The appearance of new ideas such as the clamor for open, informal schools does not cancel out old ideas. "Open education" will be a sham unless those supporting it also address themselves to recurring, fundamental problems, such as the basic inequality and racism of our society. The most pressing American educational dilemma is not the lack of informality in classrooms: It is whether we can build a more equal, multiracial society. Issues like school integration and community control have not disappeared, to be replaced by issues like open education. The agenda simply gets more crowded. It will be all the more essential, however, to keep alive in troubled times a vision of the kind of education that all wise parents want for their children.

JANICE: Many of the things about open education we've been discussing in our group and some of the things I've read really make sense. And, some of the things I've tried with my children really have made my classroom a more exciting and rewarding place for them, but what really bothers me is that when I was in college very little of what I now know was discussed in my methods classes, and really none of it was demonstrated by my college teachers.

DR. CARSWELL: Many colleges of education are changing, Jan; in fact, I've really been impressed with many of the things I've observed and read about throughout the United States.

JANICE: Perhaps, but I've only been out of college for two years, and I know that my college hadn't changed as of two years ago.

DR. CARSWELL: Dr. Roubinek and I have been more fortunate. We have the kind of department head and dean that support changes, so we've been involved in a program that is attempting to create an environment that is conducive to the development of open learning environments.

CELLA: I'd like to hear more about that, Dr. Carswell. What's different?

DR. CARSWELL: We think that we are creating a more cooperative venture between the public schools and the university. What we see happening is a team of people from various parts of the total educational system—elementary teacher to university teacher—who share a common goal and who share their skills and knowledge with other members of the team.

HERB: Is this for in-service education?

DR. CARSWELL: Our basic goal is preservice; however, we have all become somewhat involved in in-service as well. We have organized what we call the "open education" block program for students who have not yet taken their methods courses and student teaching. The first semester of the block deals with methodology and application, and the second semester of the block involves student teaching with methodology critiquing.

JANICE: With the exception of a common goal, is not this program very similar to most professional programs with methods one semester and student teaching the next?

DR. CARSWELL: In many ways it is very similar to other programs. However, we feel some very significant unique activities have been included.

JANICE: Tell me just a few major characteristics of your open education block, please.

DR. CARSWELL: Surely.

1. During the first semester, the students spend approximately half their time in stations in the public schools, bringing back to the methods classes results of their observations, planning, teaching, and evaluations.

2. The college professors are committed to making their methods courses more consistent with the concepts of open education. For example, they are working as a team and provide students with many choices and alternatives.

3. The college professors and the classroom teachers are also performing as a larger team, and as a team, they plan classroom experiences for students that will help provide students with concrete experiences during the methods semester.

4. The college professors also become part of the classroom, and in this respect, provide in-service experiences for classroom teachers and building principals. For instance, when each student went into his learning station just before school opened in the fall, each took a "bag of tricks"—techniques to use with children in art, math, literature, physical education, music, and any other specialities each uniquely possessed.

5. The college purposely invited teachers in a variety of learning environments to participate so that their students could have a choice of types of stations in which to work. The public school team consists of teachers in self-contained classrooms with aides; in teams of two, three, or four professional persons; and in schools with a variety of open spaces.

JANICE: Does the college of education provide their students with just this block?

DR. CARSWELL: No. There are several block programs involved with other public schools, and there are also the traditional on-campus methods classes followed by student teaching.

JANICE: This really makes sense to me. We know that elementary school children learn in different ways, but at the college level, we have apparently assumed that all education majors learn only one way. What really makes me feel good is to know that I'm not alone in my feeble attempts; other people are also trying, even colleges of education. HOW NEAT!!!

OPEN EDUCATION AT THE
UNIVERSITY LEVEL
by
Evelyn Carswell and
Darrell Roubinek

In an article published by the **National Elementary School Principal** for September, 1972 ("New Ways to Build—or, How to Get Your School Built Before You Retire"), Jonathan King suggests that "changes in school design during the sixties produced a new spirit of openness and informality in the best school buildings in the decade. Team teaching, the development of nongraded schools, the interest in the British open schools, the efforts to make individualized instruction—long a cliché —into a reality, all contributed to a change in spirit in education that was reflected in the responsive schools of the era."

Evidence to support King's statement exists in Arizona. In the southern part of the state, Tucson District Number 1 built open space learning environments in approximately sixty per cent of all the new elementary school facilities; and other nearby school districts, such as Sunnyside, Amphitheater, and Catalina Foothills, have continued to expand their open spaces.

King goes on to state that "while self-contained classrooms, designed for thirty students and ranged along both sides of a double-loaded corridor, were still being built, an increasing large number of exceptions was constructed, inviting change and innovation." He also points out that occasionally these open schools were staffed by teachers who were neither familiar with how to use them nor overly enthusiastic about losing the security of the familiar classroom.

Public school administrators are becoming more aware of the need to staff these new facilities with teachers who are not only trained but who, indeed, desire to work in these environments. Classroom teachers involved in these programs are also very concerned about finding capable replacements and additional staff members. As an increasing number of schools create new types of open spaces for children the need for adequately trained teachers becomes more apparent and more acute.

At the same time that the public schools are experimenting more with open space and open education and are becoming more sensitive to special needs, colleges of education are securing faculty who have had experiences in open space and open education at the public school level. The need for different preservice and in-service programs has already been sounded at the public school level and some colleges of education have responded to this call.

Some colleges of education have recognized the pleas from the public schools and have also recognized the value of these new concepts in education for the university as well as for the elementary school. This article describes one approach underway in the Department of Elementary Education, College of Education, University of Arizona.

During the 1971-72 school year, the authors (both experienced open education public school people) visited one school each week to view the physical plant and see the organizational and curricular patterns. We talked with teachers, supervisors, program coordinators, aides, and principals about public school needs.

Facilities that offered student alternatives were visited a second time. We presented a proposal for a modified professional year's program for college seniors. Traditional block programs, offering method courses in conjunction with public school visitations, had been operating successfully at our college for some years. The modifications dealt with those teaching stations committed to open education and with needs unique to such learning environments.

We found some basic concepts to be of great importance to open education teachers: (a) children can be trusted to want to learn; (b) to learn self-responsibility, children must have many, many opportunities to practice decisionmaking; (c) the second item (b) is also true for teachers; (d) individual differences are not only very real but must be encouraged in order for democracy to function—this means valuing divergent think-

sketch by Wilton David

For three days we all learned together by participating in an intensive in-depth program on self-concept and humanizing techniques, on identifying talent, on reorganizing skills and techniques learned in earlier classes. These students emerged from this continuous session with a unique "bag of tricks"—books, games, projects, songs, and so forth—and the confidence to try to be a contributing team member.

The week before public schools opened, students spent the last day with their station teachers, preparing rooms and becoming acquainted with the teachers and the learning environments.

The first week of school was experienced in its entirety by the thirty-five students; during that week all of them became helpful team members. This was an important modification for the open education block program, according to both teachers and students. We witnessed "turned-on-to-children" attitudes that carried through the entire semester.

Following this unique beginning, the block took on a fairly consistent (though different) scheduling pattern: two full days in the public school stations; two full days on campus for methods dealing with language arts, communicative arts, mathematics, social studies, and a seminar; and one full day of student choice.

We planned coursework based on an overview of the specific disciplines and on the feedback from students working in the public school stations. The seminar was especially important since it provided the core for considering major strands in the teaching-learning process, teaching and professionalism, planned visitations to other schools, job interviews, and the like.

The methods courses include patterns found in self-contained classrooms and patterns found more often in open education environments. Behavioral objectives, student contracts, basal texts, learning centers, units, field trips, and webbing or core experience were part of the total program. **(Editor's note:** A description of webbing may be found at the end of this article.)

The second semester incorporates a half-day of student teaching in those same stations, with

ing without eliminating convergent thinking; (e) since adults have individual differences, team teaching is a preferred pattern for educating children.

Because of these changed relationships between open educators and pupils, it seemed important for us, the "professorial team" to become steeped in good relationships with students. We also considered it essential to model teacher behaviors that differed from traditional behavior.

two additional methods courses and a continuation of the seminar. Students already know much about the children, the teachers, aides and principals with whom they will work. They know a great deal about the physical facilities and the environment of each school. They've already been part of the team for half a year!

We enjoy bridging the gap between theory and practice. We regard ourselves as another team of teachers, with functions differing somewhat from our teammates, public school teachers.

Colleges of education can no longer provide only one model of pre-service education if they hope to meet the needs of public schools which are creating several alternative learning environments. At the college level we are already encountering students who express a desire to change the traditional programs and who are seeking different experiences. Each passing day clarifies that individual needs cannot be met if everyone has to traverse the same path. It is also apparent that bright young persons are not content with professors who are unwilling to model the changes which they state are necessary.

How can a college of education meet this challenge? First, the need must be recognized; second, the college must prove its desire to meet today's challenges. Assuming these conditions are met, what might some of the changes be?

It seems that the following changes are not merely in order but indeed may become realities in the near future.

Public schools and the colleges of education will extend and strengthen the partnership relationship that now exists in the professional year program. Preservice education will involve more students, earlier, in the public schools to expose them to a wider variety of experiences. In-service education will become more of an individual school endeavor: professors will go to public schools to assist teachers with problems and concerns which the teachers have identified, and the curricular content and organizational pattern for the specific program will be jointly planned. This is likely to produce an exchange system: pre-service for in-service and in-service for pre-service! In other words, in exchange for the

public school teams' expertise in furnishing pre-service experiences for college students, these teams will receive professional team expertise.

A second probability largely concerns content. All methods courses dealing with the disciplines and with educational psychology, foundations of education, counseling, human growth and development will be planned more cooperatively so that strands common throughout all these courses may be identified and studied without unwarranted repetition. This avoids the worse possibility: that they might be omitted altogether because each professor thought the other took care of a situation.

As a result of this planning and the singling out of common strands, the entire preservice curriculum will become multidisciplined—as most of life's problems tend to be!

With teams of public school teachers and college teachers working in supporting roles and with curriculum shifting to in-depth, multidisciplinary directions, new open space buildings probably will not only "invite change and innovation," per Jonathan King. These changes and innovations will, in turn, help to create additional designs that will enable us to be continuously responsive to our rapidly changing society.

The colleges of education at institutions of higher learning in Arizona must be part of that team movement!

NOTE

The webbing experience: Each student brought a recipe that might be used with the children. After each was read aloud, students recorded on long strips of paper all the how, where, why, when, what, and who questions they thought of as they examined the recipes.

They then organized the group to prepare a meal from those recipes. The questions were reorganized into the disciplines normally taught in elementary school, and the students began to search out audio and visual aids that would help children begin to find answers to the questions.

On the day the meal was prepared and served to students and guests, the questions and materials were displayed, as was a giant web showing the entire process.

THE PROPOSAL FOR OPEN EDUCATION BLOCK by Evelyn Carswell and Darrell L. Roubinek

I. Purposes:
A. To enable those cooperating teachers in open education stations to work with students who prefer an open environment;
B. To enable these same teachers to maintain a continuous dialogue with those professors who support open education environments;
C. To identify those students who prefer to have experiences in an open education environment;
D. To provide for students the kinds of methods, methods' practica, and student teaching experience unique to the open education environment;
E. To provide an additional alternative in our teaching education program;
F. To develop professional relationships between open education teachers and administrators and college professors for field input in the consideration of graduate program modifications.

II. Process of Identification:
A. At student teaching orientation, students will be exposed to the OPEN EDUCATION BLOCK information and those who may wish to pursue this route will be informed of a meeting on a given day.
B. At this OPEN EDUCATION meeting students will be informed of the hard work and changed relationships involved in open education environment. They will be given an attitude inventory.
C. A minimum of twenty and a maximum of thirty-five open education stations will be identified for those persons offering to be cooperating teachers.

   Characteristics:
   (1) Desire of teacher to move toward openness with student teacher; OR
   (2) Multi-age grouping; OR
   (3) Team teaching or teaching with parent aides; OR
   (4) Providing student choices with curriculum alternatives.
D. Those teachers whose stations are identified as open will be visited to see if they are willing to work in this block.
E. Students will be given the recommendation to take the art methods, methods for teaching elem. physical education and music methods in the junior year if possible.

III. Proposed Program:
A. Students will be asked to give a full day (8:00 a.m. to 4:00 p.m.) to the OPEN EDUCATION BLOCK for the fall semester. This time will be used for:

Language Arts in the Elementary School	3 cr.
Teaching Science	3 cr.
Teaching Math	3 cr.
Teaching Social Studies	3 cr.
Seminar-Practicum	3 cr.

B. Professors who teach in this block would expect students to apply methods being taught.
C. The second semester of this professional year would be a normal student teaching experience of eight credits plus Communications Arts in the Elementary School and whatever else the student needs to complete his degree.
D. It would be assumed that professors of this block would supervise these students in their second semester.
E. The credits assigned for student teaching would be individually prescribed in order to provide some full days of teaching for each student.

IV. Long-range View of the OPEN EDUCATION BLOCK
A. During registration and in cooperation with Child Growth and Development

course, students who are juniors and who are interested in the open education concepts will be provided with a list of stations for visitation and recommendations for volunteer work experiences with children.

B. At freshman orientation, time will be requested for showing slides of open education environments and a list of

recommended student experiences will be available for interested students. Students will be advised to gather evidence of such experiences if they seek to become part of the OPEN EDUCATION BLOCK in their senior year.

C. Avenues for getting credit for practical experience with children will be explored by professors.

AUGUST−SEPTEMBER

MON	TUES	WED	THURS	FRI
UA 28	UA 29	UA 30	PS 31	PS 1
Labor Day 4	PS 5	PS 6	PS 7	PS 8
UA 11	UA 12	UA 13	PS 14	PS 15
UA 18	UA 19	UA 20	PS 21	PS 22
PS 25	PS 26	UA 27	UA 28	UA 29

OCTOBER

MON	TUES	WED	THURS	FRI
PS 2	PS 3	UA 4	UA 5	UA 6
PS 9	UA 10	UA 11	UA 12	PS 13
PS 16	UA 17	UA 18	UA 19	PS 20
23	½ UA ½ PS 24	½ UA ½ PS 25	½ UA ½ PS 26	½ UA ½ PS 27

Key: UA = days on campus for methods courses
      PS = days at a public school station
      UA prep = preparation time to be used at students' discretion
      ½ = half day

NOVEMBER

MON	TUES	WED	THURS	FRI
UA **6**	UA **7**	UA prep **8**	Visit Menlow Park Hudlow PS Sunrise **9**	Visit Erickson PS **10**
UA **13**	UA **14**	UA prep **15**	Visit ELC PS **16**	PS **17**
PS **20**	PS **21**	UA **22**	Thanksgiving Holidays	
PS **27**	PS **28**	UA prep **29**	UA **30**	UA **1**

DECEMBER

MON	TUES	WED	THURS	FRI
PS **4**	PS **5**	UA prep **6**	UA **7**	UA **8**
PS **11**	PS **12**	Finals ——————		
		To Be Announced		

Student Reaction Comments To The Open Education Block

The Open Block initiated this year is aimed at providing students with as much open classroom experience as possible while studying at the University. . . . The blocks of time can be divided in any way, a welcome deviation from scheduled, rigid classes.

—d.h.

By initiating actual classroom participation early in the year, I have been able to feel more secure about undertaking my student teaching position. University classes have become more meaningful, as I am able to apply my knowledge immediately in the classroom. Most important, I am learning through actual experience—the most impressive prof of all!

—d.r.

The open education block has given me the type of experience that I think all education majors should get from the moment they enter the University.

—n.v.

The most important aspect of our education, the children, is being dealt with firsthand.

—g.h.

We, in the open block program, are attempting to orchestrate all aspects of learning into real life experiences.

—m.c., p.m., e.h., n.r.

The children in these schools, because of their classroom background, are exciting and stimulating. They have a freedom that has encouraged individuality, responsibility, and enthusiasm. The open classroom concept inspires this in a child. He becomes a learner because he is a doer.

—r.g.

Instead of going to lectures in larger classes of forty to fifty students every day at different hours of the day, and perhaps knowing three or four students and probably not the professor, the open education block student is with one solid group of students, knowing each other rather well, and best of all, knowing the professors and knowing the professors know us! I feel a union of the "real world" and the "academic world" of the University. This is a **new** experience!

—p.c.

Dr. Carswell and Dr. Roubinek have just returned from an evaluation committee meeting, and both are concerned with what they think of as one-level thinking about open education.

DR. CARSWELL: Darrell, sometimes I get really frustrated as I try to help other educators see my interpretation of open education possibilities. You know I am a "graphics" person, and you've seen how often I try to sketch out some idea in visual form. Yet I can't seem to really find either words or sketches to help to think on more than one level at a time.

DR. ROUBINEK: I noticed you showed some frustration when you gave one example of how to provide a more open learning environment and several people latched onto it as if they had "the" answer—now they could define open education.

DR. CARSWELL: That's right! When I go into a specific school to work with the teachers and all of the other components, it is fairly easy to find some starting points and to help them develop plans for movement, but when we get into "generalized" kinds of discussions, I can't get enough levels of thinking into play. Too often too many people want to tie open education into one neat package.

DR. ROUBINEK: So, Evelyn, what I think I hear you saying is that just as you and I and our friends in Open Education have explored this movement in directions that often seem quite different, so each school must likewise anticipate not finding one right direction.

DR. CARSWELL: So it seems to me, Darrell. For instance, Dr. Ted Hipple offers one start in the next article. He suggests "participatory education." Have you read it?

From "Participatory Education: Students Assist Teachers" by Theodore W. Hipple

I propose that those who administer America's education begin offering, as many already have, approved programs for school credit that will permit students to leave their own schoolrooms and go to work for part of the day in another room in their own school or in another school altogether. Why must a trained kindergarten teacher have to sift through 60 boots, 30 scarves, 30 stocking caps, and 59 mittens each wintry day when it is time for her charges to go home? Two fifth graders from the class down the hall could be released from their work to help her. Why must several reading groups in a primary grade sit idly by while their busy teacher works with just one group? Certainly a seventh or eighth grader could listen to some of the reading groups part of the time and thereby extend their reading exposure; also the teacher, freed from having to create some seatwork material, would have more time for teaching reading.

A high school math whiz could leave school one hour early one day a week (this arrangement could be built into his schedule) and grade papers for the seventh grade math teacher or privately tutor some of his students who need special assistance. Two business students from the high school could go to an elementary school and help teachers there complete attendance records or balance milk money accounts. Several members of the high school future teachers club could be released to a grade school to offer their services in whatever capacity the schools can use them.

On the college level, where most students have transportation and reasonably flexible schedules, the opportunities are limited only by the extent of the imagination employed in the program. I suggest that college students be allowed to enroll each term, for credit toward graduation, in a program that places them in local schools for at least two hours each week, there to use their talents in helping the teachers and students alike. The college senior majoring in French could provide content help for the high school French teacher whose professional training included only a minor in French, completed 20 years ago. The college theatre major could help the overworked English teacher direct the school play. The library science student could work in a school library, the future chemists as special assistants in a high school chemistry lab, the prospective engineers in a shop program, and on and on. These college students of whom I write are not prospective teachers; future teachers, with their special talents and commitments, could be utilized even more, and possibly be allowed to earn credit for four or six hours a week.

In short, what I am proposing is a massive involvement of students at all levels of education above fourth grade with students at all lower levels. This proposal, for what I call "participatory education," can, I believe, be the means of effecting significant educational and social improvements. I am not proposing a volunteer system at all, in which the only rewards are personal satisfaction, but rather an elective system which offers, in addition to that personal satisfaction, some substantial coin of the educational realm: credit toward promotion or graduation. It seems sensible to me that our schools, which now teach virtually everything, also should present students with opportunities for helping fellow students and for doing so for credit. If the development of good driving habits is an appropriate function of the schools, and I believe it is, then surely the development of good living habits, including those of helping other people, is equally legitimate. The ideal, I suspect, is somewhat tarnished by my system of offering credit for this help; to do less, however, is to continue to rely on a voluntaristic behavior that most students, regardless of their altruistic inclinations or lack of them, do not have time for. When the students can earn credit for helping students at lower levels in the schools, I think they will jump at the chance to participate.

PART-TIME TEACHERS by Alex Groner and Carlyn Brall

With the opening of a new school year, a Detroit principal found he had a kindergarten class, a kindergarten classroom, eager kindergarten parents—but no kindergarten teacher, and none available on a full-time basis. He solved his problem by employing two fully trained, certificated teachers to share the kindergarten job. Both had left teaching to marry and raise children. Neither could work full-time, but each could work part-time. "If it hadn't been for them," the principal said, "we would have been in a bind."

The bind he spoke of is no different from that in which many other administrators find themselves—not enough teachers to go around. The few who have tried using qualified people as part-time teachers have met with heartening results. Not only do part-timers help the schools meet their needs, but the women in this vast and largely untapped reservoir of talent are more than happy to put their skills to use.

In 1965, Catalyst, a national nonprofit organization that tries to persuade employers to meet their needs for college-level personnel through flexibility in hiring and in developing work schedules for qualified women, surveyed some 700 school systems to find out how many used part-time teachers. About 40 percent of the systems surveyed reported that they hired part-time teachers. However, the total number of part-timers employed was exceedingly small when compared to the full-time teaching staff and, by and large, part-timers were used unimaginatively by the systems that did hire them.

The study showed that administrators with no experience in using part-time teachers tended to raise the most strenuous objections to their employment. They felt that hiring and scheduling part-timers would increase the administrative load, or they feared that students would be confused by the arrangement or that part-timers would be unprofessional in their approach. Administrators who did hire them, however, found that these fears were not justified.

This 1965 study opened avenues for further

research, and two years later, Catalyst made a special study of five systems that used part-timers —Niskayuna, New York; Framingham, Massachusetts; Cedar Falls, Iowa; Detroit; and Miami.

These school systems have used part-time teachers in a variety of ways. Some of these teachers teach classes for children who are partially sighted, mentally retarded, or emotionally disturbed, while others instruct courses that most school systems would never be able to offer on a regular basis. For example, in one Miami school, part-time teachers made it possible to have courses in Chinese and Asian studies and in Arabic.

Using part-timers also makes it possible for teachers to compare notes on the same pupils. Their shared insights can bring about better understanding of the children and their problems—and parents are often more willing to admit the existence of problems when two teachers have come to the same conclusions about a child.

In commenting about part-timers in Niskayuna, a junior high principal explains, "We have pieces of jobs that are important but that don't really fit together, and that's where part-time teachers come in handy. They allow me to schedule better." Another administrator points out that part-timers make excellent interpreters of school matters to their fellow citizens because they have special insights as a result of working in the schools and are able to spend more time out in the community than can full-time teachers.

Niskayuna, which has a teacher shortage, finds that part-time teachers help to make programs work better, fit well into teaching teams, and allow the schools to offer subjects for which full-time teachers are unavailable. Most principals have found that part-time teachers create no special administrative problems.

Framingham, one of Boston's bedroom communities, is a community that uses part-time teachers by design, rather than out of desperation. At the urging of Nona Porter of the Women's Educational and Industrial Union in Boston, the Framingham system decided to try "partnership" teaching, in which two fully certificated teachers shared one full-time teaching job, each working half a day.

With some backing from the Carnegie Corporation and the Permanent Charity Fund of Boston, the agency took over and administered the entire project. Starting in 1965, Mrs. Porter and her staff launched a special advertising campaign to inform the public that her agency was looking for qualified women who were interested in part-time teaching. By the fall of 1968, more than 1,000

women had responded, and 170 part-time teachers were placed in Framingham and other Massachusetts communities.

A number of school administrators were skeptical about the experiment at first, for as one principal remarked, "It would be like having two women in one kitchen." As it turned out, however, since care was taken in their selection, the paired teachers usually worked well together and often complemented each other. An older teacher might be matched with a younger one, a quiet teacher with one who is outgoing, an experienced teacher with one who has little or no classroom background, a teacher skilled in language arts with one who is strong in mathematics.

The idea of partnership teaching has started to spread from the original Massachusetts communities to other systems in the state and to other parts of the country. Whenever the groundwork —planning, organizing, and preparing key individuals and groups—has been carefully laid, it seems to work out successfully.

Cedar Falls, the other system in the study which used partnership teaching, has employed part-timers to teach such subjects as language arts, science, and remedial reading for about ten years. Part-time teachers there have worked with individual pupils or small groups who were ahead of or behind the class in reading level, freeing the regular teacher to work with the larger group, which could then proceed at its ordinary pace. If the budget permitted, Cedar Falls would employ many more part-time teachers, because they are considered an integral part of the school system, not just a temporary expedient. "We don't get enough of them," is the only complaint of an elementary school principal.

In Miami, the school system's central offices have only scanty records on part-time teachers, and administrators have little to do with their recruitment. Many school principals, on the other hand, are enthusiastic about part-timers and have felt free to hire them on their own.

There are, of course, obstacles to be overcome in the use of part-time teachers. Some are created by the arbitrariness of local official regulations; some, by the part-timers themselves; and still others by a combination of the two. For example, the hours prospective part-time teachers would like to work may not coincide with the time when they are most needed. Many who have young children wish to work only in the morning, and some are willing to work only certain days each week rather than certain hours each day.

Whether teachers work full-time or part-time, obtaining necessary certification sometimes presents difficulties, although significant progress is being made both in reciprocal certification arrangements between states and in facilitating ways of qualifying for certification. Under the state grants program of the Education Professions Development Act, federal funds may be used for the recruitment and training of teachers, both part-time and full-time, and this support can help substantially to correct the situation.

In spite of some difficulties, the pool of available and eager part-time teachers offers a rich resource for most communities. Their effectiveness will be greatest where they are considered as regular members of the faculty on a reduced teaching schedule, whether or not they teach in pairs, and whether or not they teach special courses, or subjects which have always been part of the school's curriculum.

Not only can the use of part-time teachers help alleviate the teacher shortage, but in most cases the character and quality of education can be significantly improved. And as for those teachers now in full-time service who are planning to leave work and raise families, the prospect of being able to come back and use their skills again, even on a part-time basis, is especially meaningful.

Perhaps the best marks given to part-time teaching came from a normally taciturn New England mother, who said, "The results have been outstanding socially and academically. This has been a superb educational experience for Susan." Then, somewhat taken aback by the extravagance of her praise, she paused and added, "I don't usually use words like that, but both my husband and I feel the same way."

From "Options in Public Education: The Quiet Revolution" by Vernon H. Smith

During recent years a new concept has emerged in public education. In many communities today students, parents, and teachers are accepting and even demanding options in public education. Alternative public schools are currently operating in several hundred communities in over 30 states and Canada. Many more communities are exploring, planning, and developing alternative public schools. These alternatives have developed with little or no communication with each other and without national or state coordination. They have not come as a response to educational crisis, but have been developed to meet specific needs within their local communities.

A few alternative public schools have captured the attention of the media—Philadelphia's Parkway, Chicago's Metro, Berkeley's 24 alternative schools. So much attention and publicity have been devoted to a few that they may be perceived as bizarre experiments, thereby concealing what Mario Fantini called in a recent speech "the only major movement in American education today."[1] Because each alternative has developed as a response to an individual community's educational concern rather than as a response by the mainstream of the profession to a concern for the national interest, the alternatives represent the first evolutionary thrust in public education at the grass-roots-level.

TYPES OF ALTERNATIVE SCHOOLS

What types of alternative public schools are in operation? The outline below suggests the variety.

Open Schools—with learning activities individualized and organized around interest centers within the classroom or building.

Schools Without Walls—with learning activities throughout the community and with much interaction between school and community.

Magnet Schools, Learning Centers, Educational Parks—with a concentration of learning resources in one center available to all of the students in the community.

Multicultural Schools, Bilingual Schools, Ethnic Schools—with emphasis on cultural pluralism and ethnic and racial awareness.

Street Academies, Dropout Centers, Pregnancy-Maternity Centers—with emphasis on learning programs for students in targeted populations.

Schools-Within-a-School—could be any of the above organized as a unit within a conventional school.

Integration Models—could be any of the above with a voluntary population that is representative in racial, ethnic, and socioeconomic class makeup of the total population of the community.

Free Schools—with emphasis on greater freedom for students and teachers. This term is usually applied to nonpublic alternatives, but a very few are operating within public school systems today.

WHAT THEY HAVE IN COMMON

While each alternative public school has been developed within its community in response to particular local needs, most of the alternatives share some or all of the following characteristics:

1. They provide options within public education for students, parents, and teachers. Usually these choices are open to all, but there must always be a choice for some so that the alternative schools have a voluntary clientele. There are many promising innovative schools throughout the country, but if there is no choice of schools within a community they cannot be included in alternative public schools as defined herein.

2. The alternative public schools have a commitment to be more responsive to some need within their communities than the conventional schools have been.

3. The alternatives usually have a more comprehensive set of goals and objectives than their conventional counterparts. While most alternatives are concerned with basic skills development and with college and vocational preparation, they are also concerned with the improvement of self-concept, the development of individual talent and uniqueness, the understanding and encouragement of cultural plurality and diversity, and

the preparation of students for various roles in our society—consumer, voter, critic, parent, spouse.

4. They are more flexible and therefore more responsive to planned evolution and change. Since they originated in today's scientific age, the alternatives have been designed to rely on feedback and formative evaluation as they develop and modify their programs.

5. The alternatives attempt to be more humane to students and teachers. Partly because they tend to be smaller than conventional schools, alternatives have fewer rules and bureaucratic constraints for students and teachers. In many cases the alternative has been designed to eliminate those aspects of the culture of the school which are most unpleasant and oppressive to its clientele.

From "Alternatives Within Public Schools" by Mario Fantini

Alternatives also enable a more humanistic process of education to evolve. Smaller structural units replace the mass production, factory-like nature of today's schooling. Education options assume their own sense of community. Both teacher and student assume a new identity as part of a common, often more personalized, social system.

The small size of alternatives, together with the right of choice, takes us a giant step closer to humanizing our public schools.

Expanding the framework of public education to include a wide range of legitimate educational alternatives seems the most feasible route to reforming our schools for the following basic reasons:

1. **Educationally**—The introduction of alternatives enhances the capacity of the school to tailor or individualize. Students can match themselves with a range of differing educational environments. If one is not compatible, there are others. Alternative schools adapt to the learner, not the other way around.

A teacher connects with the alternative that best enhances his style and talent. He is more nearly matched with students who prefer his approach. This should increase educational productivity, one of the major concerns of the American public at this time, and should reduce conflict between teachers, parents, and students.

Alternatives also have a renewing affect on the school as a major institution. That is, as certain alternatives prove to be more productive than others, they will be increasingly demanded. Other alternatives will be introduced as the less effective schools fail. Those that produce will be retained, triggering a continuous cycle of renewal.

Optional education gives priority to staff development, which is now clearly tied to helping professionals retool for "their" alternative.

Alternatives deal with the very substance of education. By creating a range of education environments, they also break down the impersonal system of education. Alternatives provide the basis for creating more intrinsic, humane units within our schools.

2. **Politically**—Alternatives reduce intra- and extra-institutional political conflict. Since alternatives are a matter of choice, none is imposed on any party—teacher, parents, or student. Further, since the rights of the **individual** (teacher, parents, student) are made salient by alternatives, group-oriented politics are reduced, e.g., the politics of parent bodies, teacher associations, etc. Since parents, teachers, and students connect by choice and together help develop the alternatives, a new spirit of cooperation can emerge. Consumer choice and satisfaction in alternatives respond directly to the call for educational accountability.

3. **Economically**—Alternatives do not depend on large inputs of additional money. Rather, they are based on a reutilization of existing resources. For example, existing teachers have more opportunities to regroup themselves according to the preferred alternatives. Space is utilized differently, as in schools-within-schools. Federal and state funding now used for compensatory, add-on programs can be converted for use as seed capital for alternative education.

From "Alternatives As Education"
by John Bremer

Perhaps the most important lessons to be learned from our recent past are that we can only survive through cooperation, through community, and that community cannot be based upon force, but only upon learning, upon the mutual respect that comes from public discussion of probabilities.

In spite of the size of societies, there is reason to hope. The media—radio and pre-eminently television—make possible a public place for the presentation of views and for the interchange of debate and discussion. The fact that the media are presently controlled by the very commercial interests whose values need to be subjected to scrutiny is only an interim phase. In the long run the media must be publicly controlled and will be. Congress and Parliament are not now public bodies deliberating about the common good but battlefields for pressure groups; nobody expects the common good to be promoted (or even mentioned) in such settings. But sooner or later the citizen feelings of disgust and impotency will vanish and the media will become a public meeting place, serving, in time, the function played in the ancient world by the agora and forum.

It is also becoming clearer that the politics of pressure groups, power politics, does not provide a satisfactory way for dealing with the real problems of society as a whole, and with this comes the realization that help lies in our capacity to weigh evidence, to judge character, to create value, and to decide accordingly. In other words, persuasion, if a kind of force, does invite the assent of the hearer. It is precisely this assent that defines the minimal freedom in any political situation. Audiences can still be seduced, of course, but they cannot be raped, although they can still suffer from the effects of an earlier encounter.

Education, mirroring society as it does, has tended more and more to the use of overt force and control in its attempt to renew society by the preparation of the young. The structure of society must be imposed upon by the young, since it is not believed that society could attract them by its beauty and justice, and this belief is probably correct. Unfortunately, even when control is successful, we fail, because society cannot be maintained by force. There are never enough guards. **Quis custodiet ipsos custodes?** (Who will guard the guards)? All governance is built upon trust, and trust cannot survive in a tyranny. Or, as a cynical politician once remarked, you can do everything with bayonets except sit on them.

I am often asked whether I approve of compulsory education, and I usually reply that I do and that I wish we had it; we only have compulsory attendance. It would be folly for our society to give up the notion of compulsory education, which is presumably what was in mind when attendance was required, but the compulsory nature of the enterprise lays a strong moral obligation upon society, upon educators. For, if a student comes initially because he must, he should continue to come because he benefits, and, if the benefit is not felt, then the educational program (not the student) needs adjustment. It should be added that being in an educational program is not necessarily the same as being in school. Perhaps it would be a safe rule that after the requirements that education take place, and that learning take place, no further absolute regulation should be imposed. This would entail the provision of alternatives and the creation of means by which students could create more alternatives. Every student would be expected to choose his learning pattern, with obvious beneficial results on motivation. Of course it will be said that students do not know how to choose, and this is often correct; but the consequence to be drawn is not that the professional educator should make the decision but rather that we have identified a learning area for the student. He must learn how to choose. But he will make mistakes, you say. Of course he will, because he is learning and is not pretending to be omniscient. But an educational mistake is merely something from which we did not learn. The student cannot learn anything except obedience from following the orders of another (whether those orders are correct or mistaken), but he will learn from carrying out his own decisions (again, whether correct or mistaken). The student must learn how to be free, which involves choosing from among alternatives, and he must learn to be responsible for his choice, which is the sign of maturity. However, it should be emphasized that the consequences of a choice must be determined by the nature of the choice and the circumstances in which it was made, and not artificially by the educator. Accountability is intrinsic, not extrinsic.

As the student learns how to choose, his choices will become more and more complex, involving more and more people. His choices are no longer about his own individual learning, but also about the human context in which it takes place and about the social consequences of his learning. In short, he becomes more political, and he will have to learn to discuss and debate, to persuade and to be persuaded; and as he does this, he will learn to live in a world of probabilities, in a world in which opinion (not claimed omniscience or force) is to be respected. He will learn that certainty is chimerical, that he can only consider the probabilities, and then, living with his doubts, choose to act upon the best opinion, holding himself responsible for the outcome. He will also learn to safeguard the freedom which enables him to choose, to keep it pure and uncorrupted, lest he become a mere commodity to be bought and sold.

It would be easy to justify this from a humanistic point of view, in terms of what it does for the individual student. What it does for society is what makes it so important, however; for survival depends upon the widespread existence of decision-making powers throughout society. But we learn how to make decisions by making decisions, and to make decisions requires the existence of alternatives, and it is thus that we must come to see alternatives as education.

BERKELEY EXPERIMENTAL SCHOOLS
by Diane Divoky

The world's biggest Afro whizzes by on a ten-speed bike. A skate-boarder figure-eights his way down the street, and a frizzy-headed woman in white opaque pajamas tries to hitch a ride. Other hitchhikers stand, sit, and lie near the intersection, holding signs asking to be taken to Oregon, Texas, Maine, East—anywhere. I'm on University Avenue, heading into Berkeley, California. I park for a look around. Over an old poster of a smiling black politician, words have been scrawled in lipstick: "Tom, outrageous Tom." Back in my car I find fistfuls of handbills stuck under the wipers: "Support African Liberation Day," "Protest GM and ITT's involvement in South Africa." "Sign up for a new alternative school, family and community-oriented—multi-ethnic. . . ."

Berkeley, California, pop. 116,716. Berkeley, California, pop. white university professors and white dropouts, black welfare mothers and black executives, superfreaks and superstraights. Once home of the Free Speech Movement, the Yippies, the People's Park. Still home of the University of California—probably the best public system of higher education in the world. In the rich and pretty hills overlooking San Francisco Bay, Berkeley has many fine homes and one of the nation's first cyclotrons. Down in the flatlands of the Bay shore it has a new participatory politics that works, sometimes—an elected City Council that on some issues fields a radical majority.

Berkeley: It's different here, some say. Berkeley's public schools—45 per cent black, 44 per cent white, and 11 percent Chicano and Asian—sure are different. The system was desegregated, voluntarily, a full four years ago when 3,550 elementary school pupils were bused all over town (SR, Dec. 21, 1968). Today, the schools thrive on variety and controversy. Where else could one group of parents charge that Snow White is a racist story, while another argues that a Malcolm X comic book is sexist? This fall the Berkeley public schools are probably the most diverse and experimental in the country.

Most of Berkeley's experimental schools got under way last year as part of a five-year project sponsored by the U.S. Office of Education, although the Ford Foundation had started underwriting some alternative schools a few years before that. The federal Experimental Schools

Project also made grants to school systems in Tacoma, Washington (to test individualized instruction), and in Minneapolis, Minnesota (to test autonomous administration), but the Berkeley project—designed to challenge all the old assumptions about how public schools operate—is by far the most ambitious. "It's everything you always wanted to know about change but were afraid to ask," says Richard L. Foster, Berkeley's superintendent of schools.

The experiment in Berkeley centers on twenty-four alternative public schools. All told, they enroll approximately 4,000 elementary and secondary school students—more than one-fourth of the city's entire school population. Some of the new alternative schools are on the grounds of the regular public schools; others are in former factories, homes, churches, and storefronts. Some are deliberately intimate, with a limit of fifty students; others are larger than the traditional schools from which they've drawn their students. Some emphasize multicultural studies; others are racially exclusive. In some, parents are required to participate; in others, they aren't even courted. All twenty-four experimental schools, however, say that they share two priorities: the elimination of institutional racism and the delivery of basic academic skills.

Whatever the neat phrases mean, they capsule Berkeley's heightened sensitivity about race. In the school system, it seems, every act has racial implications. When ten out of eleven students signing up for dramatics group at one experimental elementary school are white, the staff grows a bit edgy: Why don't the black students want to participate? At another alternative school the black principal notes that white parents feel free to criticize white teachers but make no comment about a weak black teacher. The very alternative schools that were designed for alienated white students anguish over their inability to attract blacks.

The fact of race overrides considerations of social class, economic status, and individual differences. It also created a new set of stereotypes, peculiar to Berkeley. If a white is on welfare, it must be "by choice." On the other hand, a black teacher, a third generation of college-educated bourgeoisie, describes herself as "just another Third World person."

The day before a school holiday to honor Malcolm X, thousands of black and white elementary school pupils—from both the experimental and the traditional schools—come to the high school theater for a special program. Inside the huge, darkened auditorium a man in a green dashiki introduces an ensemble of black fourth-, fifth-, and sixth-graders who play African drums. With none of the awkwardness common to most elementary school performers, they start to play. They are very good; rhythm flows through the audience.

The master of ceremonies takes over. With some contempt he says that white girls have to go to finishing schools to become ladies and learn how to walk, while black African girls have a natural, graceful walk because they must balance heavy loads on their heads.

After another drum number he introduces the audience-participation section of the program, explaining that an audience simply listening to a performance is a white, European kind of entertainment, while in African entertainment everyone joins in. He leads the audience through a fast-moving chant. After each phrase the kids shout "black" louder and louder, sassier and sassier.

Whatever their success in living up to their labels, Berkeley's alternative elementary schools are brighter, more intense, more interesting institutions than the "experimental schools" in most other communities. The hall displays, for example, include photographs taken by students, pictures illustrating a spring dream ("I wish to be a horse, and kind, and a sun"), stories of a field trip ("Tripping to Santa Cruz"). Teachers have the sophistication to provide all kinds of materials—records of Leadbelly wailing and Indians whooping, chemistry kits and origami packages, terrariums and tape recorders, Spanish readers and science centers. In Berkeley it's all there. Last spring I visited most of the experimental schools. Here are some impressions—and some tentative conclusions—about them:

JOHN MUIR: So many parents opted for the open classroom alternatives in John Muir's lovely, old Tudor-style building that only a few rooms remain organized in the traditional way. Outside, in the playground, a young black man in tight, purple pants and a felt hat closes down a recess basketball game: "Okay, you guys, back to class." Inside, students go about their business in classroom after classroom—reading, cooking, drawing, measuring, counting, typing, pounding, painting, using clay and dictionaries and aquariums and blueprints and counting rods and workbooks. In a bungalow the primary students do a spontaneous choral reading for the visitors.

LINCOLN: This is the home of the Environmental Studies Program, an alternative for some 200 fourth-through-sixth-graders with a predominantly black staff. The school is trying out trips to the beach, explorations in the community, music, dance, karate, dramatics, photography, almost anything, to get "unteachable" kids to learn.

"We get pushouts and lots of problem kids," says Mrs. Robbie Burke, the mother of six who has been with the alternative for a year. "We get Johnny already turned off by school. We let him act out, if it's not destructive to other students. But there are no sympathy trips. We expect as much from black kids as from whites, and we keep a tight watch on progress. If Johnny's folder shows he's not doing long division now, and two weeks from now he's still not doing it, we talk to the teacher and then deal with it at the staff meeting.

"The rewards are very small—maybe just a child completing a paper or smiling some morning. With one child, who came here very withdrawn and scared, my reward was watching the first time he went up and punched another boy. I was well pleased."

The assignments can be unusual, too. In one math project a student wrote the school superintendent to find out why he earned more than a teacher.

KILIMANJARO: If Berkeley has a counterculture elementary school, Kilimanjaro—in a residential area just north of the university campus—is it. The buildings are being removed by the People's

Architects. The school, limited to fifty elementary pupils, attracts white "welfare-by-choice" parents.

Michael Cohen, Kilimanjaro's co-director, greets visitors in the school's charmingly scruffy basement office, wearing a thermal undershirt. "There is a strong contingent of single mothers," he says. (To indicate diversity in the student body, teachers point to one student whose father works in the post office.)

The school is run by parents, and all decisions are made by consensus. There are no attendance rules, no grades. Kilimanjaro began with a rule that all parents had to participate five hours a week, but this proved unrealistic. So did a nonstructured approach. "The kids ran around and screamed for three months," Cohen says, "and then they and their parents requested more structure."

The curriculum is heavy on crafts, humanizing, and physical contact. "Sometimes I'm a human tree," Cohen says. A few moments later kids came into the room through windows and doors to hug a teacher or sit on her lap.

The staff believes that basics—such as reading —depend not so much on methods or materials as on a child's sense of himself. "Reading has to do with the environment and self-concept," Cohen says. "I never knew a kid who couldn't learn to read if he believed he was worth something."

A boy, the kind of tense fidgeter who is labeled disruptive in many schools, breaks up a math game that three girls are playing and announces, "I want to stay in here and make trouble." Cohen takes him away. Elsewhere a handful of kids work on individual projects, but others seem to be roaming around, looking for something to do.

Most of the alternatives for high school students are at Berkeley High—a massive institution with 3,000 students, including 1,200 enrolled in one or another of the six alternative schools on its six-block campus. Three of these are: Model A, which emphasizes basic skills; On Target, geared to "job awareness experiences"; and the School of the Arts, heavy on drama, music, and dance. The others:

COMMUNITY HIGH (GENESIS): Actually, Community High started three years ago—before the federal experimental schools program—as a free-flowing school for middle-class kids who were turned off by the routine and impersonalization of the big high school. José Romero, its former director, says it "was founded with the idea of lots of humanization and personal contact. It was the school with the flower power staff, the Spock generation of teachers. It worked for a few years, but it's a long shot from working now. Staffs have come and gone. The new black staff has provoked the black kids, helped polarize all the students, and the whites are overcompensating. The racial thing still isn't worked out. The tribes—the working units of students—dissolved, and everything's at a point of real apathy."

Last spring the vibes around Community High no longer felt right to many people in Berkeley, and they wondered how long it would take for things to change. Why should there be a school for alienated white kids when black kids still aren't learning to read? Is there something wrong with a school that suits whites better than blacks? The good feelings about free schools and kids doing their own thing that flowered in the late Sixties made Community High an exciting proposition three years ago; now it is worried about finances and racial balance and motives.

At a staff meeting a black student representative asks that the school's name be changed from Community High to Genesis. The motion carries with no discussion. The student then puts in his own name as director of the school for the coming year; the self-nomination is accepted. Then the real business at hand gets under way—money and autonomy. Because of a budget cut at Berkeley High, Community High is faced with cutting its staff from eight to three teachers.

"The more we compromise, the more we become a department of Berkeley High and not an alternative school."

"Maybe we should go up to 225 students, if we can get enough blacks."

"Who's going to recruit?"

The talk is tired, and over the room hangs the question of whether Community High will—or should—continue to exist. Some students explain that they will return to Berkeley High this fall.

"Going to Community High involves more of a commitment than going to the regular school," says one, "but not enough people will make that commitment. I've decided that school is something I just want to get through."

A black student defends Community High's approach. "Here you learn what's really going on, and teachers and students learn from each other. They don't treat you like a child, and they don't grade as hard." But a girl, about to graduate after two years at Community High, has some reservations. "I can't stand classes where the teacher comes in and asks the students what they want to do," she says. "They're supposed to have the expertise. My best class here was the most formal. I used to think kids could learn without structure or pressure, but I don't anymore."

AGORA: Designed to teach an appreciation of racial differences, Agora keeps its staff and enrollment balanced at one-quarter each white, black, Chicano, and Asian, promising a structured multicultural experience for its 120 students. The courses run from Egyptian hieroglyphics to sailing but all carry an overlay of cross-cultural studies. Each student, as part of a class that is racially mixed, is required to take four sections of multicultural experience, each from the perspective of one of the four racial groups and taught by an instructor of that race. At the end of the rotation the students go off in separate racial groups to evaluate the courses freely, and then come together again for an integrated evaluation.

The black and Chicano courses, according to some staff members, have fared better than the others. In fact, Agora has emphasized black and Chicano unity, showing how the two groups have been pitted against each other in the past, and how the similarities between them might be used for cooperation. "We've really been getting Third World people together, academically and socially," a teacher says.

Not surprisingly, the white multicultural courses such as "white psyche" have turned into heavy guilt trips for many white students. So now the teacher of the white studies courses tries to use materials that show that whites, too, can be down-and-out (readings on immigrants), isolated (Appalachia), and tortured (**Death of a Salesman**). COLLEGE PREP: Started in the middle of last year for 150 students (almost all black), College Prep carries a firm structure—and imparts even firmer basic skills to students who have the ability to go on to college but probably wouldn't get there without some extra help. It enrolls tenth through twelfth graders, and is designed to motivate, counsel, and drill them on to higher education.

Ronald Fortune, College Prep's young black director, talks about teaching kids what he calls "college survival skills"—how to take standardized tests, use reference materials, study. A set of review notes are part of the program, he says, so students will know how to pass a test on Shakespeare, for example, without actually having to read very much Shakespeare. The content of the curriculum is fairly traditional, but it is taught from an "Afro-American oriented approach."

WEST CAMPUS WORK STUDY: Here, Director Arnold Lockley holds the hands of fifty or more ninth-graders who already are in trouble. He finds the losers, the dropouts, the pushouts, the first offenders at Juvenile Hall and offers them a half-time school program, gets jobs for them in the afternoons, and, in effect, shadows their lives.

"We do a kind of brainwashing here," says Lockley, a black former science teacher. "We tell the kids we don't want to hear about their past; we want them to take each day one at a time. But there will be no excuses here. They have to be in class, every day, every period, and they have to be polite. If a kid's having a problem in a class, we go and sit through it with him. If a teacher's ripping him off, we'll move him out. But we push the kids. We come down on them now rather than have them get killed two years from now. And they will get killed, the way they're going when we get them. Right now eleven of our kids aren't making it, but eleven others are on the honor roll."

EAST CAMPUS: Started five years ago when a group of liberal teachers decided to remodel what used to be merely a continuation school, East Campus now is one of the system's most stable alternatives, offering students a last chance to pick up a diploma. East Campus is housed in an airy mesh of sunny classrooms and raised outdoor runways across town from Berkeley High.

On one ramp two students are locked in a dramatic embrace as others move by to classes. In an English class two boys earnestly debate whether the right clothes can get someone a job as a **Playboy** photographer. Next door students read paperbacks silently until Tom Parker, the director, enters with visitors. "Who didya bring, Uncle Tom, the FBI?" asks a bereted student. Much laughter and shouting. East Campus students must enroll voluntarily—and there is a waiting list. The program emphasizes individualized work on basic skills. Students must go to class—or face dismissal. "Kids can't get away with jiving or running down games like they did at other schools," Parker says.

CASA DE LA RAZA: At first glance Casa seems the shabbiest of the alternatives. Classes are held in a series of old wooden sheds at the far end of a stark parking lot behind a junior high school. But some of Casa's 150 Chicano students, as part of an Aztec art project, have painted joyful revolutionary scenes and slogans on a high fence outside the bungalows. The two outdoor toilets have been covered with red, white, and blue stars and labeled, "This is America." Inside, Casa has a sense of humor, a warm camaraderie that flows through the school; indeed, Casa has a reputation in Berkeley as a warm, child-oriented, Chicano-flavored open school that is particularly strong at the primary level. (It houses pupils from kindergarten through the twelfth grade.)

Casa, a family-style bilingual institution, is run by a parent-teacher-student governing board; it is open all year. At the start of summer school a film teacher, taking some time off from Stanford, greets mothers coming to register their children. The science teacher arrives with an armful of material, eager to explain his program—the telescope and rockets students have made, the laser in progress, the kitchen physics, the ham radio, the Mayan and Aztec astronomy, the "whole bunch of electronics projects" the kids have completed. Whatever its exterior, a lot is going on inside Casa.

BLACK HOUSE: While Casa is open only to Latinos, Black House is open only to blacks. As a result, both institutions are in constant negotiations with the U.S. Office of Education about possible violations of the Civil Rights Act. Its teachers are all black, its courses are taught from "the black perspective." Horace Upshaw, the bearded, young black director of Black House, says its goal is to make its sixty students "responsible to the black community."

It is difficult to learn what is happening in Black House; representatives of the "white media" are not allowed in. Second-hand reports indicate that the classroom style is traditional, except that the guiding philosophy is that the teacher himself is the course and not just a conveyor of information.

The style of Black House—a racial consciousness raising, an independent assertion of identity —holds a good deal of appeal to other minority people in Berkeley. Another alternative school, Black Perspective, has opened along the lines of Black House, but with enrollment open to all races. The Marcus Garvey Institute, which author-teacher Herb Kohl started several years ago as Other Ways, has become overwhelmingly black in enrollment and tone, and has become a "survival center" next to Black House. An all-Asian school, New Ark, also has emerged. Now New Ark, Black House, Odyssey House—a multiracial alternative for junior high kids—and Casa have combined in a loose federation to try to satisfy civil rights requirements. But separatism seems to be a growing phenomenon in Berkeley.

At a central staff meeting for all of Berkeley's experimental schools, people are talking—with deep feeling—about how they are going to talk to each other. Define, lay it out, replay, communicate, rap, respond, relate. Input, output, dynamics, data, structure, restructure, manage, organize, implement. The language of computers straining to make sense in the ill-defined world of children and learning. Finally, the decision about a staff crisis falls to Larry Wells, director of the experimental schools project. Silence holds the room as everyone waits for his opinion. "My honest response is a nonresponse," he says with great seriousness. Why can't anyone in Berkeley say

he doesn't know the answer?

It is difficult for anyone to find the answers in Berkeley. Technically, the experimental schools are a research model, not a demonstration project. The U.S. Office of Education has awarded a $748,000 "out-of-house" grant for an evaluation of the Berkeley schools due next year.

After only one year the existential questions are still coming: How can you test uniqueness? What is progress? What is success? What do you test? Five alternative schools—the ones committed to delivering basic skills—flatly refuse to use any standardized tests on their students, saying the tests are racist, culturally biased, and/or inconsequential. As replacements, they offer alternative instruments such as teacher evaluations, attitudinal surveys, and audio tapes.

The Experimental School staff has formed an evaluation team to devise some tests to measure the delivery of skills. But even they are having trouble with Berkeley's ambiguity. "No one here will agree on what basic skills are," says one researcher. "For some people it means reading well enough to get a job. For others it means reading well enough to understand Frantz Fanon." And any evaluation of a school system that is changing as fast as Berkeley's is delicate at best. "We're trying to paint a moving train in about four colors," says another staffer. "And suddenly we're on the train, not in the railroad station."

In Washington, Cynthia Parsons, program director for Berkeley's experimental schools in the U.S. Office of Education, will buy none of the line that Berkeley is a unique place. "In spite of its hip educational image," she says, "the Berkeley public school system is like any other. It's a big mess. The poor old system reflects the rest of the country. It doesn't teach minority kids as well as it teaches middle-class kids.

"Once you cut through the verbiage, the experiment is relatively uncomplicated. Can you give parents and students a clear, viable choice of schooling? We've asked them to select certain experimental schools that they'll really test over the next four years. I don't blame the schools for having problems living up to their rhetoric. They've made grandiose claims, and yet in new situations people tend to do what they were taught in the past. There's a real gap between the rhetoric and the ability to deliver. But they've got four years."

At the end of June Berkeley's experimental school staff submitted a progress report to the Office of Education. It listed nine ways the alternative schools had positively affected the local school system, but more than balanced them by also listing twenty-eight problems—ranging from frustration, intolerance, inflexibility, and paranoia to lack of community information and teaching materials. Every problem that school people could find to complain about was laid out, plus some that only school people in Berkeley could find.

By contrast, consider the experimental school project in Tacoma in which everything is neat, controlled, predictable. Tacoma isn't going to make any big mistakes, and Berkeley is making them all the time. But Tacoma isn't asking any of the big questions either and isn't likely to make a major change.

For all its rhetoric and self-importance, Berkeley is bold enough to question a lot of the assumptions that have kept American public schools going for so many years. Berkeley is looking for a new direction—and some better answers. It isn't going to find all of them in the next four years. But if it finds a few, it will be way ahead of the same old game the public schools are playing out for children in most other cities.

From "The Schools and Equal Opportunity" by Mary Jo Bane and Christopher Jencks

Implications for Educational Policy

These findings imply that school reform is never likely to have any significant effect on the degree of inequality among adults. This suggests that the prevalent "factory" model, in which schools are seen as places that "produce" alumni, probably ought to be abandoned. It is true that schools have "inputs" and "outputs," and that one of their nominal purposes is to take human "raw material" (**i.e.,** children) and convert it into something more "useful" (**i.e.,** employable adults). Our research suggests, however, that the character of a school's output depends largely on a single input, the characteristics of the entering children. Everything else—the school budget, its policies, the characteristics of the teachers—is either secondary or completely irrelevant, at least so long as the range of variation among schools is as narrow as it seems to be in America.

These findings have convinced us that the long-term effects of schooling are relatively uniform. The day-to-day internal life of the schools, in contrast, is highly variable. It follows that **the primary basis for evaluating a school should be whether the students and teachers find it a satisfying place to be.** This does not mean we think schools should be like mediocre summer camps, in which children are kept out of trouble but not taught anything. We doubt that a school can be enjoyable for either adults or children unless the children keep learning new things. We value ideas and the life of the mind, and we think that a school that does not value these things is a poor place for children. But a school that values ideas because they enrich the lives of children is quite different from a school that values high reading scores because reading scores are important for adult success.

Our concern with making schools satisfying places for teachers and children has led us to a concern for diversity and choice. People have widely different notions of what a "satisfying" place is, and we believe they ought to be able to put these values into practice. As we have noted, our research suggests that none of the programs or structural arrangements in common use today has consistently different long-term effects from any other. Since the character of a child's schooling has few long-term effects, and since these effects are quite unpredictable, society has little reason to constrain the choices available to parents and children. If a "good school" is one the students and staff find satisfying, no one school will be best for everyone. Since there is no evidence that professional educators know appreciably more than parents about what is good for children, it seems reasonable to let parents decide what kind of education their children should have while they are young and to let the children decide as they get older.

HANSEL AND GRETEL by Arthur Pearl

Hansel and Gretel lived with their father, Fred, and stepmother, Mary, in a neat little suburb where houses looked much like each other and lawns were well manicured and dogs were big, friendly, and obedient—which was more than could be said of the children! Hansel and Gretel's father wasn't poor; he had a good job that required his presence five days a week for eight hours a day, and he worked very hard, and he had his own secretary and a key to the men's room and was on a cordial first-name relationship with the vice-president.

Unfortunately, however, he owed everybody money. The nice, neat, manicured house he lived in would be paid for after 303 more easy payments. His first wife agreed to be warm, friendly, and cordial; in exchange she received a sizable portion of his monthly check. The new car he drove would be his in thirty-one more payments; the old car his wife drove would be his in seven more payments (but it was getting pretty run-down and would probably run out before he could claim it). But money wasn't his biggest problem—Hansel and Gretel were. They did not like school. It was dull, irrelevant, dreary, and dumb. Hansel's teacher was "icky"; Gretel's was downright mean. As a result, the children grew distant, hostile, moody, unhappy, and even got into trouble. But Hansel and Gretel's stepmother was young, together, and hip. She was not caught up in "things"—she wasn't trapped by middle-class values.

So one day she came home with some terrific news. She had discovered an alternative school —a school deep in the woods where exciting things occurred. There were ecological projects in the wilderness; there were art and music and theater and rap sessions; it was a place where children made things and went on field trips. She asked the children, would they like to go there? Hansel and Gretel were insistent, and they promised everything—they even promised to be good if they were allowed to go to the new, exciting alternative school. That night, after Hansel and Gretel went to bed, Fred and Mary talked about the new school. Fred protested, and the more Fred protested, the more Mary insisted. Fred said it cost too much money and, second, it seemed like giving in to the children and, third, he was afraid of such a loose, permissive place. But Mary was persuasive and pointed out that the children were not doing well in traditional school and if they kept it up they were going to get into serious trouble, and Fred finally agreed.

So early the very next morning Mary, Hansel, and Gretel drove to the new school. It was exciting! "Wow!" said Hansel; "Far out!" said Gretel. The school was tucked into a lovely little setting of woods surrounded by wild flowers, and while it was made of redwood, it looked like it was made of gingerbread, cake, and sugar. Children were running inside and outside, and teachers were running with them, and everybody looked like they were happy. Above the door of the new school was inscribed the motto: "Man was born free, and everywhere he is in chains." "Wow!" said Hansel; "Far out!" said Gretel. The children walked into the office of the headmaster, whose name was Thomas Superwitch, who welcomed the children by saying that he was "Tom," and he told the children, as he sat on the corner of his desk and puffed on his pipe, about the philosophy of the school. "This school is for you to have fun, and all your teachers are here to be your friends and help you have fun. There are no tests, no grades, no lectures—students can do almost anything they want." "Far out!" said Hansel; "Wow!" said Gretel. Hansel and Gretel were then introduced to one of their teachers, John Holtwitch—who told them to call him "John," and they did. And John said, "What would you like to do? The one thing we want you to know here is that there is no way you can fail—there is no way anybody can fail—so what do you want to do?" So Hansel and Gretel said that they would like to go out there and play with the sheep and milk the yak and do all the wonderful things that other kids were doing out in the yard. And John said, "Fine." He said, "Anything you want to do is fine with me as long as you don't hurt yourself and don't hurt others." And they promised they wouldn't hurt anybody, and off they ran to join the others. Hansel and Gretel thought they were in paradise. They thought the desks they sat in were just like soft, feathery beds to sleep in and the classes every morning to every afternoon were just like having creamy milk to drink and rosy apples and honey cake to eat. And John Holt-witch seemed to want them to eat and think and do good things, and he would never accept any thanks. He said, "You please me best if you do as much of what you like and as much of what you want to do. There is nothing I like better than to see happy little boys and happy little girls."

And Hansel and Gretel would go home and tell their parents about the great school, and they would bring back various little things that they had made, and they would talk about the rap sessions they had had about Vietnam and racism and things like that. And they would talk about the plays they had been in, and even Fred had to admit that the school seemed like a good thing, and everything seemed to be going well, and the fact that he had found a peculiar little wrinkled, brown cigarette-looking thing in Hansel's room didn't bother him too much, and the fact that Gretel seemed to be a little bit more distant and a little bit all wrapped up in herself more than she used to be didn't bother him too much because they weren't getting into trouble. And the fact that the school was maybe a little expensive didn't bother him too much because they weren't getting into trouble.

John was not the only teacher they had. **All** of the teachers turned them on—which was their sole criterion for teaching excellence (more and more in their own eyes Hansel and Gretel became electrical appliances). They talked about the other teachers—Neal Postwitch, who pointed out they didn't have to read. He was a "heavy dude," said Hansel. "For sure," said Gretel. There was George Denniwitch, who said that they didn't have to think about the future. He was a "heavy dude," said Gretel. "Really," said Hansel. There was yet another "heavy dude"—Bill Glasswitch, who turned them on because he said, "Humans are

role-oriented, not goal-oriented," and had them sit in circles and discuss "heavy" things. And finally there was Ivan Illwitch, who said that there should be no schools at all, and he was a "very heavy dude," said Hansel and Gretel. "For sure," said Mary. And Fred said, "I have a headache," and went to bed—but it was worth it because the children didn't get in trouble.

Finally, the time came for graduation—what excitement, what joy, what a different kind of graduation!—students wore what they liked, and you never saw such an array of color and variety of clothes. The stage, where the children were garlanded with flowers, mostly wild, plucked from their natural origins near and not far from the school itself—and the smell of the flowers blended neatly with the aroma of those funny, brown cigarettes that most of the children smoked more openly now (and that made them somewhat different from kids in regular schools, who still did those kind of things clandestinely). And although they were aware that they were violating the law, they didn't care because unjust laws did not need to be obeyed—and that was only one thing that they had learned at school.

Then came the final moment, and Tom Super-witch turned them on for the very last time—he recounted the great times that they had had together; he rode on excitedly with nostalgic metaphor, and they encouraged him in choruses of "ride on," and Hansel and Gretel rode on to attack the real world—of work, politics, leisure, culture, and personal encounters.

But they didn't go to work—work was dull, work was wrapped up with a "Protestant ethic" and middle-class values, work was a "rat race of bureaucracy," and, besides, work just helped the wealthy get wealthier. They didn't mind work, you understand, and if a good job came along, which turned them on and fulfilled them, they would take it in a minute. In the meantime they needed very little money, except for records and a subscription to **Rolling Stone** and organic foods and leather things and, of course, tickets to flicks and concerts. (Fred's headaches seemed to be getting worse, and even Mary's patience was wearing thin.)

Hansel and Gretel were political—make no mistake about that; they marched, they baited policemen, they chanted slogans and demonstrated (although, in truth, there were not too many demonstrations any more). They were too sophisticated for traditional politics—they weren't going to be sucked into supporting "bourgeois" liberals—and while they were as pure and uncorrupted as the organic food they ate, Presidents continued to preside, governors to govern, and legislators to legislate. And thus it was that even more hundreds of billions of dollars were appropriated for defense, taxes were paid by the poor to support the profit-making activities of the rich, the nonwhites (with whom Hansel and Gretel identified through concerned inactivity) continued to receive less than their fair share at home and abroad, and the environment that Hansel and Gretel loved continued to deteriorate.

In culture and leisure Hansel and Gretel, for all their school involvement, found little to enjoy. They strummed their guitars less and less; they dabbled with paints almost never at all. They never learned that hard work was important if one were ever to master anything.

They weren't good company either. They didn't like very many people, and not very many people liked them. They tended to be dull, self-centered, remote, and ill-tempered. They didn't belong to anything; they didn't contribute to anything.

And so it was that when Hansel and Gretel entered the real world, they were eaten up.

There is, however, something more to be said. Hansel and Gretel's counterparts—the children who stayed in regular schools—didn't fare too well either: they, too, found work adjustment difficult; they, too, were politically impotent; they, too, failed to contribute to cultural activities; they too, had difficulty in belonging, contributing, and feeling competent.

And the parents of Hansel and Gretel and the parents of the children who went to regular schools—they, too, weren't doing too well. They, too, found work adjustment difficult; they, too, were politically impotent; they, too, failed to contribute culturally; and they, too, had difficulty belonging, contributing, and feeling competent.

So there you have it. Children educated in both traditional and open schools, and their parents, end up much the same. There must be a moral there someplace.

OPENERS
FOR TEACHERS

Closed door ————————→ open doors

    Closed-circuit learning————————→ series learning (one thing leads to another)

       Closed-room arrangement ————————→ many kinds of arrangements

       Closed-teaching style ————————————→ many styles of teaching
          (your collection + all your children)

1 room ————→ entire school

   1 text ————→ many resources

     1 answer ————→ many possible answers

       1 kind of evaluation ————————→ many varieties of evaluations

1 grade level ————→ nongraded learning

   3 groups in reading ————→ grouping for specific goal

1 teacher ————→ many teachers

   1 kind of education ————————→ great divergency with convergent thinking toward
       goals for the good of society

CHAPTER EIGHT

Humanizing

From *The People, Yes* by Carl Sandburg

(From Section 107)

The people will live on.
The learning and blundering people will live on.
They will be tricked and sold and again sold
And go back to the nourishing earth for rootholds,
The people so peculiar in renewal and comeback,
You can't laugh off their capacity to take it.
The mammoth rests between his cyclonic dramas. . . .

This old anvil laughs at many broken hammers.
There are men who can't be bought.
The fireborn are at home in fire.
The stars make no noise.
You can't hinder the wind from blowing.
Time is a great teacher.
Who can live without hope?

In darkness with a great bundle of grief the people
     march.
In the night, and overhead a shovel of stars for keeps,
     the people march:
                              "Where to? what next?"

Man's inhumanity to man makes countless thousands mourn.

From "Man Was Made To Mourn,"
by Robert Burns

A person
who is alien to
some part of himself
is
invariably
separated from anyone
who represents that alien part.

—Esalen

In its highest sense, humanizing is a feeling that a teacher has when he looks at a student and thinks, "I believe in the perfectibility of this student and since I care for him, I will help him to grow toward the full potential of his being while I am his teacher."

From "Humanizing The Social Studies In the Elementary School," by Max Poole

---

The message is clear: schools can be centers for human development if schools are willing to accept the challenge of humaneness.

—Donald H. Eichhorn

A fool must now and then be right, by chance.

From **Conversation** by William Cooper

Once the idea is accepted that the student is, to use one principal's words, "a Product," then we cease to consider students as human beings. When they are to become "products" we can then shape them to our own liking, our whim, in short, to be just like us. We are training good Russians but not good Americans. We are teaching for conformity, sameness and as Silberman titles one chapter, "Education for Docility." If this is realized our schools finally begin to make sense and the absolute cruelty and personal destruction which must follow falls into a logical pattern.

From "Is There A Chance For Your Child?—Creative, Open Classrooms,"
by David N. Campbell

Students are citizens . . . They already have all the rights that older people do, and the burden of proof is on us if we take away any of those rights because students are "immature."

—Delmo Della-Dora

While we value change, we often seem more receptive to changes in the technological realm than in the realm of personal values and social relationships.

From **A Man For Tomorrow's World** (ASCD 1970)

Activities for Humanization

Every time you plan to use someone's language other than yours and the children's with whom you are working,

S T O P — Think! ! !

Would it be more humane to use your own language patterns or theirs?

Every time you plan to use math problems written by someone else,

S T O P — Think! ! !

Would it be more humane to write (with the children) your own, relevant math problems?

Every time you plan to test the children on someone else's ideas,

S T O P — Think! ! !

Would it be more humane to evaluate the children's own ideas in light of their own experiences and then help them transfer these ideas to others' experiences?

Erik Erikson's characteristics formulated for Julian Huxley's **Humanist Frame:**

Basic Trust vs Basic Mistrust: Drive and Hope
Autonomy vs Shame and Doubt: Self-Control and Willpower
Initiative vs Guilt: Direction and Purpose
Industry vs Inferiority: Method and Competence
Identity vs Role Confusion: Devotion and Fidelity
Intimacy vs Isolation: Affiliation and Love
Generativity vs Stagnation: Production and Care
Ego Integrity vs Despair: Renunciation and Wisdom

These are the strengths which emerge from a favorable ratio for each of the psycho-social stages.

Erik Erikson, **Childhood and Society,** 2nd Ed. (N.Y.: W. W. Norton & Co., 1963) p. 274

These emerging strengths constitute a healthy personality and are essential for a happy productive life. It is not only psychoanalysts who are concerned with a healthy personality characterized by hope, competence, devotion, and wisdom, but any humanist or educator.

From "Curriculum Development from a Psychoanalytic Perspective," by Louise L. Tyler in **The Educational Forum**, 36 (January 1972): 173-79.

The child learns who he is from what happens to him,
    from the language that surrounds him,
    from the people who are dear to him,
    from the opportunities to deal with the objects and events in his immediate world
        and
    from his own responses to the welter of stimuli.
His self-esteem represents his unique organization of his own biological make-up,
    the evaluation made of him by significant adults,
        and
    his own learning from trial and manipulation
        and
    feedback from his world.
Cognitive development is inseparable from personality development.

From "The Beginnings of the Self: The Problems of the Nurturing Environment," by Ira Gordon

---

No printed word or spoken plea
Can teach young minds what men should be,
Not all the books on all the shelves
But what the teachers are themselves.

          —Anonymous

SCENE: The entire group gathered for discussion.

TONY: I'd like to ask each of us to take time to jot down one or two of the most humane experiences each of us has ever had in school. Then I would like for us to jot down words or phrases that indicate some dehumanizing experiences.

HERB: Tony, don't you think a lot of what some authors might call "dehumanization" is really like castor oil—good for us, even though we might not like it?

TONY: I have my views on that—I'd like to know yours. What to you, Herb, is humane and what is dehumanizing? You tell me that, and I might be able to make a guess as to how open a teacher you are. I may be wrong, but would you be willing to try this little activity?

Now it's your turn:

HUMANE EXPERIENCES

DEHUMANIZING EXPERIENCES

From "Is Rational Man Our First Priority?"
by Joseph S. Junell

It is not our intent to discredit the need for reason, nor to elevate the position of emotions. Our thesis is simply that because attitudes function in the peculiar way they do, the emotions of young children must be made the primary target of public education, and the educator who wishes to improve the human condition without full recognition of this fact is merely whistling in the dark. He must be able to distinguish between attitudes which are liberating and those which are imprisoning; between the ones which most fully enable the child's imagination to range free and those which slam the door shut on him, so that often he stands outside it, not even wondering what lies beyond. The educator must be made to realize that the imprisoned mind is, in some respects, as much the product of Scarsdale as it is of Harlem and that college credentials are by no means a guarantee against it. He must have some inkling, finally, of the forces which affect attitudes and the important principle under which these forces operate.

Unfortunately, our knowledge of such matters is still painfully limited. We know a great deal more, for example, about how to teach a highly complex idea, such as the relationship between climate and culture, than we do about instilling so simple a belief as integrity. Although research has shown us that attitudes can be formed or modified through a principle called identification, we are not at all sure what happens when identification takes place.

We do have some understanding, however, of one or two of its peculiarities and the conditions under which it is most apt to occur. We know that, unlike intellectualization, in which the gestalt of conceptual learning must be in large part independently achieved, the learning of an attitude seems to be far more an act of sheer dependence. Sometimes it may be dependence on the quality of experience which introduces the element of pleasure or pain. More often it is dependence on specific human models or types, either fictional or real, with which the learner establishes a strong emotional affinity and whose characteristic behaviors he uncritically accepts and makes a part of his own way of perceiving the world.[1]

Because identification takes on a major dimension in our problem, establishing an atmosphere most conducive to its operation is crucial. Such an atmosphere is achieved only through a number of uniquely **human** characteristics within the teacher and his curriculum. This sounds harmless enough, but in fact it contains ramifications which, when considered in their entirety, may be sources of embarrassment and trepidation.

Let us first of all look briefly at the teacher. In our scheme of things, if he were to possess but one dominant trait, it would be his spirit of reverence for children. Although this is a quality which hiring personnel widely subscribe to in theory, they make little effort in practice to insure its presence in the candidate and often give higher priority to scholarship and organizational ability. Yet, to repeat after the eminent analyst, Erich Fromm, it not only stands as the single most important ingredient within the teacher's repertoire of personal characteristics, but is one which our own materialistic culture has largely ignored. In his own words, "While we teach knowledge, we are losing that teaching which is the most important one for human development: the teaching which can only be given by the simple presence of a mature, loving person. In previous epochs of our own culture, or in China and India, the man most highly valued was the person with outstanding spiritual qualities. Even the teacher was not only, or even primarily, a source of information, but his function was to convey certain human attitudes. . . ."[2]

But reverence for children by itself will not do; it is frequently too passive in character. What is needed, if things are to happen between teacher and pupil, are certain talents which serve as catalytic agents in a chemical reaction. High among these is the teacher as dramatist—not in the sense of the accomplished actor, but one skillfully trained to recognize those parts of the curriculum which lend themselves to dramatic treatment. I am not suggesting that we abandon the teaching of rational processes, but simply that we place them whenever possible within an emotional context, employing such elements as narrative, conflict, and denouement. In order for attitude formation to occur, teachers must espouse the arguments which favor the attitude we wish to instill.[3] If this seems like a hard saying, suggestive of indoctrination, we should perhaps reexamine the attitude in question, or abandon our efforts in this area entirely. What exerts the greatest impact on children's attitudes is not that their motivations, either rational or irrational, are exposed to reason, but that children are exposed to dynamic teachers.

In an age of vast social change and upheaval, the teacher as social critic is indispensable to the program. The notion that small children cannot identify with social issues involving the most fundamental human rights is sheer nonsense. Awakening children to feelings and attitudes which are couched in sophisticated language is not easy; but it is not impossible. What child has not felt the iron barb of rejection by his classmates or teacher through no fault of his own, or the panic fear that comes from having voiced an unpopular opinion, or the bitterness of isolation in a contest of unequal opportunity? These, it seems to me, are the very stuff on which human rights are built.

The teacher must also possess the temper of the liberal mind if his presence before children is not to exemplify a highly dogmatic and opinionated view of life. By the liberal attitude we mean one which is trusting and accepting of others, however bizarre their ideas or appearance, and unfearful of losing face when found wrong. It is the attitude which in turn enables children to express themselves, not anarchistically but fearlessly, so that they need not build insular detachments and hostilities in defense of their own errors, which so often leads to the narrow, prejudiced outlook. The learner whose responses are purposely disruptive, or who maintains frigid silence, is the product of teachers (and parents) who have themselves squirmed under the lash of the authoritarian's scorn.

Except for the temper of liberalism, which is sometimes sadly lacking in the very youth whose courage and dedication we so much admire, the teacher we speak of might well be drawn from the ranks of articulate young radicals. He might

be something of a firebrand, uncomfortable to live with, a bane to his principal but a joy to his children, who see him as the champion of their own unredressed grievances against the adult world. Teachers who are the least popular with school boards and administrators are most frequently lionized in the classroom. Recently I witnessed a young professor ceremoniously announce his resolution to resign if his department did not agree to changes which he firmly believed were imperative to the welfare of his students. A number of his colleagues considered such an announcement not only premature, but the benefits to be derived hardly worth the risk. The favorable impact on students, however, was instantaneous. Their roar of approval brought the house down. "He's a fool," I overheard one of his older colleagues whisper, "but he is enormously popular with these kids."

For the teacher deeply concerned with children's attitudes toward the world they live in, the style and content of much of today's elementary curriculum must be vaguely disappointing. Except for a small but growing volume of library fiction, the reading which takes up so large a part of the child's school time is quite devoid of all but the most innocuous kinds of social learning. The readers, especially at the lower elementary levels, are still largely occupied with community helpers, lost pets, animal characters, and trite mysteries. Apart from the occasional child's classic or story written by the established writer, their only claim to drama is that they employ the technique of dialogue whose banalities are frequently matched only by those of the plot. Much of a child's life is involved with misplaced puppies and make-believe journeys to the moon, but these cannot be the whole of it. Deep attachment, deep loss, hate, fear, rivalry, and revenge are as much a part of his life as they are the adult's.

1. Ives Hendrick, **Facts and Theories of Psychoanalysis.** New York: Alfred A. Knopf, 1958. pp. 156-67.

2. Erich Fromm, **The Art of Loving.** New York: Bantam Books, Harper & Row, 1963, p. 98.

3. Muzafer Sherif and Carolyn W. Sherif, **An Outline of Social Psychology.** New York: Harper and Brothers, 1956, p. 560. The authors describe an experiment in which specific attitudes emerge only when the teacher "draws conclusions" for learners rather than leaving an issue supended between several alternatives.

MARTHA SUE JACOBS, from Benfield Elementary School, says, "Teacher is . . . like a football player—always trying to get through to you."

Teacher is trying to get through to children: to teach them reading, mathematics, and even "the little bird walk." Each of these things is another way of saying that teacher is trying to give his students not only the basis for a productive adult life, but teacher is teaching ways to make life livable in the twenty-first century.

Sometimes, it's a funny job; sometimes, it's a job requiring intense concentration and patience; but all the time it's hard work that requires special people with special talents. Indeed, teacher is . . . always trying to get through to you!

To know students well, to open up the way for some, to prod others, or simply stand aside and watch in wonder as some accomplish near miracles—this is teaching.

—Mary Harbage

DISCUSSION, both with other children and with teacher, is of **first importance at all stages.** It is a most reliable instrument for assessment and diagnosis.

From **Inside The Primary School** by John Blackie

All societies educate their children. In more developed societies a formal school system is developed so that the youth are able to learn most efficiently. That there is a relationship between a particular society and its school system is obvious, but what the nature of its specific relationship should be may be a matter of disagreement. This writer makes two assumptions: (1) that the function of the school is to provide an educational program that develops the potentialities of all members of the society and (2) that while a very subtle balance exists and is necessary between man's requirements and society's demands, man's requirements have priority over the demands of a particular society.

From "Curriculum Development From A Psychoanalytic Perspective," by Louise L. Tyler

---

. . . it would seem that the old saw about "what reading is doing in Johnny" rather than "what Johnny's doing in reading" contains considerable professional wisdom. Since reading is a distinctive, human enterprise embedded in the large contexts of communication and language, its importance emanates from its usefulness to the person doing it. Since reading does not really exist outside a person in the process of doing it, the whole person is involved in it as a fully functioning human being. Since the school takes the major responsibility for teaching reading, the ways in which the child is taught to read have direct bearings on both his productivity as a reader and his aspirations about being a reader.

If what reading is doing in Johnny puts him further in charge of his life and increases his authority over it, it enhances his humanness. If reading in Johnny confirms and extends his ways of knowing about his world and those who live therein, he can at least potentially increase his humaneness. Then the right to read is matched by the rightness of the handling of that right. That is what schools must do.

From "Humanism in Teaching Reading," by Leland B. Jacobs

A Teacher's Prayer

Lord, make me an instrument of Thy unrest.
Where there is complacency, let me sow turbulence,
Where there is benevolence, discipline.
Where there is faith, truth,
Where there is mass thinking, the loneliness of an idea
Where there is a recognition of the strength
    of physical force, There will be realization
        of the power of an idea.
And where there is joy of self advancement
A sensitivity and involvement with those less fortunate.
Divine Master, grant that I may not so much
    seek to placate, as to educate,
Not only to understand, but to be understood.
To feel empathy as well as sympathy,
For it is in the disturbing the minds of youth
    that they are taught.
It is through the raising of questions that they learn.
And it is in their meeting a challenge of
Thought that eternity is blessed.

—Stuart Baller

Note: The writer, through his admiration
for the Prayer of St. Francis of
Assissi, has written **A Teacher's Prayer.**

From "Primary Education in England: An Interview with John Coe," by Vincent R. Rogers

ROGERS: Since we're talking about reading, I think there's a phenomenon that's going on in America that I'd like to get your reaction to. In a school system not far from where I work, a company has come into the system and has guaranteed to raise primary children's reading levels if they're allowed to work with the children so many minutes per day on a regular basis throughout the year. These gains, of course, are measured by standardized achievement tests, and the school system pays the company only if the level has been raised to a certain degree. As you probably know, the techniques used in programs like this feature immediate reward offered in terms of tangible things—sometimes a token, sometimes candy bars, and sometimes, I gather, even things like transistor radios. Would you give us your reaction to this development?

COE: I am cautious about reacting to something happening in your country of which I have no direct knowledge. But there are some questions which, if I were an American teacher, I would want to ask about this particular development. The aim seems to be to achieve a measurable growth in a skill, notably reading. And the aim seems to be that this be achieved over a fairly short time, and that there be payment by result, not only for the firm concerned, but for the children.

As an American teacher I would want to ask about the long-term results of this, because we all know as teachers that learning can be lost as well as gained. If you measure the increase in the reading age after six months you might well get a different result than if you measured the reading age after two years. And the sort of learning that we want to encourage in our children is learning which is deeply fundamental to growth, learning that will stay with the child always. If the attack on the basic skill is a head-on attack, then no doubt (and as teachers most of us have done this) you can achieve a measurably significant improvement. But time and time again we have seen our children in later life fall back because their hold on the newly learned skill was too tenuous, too immediately reflective of the pressure to which they have been subjected. Thus as an American teacher I would want to inquire about the long-term results in the learning of children. My feeling, of course, is that learning is a far more complex and subtle matter than can be revealed in a reading quotient or any other kind of objective measure.

There is one other major question which I would wish to ask—and this concerns the reasons that the children are given for increasing their skill. You said in your question that very often there were immediate rewards for the children, tangible things that they were given. My experience as a teacher is that children learn more from the assumptions which we as adults have about life than they do from the words that we use. How many of us, when we were adolescents, were given homilies by our teachers about the evils of smoking and then watched them light their cigarettes as they left the classroom—and which lesson spoke loudest to us? Our children learn from us as human beings—the most important part of the environment which surrounds a growing child.

If you offer a child an immediate reward, a candy bar, for reading a page or a book, what is the assumption you are making in human terms about reading? It is that reading is worthwhile because you get a reward for it, that there is little value implicit in the reading itself. Is this an assumption that we will want our young people to have when they have left school? That they must only read for candy bars or their equivalent? Isn't reading a wonderful skill, a rewarding skill in itself, not because of any other added rewards? If we're going to get good attitudes toward reading and toward books, if we're going to get educated adults, then let the skills be valid enough in themselves.

What I want to sketch here is the role filled by a teacher in a school run on fairly up-to-date lines. He will first of all want to know the children as individuals. This takes a little time since it will not just be a matter of knowing their names, or even what they can do, but will mean getting to know them as people. This means establishing a relationship with them. Ideally this will be a relationship of mutual trust and respect, in which coercion and punishment have no place and where marks and rewards are unnecessary. Such a relationship is not always easy to establish and there may be individuals and sometimes whole groups with whom it is so difficult as to be practically impossible. But do not write it off as pie-in-the-sky. There are schools where it is the established relationship and many more in which at least something of it exists, and it is the ideal towards which very many teachers are striving. Where it exists a very favorable atmosphere for learning has been created. The children feel free and relaxed and at the same time, in the care of someone whom they respect and to whose authority they can trust themselves. It is not possible to reduce this sort of thing to a formula.

From **Inside The Primary School** by John Blackie

**How do you respond to
coercion?
Remember an experience with
certain kinds of salesmen, or
an experience with an administrator who was trying
to force
you
into behaving in a certain
manner?**

**Have you practiced
coercion
with children in your
classroom?
How do you think the children
felt? How did they feel
toward YOU?
Are you desirous of interacting
again with the salesmen who employed
coercion? Are children any different?**

From "Illuminating the Lives of Children: More Effective Use of Resources in the Elementary School," by Leland B. Jacobs

Now we've got three kinds of "teachers" in classrooms so far as I'm concerned. They all pass under the name of teacher, but they aren't all teachers from my point of view.

THE SCHOOL KEEPER

The first kind of person who is in a classroom with children, I would call the school keeper. Now school keepers have got one job in mind as I see it. Their job is to form things. Oh, they have the best looking bulletin boards in a whole lot of the schools in America. Of course in April, it is little ducks with umbrellas all marching across the bulletin boards, but they're straight—they're in order. And of course, no child could pick out his own unless he turned it over and read his name on the back of it. The job of the school keeper of America is to order things, to form things. They even pat the children into line.

THE INSTRUCTOR

The second kind of person who in elementary education goes under the name of teacher, I call instructor. The instructor is a person who loves his content. He dearly loves his content, and he loves it so much that he wants children to love it like he does. And so he sneaks up on them. He uses all kinds of sneaky devices to get them to

like the subject matter. He adds method to content not because method is important for its own sake, but because method gets him to where he wants to go with subject matter.

THE REAL TEACHER

And then we've got the real teachers. And whereas the job of the school keeper is to form, and the job of the instructor is to inform, the real teacher knows that the main job of teaching is to influence what takes place within the child. The truth of the matter is that every real teacher I know, whether he can verbalize it or not, knows that it isn't a "teaching-learning" continuum that we are concerned with but a "teaching-feeling taught so you can learn" continuum.

**What label
would you give
yourself?
What labels
do you think
others would
give you?**

TONY (to Cella, Janice and José): Several meetings ago we all agreed that to classify children is a mistake and yet none of you have voiced any reaction to Jacobs' classification of teachers. Personally, I think it's just as wrong to classify teachers as it is to classify children.

CELLA: The difference I see, Tony, is that when a teacher classifies children, such as slow learners, average learners, and fast learners, she often treats them differently. For one thing, she might organize ability grouping patterns which we know affects the self-concepts of children. I see Jacobs' classification as being like the classification of children. Have any of you experienced a situation where teachers were classified and subsequently were treated differently?

JOSÉ: Last year I felt that my principal had made some type of classification of the teachers in my building. For one thing, he always took visitors to just a few rooms and only to those rooms. He also spent more time in some teachers' rooms. We all felt as if he had made a judgment about us and had classified us.

TONY: It's possible that your principal might have personally liked some teachers more than others, or perhaps he felt like he needed several "showcases" for visitors. José, how did the teachers react to this?

JOSÉ: Some teachers talked about the situation and were concerned about it.

TONY: Do you think it affected their performance?

JOSÉ: That's hard to tell, but it did appear to shake some teachers' confidence about their performances.

TONY: I think José has just proved my point—basic human needs are basic to all people regardless of age. People of all ages need to feel wanted, needed, and worthwhile. How can a principal hope to have "humane" teachers when he doesn't demonstrate "humaneness" himself? I find it difficult to feel like a loving person after being kicked in the seat of the pants.

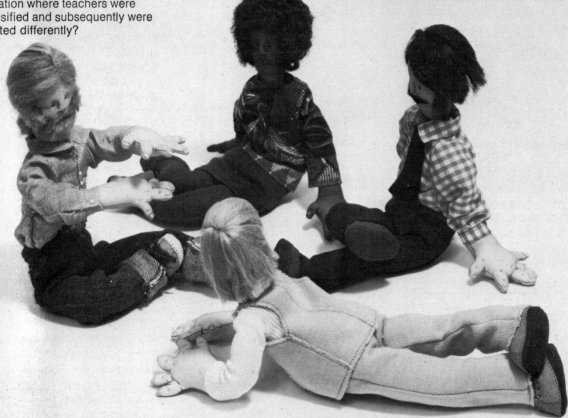

Don't be a damned warehouse of information. Be a person—with knowledge, yes—but with impact!

From "Can Schools Grow Persons?"
by Carl R. Rogers

From *Humanizing the Education of Children* by Earl C. Kelley

HUMANIZING—
The quality of openness is an asset to a teacher, for the learners in turn become more open. The teacher who threatens and behaves in a distrustful manner causes children to close up; and communication, the business of teaching, becomes much more difficult because children are quick to detect hostility as well as love. They soon see the difference between a teacher who is a helping person and one who is threatening. They are drawn to the one and repelled by the other.

To humanize education, then, the teacher must learn to care for the children and show that he has confidence in them, that he trusts them.

TEACHER NEEDS—
If he is to humanize education, the teacher, too, has certain needs. He needs to be free to be himself. Teacher freedom is limited in both real and imagined ways: fear of the next teacher, subject matter requirements, the quiet room, the parents' expectations, and many others.

Every teacher should take a good look at himself and ask how many of his fears are genuine and how many are fancied. Thus, he may reduce his load of fears and begin to foster openness in the children under his care through more humanizing experiences.

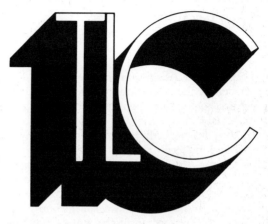

Tender Loving Care

Make a list of the children in your classroom who appear to have experienced the least amount of "tender loving care." Create a "T.L.C." schedule. Give some T.L.C. to every child on your list every day.

Remember, "T.L.C." comes in many forms:

a hug	praise	showing trust
holding hands	a smile	showing faith
timely comfort	a wink	a compliment
support	a touch	

Don't forget your peers. They, too, need **T.L.C.**

When a child feels failure, he doesn't just feel failure here, there, or someplace else; it pervades his whole system.

From "The Effect of School Failure on the Life of a Child," by William Glasser

**From "New Day in North Dakota:
Changing Teachers and Changing Schools,"
by Clara A. Pederson**

NEW SCHOOL CLASSROOMS

To enter one of the New School classrooms is to enter a sea of activity; children are involved simultaneously in a variety of operations. Some are working individually; others with partners, in teams, and in small groups. Older children are tutoring younger children. Fives and sixes may be together in one classroom with the seven-and eight-year-olds together in another room. Also noticeable is the flow of children from one room to another. A hum of industry permeates the classrooms. You can readily observe that the emphasis has shifted from teaching to learning.

Since children often need long uninterrupted periods to complete projects, some of the classrooms have eliminated boundaries of time and have what could be called a seamless curriculum; children change their work at a time when most convenient for them. Rigid division of the curriculum into subject-matter areas has been eliminated by some of the teachers because it tends to interrupt the child's train of thought and may interfere with his solution to a problem.

The children live in an environment that provides incentives for them to **want** to learn, to discover, to read, and to solve problems. The classroom atmosphere is relaxed—with a sense of fun in relation to learning, a willingness on the part of increasing numbers of children to get deeply involved. Emphasis is upon children being encouraged to set their own pace for learning and to pursue their own areas of interest. By having available for children learning centers where they may go to do their work and discover answers to their questions, an environment is created where children learn primarily to satisfy their own natural curiosities rather than the expectations of the teacher. Included in these centers are areas for working with sand, water, wood; for listening, viewing, puppet-making, role-playing, cooking; for integrating work in the arts, mathematics, science. And they vary throughout the year. In order for the centers to be most effective, they are changed frequently. Children and teachers together plan and contribute to these learning centers.

ROLE OF THE TEACHER

In such a learning environment the role of the teacher has changed. He is now guide, adviser, observer, catalyst—one who asks the right question at the right time in order to extend children further in searching for information and in solving problems. The teacher is busily observing, assisting and stimulating children in their learning and helping them discover explanations for themselves. Emphasis is upon teaching children to think and allowing them to participate actively in the learning process.

Sources of Authority—

The arbitrary authority of age and degrees and expertise is out; to learn "that there's no one over you" is now an acknowledged goal.

School is seen as a place for finding out **who** you are, not for learning to accept others' standards.

For the teacher, this means presenting himself as an essentially neutral resource, not as a cajoling, demanding, ego-involved participant in the child's learning process.

For the student, this means crafting his own yardstick, not measuring himself by someone else's.

From "Assessing The Alternatives," by Charles H. Rathbone

**From *Teaching As A Subversive Activity*
by Neil Postman and Charles Weingartner**

It is the thesis of this book that change—constant, accelerating, ubiquitous—is the most striking characteristic of the world we live in and that our educational system has not yet recognized this fact.

The most important intellectual ability man has yet developed—the art and science of asking questions—is not taught in school.

The new education has as its purpose the development of a new kind of person, one who—as a result of internalizing a different series of concepts— is an actively inquiring, flexible, creative, innovative, tolerant, liberal personality who can face uncertainty and ambiguity without disorientation, who can formulate viable new meanings to meet changes in the environment which threaten individual and mutual survival.

From *Humanizing The Education of Children* by Earl C. Kelley

FREEDOM—
Freedom is a requirement for being truly human. This is because all living tissue—especially the human organism—is uniquely purposive. There is no point in one's being purposive if one is not free to make choices. Purpose shows the path down which unique energy can be spent.

No one has the right to do just as he pleases if what he pleases infringes on the rights of others. That is not what is meant by freedom. In a sense, as long as a human being lives anywhere near another, his freedom to do just as he pleases is reduced. In the present world, few of us live completely free. I hasten to insert this because there will be those who will think that I want everybody, especially children, to have a form of freedom that is difficult to distinguish from anarchy. Not so, but every individual must have a chance to make choices, to learn, and to bear the consequences. Little children need much freedom; but the farther they go in school, the less they are given opportunities to make choices.

The trappings of enslavement are all around the school. The superintendent, the principal, the supervisor, and the teacher have many devices. The lesson set out to be learned is one device—usually represented by the textbook, usually prepared with regard only for the subject matter.

The trappings of enslavement are evident in the school room itself. It is built to keep our children from looking out. . . . . The seats in which our young are imprisoned, ..., allow the learner (as long as he "behaves himself") to see the back of the neck of the person in front of him—definitely not the most attractive part of the anatomy.

Man's most valuable asset and his definitive feature is his ability to weigh and to make choices. But this ability can be eroded or destroyed completely. The most obvious examples of "brainwashing" occur during wartime, but less realized is the brainwashing done by the authoritarian teacher. Our young manage to escape in many ways, however: by daydreaming while in class, by going home at the end of the day, or by becoming dropouts.

There is also the matter of conditioning. A child can be conditioned, and in limited areas conditioning perhaps helps because it would be quite burdensome to have to think about every move. But in a broader sense, in important areas, conditioning is the opposite of education. Conditioning calls for the repression of responses. Education, on the other hand, is or should be the encouragement of responses.

One learns to use freedom only by using it. Freedom, like anything else, has to be learned. Every individual must have a chance to learn to make choices and to bear the consequences. And we teachers must learn how to provide the alternatives. For if freedom dies, so does our way of life.

On a Picture of Poverty in Appalachia:
3 Year Old and Doll

With jelly on her face
    (and a three year old hand),
that so easily laughs in a giggle
    (patting the plump belly of the dry rag doll);
She does not know yet of rickets, boney legs,
the swelling in the belly—
or of professors of economics
    and the sensuously curved GNP;
Rather, Politics
is a word
    (and meat is a happy surprise);
so
to her, the matter of this poem is of no concern
for her smile at me
is that of one to a funny friend
from the face of one that has not yet learned to envy
    the doll.

—Sam Hamod

THE HUMAN SIDE OF LEARNING
by Arthur W. Combs

Anyone who doesn't know that education is in deep trouble must have been hiding somewhere for the last fifteen years. Somehow we have lost touch with the times, so we find young people opting out, copping out, and dropping out of the system. The processes of education have become concerned with nonhuman questions, and the system is dehumanizing to the people in it. Earl Kelley once said, "We've got this marvelous school system with beautiful buildings and a magnificent curriculum and these great teachers and these marvelous administrators, and then, damn it all, the parents send us the wrong kids."

For a number of generations now, we have been dealing with learning from a false premise. Most of us are familiar with Pavlov's famous experiment conditioning a dog to respond to a bell. The principles he established then are the ones we still use to deal with the problems of learning

in our schools today. But Pavlov's system depended on: (1) separating his dogs from all other dogs, which made the learning process an isolated event; (2) tying his dogs down so that they could only do precisely what he had in mind, a technique not very feasible for most elementary teachers; (3) completely removing the dogs from all other possible sources of stimuli, a hard thing to do in a classroom.

This point of view has taught us to deal with the problem of learning as a question of stimulus and response, to be understood in terms of input and output. Currently it finds its latest expression in behavioral objectives, performance based criteria for learning that systematically demand that you: Establish your objectives in behavioral terms; set up the machinery to accomplish them; and then test whether or not you have achieved them. Such an approach seems straightforward, businesslike, and logical; and that's what is wrong with it. I quote from Earl Kelley again, who once said, "logic is often only a systematic way of arriving at the wrong answers!"

I'm not opposed to behavioral objectives. Nobody can be against accountability. The difficulty with the concept is that its fundamental premise is only partly right. The fact is that behavioral objectives are useful devices for dealing with the simplest, most primitive aspects of education, the things we already do quite well. Unfortunately, they do not serve us so well when they are applied to other kinds of objectives, such as intelligent behavior requiring a creative approach to a problem. Behavioral objectives do not deal with the problem of holistic goals. They do not help us in dealing with the things that make us truly human—the questions of human beliefs, attitudes, feelings, understandings, and concerns—the things we call "affective." Nor do they deal with the problems of self-actualization, citizenship, responsibility, caring, and many other such humanistic goals of educators.

Using this approach, we are evaluating schools and circumstances on the basis of what we know how to test. As a result, we are finding that our educational objectives are being established by default because the things we know how to test are the simplest, smallest units of cognitive procedures, which don't really matter much anyway.

We are spending millions and millions of dollars on this very small aspect of dealing with the educational problem, while the problems of self-concept, human attitudes, feelings, beliefs, meanings, and intelligence are going unexplored.

Although I do not oppose behavioral objectives, I do believe that those who are forcing accountability techniques on us need also to be held accountable for what they are doing to American education.

Performance-based criteria is the method of big business, a technique of management, and we are now in the process of applying these industrial techniques to education everywhere. We ought to know better. When industry developed the assembly line and other systematic techniques to increase efficiency, what happened? The workers felt dehumanized by the system and formed unions to fight it. And that is precisely what is happening with our young people today. They feel increasingly dehumanized by the system, so they are fighting it at every possible level. Applying industrial techniques to human problems just won't work. A systems approach, it should be understood, is only a method of making sure you accomplish your objectives. Applied to the wrong objectives, systems approaches only guarantee that your errors will be colossal.

The trouble with education today is not its lack of efficiency, but its lack of humanity. Learning is not a mechanical process, but a **human** process. The whole approach to learning through behavioral objectives concentrates our attention on the simplest, most primitive aspects of the educational endeavor, while it almost entirely overlooks the human values. I believe we can get along better with a person who can't read than with a bigot. We are doing very little to prevent the production of bigots but a very great deal to prevent the production of poor readers.

Learning is a human problem always consisting of two parts. First, we have to provide people with some new information or some new experience, and we know how to do that very well. We are experts at it. With the aid of our new electronic gadgets, we can do it faster and more furiously than ever before in history. Second, the student must discover the meaning of the information provided him. The dropout is not a dropout because we didn't give him information. We told him, but he never discovered what that information meant.

I would like to give an alternate definition to the S-R theory most of us cut our teeth on: Information will affect a person's behavior only in the degree to which he has discovered its personal meaning for him. For example, I read in this morning's paper that there has been an increase in the number of cases of pulmonic stenosis in the state of Florida in the past two years. I don't know what pulmonic stenosis is, so this information has no meaning for me. Later in the day I hear a friend talking about pulmonic stenosis, so I look it up and find that it's a disorder that produces a closing up of the pulmonary artery. It's a dangerous disorder, and it produces blue babies. Now I know what it is, but it still doesn't affect my behavior very much. Later in the day I receive a letter from a mother of one of my students who says, "Dear Teacher, we have taken Sally to the clinic, where we learned that she has got pulmonic stenosis, and she's going to have to be operated on when she reaches adolescence. In the meantime, we would apprciate it if you would keep an eye out for her."

This information has more meaning to me now because it's happening to one of my students, and my behavior reflects that meaning. I protect the girl, and I talk to other people on the faculty: "Did you hear about Sally? Isn't it a shame? She's got pulmonic stenosis. Poor child, she's going to have to be operated on."

Let's go one step further. Suppose I have just learned that my daughter has pulmonic stenosis. Now this information affects my behavior tremendously, in every aspect of my daily life.

This explains why so much of what we do in school has no effect on students. Sometimes we even discourage them from finding the personal meaning of a piece of information. We say, "Eddie, I'm not interested in what you think about that, what does the book say?" which is the same as telling him that school is a place where you learn about things that don't matter.

What do we need to do, then, if we're going to humanize the business of learning? We have to see the whole problem of learning differently. We have to give up our preoccupation with objectivity. In our research at the University of Florida, we find that objectivity correlates negatively with effectiveness in the helping professions we have so far explored.

Freud once said that no one ever does anything unless he would rather. In other words, no one ever does anything unless he thinks it is important. So the first thing we must do to humanize learning is to believe it is important.

Let me tell another story by way of illustration. In the suburbs of Atlanta there was a young woman teaching first grade who had beautiful long blonde hair which she wore in a pony tail down to the middle of her back. For the first three days of the school year she wore her hair that way. Then, on Thursday she decided to do it up in a bun on top of her head. One of the little boys in her class looked into the room and didn't recognize his teacher. He was lost. The bell rang, school started, and he didn't know where he belonged. He was out in the hall crying. The supervisor asked him, "What's the trouble?" and he said, "I can't find my teacher." She said, "Well, what's your teacher's name? What room are you in?" He didn't know. So she said, "Well, come on, let's see if we can find her." They started down the hall together, the supervisor and the little boy, hand-in-hand, opening one door after another without much luck until they came to the room where this young woman was teaching. As they stood there in the doorway, the teacher turned and saw them and she said, "Why, Joey, it's good to see you. We've been wondering where you were. Come on in. We've missed you." And the little boy pulled away from the supervisor and threw himself into the teacher's arms. She gave him a hug, patted him on the fanny, and he ran to his seat. She knew what was important. She thought little boys were important.

Suppose the teacher hadn't thought little boys were important. Suppose, for instance, she thought supervisors were important. Then she would have said, "Why good morning, Miss Smith. We're so glad you've come to see us, aren't we boys and girls?" And the little boy would have been ignored. Or the teacher might have thought the lesson was important, in which case she would have said, "Joey, for heaven's sake, where have you been? You've already two pages behind. Come in here and get to work." Or she might have thought that discipline was important, and said, "Joey, you know very well when you're late you must go to the office and get a permit. Now run and get it." But she didn't. She thought little boys were important. And so it is with each of us. We have to believe humanizing learning is important.

To humanize learning we must also recognize that people don't behave according to the facts of a situation, they behave in terms of their beliefs. In the last presidential election, those who thought that the Democrats would save us and the Republicans would ruin us voted for the Democrats. And those who thought the Republicans would save us and the Democrats would ruin us voted for the Republicans. Each of us behaved not in terms of "the facts," but in terms of our beliefs. A fact is only what we believe is so. Sensitivity to the beliefs of the people we work with is basic to effective behavior. In our research on the helping professions, we found the outstanding characteristic of effective helpers was that the good ones are always concerned with how things look from the point of view of the people they are working with.

Let me give another illustration of what I mean by being aware of the other person's point of view. A supervisor and a teacher were talking about a little boy: "I don't know what to do with him," the teacher said. "I know that he can do it; I tell him, 'It's easy, Frank, you can do it,' but he won't even try." The supervisor said, "Don't ever tell a child something is easy. Look at it from the child's point of view. If you tell him it's easy and he can't do it, he can only conclude that he must be stupid, and if he can do it, you have robbed it of all its thrill! Tell him it's hard, that you know it's hard, but you're pretty sure he can do it. Then if he can't do it, he hasn't lost face, and if he can do it, what a glory that is for him."

So much of what we do in teaching is not concerned with people. It is concerned with rules, regulations, order, and neatness. I visited a school some years ago, and as I sat in the principal's office one of the bus drivers came in with a little boy in one hand and a broken arm from one of the seats of the bus in the other hand. How did this principal behave? He became very angry. It was as if the little boy had broken the principal's arm. And, in a sense, the boy had, I suppose.

In contrast to that, I am reminded of a visit I made to a school in Michigan. As I walked down the hall with the principal, a teacher and a group of children came out of one of the rooms of this very old building. We walked into the room and saw that it was in complete havoc. The principal said, "It's a mess isn't it? And it can stay that

way. That teacher has raised the reading level of her classes by two grades every year she's had them. If that's the way she wants to teach, it's all right with me!"

We walked along to the gymnasium and looked in. He said as we looked at the floor. "That's the third finish we've had on that floor this year. We use it in the evenings for family roller skating!" There is a man whose values are clear. He is more concerned with people than things.

There are hundreds of ways we dehumanize people in our schools, and we need to make a systematic attempt to get rid of them.

In **Crisis in the Classroom,** Charles Silberman says that the believes one of the major problems in American education is "mindlessness." We do so many things without having the slightest idea of why we're doing them. One dehumanizing element is the grading system. Grades motivate very few people, nor are they good as an evaluative device. Everyone knows that no two teachers evaluate people in exactly the same terms. Yet we piously regard grades as though they all mean the same thing, under the same circumstances; to all people at all times.

I remember my son coming home from college and asking, "Dad, how can you, as an educator, put up with the grading system? Grading on the curve makes it to my advantage to destroy my friends. Dad, that's a hell of a way to teach young people to live." I'd never thought of it that way before.

Another thing we need to understand is the serious limitation of competition as a motivational system. Psychologists know three things about motivation:

1. The only people who are motivated by competition are those who think they can win. And that's not very many. Everyone else sits back and watches them beat their brains out.

2. People who do not feel they have a chance of winning and are forced to compete are not motivated. They are discouraged and disillusioned by the process, and we cannot afford a discouraged and disillusioned populace.

3. When competition becomes too important, morality breaks down, and any means becomes

justified to achieve the ends—the basketball team begins to use its elbows and students begin to cheat on exams.

Grade level and grouping is another mindless obstacle to humanizing. All the research we have on grouping tells us that no one method of grouping is superior to any other. And yet we go right on, in the same old ways, insisting that we must have grade levels. As a result, we might have an eleven-year-old child in the sixth grade reading at the third-grade level. Every day of his life we feed him a diet of failure because we can't find a way to give a success experience to such a child.

If we want to humanize the processes of learning, we must make a systematic search for the things that destroy effective learning and remove them from the scene. It we're going to humanize the processes of learning, we must take the student in as a partner. Education wouldn't be irrelevant if students had a voice in decision making. One of my friends once said that the problem of American education today is that "all of us are busy providing students with answers to problems they don't have yet." And that's true. We decide what people need to know and then we teach it to them whether they need it or not. As a result some students discover that school is a place where you study things that don't matter and so they drop out. It's intelligent to drop out. If it isn't getting you anywhere, if it doesn't have any meaning, if it doesn't do something for you, then it's intelligent to drop out. But we seldom think of it that way. Most of us regard the dropout as though there is something wrong with him.

Part of making education relevant to the student is allowing him to develop responsibility for his own learning. But responsibility can only be learned from having responsibility, never from having it withheld. The teacher who says, "You be good kids while I'm out of the room" is an example of what I'm talking about. When she comes back the room is bedlam. "I'll never leave you alone again," she says. By this pronouncement she has robbed the children of any opportunity to learn how to behave responsibly on their own.

Not long ago, I arrived at a school just after the election for student body president, and the teachers were upset because the student who was elected president had run on a platform of no school on Friday, free lunches, free admissions to the football games, and a whole string of other impossible things. The teachers thought it was "a travesty on democracy" and suggested that the student body have another election. I said, "If you do that, how are these kids ever going to discover the terrible price you have to pay for electing a jackass to office?'

We know that what a person believes about himself is crucial to his growth and development. We also know that a person learns this self-concept from the way he is treated by significant people in his life. The student takes his self-concept with him wherever he goes. He takes it to Latin class, to arithmetic class, to gym class, and he takes it home with him. Wherever he goes, his self-concept goes, too. Everything that happens to him has an effect on his self-concept.

Are we influencing that self-concept in positive or negative ways? We need to ask ourselves these kinds of questions. How can a person feel liked unless somebody likes him? How can a person feel wanted unless somebody wants him? How can a person feel acceptable unless somebody accepts him? How can a person feel he's a person with dignity and integrity unless somebody treats him so? And how can a person feel that he is capable unless he has some success? In the answers to those questions, we'll find the answers to the human side of learning.

From "The Death of the Textbook," by Eileen M. Oickle

This fall much-needed funerals are being held throughout the county. These obsequies herald the death of the textbook. Teachers are now handling and viewing their students as individuals with individual needs. From the Sputnik-age craze over why Johnny can't read, the pendulum has swung to the thought does Johnny always need to read?

For centuries man has learned in many ways from a variety of experience. Yet pedagogical methods have tended to ignore these natural approaches to learning and have kept teacher and students tied slavishly to a tired textbook as the main avenue to knowledge. At its worst, the role of a teacher was that of an orator giving a recitation of the text; at its best, the role of the teacher was that of an artistic performer enlivening a lesson which was still reinforced with and oriented to a textbook. Now however, the teacher has resigned stage-center.

Teaching emphasis has switched from what the teacher does to how the student learns. The teacher knows that the student acquires much knowledge before he ever meets a textbook. He analyzes various avenues to comprehension and helps the student choose from among them. Thus, the teacher's role has switched from that of a leading actor in education to that of the informed creative director of learning.

The teacher of today employs a variety of media and situations for student development. The classroom has many activities and performances instead of a single act. To establish a variety of learning situations, the teacher calls upon modern technology as an assistant for her professional knowledge. Creatively arranged processes of learning pace the student's development and ability.

First the teacher selects a form of instruction which will best meet the objectives the student should be able to accomplish. By using an assortment of instructional techniques that provide motivation and objectivity for the learning situation, the teacher helps the student in his task. Then, through the use of a variety of instructional aids which involve auditory, visual and sensory perceptions, the teacher chooses and organizes various materials and instructional techniques to correlate with theories of learning. Strategically, the teacher has designed the approaches for comprehension.

Now the teacher circulates throughout the room observing the learning situations. Pausing to answer a question of a student listening to a tape; stopping to help a student correlate a slide carousel and a record player, the teacher moves along evaluating the progress: Susie is animatedly talking to Johnny about the answer to a problem presented on the tape, while Dorothy's face reflects her rapt attention as she observes a sound and sight presentation of a lesson. Brian, Tom and Jim are busily planning a dialogue that they will present. At the same time, Kevin and Bob are viewing cartoon transparencies which demand interpretation.

As the teacher observes the students acquiring skills and understandings by a variety of methods through electronic media, her mind jumps ahead envisioning new ideas for lessons for the next unit. . . . The students have become active participants in learning rather than a passive audience in monotony. Looking at the eager faces filled with life, the teacher can't help but rejoice at the death of the textbook.

From "Special Instructors—A Highly Individualistic Teaching Style," by Margaret Adams

Have you ever wondered how, at school, a teacher can get your child to make a perfectly tailored two-piece suit or build a complex stereo set; do intricate art work or even interpret a tough passage of Beethoven, when you can't even get the same child to hang a towel up straight at home? If you've ever wondered that, you've probably concluded that they're special teachers. And they are. In the Anne Arundel County Schools (Maryland) five disciplines are considered areas for special teachers. The subjects are home economics, art, music, physical education, and industrial arts.

Each instructor in these fields has a highly individualistic teaching style. This style and his subject matter form an inseparable whole which motivates young people to maintain an interest and an involvement in the aesthetic aspects of living.

The teachers in these special subjects have a diversity of interests, skills, and talents, and each program has its own specific goals. However, they do have several goals in common:

- humanizing education
- offering opportunities for both vocational and avocational pursuits
- stimulating and guiding creative abilities
- opening doors to the expression and interpretation of emotions
- promoting a sensitivity to an aestheic environment
- involving students actively with the tools appropriate to the learning situation
- developing in-depth skills which enable the students to become increasingly independent in actions and thoughts
- encouraging continued interest and participation in the fine and practical arts through later years.

SO YOU WANT TO BE A REAL TEACHER?
by Richard W. Calisch

Over the years, literally thousands of young people have neglected to write and ask my advice as to whether they were making a mistake in preparing to be teachers. By now, hundreds and hundreds of them (many no longer quite so young, of course) are moving about in the world of the classroom. With more brashness than modesty, I have finally decided to speak out to them, and to all teachers and would-be teachers everywhere. Although I'd run for cover if anyone started deciding just how qualified I am to be a career teacher, I'm prepared to list what I think those qualifications ought to be. Many people will undoubtedly disagree with one or several items on my list, but here goes, anyway.

In the first place, if you're not a brainy, top-level, creative student, consider doing something else. Good teaching is done by good students, by people who themselves are compulsive about learning. It takes intelligence; it takes the ability to read and to write well.

Good teaching takes the kind of person who wants to know just about all there is to know about his subject and who tops everything off with a strong desire to help his students acquire knowledge. You can't be content to keep just a few pages ahead of them. You must really know the field, whether it be mathematics or physical education, literature or cooking. (This calls for even greater emphasis on subject matter courses in college.) You need to be an expert, a specialist, a scholar, a consistent learner, in order to be a teacher. Teaching is, after all, primarily an intellectual art.

Being an intelligent specialist isn't enough, however. You must also have a wide range of adult knowledge and interests. It goes without saying that a teacher of any subject should be well-versed in the literature, music, art, and history of his world, as well as alert to the newest of the new. He should be hip to the world around his eyes and ears—knowledgeable about the latest cars, movies, fashions, books. You may not be able to answer all your students' questions or participate in all their discussions, but at least you should know the terms they use. A teacher who can't rap with the guys on their ground isn't going to educate them on his.

But—and this is important—never forget that you are there to bring young people up the educational ladder, not to bring yourself down.

A teacher must understand students' likes and dislikes, hopes and fears, but at the same time, he must teach as an adult. Sometimes it takes courage to tell a youngster he is wrong; but when he **is**, pretending he **is not** is a grave sin, in **my** mind. I guess what I am saying here is that I wholeheartedly endorse the client concept of education, in which the teacher has the obligation to know his subject and much more besides; in which the student comes to the teacher as a client to absorb what he can, to learn what the teacher has to teach.

Your responsibility is to make your teaching relevant to your students, but you must not succumb to the pressure to tell them only what they want to hear because that way is easier.

Treating children childishly produces childish grown-ups. To avoid doing this, you must use all of the intelligence, knowledge, and expertise that you possess. You must be in command, and this takes that added combination of confidence, wit, maturity, and strength of character. If you lack these attributes or are satisfied with your present attainment of them, there is another occupation for you.

I have stressed the teacher's need to **have** knowledge and intelligence. Hand in hand with these attributes go two others: creativity and imagination. A teacher needs to be an idea person. You must be able to make use of any idea, from any source, and turn it to a thought-producing teaching technique.

When Georgy asks, "Why?" when Suzy says, "What for?" when Mary says, "Are you kidding?" you've got to be able to come up with answers, and they aren't always in the book. Answering a question, such as "What good is this ever going to do me?" from a belligerent, bored, boorish troublemaker is going to take creativity and imagination, as well as a conviction on your part that whatever it is **will** do him some good. This conviction can arise only if you yourself are an expert in whatever field you teach.

In summary, a teacher, first and foremost, must be intelligent, knowledgeable, creative, and imaginative. I know that's not the standard definition, but if Mr. Binet doesn't complain, I won't knock his test. Score yourself one point each for intelligence, expertise in your subject matter, creativity, and imagination. If you don't have four points now, quit here.

My next bit of advice will seem strange, but take it anyway. Sometime when you're feeling up to par, find a quiet, secluded room with no books, no TV, no transistor radio, no cokes, no tasty snacks. Go in, sit down, and stay for an hour. Ask a friend to let you know when the time is up. If the hour seems like a year or if you fall asleep, forget about teaching.

If your inner resources are not enough to keep you interested in yourself for one class period, imagine how you will affect your students. Your subject matter is only subject matter until **you** add the vital ingredient to it—you. And if your **you** isn't enough to make that hour of solitude pleasant and interesting it is going to be hell for

the 30 or so squirming students who have just straggled in after an hour's ordeal with some other dull pedagogue.

That hour you spend alone in the empty room may be the most eye-opening hour of your life. You'll find out whether someone could possibly spend 60 minutes in your company without going out of his mind from simple boredom.

If you've read this far and still think you want to teach, test your weirdo quotient. Every good teacher has in him the confidence and self-reliance to be a weirdo. From Socrates to "Sock it to me!" the memorable lessons have been taught by showmen who knew the value of a vivid performance. The classroom is a stage and the teacher is the player: hero, villain, clown and the whole supporting cast of the greatest long-run, hit show ever to play off Broadway or on. And it's a show whose script changes daily, without notice, and usually without consultation with the cast.

In every good classroom personality, there is some of P. T. Barnum, John Barrymore, Ringo Starr, and Houdini. Are you afraid to stand up and sing with a wastebasket over your head, to demonstrate the various qualities of sound? Can you be King Richard bawling "A horse! A horse! My kingdom for a horse!" or act out photosynthesis, playing all parts yourself?

Think back to your own teachers. From which did you learn the most? Certainly not from the sit-behind-the-desk mumblers who read their lectures from neatly typed notes. Teaching involves a great deal of showmanship and salesmanship, and the great teaching personalities are those that are not afraid to be different, unusual, or what the current jargon styles "weirdo." Classroom spontaneity and showmanship take confidence and a degree of cool that the average person doesn't possess; but, then, a teacher isn't an average person.

Have you ever tried to talk a died-in-the-wool Democrat into voting for a Republican, or a vegetarian into eating meat, or a Card fan into cheering for the Cubs? How did it come out? Probably it produced a humdinger of an argument—one with sparks, flames, daggers, and music played by the brasses. Or else the person you were talking to just turned you off, wouldn't even listen.

Those two responses to persuasion are most typical, because people just don't like to have their cherished beliefs challenged and will protect them from attack in any way they can. Yet teaching involves challenging the sacred beliefs of the student and asking him, forcing him if necessary, to examine them.

Each student brings to the classroom a whole complex of his own folk beliefs about those aspects of life of which he is ignorant. Typically, his attitude will be that if he has never heard of it, it either isn't true or is unimportant. He will cling to his preconceptions like the proverbial drowning man to the proverbial log. Your job is to push him off the log and see that he stays afloat. Don't expect him to be overjoyed about it. Don't expect him to love you for it. If he learns from you, if he matures and gains confidence under your direction, then you have achieved success. If you also want love, get married.

I tell my pupils that if I can't send them home muttering darkly at least once a week, I've failed. And I mean that. An exasperated student will think, ask, read, search for answers—and that is education. Even though he may come up with answers that disagree with your beliefs, you have done your job as a teacher if he has arrived at those answers through intelligent thought.

What students need is some answers and a lot of needling questions. So I agree with Socrates that a teacher must try to be the most irritating person for miles around. (You can expect hemlock as your reward.)

Most books I've read about teaching indicate that the prime requisite for a teacher is a "love of children." Hogwash! That bit of misinformation has probably steered more softhearted and softheaded Mr. Peeperses and Miss Brookses into our art than any other deception ever practiced on the mind of man. What you must love is the vision of the well-informed, responsible adult you can help the child become.

Your job as a teacher is to help the child realize who he is, what his potential is, what his strengths are. You can help him learn to love himself—or the man he soon will be. With that kind of under-standing self-love, the student doesn't need any of your sentimentality. What he needs is your brains, and enabling him to profit from them calls for decisive firmness. "I must be cruel only to be kind," say Hamlet and many a good teacher. Discipline and firm guidance are often called meanness by those subjected to them, but in my experience they are the kind of loving care most likely to produce intelligent, knowledgeable, perceptive adults who can do a better job of coping with the problems of the world than did those who taught them.

The fact that real teaching is an art is too often pooh-poohed. Some critics place teaching in the same category as baby-sitting; and far too many people enter the field because it seems like an easy way to earn a fair living. Girls may look on it as a pleasant way of biding their time until they capture husbands.

But the kind of teacher I have been talking about is a dedicated person who plans to stay in teaching despite its drawbacks. He looks upon his work with individual children as an art to which he brings his talent, his craftsmanship, his experience, learning, intelligence, and that indefinable something called inspiration.

I hope, prospective teachers, that as you take an honest, searching look at yourselves you can sense that you have the potential for being this kind of teacher.

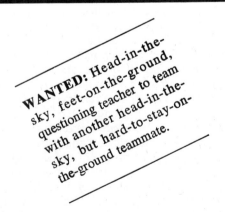

WANTED: Head-in-the-sky, feet-on-the-ground, questioning teacher to team with another head-in-the-sky, but hard-to-stay-on-the-ground teammate.

CELLA (to total group): What was your reaction to "So You Want To be A Real Teacher?" I'm both surprised and upset by it, in general. For years I've seen teachers bully children and then rationalize their behavior with a simple "they need it."

TONY: Cella, I share your concern. To me the article encouraged teachers to physically and psychologically beat children.

MORNING STAR: I didn't get the impression that the author was talking about physically beating children. You know how easy it is for a beginning teacher to lose control over a group of children because the teacher wants children to like him. I thought this was good advice for a beginning teacher.

TONY: Perhaps you're right, Morning Star, but if he didn't intend to give this impression why didn't he explain his position better? How about this statement,

"a love of children, hogwash!" I'm sorry, Morning Star, but I think that is terrible advice. For me, *love* is a prerequisite for teaching and for living.

MORNING STAR: Tony, many people are saying that educators who advocate a more humanistic approach to education are copping out. They feel we are not realistic about society and are hiding behind humanism in order to avoid situations such as giving tests, grading, and making decisions about the competency of our students.

TONY: That's not true! I can't for the life of me, understand how anyone can say that people who are concerned about self-concepts of children, children's attitudes, and children's values are copping out. If anyone is copping out, they are!

MORNING STAR: Tony, I'm sure we all agree with you. The point I'd like to make is that we may be

reading more into this article than the author intended. Perhaps he desired to have people think about humanism and its relationship to education and to discuss their concerns with others.

TONY: If that was his purpose, he certainly was successful with me.

CELLA: Wouldn't it be nice if we could sit down with Mr. Calisch and discuss his article and our concerns?

TONY: Well, Cella, we may never live to see it, but someday communications will allow teachers to enjoy such a discussion with authors like Mr. Calisch from the comfort of their own living rooms.

MORNING STAR: In loving, living color, Tony?

TONY: Certainly!

CELLA: And wouldn't it be nice to have someone like John Holt in on the conversation as well!

TONY: SOMEDAY! And as far as I'm concerned it can't happen too soon.

Think about your most
   recent teaching day.
How many times did you expect
   a superficial direction
   or answer?
How often did you hope the
   class would be passive,
   good, quiet?

Now think about yourself as a
   student—an adult returning
   for more learning.
How many times were you expected
   to give a superficial answer?
How often did you sit in class
   and know that your thoughts
   were afar?
How "turned on" were you?

Learning Opportunities. Films, texts, slides, discussion, field trips, role-playing, charts, maps all can be thought of in light of two concepts that have psychological ramifications: interpersonal relationships and activity. Most of the learning opportunities utilized in schools eliminate interpersonal communication on any other than a superficial level of direction-giving and answer-giving. The textbook is the focus of most classroom instruction and its use eliminates interpersonal communications of a significant nature. Secondly, most of the learning opportunities engender passivity. Students are not active intellectually or behaviorally. A textbook, film, filmstrip usually gives at best a prepackaged description of the problem, ways of solving the problem, and solutions. The student who is accustomed to "prepackaged" descriptions, explanations, and solutions loses the capacity to produce them for himself. In other words, his passivity has been constricting his development, his "activity" is greatly shaped by his environment.

From "Curriculum Development From A Psychoanalytic Perspective," by Louise L. Tyler

Humanizing Your Classroom:
Tips for the Teacher

**Encourage students to set their own standards and compete with themselves, not with others.

**Express respect for people and their differences.

**Refrain from stereotyping groups of people but don't ignore the differences children bring to school.

**People usually ridicule from ignorance. Teach for understanding.

What are your attitudes? Do you assume things about people based solely on the group they belong to? **Explore your own attitudes.

**Be careful of what you say in the classroom. Avoid remarks that compare groups of people.

**What do you expect from certain children based on race, sex, or socioeconomic status? Evaluate each as an individual.

FOR TEACHERS

Take a piece of paper.
Think about your professional life.
Begin with your preservice years.
As you remember your experiences, begin drawing a line across your paper, making peaks and valleys to represent good and bad experiences.

Describe your peaks and valleys.
Can you discover any consistent pattern in your peaks and valleys?

What part of your peaks and valleys were influenced by a teacher of some kind?

List those characteristics you possess that you feel make you a good teacher.
Ask your children to identify things about you that they feel make you a good teacher.

Compare
Or

List those characteristics that you feel would help make anyone a good teacher. Ask your children to do the same.

Compare

Think of your school and your classroom.
Are there some things you'd like to change?
List what you feel needs to be changed.
Identify why it can't be changed.
Do you have realistic reasons for thinking things can't be changed?
Share your thoughts with others, see if they agree.

Reality—Excuses—Fears—Courage

What is a good student?
Take a few minutes and describe in your own words the characteristics of a good student.
What kind of student were you?
Take a few minutes and rediscover yourself as a student. Describe yourself as a student. Would you like to teach a child who was a student just like you? Why?

Consider This

You are having a dinner party. Your best friend's husband spills a drink on your favorite chair. What would you say to your best friend's husband?

Now Consider This

A child in your classroom, while attempting to direct attention to himself (perhaps just like your friend's husband) spills paint over several pictures and the floor. What would you say to this child? Would you treat your best friend's husband any differently than a child in your classroom? If so, could you justify your behavior?

Open Sesame

CHAPTER NINE

To begin is never easy. Having assessed the alternatives and having looked squarely at one's own motives, having evaluated the odds and sized up the opposition, having decided the cause is just, one needs but the courage to act. At the end of the final chapter of **What Do I Do Monday?** John Holt puts it bluntly:

"Every day's headlines show more clearly that the old ways, the tried and true ways, are simply and quite spectacularly not working. No point in arguing about who's to blame. The time has come to do something very different. The way to begin is— to begin."

From "Assessing The Alternatives," by Charles H. Rathbone

CREATES (Cultural Resources Exploration: Awareness Through Educating the Senses) by Myra Danielson, CREATES Coordinator

It's 9:15, homeroom is over, and the line to the check-in and supply counter in CREATES looks like waves in motion as it flows from the hall into the Center. Approximately fifty children ranging in age from five to twelve are lined up to check into CREATES to do their "thing."

Jack, with a chicken in his arms, stands at the counter and announces that he is going to work on his "chicken project." "I gotta check the eggs in the incubator, then I think I'll draw a picture of my hen. She sure is neat, huh!" With this announcement Jack is off to begin another day of self-directed learning. This type of interaction is repeated until the initial flood of children are checked into the Center, their unfinished projects handed out, and supplies dispensed.

The room is a hive of activity. The noise is that of children doing and learning. Children flow in and out of CREATES all day. No child has to come to CREATES, but most children choose to come at one time or another during the day or week. The atmosphere is one of informal relaxed freedom.

How a child learns in CREATES is a very personal thing—he will learn in his own way, at his own pace, exploring his own interests, for his own purposes. Possible happenings in CREATES on a typical day at any given time are as follows: Jack and two others who have become interested, sit at a table drawing pictures of a chicken using the hen as a model. Two boys build a boat model from scrap lumber and discover that if you soak wood it becomes flexible and you can bend it. A group meets and works on plans for setting up a center and teaching a mini-course on ecology. The group has gathered materials, talked to resource people and researched the topic for a month. They now are chatting and working on posters to advertise the mini-course and center. Another group is watching filmstrips and listening to records. A child is curled up on a pile of pillows, reading, while next to him several children are working with a student teacher building structures from various materials and testing them for strength of design. A group works at the tinker table exploring and investigating a car transmission and other assorted machines. Two boys talk to the teacher about insects while two others play chess. So goes a normal day in CREATES!

With the diversity of projects and the wide range of explorations going on at one time the teacher's role is that of facilitator. The teacher moves from one group to another or to an individual—listening, questioning, suggesting, accepting. The questions that a teacher would plan to have children explore usually come from the children through their own discoveries while exploring whatever "things" or interests they are working (or playing) with. Children feel free to approach any adult in the environment and their peers for help.

The CREATES environment is rich with an abundance of varied materials, "things" and resources available to all children regardless of age level. Curiosity, individual interests, and the uniqueness of each child is highly valued. The emphasis is on the child, not the subject matter.

In CREATES everyone is a learner and everyone is a teacher. CREATES really means CREATES—children creating learning environments for other children and for adults, and adults creating learning environments for other adults and for children.

—Exploratory Learning Center Tucson District #1

plea

New Symbols

zrr

shun

ist

itza

ax

ur

hmp

zak

prt

bl

mt

shm

ims

gnerg

Arroba

onk

twize

um

weem

twims

lop

sloot

twiggle

New Words

Sherlock Holmes and others

New Ideas

RECIPES FOR SUCCESS

SUPPORT

1. Take one willing teacher or a team of teachers who want to create an open learning environment.
2. Add other adults who share their ideals and have experienced openness in a classroom.
3. Mix together professionally and socially.
4. Surround yourself with supportive people—allow yourself the luxury of positive support!

MOVEMENT

1. Take an aspiring open classroom teacher.
2. Add movement-toward-openness at a rate that is comfortable for that teacher.
3. Mix time for thinking, for exploring, for evaluation, for choices, for problem solving, for observing children, and for more evaluation.
4. Add support, assistance, and self-appraisal as requested.

CURRICULUM

1. Take skills and knowledge that appear to be necessary for successful living in our society.
2. Add the interests, needs, and concerns of children.
3. Mix together these ingredients for each child, adding skills and knowledge to the interests, needs, and concerns of children.

WARNING: Do not premix before knowing each child!

SELF-APPRAISAL

1. Take teachers interested in open education.
2. Add: (a) open education materials of all kinds.
    (b) visits to open classrooms
    (c) professional meetings and in-service programs
    (d) college seminars and classes on open education
    (e) private discussions with professionals
3. Mix these ingredients together with a serious evaluation of each teacher's beliefs about children, learning, society, knowledge, and education.

PARENT INVOLVEMENT

1. Take an aspiring open classroom teacher, a classroom of children, a supportive principal and parents.
2. Add informal coffees for parents, parent visits, classroom newsletters, and parent aides.
3. Mix ingredients with honest open communication and dialog.
4. Add patience, understanding, empathy, concern, and appreciation as needed.

ASSISTANCE

1. Take one open teacher or an open teacher team.
2. Add: (a) principal support and assistance
    (b) one or more teacher aides
    (c) parent assistants
    (d) cross-age helpers
    (e) supportive curriculum specialists
    (f) interested and knowledgeable professors
    (g) local community resources
3. Mix ingredients together in the amount that best fits needs of the children and teachers.

FOR TEACHERS

A Way To Encourage Interaction among Children.

Write on index cards the names of famous explorers. Pin a card on the back of each student. By asking only two questions of each person, which can only be answered by a yes or no, each child is to try and figure out who he is.

Other ideas:
names of occupations, birds, sports personalities, names of pets.

Beyond Manila-Folder Learning Centers

Create learning centers with a lot of manipulative materials. Store the materials in boxes. Label your boxes. Allow children to explore the boxes as they become interested in the topic or materials or introduce children to the boxes as you see interest or need.

Beyond Teacher-Made Learning Centers

Provide children the opportunity to create learning centers for themselves and others. After all they probably know more about what children are interested in than you, the teacher!

Beyond Show and Tell

Create several sharing stations. Rather than having all children listen to everyone share, announce what is to be shared and where the sharing will take place. Provide children the opportunity to visit all or none of the sharing stations. Don't forget that the teacher draws a crowd so get around to all stations. That way no one will be without an audience.

Beyond the Call of Duty

As teacher, do something in the room that you would like to do even if the children were not there. Like read, paint, knit, work on your picture file, etc. You'll be surprised what a positive effect it will have on your feelings and attitude, plus, children will have the opportunity to see you as you really are. Who knows, some of your children might get involved as well. Wanta bet??

Parent Involvement

Survey Your Parents
Discover
1 occupations
2 hobbies
3 travels
4 interests
5 concerns
Find ways to use this expertise in your classroom!

Don't overlook the mother with a new baby—invite both of them to school.

Don't forget fathers!!

Don't forget grandparents!!

Don't forget older brothers and sisters!!

Ask parents to assist you with:

Learning centers

Crafts projects

Field trips

Listening to children
read, share, or
just talk.

Routine paper work

FOR TEACHERS

A Way To Facilitate Communication:

Encourage children to write notes to each other—notes that are positive and constructive in nature!

Dear Darren,
Thank you for being my friend
from Bill

Dear Mrs. James:
I don't feel that you treated Mark right today. Mark acted worse after you punished him.

Dear Mrs. James,
Thank you for giving us choice centers. School is a lot more fun now!
Love
xxxx Karen

Dear Mrs. James, I love you

The teacher should also write notes to children!

Dear Mary
How pretty you look today. Your dress looks beautiful!
Mrs James

Dear Kerry,
I would really appreciate it if you would not bother Mike so much. He told me that he likes you but you tease him too much.
Mrs James

Dear Mary,
I really appreciate the help you gave John and Sue. I don't know what I would do without your help. Thank you!
Mrs James

Where Do We Go From Here?

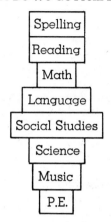

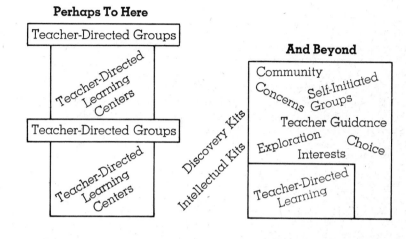

Emphasis	Emphasis	Emphasis
1. Textbook Orientation	1. Textbook and Experiential Orientation	1. Experiential Orientation
2. Content Centered	2. Content-Person Centered	2. Person Centered
3. Logical Sequence	3. Logical-Psychological Sequence	3. Psychological Sociological Logical Sequence
4. Teacher Directed	4. Teacher Directed with some shared Responsibility	4. Shared Responsibility
5. Abstractions	5. Abstraction with some Action	5. Action/Abstraction
6. Group Norms	6. Group and Individual Norms	6. Individual Norms
7. Segmented Time	7. Less Segmented Time	7. Large Blocks of Time
8. Separate Disciplines	8. Cross Discipline Relationships	8. Integrated Curriculum
9. Predetermined Curriculum	9. Predetermined Curriculum with Modifications	9. Emerging Curriculum

SELF-SELECTION CLASSROOM
by Zilpha W. Billings

In the days when I did much substitute teaching, I realized that the teacher talk I heard in many different schools often centered around problem children—the slow child, the lazy child, the day-dreamer, the underachiever, the emotionally disturbed child.

As I listened to the discussions, I wondered whether methods of teaching were at least partly responsible for these children's problems.

When later I became the regular teacher of a fourth grade classroom, I ran head on into the problem children I had heard about in the teachers' lounge. Most of my pupils were eager to learn, but a few of them had already turned school off and tuned teachers out. I wondered why this should be the case with boys and girls who were only nine years old.

When I questioned children about their turned-off, tuned-out attitudes on school, they acknowledged such reactions as "afraid of seeming dumb" and "afraid of teachers."

That responses bothered me, and, as time went on, I kept asking myself: are there teaching methods that can enable **all** children to develop a positive self-image? How can I develop a classroom situation that will build **all** children's self-confidence and self-esteem?

I began to find an answer to my questions while teaching a sixth grade at Flynn School in Burlington, Vermont, under a fine principal who believed that teachers often had better ideas than the textbook manual and encouraged and supported them in being creative. This atmosphere fostered the development of what I later called the "self-selection laboratory."

As the classroom climate changed from emphasis on teacher to emphasis on pupil, I was excited and amazed to see changes in pupils' attitudes toward themselves, each other, and me. It seemed a big step to me when pupils were freed to select **which** story they'd read **first** in a basal reader. It was an even bigger step when they could select which story they would **not** read in the text. The step to individualized reading was easier as I became aware that boys and girls wanted to read about **living**—not stories with unreal endings.

I had experienced the satisfying, exciting results of offering children the opportunity to learn without the pressure to do so at a teacher-set time. So, when the call came from the school administration, "Put ideas into action," I was ready to draft a proposal for organizing and putting into effect a self-selection laboratory for a year. The superintendent and the school commissioners approved the proposal. I was off!

The first experimental year began with a completely heterogeneous group of 40 sixth graders and a teacher aide. Early in the school year I arranged meetings with the students' parents to explain the self-selection concept. When parents understood that the student's choices were not in the area of whether to work or not, but rather what subject he'd work in at what time and with what materials, with the goals of self-motivation and development of good study habits, they felt safe to let their children try.

I explained self-selection goals to the school staff and asked for their appraisal as the year went on. Any program that is pioneering in relatively new and unknown areas usually creates anxiety and fear—fear of failure, fear of what others will think and say. Self-selection was no exception, but the positive attitudes, concern, and understanding of all the staff and my teacher aide made the first year a relaxed, fulfilling one.

In an orientation workshop at the start of school, the students and I planned together to develop an understanding of the privileges, responsibilities, and duties each member must assume. We discussed the role of the teacher as catalyst, resource person, guide, and friend and the student's role as a unique individual with his special strengths, needs, goals, and purposes.

The teacher aide and I instructed the students in the proper use of all media in the classroom. I helped them acquire procedures for evaluating their own learnings and identifying their own needs. Each child received curriculum guidelines to help him establish his goals. Because of the wide diversity in students' abilities, I took care to provide meaningful guidelines within which all children could meet varying degrees of success each day.

To facilitate maximum use of all materials, I divided the curriculum into four areas: language arts, mathematics, science (man's place in sciences), and social studies (a problem approach to man and his world). I collected the materials for all these areas with totally individualized teaching in mind. Consequently, reading levels of the materials started with a low fourth and advanced in some cases to college level.

I also prepared a short, concise summary of minimum achievements in each area to help the student find out where he presently was and where he might hope to go. Thus, a student who might be working on fractions in the math area could take the following routes: (a) any one of as many math books as I could obtain with a teacher's edition for self-correcting, (b) a game dealing with fractions, (c) an electric fraction board, (d) matching equivalent fraction line, (e) solving teacher-prepared, real-life problems dealing with fractions, (f) constructing and putting up a teaching fraction bulletin board, (g) discovering with manipulative fraction pieces, (h) working with a programed prepared kit on fractions, (i) working through a visual package of transparencies on fractions, (j) making and solving his own fraction problems, (k) selecting a peer to teach or to be taught by, (l) listening to a tape while watching a filmstrip on fractions, (m) working on a page from a teacher-prepared, programed math kit. This example typifies our attempt to have many different media for doing the same thing successfully so each child could find a way that worked best for him.

By means of portable room dividers, we organized the room into four flexible areas: mathematics, science, language arts, and social studies. to facilitate free flow in the classroom, we replaced desks with tables and stacking chairs.

Pupils preplanned their day within varying blocks of time according to their needs and interests. For evaluation we used many kinds of testing. Sometimes the teacher alone did the evaluating; sometimes the pupil alone; sometimes the two **together.**

The pupils selected the area they worked in, the materials they used there, and the length of time they stayed before moving on to another area. Each student worked through his preplanned schedule until he encountered difficulty, at which time he requested help. Changes in the original planning occurred as pupils gradually began to comprehend the actual degree of their involvement in the classroom.

The interest and response of fellow teachers was rewarding: By the end of the first year, several levels were trying self-selection. As the second year continued, more and more teachers were experimenting with various methods of adaptation. Those who elected to change were both experienced teachers and new teachers, ranging from kindergarten through sixth grade. Their approaches to self-selection varied with their experience and daring.

Interested teachers began to collect curriculum material for one area at a time. Since only regular budget money was available for this project, teachers became very creative in finding many ways to reach the same end. They pored through trade catalogs to find more materials to meet children's diverse needs. We divided books and existing materials among many classrooms. In individualized teaching, no area needs materials for more than six or eight pupils at a time. Thus we could divide many programmed kits equally among two or three rooms.

Teachers began assembling a variety of work sheets from as many sources as possible to set up their own programmed kits. They made some work sheets into transparencies to use on an overhead projector or at a child's seat; others, they covered with X-ray film or laminating film to be written on directly and then erased. Each kit provided many levels of nonconsumable, sequential-skill-development practice sets.

When a teacher had collected enough materials in the area in which he felt most comfortable, he talked over the change with his students, and self-selection began. Once a small beginning had occurred evolvement into total self-selection seemed inevitable, for teachers feel rewarded when they see busy, happy children working responsibly.

As I visit classrooms where self-selection is in effect, I see many common values that I believe are important to children while they seek new knowledge and skills. Let me share these with you:

• The atmosphere is relaxed and happy as thirty or more youngsters work on their own, communicating ideas with the low busy hum of a beehive.

• Instructional grouping is flexible. Large group instruction and participation occur when they prove to be more effective than individual instruction. Grouping in self-selection may be teacher- or student-initiated to meet a particular goal. No grouping is permanent as the children's rates and levels change from day to day and from week to week.

• Individualized reading is used to help each child reach his potential. Mini-books, made by taking apart basal readers and color coding a paper cover for each story according to reading level, allow each child on any level to become involved with a book the first day of school.

• As often as possible, the carefully selected curriculum materials are self-directing (to let a student feel his own inner strength) and self-correcting (to immediately reinforce correct work habits and to help him assess his need to ask for assistance).

• Students organize their day. Children on the primary level work with a weekly schedule in planning their day. During pupil-teacher conferences they set reasonable goals for daily achievement. Children must be helped to determine what they ought to learn. When a child consistently avoids an important area, the teacher helps him understand its value and encourages him to undertake it in a way that interests and concerns him.

Intermediate-level children accept the responsibility of writing their own schedules each day. The teacher offers exactly as much help as each child needs in order for him to become proficient at this.

• Grouping is heterogeneous. We deliberately group each level heterogeneously according to chronological age to create a mini-world in which real-life problems arise and can be handled with the help of an alert teacher.

• The children have time to think new thoughts uninterruptedly, to envision unknown frontiers, to create in styles peculiarly their own, to question established ideas and facts, to decide **who** they are and **what** they are in their world.

Now, if you agree that all children can and want to learn, all children can identify real purposes for learning, all children can learn to identify their needs all children can be self-directing in their learning, all children can learn to evaluate their own learning, then, self-selection may be for you.

FOR TEACHERS

TEACHING OBJECTIVE—SEQUENCE SKILLS

RATHER THAN THIS:

(NO CHOICE)

Draw a picture describing an experience in a cave. Your picture must have a beginning—a middle—and an end.

WHY NOT THIS:

(SOME CHOICE)

1. You may draw the picture
   or
2. Work with this box of pictures. After you have explored the pictures put them in an order that tells a story. Share your story with a friend.

AND BEYOND TO:

(MANY CHOICES)

3. Find someone who would like to act out your story—organize your play into parts.
4. Listen to the three story versions on the tape recorder and choose the version you like the best—share your choice with others.
5. Use the puppets to act out a story you would like to share.
6. Draw several pictures about our last moon mission—make sure your pictures show different things that happened throughout the entire mission. Let other children try to put the pictures in the order in which they really occurred during the mission.
7. Work with the "life stages of the butterfly" models and see if you can put them in the order that they occur in real life—begin with any stage you want to—have a friend check to see if he agrees with you.
8. Draw some pictures of the things you do when you get up and get ready for school—have some friends guess the order in which you do them—perhaps some of your friends would like to do the same thing—ask them.
9. Draw some pictures or act out with some friends several specific things your mother does in the morning while she is preparing breakfast—make a list of kinds of breakfasts that your mother might prepare and choose one.

DON'T FORGET:

Children have different learning styles—
Children have different interests and concerns!

Don't put all your eggs in one basket—
Provide a variety of activities!

From—Learning Centers

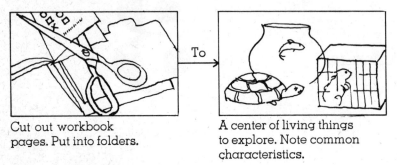

Cut out workbook
pages. Put into folders.

To

A center of living things
to explore. Note common
characteristics.

From—Activity Cards

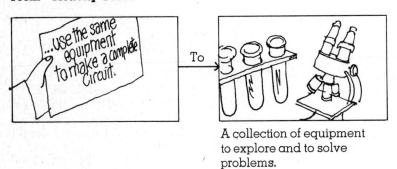

To

A collection of equipment
to explore and to solve
problems.

**To—Intellectual Kits
    Discovery Kits**

Collection of
shoes
lids
buttons
tools

Collection of hats

Box of cultural items
from Japan

FOR TEACHERS

Open Up Your Classroom!

There is nothing magical about the quality of classroom learning.

Allow the total community to become a learning center for your children.

Consider for a moment all the potential learning opportunities represented by these sample community resources.

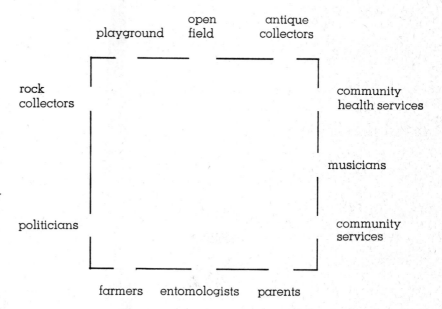

playground   open field   antique collectors

rock collectors   community health services

musicians

politicians   community services

farmers   entomologists   parents

Reading—

From: Mother-hen-and-her-baby-chicks concept of teaching reading	To: A Wider Range of Reading Materials	To: A wider range of materials and activities	To: Student Self-Pacing	
Emphasis	Emphasis	Emphasis	Emphasis	
Basal Reader				Listening centers
Oral Reading	Individualizing materials			Creative-writing centers
Teacher-Directed Learning	Teacher directed		Communication skills	
Student Dependence	Some student choice of materials	Individualizing materials	Child directed	Art center
Reading Circle	Individualizing activities	Personalized	Library center	
Departmentalized	More activities	Language Development	Teacher guidance	Publishing center
Seat Work	Departmentalized		Independence	Drama center
			Integrated	Music center

Writing—

TITLES

I can write five sentences.

My Own Book

CHARACTERIZATIONS

Words—
action
color
descriptive
3 syllables

choose phrases to describe

PLAYS

about yourself as the
person or object in
the picture

match words to pictures

rewrite a story substituting as
many words as possible while
keeping the same message for
the same picture

develop sequential
actions—before
picture and after
picture

SLOGANS

COMMERCIALS

comic strip for a picture

outline for describing a picture

write how a picture would look to you if you were a giant. Then write
how it would look to you if you were a small insect.

Listening—

. . . to someone **naming** objects or people in photos or pictures.

. . . to someone **listing** all things that begin or end alike.

. . . to someone **name** and **count** all feeling words or color words or doing words, etc.

. . . to someone **tell** a story about the picture, or begin a story for someone else to end.

. . . to several different **versions** of the same title for a picture.

. . . to **hear** how many questions a group can think to ask when looking at a picture.

. . . to **identify** the characters or persons in a picture who might be speaking and to suggest what they are saying.

. . . to **intonations** of ideas or expressions to accompany pictures.

. . . to **hear** great variety of possible titles for any one picture.

. . . to **conversations** inspired by pictures.

. . . to **slogans** that might be appropriate.

. . . to ideas for **discussions** about pictures.

. . . to "what if" **kick-offs** from pictures.

. . . to **ways** pictures might be altered to produce different results.

. . . to **sounds** made by fingers being run over or rubbed on different kinds of surfaces.

Telling—

... how things in the pictures feel, taste, smell, etc.

... why things look as they do.

... what the picture does to me, or for me.

... what the picture could look like "if"...

... how many words I can think of to talk about this picture.

... how science, social studies, math, English all can be found in a picture.

... what ideas are stimulated by a picture.

... what pictures you could make from parts of other pictures.

... what commercials can be made to sell a picture or its components.

... how I would make my art museum.

... the artist's viewpoint or the photographer's story.

... why I chose this picture.

... poetry inspired by a picture.

... "Once upon a time" stories of pictures.

... resumés of literature that a picture brings to mind by dramatizing or pantomime.

Seeing—

facial expressions   focus   events   stories   behind the scenes
  body postures   background   action   captions   what might be next
    kinds of movements   hidden ideas   diagrams   descriptions
    patterns
     shadings

KEEP YOUR EYE ON THE WANT ADS—

820 Drawings	841 Photographs	862 Pictures	878 Cartoons

These are categories in the want-ad section of the newspaper that we use for stimulating creative activities.

This then led to the use of other kinds of paper products to be used:

1. As background on which to paste things.
2. As foreground on other backgrounds.
3. As content in stories, jokes, poems, other ideas.
4. As individual letters from which to form words, etc.

One of our many "do-not-throw-away-until every-possible-use-is-made-of-it" activities!

—emc

wallpaper
  book covers
   record covers
newspapers
  periodicals
   posters   Christmas, birthday and other cards
    school photographs   place mats, napkins, table cloths
     pictures taken by the class   cereal boxes, labels from cans
     pictures made by children
      tactile pictures—mud, string, glue, paint etc.   wrapping paper
      art work   bags from various stores
                  sheet music
                  letterheads
                   toy boxes and wrapping
                    garment bags from cleaners

"HOW-TO" BOOKLETS

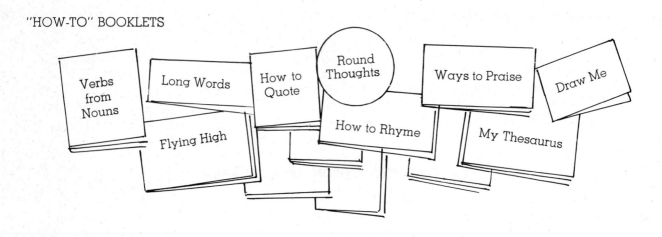

Verbs from Nouns

Long Words

How to Quote

Round Thoughts

Ways to Praise

Draw Me

Flying High

How to Rhyme

My Thesaurus

WRITING CENTER

ACTIVITY CARDS

Games   Puzzles   What if?   Book jackets

CORRESPONDENCE DESK
Assortment of writing paper.
Zip code booklet.
Pen(s).
Stamps.
Dictionary.

Find others like me
One for me and
One for my friend

PUBLISHING PEN
Titles to be expanded,
illustrated or substituted.
Tapes to be typed.
Stories to be taped.
News to be organized.

Stories to be titled, illustrated,
edited, or completed.

ACTION BULLETIN BOARDS
Listening
Speaking

Writing
Reading

How do you work with Writing Skills?

Rather than: Underlining or encircling errors in red.
  Holding formal writing lessons for the entire class,
    Facing wide discrepancies between penmanship papers and the daily papers.

Build a:

writing center—an
attractive desk with a
variety of writing papers
(personal—not school paper)
and implements with which
to write, as well as ideas
for personally meaningful
reasons for writing.

bulletin board
with postmarks,
cancelled stamps, and
interesting examples of penmanship.

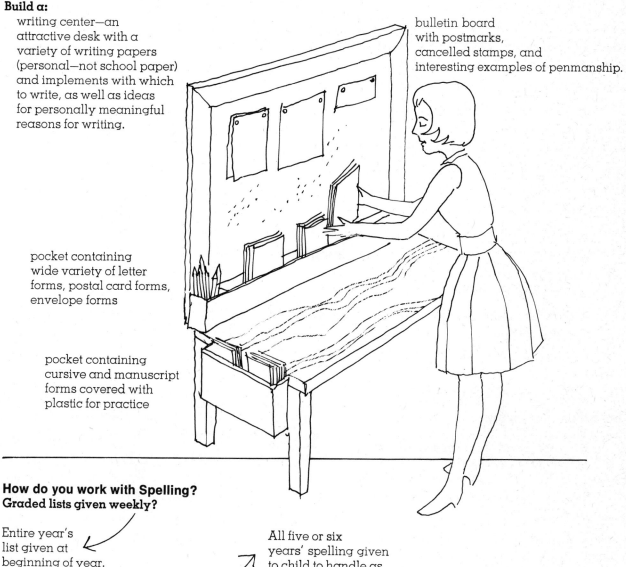

pocket containing
wide variety of letter
forms, postal card forms,
envelope forms

pocket containing
cursive and manuscript
forms covered with
plastic for practice

How do you work with Spelling?
Graded lists given weekly?

Entire year's
list given at
beginning of year.
Children divide "unknown"
words into weekly lists
with weekly testing.

All five or six
years' spelling given
to child to handle as
expediently as possible.
(Frees teachers to work
with individuals.)

How do you work with Math?

From graded texts
with many topics
touched upon each year.

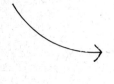

Sharing with children
the six years of texts
and enabling them to
pursue topics in depth if
desired.

Identifying basic math
topics and encouraging
children to pursue each topic
in depth, and in order of
learner's preference.

Solving problems,
keeping diary of math
learned as problems are
solved.

 **FOR TEACHERS**

Let's think about social studies for a moment!

Rather than using these kinds of typical social studies units:

Indians of the Southwest   Hot Wet Lands

Mexico   Community Helpers   Canada

Northeastern States

Why not provide your children with some of these theme choices?

music   producer   fun   pets   food

frontiers (past and present)   seaport cities

games   peace   precious gems   emotions

love   consumer   change   leisure time

innovation   work   plan

leaders and leadership   superstitions

CONSIDER: 1. What is really important for children to learn?
                    2. What kind of society will our children spend their adult lives in?

How do you work with Science?

Short science lessons ——————— S ———→ Science learning centers
twice a week.   as part of daily work.

Science indoors. ————————— C ———→ Science outdoors.

Reading as large part of science ——— I ———→ Doing as largest part
curriculum.   of science curriculum.

Discussions from random ————— E ———→ Provisions of many good activities
experiential backgrounds of   to provide rich experiential background.
children.

Light-touch, oft-repeated units ——— N ———→ School-wide planning of rich, in-depth
(i.e., Magnetism, Seasons, etc.).   science explorations.

Large group (We're **all** interested —— C ———→ Individual and small-group science.
in orchids!) science.

Learning about science. ————— E ———→ Learning to use scientific knowledge
                                               in daily life and to use daily life for
                                               learning more scientific knowledge.

SCIENTIFIC SKILLS

Do you use, and encourage children to use these skills for all activities?

observe	observe differences	observe differences	and on
record	record	record	and on
test	test	test	and on
retest	retest	retest	
conclude	conclude	conclude	

ANIMALS

Children throughout an elementary school
experience should have many chances to care
for a wide variety of animals and
to know they can help, hurt, or cause
a smaller creature to die.

PLANTS

Regardless of whether you teach in the city
or in the country, chances are that if you
examine a one-mile square area around your
school, you'll find small plants and trees that
neither you nor your children will know. Why
don't you know them? Think of the math, science,
social studies and language arts involved in
mapping out and identifying plant life
in such a mile.

A Large-Group Exploratory Experience with Elementary School Children

1. Children of third through sixth year were brought together and shown a painting of an American Revolution scene on the opaque projector. They called out what they saw (no raised hands, just polite behavior, watching and listening for a turn.)

2. Children were told the teachers wanted to see what would happen if during certain portions of each day of the next five weeks they would explore one question—"How was it possible for the small thirteen colonies to defeat the great British Empire?" They could work alone or in small groups and could seek help from any teacher or teachers in the school. The sixth week could be "share" so conclusions could be drawn.

3. The results were fantastic! There were plays and authentic dress; governmental debates; models of ships with accurate sizes and kinds of cannon; charts and models of food-carrying limitations; mock-ups of British soldiers under-limitations; mock-ups of British soldiers as compared with American woodsmen and Indian allies; etc.

4. In reaching conclusions, no small paragraph of six major reasons was possible. Children quickly saw that a "historical fact" represented hundreds of complex events—and they could even see that in winning the war, we lost many good things.

—emc

A FEW WORDS ON CAREER EDUCATION
by Paul Anthony Mihalik

Educators, as of this writing, still do not agree on a definition of career education. Most can agree, however, on the goals and objectives behind this thrust in education. Briefly stated, proponents of career education generally agree that a number of elements must be developed in the student for adequate career preparation. These elements are: (1) self-awareness, (2) career awareness or career opportunities, (3) educational awareness and opportunities, (4) appreciations and attitudes concerning the work ethic, and (5) an understanding of the decision-making process.

My experience in one of the federally funded exemplary projects has been with fifty-four elementary school teachers (in grades kindergarten through six) in five elementary schools. Our efforts have been quite experimental in the attempt to integrate the goals and objectives of career education into the regular classroom curriculum, and I can describe this attempt as one of the most interesting, motivating, and encouraging educational experiences of my career in education.

Since children would prefer to be involved in an action activity that holds their interest, we find that field trips, hands-on activities with tools, kits of occupational interest, and research activities into careers can be beautifully integrated into the language arts, mathematics, social studies, and arts and crafts curricula. When the youngsters see for themselves that there is a very relevant tie-in between the school curricula and the world outside the school building, they simultaneously discover that school can and does serve a very personalized service to them. Isn't this what the parents really expect of our educational institutions? Isn't a "functional citizen" the ultimate goal of every teacher's efforts? Most of us, I believe, are striving to help our youngsters to become aware of the realities of life and to help them tackle these realities with as realistic a preparation as possible. Career education might well be one of the means by which educators can achieve their goals and their students' goals.

One aspect of career education that gives it a better than average chance for survival among the current innovative trends is its primary goal of career development. Whether you are team-teaching, in an open classroom, self-contained, or whatever your approach, you can introduce the career education concept into your curriculum. It's really a frame of reference or point of view that permeates your curriculum presentation. It **is not** another subject to be taught in the sense of another textbook to use. You'll find yourself using your textbooks as a career-awareness tool. You'll find it almost impossible to turn a page in any text without seeing a relevant connection to an occupation or a vocation. The imaginative and creative teacher will find that there really is a substantial platform from which to launch her curriculum, and it will be a fresh viewpoint of the textbooks that can make the vital difference to education and to students. Career education serves not as an impediment to the teacher's efforts within a very crowded time-frame, but as an incentive, a motivator, and a relevant assist to our younger people who are thirsting for meaningful experiences. We owe them at least that much while they are entrusted to our charge.

Note: Paul Anthony Mihalik is on Elementary Resource Person, Tucson District #1. Paul, with others, has developed "HANDS-ON" kits in foot lockers. These kits enable children and teachers to explore feelings, actions and materials that adults use to earn a living. Some kits are:

Cooking kit (everything but the food to make a complete meal)

Medical kit	Plumber's kit
Transportation kit	Garden kit
Mineralogy kit	Workbench

A Webbing Experience for
Open Education Block Students

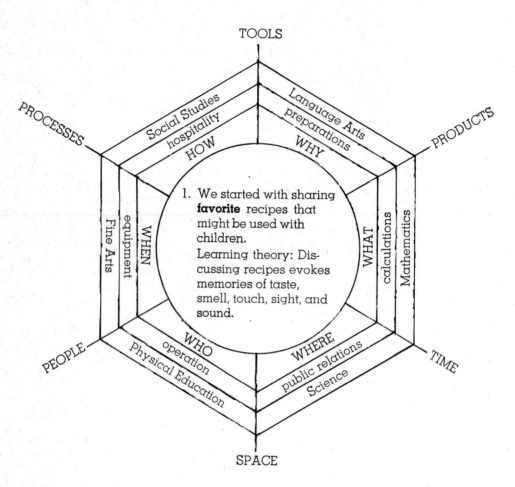

1. We started with sharing **favorite** recipes that might be used with children.
   Learning theory: Discussing recipes evokes memories of taste, smell, touch, sight, and sound.

2. We listed all the questions we thought about as we discussed our favorite recipes.
3. We formed committees to make a full meal for ourselves and guests (to test these recipes).
4. We reorganized the questions to see how they would fit the subject matter areas found in the elementary schools.
5. We "discovered" common strands.
6. We concluded:
   a. Total involvement is FUN!
   b. Much learning occurred.
   c. Most learning is actually cross-disciplined rather than segmented.
   d. An open teacher could really start from any experience or idea and go to any place—thus meeting the learning paces and styles of children. All she needs to know is the basic structure of the school's curricula.

As we end this Primer on Open Education, we
are well aware that we still have not given you a formal
definition of Open Education. We do feel, however,
that we have offered you, through excerpt, dialog,
and illustrations, many examples of open education.
We believe our chapter titles offer you the basis for
developing open learning environments and we
think that each of you must determine the pacing
and styling of each of these important elements.
There is one thing we can say for certain—your
exploration of providing alternatives for children will
keep life from being dull.

—Evelyn Carswell and Darrell Roubinek

Acknowledgments

viii Photo courtesy of Office of Education.

3 From Lillian Weber, *The English Infant School and Informal Education* (Englewood Cliffs, N.J.: Prentice-Hall).

4 From William D. Romey, "The Curriculum-Proof Teacher," *Phi Delta Kappan,* February 1973.

From Dr. Haim Ginott, *Teacher and Child,* copyright © 1972 by Congruent Communications, Inc. Reprinted with permission of the author and of Macmillan Company. Dr. Ginott is also the author of *Group Psychotherapy with Children* (McGraw-Hill) and of the best sellers—*Between Parent and Child* and *Between Parent and Teenager* (Macmillan).

4 From Kahlil Gilbran, *The Prophet,* with permission of the publisher, Alfred A. Knopf, Inc. Copyright © 1923 by Kahlil Gilbran; renewal copyright 1951 by Administrators C. T. A. of Kahlil Gibran Estate, and Mary G. Gibran.

5 Janet Bauer, "The Magic Wand," *The Educational Forum,* January 1972, p. 168, with permission of Kappa Delta Pi, An Honor Society in Education, owners of the copyright.

6 From Robert J. Fisher, *Learning How to Learn* (New York: Harcourt Brace Jovanovich, © 1972), reprinted with permission of the publisher.

6 From Albert Schweitzer, *Memoirs of Childhood and Youth* (New York: Macmillan, 1949). Reprinted with permission of the publishers, Macmillan, and Allan and Unwin, Ltd.

7 Photo by Alan Mercer.

From Leila Berg, *Look at Kids* (London: Penguin Books, 1972), Penguin Education Series, copyright © 1972 by Leila Berg, reprinted with permission of the publisher.

10 From Don Fabun, *Children of Change.* Copyright © 1969 by Kaiser Aluminum & Chemical Corporation. Reprinted courtesy of Glencoe Press.

Alwin W. Howard, "Disciplin is Caring," *Today's Education,* March 1972, reprinted with permission of the publisher and author.

12 From Theodore Roszak, "Educating Contra Naturam," *A Man For Tomorrow's World* (Association for Supervision and Curriculum Development, © 1970), reprinted with permission of the publisher.

14 From Carl R. Rogers, "Toward Becoming a Fully Functioning Person," *Perceiving, Behaving, Becoming: A New Focus for Education* (Association for Supervision and Curriculum Development), reprinted with permission of the publisher.

Excerpted from John Holt, *Why Children Fail* (New York: Pitman Publishing Company).

15 Photo courtesy of Gordon Menzie.

16 From Earl C. Kelley, *In Defense of Youth* (Englewood Cliffs, N.J.: Prentice-Hall, © 1962), reprinted with permission of the publisher.

18 From Dr. Haim Ginott, *Teacher and Child,* copyright © 1972 by Congruent Communications, Inc. Reprinted with permission of the author and of Macmillan Company.

Jack E. Smith, Jr., "The Children of Summer," *The Educational Forum,* March 1972, p. 322, with permission of Kappa Delta Pi, An Honor Society in Education, owners of the copyright.

20 From Evelyn Carswell, "The Elementary Feature," *The Instructor,* October 1972, p. 17, reprinted with permission of the publisher.

From Ralph L. Mosher and David E. Purpel, *Supervision: The Reluctant Profession* (Boston: Houghton Mifflin Company).

23 Jim Gibbons, "A Peso for Their Thoughts" reprinted with permission of the author.

26 From John Holt, *How Children Learn* (New York: Pitman Publishing Company, © 1967), reprinted with permission of the publisher.

29 James A. Smith, "The Awful Beginning," *Today's Education,* April 1972, reprinted with permission of the publisher and author.

31 From Ralph L. Mosher and David E. Purpel, *Supervision: The Reluctant Profession* (Boston: Houghton Miffling Company).

Mary M. Harris, "Failure in First-Grade," *Today's Education,* February 1972, reprinted with permission of the publisher and author.

33 Kathleen Mulholland, "To Julie," *The Education Forum,* January 1972, p. 220, with permission of Kappa Delta Pi, An Honor Society in Education, owners of the copyright.

34 From Frederick M. Raubinger, "What's the Score on Pressures on Students," *Today's Education,* December 1971.

Brian Patrick McGuire, "The Grading Game," *Today's Education,* March 1969, p. 32, reprinted with the permission of the publisher and author.

37 From Don Fabun, *On Education,* Kaiser Aluminum News.

From R. Dean Gaudette, "Flexible Scheduling: An Elementary School Need," *Kappa Delta Pi Record,* October 1971, pp. 11-12, reprinted with permission of the publisher.

38 Girolama Garner, "When Jerry Listened," with permission of the author.

39 From *The Plowden Report,* The Central Advisory Council for Education, U.K.G.B.

40 Walter de la Mare, "Me," in *Bells and Grass,* copyright © 1941 by Walter de la Mare, renewed © 1969 by Richard de la Mare, reprinted by permission of The Viking Press, Inc.

From "Statement of School Philosophy," Sacred Heart School, Tucson, Arizona. Reprinted with permission of Sacred Heart School and Sister Judith Bisignano, O.P.

41 From John Holt, *Freedom and Beyond* (New York: E. P. Dutton & Company), copyright © 1972 by John Holt. Reprinted with permission of the publisher.

Beryce W. MacLennan, "Scapegoating," *Today's Education,* September 1969, p. 38, reprinted with permission of the publisher and the author.

44 Evelyn M. Carswell, "Teacher, Teacher."

45 From Diane Divoky, "Corporal Punishment in U. S. Schools," *Saturday Review,* February 1973.

From Mariam Goldberg, "Types of Programs," *Educating the Children of the Poor* (Association for Supervision and Curriculum Development, © 1968), reprinted with permission of the publisher.

46-47 Photo by Werner Wolff, courtesy OEO.

48 Mona Mouton, "A Shattered Dream," with permission of the author.

50 Photo courtesy of VISTA.

52 © 1969 United Feature Syndicate, Inc.

From Daniel N. Fader and Morton H. Shaevitz, *Hooked On Books,* (New York: Berkley Publication Corp.), copyright © 1966 by Daniel N. Feder and Morton H. Shaevitz, reprinted with permission of the publisher and authors.

From Leila Berg, *Look at Kids,* (London: Penguin Books, 1972), Penguin Education Series, copyright © 1972 by Leila Berg, reprinted with permission of the publisher.

54 From Larry Nash and Lyn Simmons, "Teacher in Individualized Instruction . . . A Relationship of Guidance Towards Discovery," *Anne Arundel Times,* November 11-12, 1970. Reprinted with permission of the publisher.

55 Stephen M. Corey, "The Poor Scholar's Soliloquy," *Childhood Education,* January 1944, reprinted with permission of the Association for Childhood Education International.

56 From Marshall McLuhan, *Understanding Media: The Extensions of Man* (New York: McGraw-Hill, © 1964), p. 301, reprinted with permission of the publisher.

56 From Dick Hubert and Peter Hauck, "How Fred Andrew Tills the Soil, with a Computer," *Saturday Review of the Society,* March 1973, reprinted with permission of the publisher.

58 From John Henry Martin, "The Grade School Come From Prussia," *Educational Horizon,* Fall 1972.

From George B. Leonard, *Education and Ecstasy* (Delta Publication Company).

From Frank G. Jennings, "Tomorrow's Curriculum: Future Imperfect," *Educational Horizons,* Fall 1972, reprinted with permission of the publisher, Pi Lamda Theta.

61 Jeanne H. Ward, "Steve, Go Wash Your Hands!" *Today's Education,* December 1970, reprinted with permission of the publisher and author.

62 H. Samuel Hamod, "Crazy Things," *The Famous Boating Party, Poems and Things* (Ceder Creek Press), copyright © 1970 by H. Samuel Hamod. Reprinted with permission of the author. Cedar Creek Press: P.O. Box 4512, University Station, Tucson, Arizona 85716.

64 "The Family Circus," by Bill Keane. Reprinted with permission of *The Register and Tribune Synicate* and the author. Copyright 1973.

65 From Kahlil Gibran, *The Prophet,* with permission of the publisher, Alfred A. Knopf, Inc. Copyright © 1923 by Kahlil Gibran; renewal copyright 1951 by Administrators C. T. A. of Kahlil Gibran Estate, and Mary G. Gibran.

© 1965 by United Feature Syndicate.

66 From Ashley Montagu, "What is a Child," *The National Elementary Principal,* Copyright 1971, National Association of Elementary School Principals. All rights reserved.

Candace T. Stevenson, "One Child," *The Educational Forum,* January 1967, p. 210, with permission of Kappa Delta Pi, An Honor Society in Education, owners of the copyright.

67 H. Samuel Hamod, "3 Ships from UNICEF," from *Where The Air is Clear.* Copyright 1973 by H. Samuel Hamod, reprinted with permission of the author.

From John Holt, *Freedom and Beyond* (New York: E. P. Dutton & Company), copyright © 1972 by John Holt. Reprinted with permission of the publisher.

From Leila Berg, *Look at Kids* (London: Penguin Books, 1972), Penguin Education Series, copyright © 1972 by Leila Berg, reprinted with permission of the publisher.

From Earl C. Kelley, *Humanizing the Education of Children,* © 1969, The American Association of Elementary-Kindergarten-Nursery Educators, Washington, D. C., reprinted with permission of the publisher.

68 Peter F. Meumeyer, "Trick or Treat," *The Educational Forum,* November 1966, p. 94, with permission of Kappa Delta Pi, An Honor Society in Education, owners of the copyright.

Anna Bird Stewart, "Treasures," *Rex and Other New and Old Selected Verses for Boys and Girls,*

Christopher Nye, "Navajo Girl," *The Educational Forum,* March 1969, p. 336, with permission of Kappa Delta Pi, An Honor Society in Education, owners of the copyright.

69 Kay Andrew, "This is a Child," © Hallmark Cards, Inc., with permission.

From Stan Steiner, *La Raza: The Mexican Americans* (New York: Harper and Row, 1970), with permission of the publisher.

71 Wron Carswell, "To Dance is to Feel," with permission of the author.

72-73 Photo courtesy of Gordon Menzie.

74 Caroline Norton, "The Eyes of a Child," *Life's Greatest Treasure,* © 1971 by Hallmark Cards, Inc. Reprinted with permission of the publisher.

Paul Engle, "To Be a Child," *Life's Greatest Treasure,* © 1971 by Hallmark Cards, Inc. Reprinted with permission of the publisher.

From Rachel Carson, *A Sense of Wonder* (New York: Harper and Row, 1956), copyright © 1956 by Rachel L. Carson, reprinted with permission of Harper and Row, Publishers, Inc.

75 Kate Douglas Wiggin, "Somewhere a Child," *Life's Greatest Treasure,* © 1971 by Hallmark Cards, Inc. Reprinted with permission of the publisher.

76 Francis Thompson, "Know You What it is to be a Child?" *Life's Greatest Treasure,* © 1971 by Hallmark Cards, Inc. Reprinted with permission of the publisher.

Samuel Taylor Coleridge, "A Little Child," *Life's Greatest Treasure,* © 1971 by Hallmark Cards, Inc. Reprinted with permission of the publisher.

Emily Carey Alleman, "Half-Past Three," *Life's Greatest Treasures,* © 1971 by Hallmark Cards, Inc. Reprinted with permission of the publisher and author.

77 Walt Whitman, "There was a Child Went Forth," *Leaves of Grass.*

80 From John Holt, *Freedom and Beyond* (New York: E. P. Dutton & Company), copyright © 1972 by John Holt. Reprinted with permission of the publisher.

Kenneth L. Patton, "Child's Country," *The Magic of Children,* © 1971 by Hallmark Cards, Inc. Reprinted with permission of the publisher and author.

81 Anna Bird Stewart, "The Dump," *Rex and Other New and Old Selected Verses for Boys and Girls.*

Frederick J. Moffit, "Thus a Child Learns," *Kappa Delta Pi Record,* December 1971, p. 55. Reprinted with permission of the publisher.

83 Photo by Alan Mercer.

84 From James L. Hymes, Jr., *Teaching the Child Under Six* (Columbus, Ohio: Charles E. Merrill Publishing Company).

From Don Fabun, *Children of Change.* Copyright © 1969 by Kaiser Aluminum & Chemical Corporation. Reprinted courtesy of Glencoe Press.

86 Cartoon © 1963 by United Feature Syndicate, Inc.

From *Radical Ideas and the Schools,* ed. Jack L. Nelson, Kenneth Carlson and Thomas S. Linton (New York: Holt, Rinehart and Winston, 1970), with permission of the publisher.

From John Holt, *Freedom and Beyond* (New York: E. P. Dutton & Company), copyright © 1972 by John Holt. Reprinted with permission of the publisher.

87 From Earl C. Kelley and Marie I. Rasey, *Education and the Nature of Man* (New York: Harper and Row).

From Earl C. Kelley, *Humanizing the Education of Children,* © 1969, The American Association of Elementary-Kindergarten-Nursery Educators, Washington, D. C., reprinted with permission of the publisher.

From John Holt, *Freedom and Beyond* (New York: E. P. Dutton & Company), copyright © 1972 by John Holt. Reprinted with permission of the publisher.

From Jonathan Kozol, *Death at an Early Age* (Boston: Houghton Mifflin Company, 1967).

From Leland B. Jacobs, *Illuminating the Lives of Children,* © 1971, The American Association of Elementary-Kindergarten-Nursery Educators, Washington, D. C., reprinted with permission of the publisher.

88 From Herbert Kohl, *The Open Classroom* (New York: New York Review Book).

Photo by Alan Mercer.

From T. Darrell Drummond, "To Make a Difference in the Lives of Children," *The National Elementary Principal,* February 1970.

91 From Caleb Gattegno, *What We Owe Children—The Subordination of Teaching to Learning* (London: Outerbridge & Dienstfrey, distributed by E. P. Dutton & Company).

92 From Lloyd W. Kline, *Education and the Personal Quest* (Columbus, Ohio: Charles E. Merrill, © 1971), with permission of the publisher.

From James S. Coleman, "How Do the Young Become Adults," *Phi Delta Kappan,* December 1972.

From Earl C. Kelley, *Humanizing the Education of Children,* © 1969, The American Association of Elementary-Kindergarten-Nursery Educators, Washington, D. C., reprinted with permission of the publisher.

93 From Earl C. Kelley, *Humanizing the Education of Children,* © 1969, The American Association of Elementary-Kindergarten-Nursery Educators, Washington, D. C., reprinted with permission of the publisher.

From *Educating the Children of the Poor* (Association for Supervision and Curriculum Development, © 1968), reprinted with permission of the publisher.

From John I. Goodlad, "How do We Learn," *Saturday Review,* June 21, 1969, with permission of the publisher.

Roy Wilson, "A Teacher is Many Things," *Today's Education,* reprinted with permission of the publisher.

From *Anne Arundel Times,* November 11-12, 1970, with permission of the publisher.

From Henry W. Ray, "Designing Tomorrow's School Today: The Multi-Sensory Experience Center," *Childhood Education,* February 1971, reprinted with permission of the author and the Association for Childhood Education International.

From James Herndon, *How to Survive in Your Native Land* (New York: Simon and Schuster).

97 "Federal Fashions," *The Education Digest,* January 1971, p. 57, reprinted with permission of the publisher.

From Jonathan Kozol, *Death at an Early Age* (Boston: Houghton Mifflin Company).

From Theodore Roszak, "Education Contra Naturam," *A Man For Tomorrow's World* (Association for Supervision and Curriculum Development, © 1970), reprinted with permission of the publisher.

From E. Joseph Scheider and Mary Kennedy, "Research Results for the Classroom," *Today's Education,* March 1973.

From Beatrice and Ronald Gross, "A Little Bit of Chaos,"

Saturday Review, May 16, 1970, with permission of the publisher.

99   Gerald T. Kowitz, "Innovation," *The Educational Forum,* November 1967, p. 38, with permission of Kappa Delta Pi, An Honor Society in Education, owners of the copyright.

100   From Kathleen Gee Haight, "Master of Arts Thesis," University of Arizona, with permission of the author.

101   From John Holt, *Freedom and Beyond* (New York: E. P. Dutton & Company), copyright © 1972 by John Holt. Reprinted with permission of the publisher.

102-103   Photo by Jane Bown, © 1974 by CRM, a division of Ziff-Davis Publishing Co. Used with permission.

106   Ella Q. Forman, "Open Education: Yes!" *Arizona Teacher,* September 1972, (Vol. 61. No. 1). Reprinted with permission of the Arizona Education Association.

111   "St. Paul Open School Goals," St. Paul Public Schools, St. Paul, Minnesota. Reprinted with permission of the publisher.

From Wayne Jennings, "St. Paul Open School: Design, Rationale, and Implementation," reprinted with permission of the author.

115   Wayne Jennings, "The St. Paul Open School," reprinted with permission of the author.

116   Art by Bunny Carter, from *Learning* Magazine, November 1973. © 1973 by Education Today Company, Inc. Reprinted with permission of the publishers.

119   From Barbara Blitz, *The Open Classroom: Making It Work* (Boston: Allyn and Bacon).

Roland S. Barth, "So You Want To Change an Open Classroom," *Phi Delta Kappan,* October 1971, reprinted with permission of the publisher.

126   From Erich Fromm, *The Art of Loving* (Hardbound edition), Volume 9 in World Perspective Series, Planned and Edited by Ruth Nanda Anshen, Copyright © 1956 by Erich Fromm. Reprinted with permission of Harper and Row, Publishers, Inc.

Excerpted from Earl C. Kelley, *In Defense of Youth* (Englewood Cliffs, N.J.: Prentice-Hall, 1962), with permission of the publisher.

From Dorothy H. Cohen, *The Learning Child* (New York: Pantheon Books).

127   From Ashley Montagu, "A Scientist Looks at Love," *Phi Delta Kappan,* May 1970, with permission of the publisher.

From Erich Fromm, *The Art of Loving* (Hardbound edition), Volume 9 in World Perspective Series, Planned and Edited by Ruth Nanda Anshen, Copyright © 1956 by Erich Fromm. Reprinted with permission of Harper and Row, Publishers, Inc.

130   Gerald T. Kowitz, "Game Theory," *The Educational Forum,* May 1972, p.514, with permission of Kappa Delta Pi, An Honor Society in Education, owners of the copyright.

Dorothy Law Nolte, "Parent's Creed," Copyright 1963 by J. P. Company. Reprinted with permission of the John Philop Company.

132   From Erich Fromm, *The Art of Loving* (Hardbound edition), Volume 9 in World Perspective Series, Planned and Edited by Ruth Nanda Ashen, Copyright © 1956 by Erich Fromm. Reprinted with permission of Harper and Row, Publishers, Inc.

133   From Ashley Montagu, "A Scientist Looks at Love," *Phi Delta Kappan,* May 1970, with permission of the publisher.

134   From Leila Berg, *Look at Kids* (London: Penguin Books, 1972), Penguin Education Series, copyright © 1972 by Leila Berg, reprinted with permission of the publisher.

From Abraham Maslow, *Motivation and Personality* (New York: Harper and Row, 1970).

Jack Frymier, "Teaching the Young to Love," *The National Elementary Principal,* November 1969, copyright © 1969 by the National Association of Elementary School Principals. All rights reserved.

136   From Ashley Montagu, "What is a Child," *The National Elementary Principal,* Copyright © 1971, National Association of Elementary School Principals. All rights reserved.

137   Jean E. Mizer, "Cipher in the Snow," *NEA Journal,* November 1964, p. 8, reprinted with permission of the publisher.

139   From Charles H. Rathbone, "Assessing the Alternatives," *Childhood Education,* February 1971. Reprinted with permission of the author and the Association for Childhood Education International.

142   From Alfred North Whitehead, the *Preface* to *The Aims of Education* (New York: Macmillan, 1929), with permission of the publisher.

H. Samuel Hamod, "A Natural High," *Where the Air is Clear.* Copyright © 1973 by H. Samuel Hamod, reprinted with permission of the author.

From Peter Marin, "Children of the Apocalypse," *Saturday Review,* September 19, 1970. Reprinted with permission of International Famous Agency and Peter Marin, Copyright © 1970 by Peter Marin.

143   From *The Plowden Report,* The Central Advisory Council for Education, U.K.G.B.

144   From Earl C. Kelley, *Humanizing the Education of Children,* © 1969, The American Association of Elementary-Kindergarten-Nursery Educators, Washington, D.C., reprinted with permission of the publisher.

Ronald Russell, "Lessons from Life," copyright 1971, AA Sales, Inc., Seattle, reprinted with permission.

From Carl R. Rogers, "Can Schools Grow Persons," *Educational Leadership,* December 1971.

145   From Norman E. Silverberg and Margaret C. Silverberg, "Reading Rituals," *Transaction,* July-August 1971.

146 A. S. Flaumenhaft, "Status Takes Over the School House," *The Educational Forum*, November 1966, p. 31, with permission of Kappa Delta Pi, An Honor Society in Education, owners of the copyright.

Val D. Rust, "Patriotism and All That Goes With It," *The Educational Forum*, May 1972, pp. 537-538, with permission of Kappa Delta Pi, An Honor Society in Education, owners of the copyright.

148 From Mary Harbage, "Human Sensitivity and Schooling," *Educational Leadership*, December 1971.

From Leila Berg, *Look at Kids*, (London: Penguin Books, 1972), Penguin Education Series, copyright © 1972 by Leila Berg, reprinted with permission of the publisher.

149 From Ruth E. Hartley, "Play, the Essential Ingredient," *Childhood Education*, November 1971, with permission of the publisher.

150 Photo by R.A. Gregoire, © 1974 by CRM, a division of Ziff-Davis Publishing Co. Used with permission.

152 Betty Jane Stielau, "Toy Talk," *Arizona Teacher*, January 1972, (Vol. 60., No. 3). Reprinted with permission of the Arizona Education Association.

Photos courtesy of *The Arizona Republic*.

155 NTL Institute for Applied Behavioral Science, "An Experiment in Cooperation," *Today's Education*, October 1969, p. 57, reprinted with permission of the publisher.

156 From Paul Goodman, *Radical Ideas and the Schools* (New York: Holt, Rinehart and Winston).

From George Henderson, "Peace; Today and Tomorrow," *Education for Peace* (Association for Supervision and Curriculum Development, 1973 Yearbook).

Geoffrey Johnson, "But Where's Our Wisdom?" *The Educational Forum*, May 1968, p. 422, with permission of Kappa Delta Pi, An Honor Society in Education, owners of the copyright.

157 From Alexander Frazier, "Human Beings as Learning Resources," *Keeping Up with Elementary Education*, Winter 1971, (American Association of Elementary-Kindergarten-Nursery Educators) with permission of the publisher and author.

From Leila Berg, *Look at Kids*, (London: Penguin Books, 1972), Penguin Education Series, copyright © 1972 by Leila Berg, reprinted with permission of the publisher.

158 From Lloyd W. Kline, *Education and the Personal Quest* (Columbus, Ohio: Charles E. Merrill, © 1971), with permission of the publisher.

From Samuel D. Proctor, "Education for Genuine Community," *A Man for Tomorrow's World* (Association for Supervision and Curriculum Development, 1970), with permission of the publisher.

160 From *A Man for Tomorrow's World* (Association for Supervision and Curriculum Development, 1970), with permission of the publisher.

Dorothy H. Cohen, "Children of Technology: Images of the Real Thing," *Childhood Education*, March 1972, reprinted by permission of Dorothy H. Cohen and the Association for Childhood Education International. Copyright © 1972 by the Association.

164 From William Glasser, M. D., *Reality Therapy* (New York: Harper and Row, 1965), copyright © 1965 by William Glasser, reprinted with permission of Harper and Row, Publishers, Inc.

166 Margaret Greer, Michael Langenbach, and Thomas W. Wiggins, "How To Kill Individuality: Two Viewpoints," *Today's Education*, December 1971, with permission of the authors and publisher.

169 NTL Institute for Applied Behavioral Science, "Team Learning," *Today's Education*, December 1969, p. 59, reprinted with permission of the publisher.

170 From Carl R. Rogers, *Freedom to Learn* (Columbus, Ohio: Charles E. Merrill).

From Barbara Blitz, *The Open Classroom: Making It Work* (Boston: Allyn and Bacon).

171 Girolama Garner and Evelyn Badger, "Helping Kids Live Together," with permission of the authors.

176 Excerpted from James Herndon, *How to Survive in Your Native Land* (New York: Simon and Schuster, 1971), with permission of the publisher.

H. Samuel Hamod, "Celebration," *The Famous Boating Party II*, (Cedar Creek Press), 2nd ed., © 1973 by H. Samuel Hamod. Reprinted with permission of the author. Cedar Creek Press: P.O. Box 4512, University Station, Tucson, Arizona 85716.

182-83 Photo courtesy of Gordon Menzie.

184 From Charles William Brubaker, "The American Schoolhouse—Historical Perspective," *The National Elementary Principal*, September 1972, copyright © 1972, National Association of Elementary School Principals. All rights reserved.

186 From Evans Clinchy, "The Vanishing Schoolhouse," *The National Elementary Principal*, September 1972, copyright © 1972, National Association of Elementary School Principals. All rights reserved.

From Robert H. Anderson, *Teaching in a World of Change* (New York: Harcourt Brace Jovanovich, 1966), copyright © 1966 by Harcourt Brace Jovanovich, with permission of the publisher.

189 From Alvin Hertzberg and Edward F. Stone, *Schools are for Children* (New York; Schocken Books, 1971), copyright © 1971 by Alvin Hertzberg and Edward F. Stone, reprinted with permission of Schocken Books Inc.

192 Photo by Jane Bown, © 1974 by CRM, a division of Ziff-Davis Publishing Co. Used with permission.

196 Leonard L. Stillwell, "Individualized In-Service Education," *Today's Education*, December 1969, reprinted with permission of the publisher and author.

199 From Joseph Featherstone, "Open Schools: Tempering a Fad, An Introduction," *Informal Schools in Britain Today* (New York: Citation Press; London: Macmillan), © 1971 by Schools Council Publications, reprinted with permission of the publishers.

202   Evelyn Carswell and Darrell L. Roubinek, "Open Education at the University Level," *Arizona Teacher*, May-June 1973. Reprinted with permission of the publisher.

209   From Theodore W. Hipple, "Participatory Education: Students Assist Teachers," *Bulletin of the National Secondary School Principal*, September 1969, reprinted with permission of the publisher.

210   Alex Groner and Carlyn Brall, "Part-Time Teachers," *Today's Education*, January 1970, reprinted with permission of the publisher.

213   From Vernon H. Smith, "Options in Public Education: The Quiet Revolution," *Phi Delta Kappan*, March 1973, reprinted with permission of the publisher.

214   From Mario Fantini, "Alternatives Within Public Schools," *Phi Delta Kappan*, March 1973, reprinted with permission of the publisher.

215   From John Bremer, "Alternatives as Education," *Phi Delta Kappan*, March 1973, reprinted with permission of the publisher.

216   Diane Divoky, "Berkeley's Experimental Schools," *Saturday Review*, October 1972, reprinted with permission of the publisher and author.

222   From Mary Jo Bane and Christopher Jencks, "The Schools and Equal Opportunity," *Saturday Review*, September 16, 1972, reprinted with permission of the publisher and authors.

223   Arthur Pearl, "Hansel and Gretel," *Saturday Review*, December 9, 1972, p. 51, reprinted with permission of the publisher and author.

228   From Carl Sandburg, *The People, Yes* (New York: Harcourt Brace Jovanovich, 1936), copyright renewed 1964 by Carl Sandburg, reprinted with permission of the publisher.

From Max Poole, "Humanizing the Social Studies in the Elementary School," *The National Elementary Principal*, April 1970.

From Donald H. Eichorn, "The School as Center for Human Development," *Educational Leadership*, October 1971.

From David N. Campbell, "Is there a Chance for Your Child?"—Creative Open Classrooms," copyright by David N. Campbell.

From Delmo Della-Dora, "What's Bothering Us?" *Educational Leadership*, December 1971.

From *A Man for Tomorrow's World* (Association for Supervision and Curriculum Development, 1970) with permission of the publisher.

229   Erik Erickson, *Childhood and Society*, second ed. (New York: W. W. Norton & Co., 1963) p. 274.

230   From Louise L. Tyler, "Curriculum Development from a Psychoanalytical Perspective, *The Educational Forum*, January 1972, pp. 173-79, with permission of Kappa Delta Pi, An Honor Society in Education, owners of the copyright.

From Ira Gordon, "The Beginning of the Self: The Problems of the Nurturing Environment," *Phi Delta Kappan*, March 1969, p. 375, reprinted with permission of the publisher.

232   From Joseph S. Junell, "Is Rational Man Our First Priority?" *Phi Delta Kappan*, November 1970, reprinted with permission of the publisher.

234   From Mary Harbage, "Human Sensitivity and Schooling," *Educational Leadership*, December 1971.

From John Blackie, *Inside the Primary School* (London: Her Majesty's Stationery Office, 1967).

From Louise L. Tyler, "Curriculum Development from a Psychoanalytical Perspective, *The Educational Forum*, January 1972, pp. 173-79, with permission of Kappa Delta Pi, An Honor Society in Education, owners of the copyright.

From Leland B. Jacobs, "Humanism in Teaching Reading," *Phi Delta Kappan*, April 1971, reprinted with permission of the publisher.

235   Stuart Baller, "A Teacher's Prayer," *The Educational Forum*, November 1967, p. 30, with permission of Kappa Delta Pi, An Honor Society in Education, owners of the copyright.

235   From Vincent R. Rogers, "Primary Education in England: An Interview with John Coe," *Phi Delta Kappan,* May 1971, reprinted with permission of the publisher.

236   From John Blackie, *Inside the Primary School* (London: Her Majesty's Stationery Office, 1967).

237   From Leland B. Jacobs, *Iluminating the Lives of Children*, © 1971, The American Association of Elementary-Kindergarten-Nursery Educators, Washington, D. C., reprinted with permission of the publisher.

239   From Carl R. Rogers, "Can Schools Grow Persons," *Educational Leadership*, December 1971.

From Earl C. Kelley, *Humanizing the Education of Children*, © 1969, The American Association of Elementary-Kindergarten-Nursery Educators, Washington, D. C., reprinted with permission of the publisher.

From William Glasser, "The Effect of School Failure on the Life of a Child," *The National Elementary School Principal*, November 1969.

240   From Clara A. Pederson, "New Day in North Dakota: Changing Teachers and Changing Schools," *Childhood Education*, February 1971, reprinted with the permission of the author and the Association for Childhood Education International.

From Charles H. Rathbone, "Assessing the Alternatives," *Childhood Education*, February 1971. Reprinted with permission of the author and the Association for Childhood Education International.

From Neil Postman and Charles Weingartner, *Teaching as a Subversive Activity* (New York: Dell Publishing, 1969), copyright © 1969 by Neil Postman and Charles Weingartner, reprinted with permission of the publisher.

241 From Earl C. Kelley, *Humanizing the Education of Children*, © 1969, The American Association of Elementary-Kindergarten-Nursery Educators, Washington, D. C., reprinted with permission of the publisher.

242-43 Photo courtesy of Gordon Menzie.

244 H. Samuel Hamod, "On a Picture of Poverty in Appalachia: 3 Year Old and Doll," *The Famous Boating Party, Poems and Things* (Cedar Creek Press), Copyright © 1970 by H. Samuel Hamod. Reprinted with permission of the author. Cedar Creek Press: P. O. Box 4512, University Station, Tucson, Arizona 85716.

Arthur W. Combs, "The Human Side of Learning," *The National Elementary Principal*, January 1973, National Association of Elementary School Principals. All rights reserved.

248 From Eileen M. Oickle, "The Death of the Textbook," *Anne Arundel Times*, November 11-12, 1970, reprinted with permission of the publisher.

249 From Margaret Adams, "Special Instructors—A Highly Individualistic Teaching Style," *Anne Arundel Times*, November 11-12, 1970, reprinted with permission of the publisher.

250 Richard Calisch, "So You Want To Be A Real Teacher," *Today's Education*, November 1969, reprinted with permission of the publisher and author.

253 From Louise L. Tyler, "Curriculum Development from a Psychoanalytical Perspective," *The Educational Forum*, January 1972, pp. 173-79, with permission of Kappa Delta Pi, An Honor Society in Education, owners of the copyright.

256 From Charles H. Rathbone, "Assessing the Alternatives," *Childhood Education*, February 1971. Reprinted with permission of the author and the Association of Childhood Education International.

Myra Danielson, "CREATES," with permission of the author.

262 Zilpha W. Billings, "Self-Selection Classroom," *Today's Education*, October 1970, reprinted with permission of the publisher and author.

277 Paul Anthony Mihalik, "A Few Words on Career Education," with permission of the author.